D0204099

MARK TWAIN INTERNATIONAL

Drawing titled "Mark Twain's Outreach" (Courtesy of the artist Judith R. Smith)

MARK TWAIN INTERNATIONAL

A BIBLIOGRAPHY AND INTERPRETATION OF HIS WORLDWIDE POPULARITY

EDITED AND COMPILED BY
ROBERT M. RODNEY

84489

GREENWOOD PRESS
WESTPORT, CONNECTICUT • LONDON, ENGLAND

FONTBONNE LIBRARY

Library of Congress Cataloging in Publication Data

Rodney, Robert M.
  Mark Twain international.

    1. Twain, Mark, 1835-1910—Bibliography. 2. Twain,
Mark, 1835-1910—Appreciation. I. Title.
Z8176.R62 [PS1338] 016.818′409   81-13441
ISBN 0-313-23135-4 (lib. bdg.)   AACR2

Copyright © 1982 by Robert M. Rodney

All rights reserved. No portion of this book may be
reproduced, by any process or technique, without the
express written consent of the publisher.

Library of Congress Catalog Card Number: 81-13441
ISBN: 0-313-23135-4

First published in 1982

Greenwood Press
A division of Congressional Information Service, Inc.
88 Post Road West
Westport, Connecticut 06881

Printed in the United States of America

10 9 8 7 6 5 4 3 2 1

FONTBONNE LIBRARY

PS
1338
. R62
1982

To the memory of
Harry Hayden Clark
Scholar—Teacher—Mentor

Contents

Illustrations

Tables

Preface

An earlier study of Mark Twain's reception in England, done under the spirited guidance of the late Professor Harry Hayden Clark, led me to believe that the international dimensions of Mark Twain's popularity, during and especially subsequent to his own lifetime, were much greater than critics, scholars, and Mark Twain devotees had suspected. Many facets of the Mark Twain phenomenon have been examined and reexamined, but to the present time there has been no comprehensive investigation of Twain's worldwide popularity based on the totality of his international publication. The discovery of his enormous popularity among British readers and his personal role in Anglo-American relations prompted a long search of bibliographical sources in America and abroad that finally culminated in the present work. I am greatly indebted to Harry Clark for his early encouragement and professional advice, and to the late Frederick Anderson, editor of the Mark Twain Papers, for his many courtesies and most helpful suggestions during my visits to the repository of Mark Twain materials at Berkeley.

In this short space it would be impracticable to mention all of the reference librarians and other specialists who facilitated my search for source materials. I am especially grateful to the staffs of the British Museum, the Huntington Library, and the Library of Congress.

The problem of coping with such a wide range of languages would have been insurmountable without the special help of Maria Maris Van Blaaderen in translating troublesome Dutch titles, Wong Tak-Wai of Hong Kong in transliterating and translating Chinese titles and prefaces, Hiroshi Okano of Tokyo in similar rendering of Japanese titles, Stephen Zirko in his rendering the titles and contents of many Russian editions, and the accommodating specialists of the Library of Congress East European Division and the University of California/Berkeley in their deciphering the titles of Slavic and Indian editions of Mark Twain's works.

Finally, I owe a very special thanks to my wife Isobel and daughter Judith for their long-continued labors in helping to search out and record vital information and for their patient help in checking the accuracy of bibliographical data and proofreading manuscript.

If the outcome reveals the full nature and extent of Mark Twain's international popularity and puts this controversial writer into better historical perspective, this work will serve its purpose.

Robert M. Rodney

Acknowledgments

I wish to express my appreciation to Harper & Row for permission to quote from the following work published by Harper & Brothers: *Mark Twain's Letters*, edited by Albert Bigelow Paine, copyright 1917 by the Mark Twain Company, renewed 1945 by Clara Clemens Samossoud.

Grateful acknowledgment is made to the following publishers for their permissions to reproduce specified materials from their editions of various Mark Twain works for illustrative purposes:

S. Fischer Verlag of Frankfurt am Main to reproduce the cover of their edition of Mark Twain, *Tot oder Lebendig. Siebzehn Erzahlungen*, copyright 1961.

Wilhelm Goldmann Verlag of Munich to reproduce the cover of their edition of *Huckleberry Finn. Seine Abenteuer und Fahrten mit Tom Sawyer*, Jugendbucher series, copyright 1962, and the cover and page 5 of their edition of Mark Twain, *Tom Sawyer. Abenteuer und Streiche des berühmtesten Lausbuben von Amerika*, Jugenbucher series, copyright 1961.

Philipp Reclam Jun. of Stuttgart to reproduce the cover of their edition of Mark Twain, *Der Berhümte Springfrosch der Provinz Calaveras*, copyright 1962; and the cover of their edition of *Ausgewählte Skizzen von Mark Twain*, Universal-Bibliothek series, copyright 1878.

Rizzoli Editore of Milan to reproduce the covers of their editions of Mark Twain, *Wilson Lo Zuccone*, copyright 1949; Mark Twain, *Il Ranocchio Saltatore e Altri Racconti*, copyright 1950; and Mark Twain, *Un Americano alla Corte di Re Artu*, copyright 1955, Biblioteca Universala series.

Plaza & Janes, S.A. Editores of Barcelona to reproduce the cover and page 5 of their edition of Mark Twain, *Tom Sawyer: Las Aventuras de Tom*

Sawyer. Huck Finn. Tom Sawyer, detective. Tom Sawyer de viaje, copyright 1964.

Rajpal & Sons of Delhi to reproduce the jacket and first page of text of their edition of Mark Twain, *Bahati Dhara*, copyright 1968.

Shinchosha Company of Tokyo to reproduce the cover, title page, and page 7 of their edition of Mark Twain, *Tom Sawyer No Boken*, copyright 1953.

I am indebted to Judith R. Smith for her graphic illustration of Mark Twain and his world outreach.

Introduction and Interpretation
of the Bibliography

*My audience is dumb, it has no voice in
print, and so I cannot know whether I have
won its approbation or only got its censure.*[1]
Mark Twain

No American writer has survived more controversy among his critics, or
more contradictory "final" assessments of his reputation by the scholars,
than Mark Twain. During one hundred years following his international
debut in 1869 he was successively "discovered," patronized, condescended
to, deplored, critiqued, psychoanalyzed, reappraised, rehabilitated, and extolled. From 1870 to 1907, when he was celebrated with an honorary Oxford University degree, reviewers delivered their judgments of his various
writings with such epithets as "amusing," "reckless," "droll," "grotesque,"
"extravagant," "inartistic," "irritating," "pompous," "absurd," "facetious,"
"quaint," "macabre," "provincial," "Rabelaisian," "coarse and vulgar,"
"audacious," "unpalatable," "profane," "wearisome and fatuous,"
"distasteful," "fantastic," "so sane," "incorrigible," "irresponsible," "offensive," and "deplorable."[2] At the time of his death in 1910 Twain was tem-
porarily elevated to "apocalyptic" and "heroic." During subsequent decades
various critics pronounced him "overrated," "irritating and astonishing,"
"shallow," "provincial," "intellectually intolerable," "unique, inimitable,"
"completely and finally bone-headed," "jejune," "erratic, mercurial," and
"vulgar and boring." This largely objurgatory chorus, coming from British,
French, and even American critics, reflects the Victorian sensitivities of the
critics before 1910 and the intellectual prepossessions of the critics following
that year, especially during the 1920s and 1930s.

In contrast to the above, literary historians, biographers, and fellow writers who perceived the larger dimensions of the American humorist took a carefully considered and more charitable view of Mark Twain, basing their judgments on the personality of the man, the totality of his work, and the milieu that produced him. Their judgments, however, reached no consensus, running the gamut from early appreciation to acceptance, rejection, commendation, deification, denunciation, and affirmation. It is at least instructive to pass in review their more trenchant observations. Between 1878 and 1910 the bolder and the more wary among them characterized Mark Twain as "a constitutional humorist" rather than a professional humorist, "an extravagant wag," "in a measure a true philosopher," "a very remarkable fellow" (Thomas Hardy), "a low comedian in literature," "this man of genius," "a microscopic rather than a penetrative intellect," "a man of literary cultivation," "one of the benefactors of the world," "the typical American," "a serious critic of life," "Ambassador at large of the U.S.A.," "the true consolidator of nations," "pure concentrated vulgarity," "by far the greatest American writer" (George Bernard Shaw), "America's greatest cosmopolitan," and a "chartered libertine of literature." In their 1910 memorials notabilities of the day eulogized Twain with such phrases as "the greatest living humorist" (William Dean Howells), "a master of English prose" (Brander Matthews), "a great Yankee rustic" (G. K. Chesterton), and "a divine amateur" (Arnold Bennett).

Subsequent to Twain's death three generations of literary historians and biographers (1913 to 1970) took a closer look at the "Mark Twain" phenomenon from various perspectives and took issue with each other's interpretations. After John Macy pronounced Mark Twain "a powerful, original thinker," the new critics of the 1920s largely deplored their discoveries that Twain was "a defeated soul" (Waldo Frank), "a balked personality" (Van Wyck Brooks), "a rough rider of literature" (Karl Bleibtrau), "America's last buffoon" (Alfred Kreymborg), "very much of an innocent" (E. T. Raymond), and "the greatest cynic and infidel that America has produced" (James M. Gillis). Other critics of the period countered with the assertions that Twain was "the grand common man" (A. C. Ward), "a thinking artist" (Friedrich Schonemann), "a great writer" (W. W. Jacobs), and "a genius" (Temple Bailey). In the 1930s analysts of Mark Twain sought to improve his image by insisting that he was "a pioneer talent" (Constance Rourke), "an artist—as American" (Bernard DeVoto), "the first American prose writer of any importance" (V. F. Calverton), "a figure of legend" (M. M. Brashear), and "an American writer who wrote like an American" (Anthony Deane); and the Mark Twain centennial of 1936 brought forth such verdicts as "the largest man of his time" (Rudyard Kipling) and "one of the greatest of American authors" (Somerset Maugham). The long controversy over what Mark Twain really was and what he represented waned during the post-World War II years, but the problem remained unresolved by the conclusions of several biographers that America's most paradoxical writer was "a dark and doubled personality" (Maxwell Geismar), "an extraordinarily complex personality" (Henry Nash Smith), and "a great artist" (Justin Kaplan).

From such conflicting and often irreconcilable judgments, Mark Twain devotees and his readers in general could hardly be expected to distill the "truth" about the man and his work. Such matters as a writer's temperament, intellectual bias, literary art, and outlook on life are too subjective for even the most ardent analyst to objectify, let alone quantify and computerize. M. M. Brashear may have come closest to the heart of the matter when she said that Mark Twain "defies final analysis."[3]

Meanwhile, another Mark Twain constituency, in their own way, had been testifying to his success as a writer. Largely uncritical and seldom articulate, five generations of silent readers—his "dumb" audience—demonstrated a continuing reaction from which a collective popular judgment can be obtained. The geographical extent and high degree of Mark Twain's worldwide popularity are phenomena that have been too long overlooked. A measure of that popularity, however approximate, can supply a much-needed dimension to Twain's stature. The purpose of the present work is to consolidate and make available the record of his international publication and to interpret what that record reveals.

1. THE WORLD SCOPE OF MARK TWAIN'S AUDIENCE

During two centuries of its growing cultural independence the United States produced a host of popular writers, many of whom earned a large measure of foreign as well as domestic popularity for a generation or so. Some of these writers not only gained critical recognition on the strength of their literary merits but also had sufficient popular appeal to sustain their reputations well past the mid-twentieth century. Among these the most notable were James Fenimore Cooper, Edgar Allan Poe, Nathaniel Hawthorne, Herman Melville, Mark Twain, Harriet Beecher Stowe, Louisa May Alcott, Henry James, Theodore Dreiser, Jack London, Sinclair Lewis, T. S. Eliot, Ernest Hemingway, William Faulkner, Pearl Buck, and John Steinbeck (see Tables 4, 5). All of these were essentially fictional writers, with the exception of T. S. Eliot and Mark Twain. The durability of a large audience for Eliot's poetry for over half a century is probably a unique case. Also unique is the case of Mark Twain, whose literary reputation and popular appeal stemmed from a few novels and a wide range of anecdotes, tales, travel sketches, and social commentaries. Twain's uniqueness becomes even more apparent when it is observed that among his earlier American competitors Cooper and Poe were his only serious, although distant, competitors for international favor, and that London and Buck were his only close rivals from the twentieth century (see Table 5). If literary success depends upon a writer's durability for more than a few decades, there is no question about Twain's preeminence among his literary forerunners, contemporaries, and successors. During the first 110 years of his publications the pen name "Mark Twain" attracted and sustained enormous audiences both at home and abroad. This generally held, but unsubstantiated, assumption is confirmed by the record of his publications. Beyond the basic fact of his popularity remain several questions. How extensive was Twain's international audience? How prolonged was his popularity in various parts of the world? How has his popularity compared with that of other American writers in recent times? What has Mark Twain contributed to the American image abroad?

The following discussion is an attempt to answer the above questions. The full and final measure of Mark Twain's worldwide audience might never be arrived at because of the unavailability of publishers' records and the incompleteness of certain bibliographical sources, but the latter (cf. Bibliographical Sources, page lxiii) have provided sufficient evidence to establish the various perimeters of that audience and its rapidly growing dimensions. All observations about these matters are based on the frequency with which editions of Twain's single works were published within comparable periods of time, in specific countries, and in various languages (see Tables 2, 3). Comparisons between Mark Twain and other American writers are based on the frequency of editions published during the middle decades of the twentieth century (see Tables 4, 5).

2. INTERNATIONAL DIMENSIONS OF MARK TWAIN'S POPULARITY

An accounting of Mark Twain's total publication during eleven decades provides an overview with the broadest perspective of his international popularity. Such an overview, of course, leads to a strictly nationalistic interpretation without regard to the ethnic distribution of his works, a consideration taken up in the next section of the discussion.

Overall, during the period 1867-1976 Mark Twain's writings in book form were published in at least 5,344 single editions issued in fifty-five countries and translated into seventy-two foreign languages (see Table 1). The record reveals that, as would be expected, Twain had his largest readership among Americans (see Table 3), averaging ten editions per year over the period of time involved. For the purpose of estimating degrees of foreign popularity, it is assumed that any writer's popularity, in terms of his total works, would be enormous at the rate of five editions per year, very strong at the rate of four editions, strong at the rate of two to three editions, and at least sustained at the rate of one edition per year during various periods. On such a scale it can be observed that beyond the United States Mark Twain's writings had appreciable popularity in the following countries:

Enormous popularity in Germany during a 102-year period.

Very strong popularity in Great Britain during a 110-year period and in Argentina during a thirty-two year period.

Strong popularity during various periods in Spain, Italy, Russia, Yugoslavia, Japan, France, Sweden, Brazil, and India in descending order.

Sustained popularity during various periods in Mexico, Czechoslovakia, Netherlands, Belgium, Denmark, Turkey, Bulgaria, Finland, Romania, and Israel in descending order.

Undoubtedly Mark Twain's popularity was also well sustained in Canada, Australia, New Zealand, and South Africa as well as other areas of the English-speaking world by virtue of the many British and American editions available in those Commonwealth countries. Similarly, Austrian readers had access to German editions and Swiss readers to German and French editions.

Mark Twain also had substantial audiences in at least twenty-three other countries, principally in the twentieth century. He was well known in Portugal and Norway for over fifty years through frequent, although not sustained, publication in those two countries. He became known in Iceland, Chile, Colombia, and Uruguay for more than forty years through a few translations published in those countries. In mainland China, where Twain had been introduced to Chinese readers in the late 1930s through translations of *Tom Sawyer* and *The Prince and the Pauper*, a spate of Chinese-language editions of ten major works were published in the 1950s after the Communist Revolution; and during the turbulent 1960s Twain continued to be available through numerous editions published in Hong Kong. After World War II multiple editions of some of his major works reached Cuba, Albania, Greece, Iran, Egypt, Pakistan, Indonesia, Malaysia, Taiwan, and Korea. And he belatedly reached Peru, Morocco, Ceylon, Burma, Singapore, the Philippines, and Thailand by the 1960s with one edition in each of those countries.

One of the most inveterate travelers of the nineteenth century, Mark Twain had explored all of Western Europe, the Mediterranean regions, and almost every corner of the British Empire. After his death in 1910 his literary legacy of the American experience continued to grow and eventually included every nationality with a publishing enterprise large enough to support the translation and publication of his various writings. Many writers have enjoyed extensive international audiences, of course, but in point of geographic coverage and duration the dimensions of Mark Twain's audience are undoubtedly a rare phenomenon.

3. MARK TWAIN'S ETHNIC OUTREACH

The geographical expansion of Mark Twain's publications is an impressive phenomenon. By 1900 foreign editions of his major works had made his writings available in twenty countries, by 1920 in twenty-five countries, by 1940 in thirty-two countries, by 1960 in forty-nine countries, and by 1976 the expansion had grown to fifty-five countries. However, a better sense of the scope and diversity of Twain's worldwide audience can be had from an ethnic overview, in which the cultural diversity of his readers is revealed by the wide range of foreign language translations of his writings.

Some early critics were doubtful that Twain's humor and his American idiom could be rendered into foreign languages, but it turned out that cultural differences were no obstacle to the translation of his works for alien peoples, whether European, Near Eastern, or Asian. Most of Twain's writings quickly became available to English-speaking peoples around the world as successive editions were issued through British and Canadian presses. From 1867 through 1976 over eighteen hundred English-language editions were published in the United States and abroad, many of them in Germany. On the Continent most of Twain's works were translated into nine Western European languages: Danish, Dutch, French, German, Italian, Norwegian, Portuguese, Spanish, and Swedish. A few editions also appeared in Catalan, Icelandic, German Spoerli, and Sorbian. German-language versions alone ran to more than six hundred editions, accommodating Austrian and Swiss as well as German readers. Over five hundred Spanish-language editions were produced for Spanish and Latin American readers. Other foreign presses turned out well over two hundred editions each in French and Italian, almost two hundred in Swedish, over one hundred in Dutch for the Netherlands and Belgium, and more than one hundred editions each in Danish and Portuguese, with a large output of the latter in Brazil. *The Adventures of Tom Sawyer*, a perennial favorite among readers of almost all ethnic backgrounds, was published in at least 174 German-language and 144 Spanish-language editions. Twain's stories and sketches, ever popular among most foreign readers, appeared in approximately one hundred German and one hundred Spanish editions.

Mark Twain was longer delayed in reaching Eastern European readers, but eventually his major works were translated into seventeen languages of that region: Polish, Finnish, and Yiddish for peoples of the northern area; Bohemian, Czech, Magyar, and Slovnik for the central area; and Romanian, Bulgarian, Croatian, Serbian, Serbo-Croatian, Slovak, Slovene,

Albanian, Macedonian, and Greek for the southern area. Twain's popularity in Yugoslavia after World War II was tremendous, where his works were published in more than one hundred Serbo-Croatian editions alone. The ethnic diversity of the Yugoslav people required translations into eight languages to satisfy their demand for Mark Twain's writings. Hungarian readers consumed at least 120 editions; Czech, Polish, and Finnish readers over eighty editions. As in Western Europe, the works most widely read were *The Adventures of Tom Sawyer* and collections of Twain's stories and sketches. Polish readers took an especially strong interest in *The Prince and the Pauper* as well as *Tom Sawyer.*

In Russia Mark Twain's appeal to a large diversity of peoples became phenomenal after the Revolution. Some Russian readers had become acquainted with Twain at the turn of the twentieth century through a Russian-language version of his collected works published in 1899. Twain's Russian audience after 1917 expanded to the point where more than two hundred Russian-language editions of his various writings were issued by 1976. These were supplemented by almost one hundred editions in eighteen other languages. The Soviet presses, following an official policy of accommodating minority peoples and their ethnic differences in that vast country, made editions of some of Twain's works available to Belorussians, Estonians, Latvians, Lithuanians, Ukrainians, Moldavians, Slovak-Croatians, and Tatars in their native languages. Translated editions were further published for the Transcaucasian peoples of Armenia, Azerbaidjan, Georgia, and Kabardin, and a few translations were made available to readers of the Karakalpak, Kazakh, Kirghiz, Tadzhik, Turkmen, and Uzbek republics of the Asian hinterland. Reader interests among Russian natonalities varied slightly, the preference among Russian readers running to *The Adventures of Tom Sawyer* and the stories and sketches, and among the ethnic minorities to *Tom Sawyer* and *The Prince and the Pauper.*

In the Near East Mark Twain's greatest popularity developed among Turkish readers, who consumed at least thirty-nine editions in their language published mainly between 1950 and 1976. Twain had been introduced into the Palestine area in 1940, where, after Israel became established as an independent nation, local presses published several of his major works in at least twenty-four Hebrew editions. During these same postwar years several works were also translated into Arabic and Persian for Egyptian and Iranian readers. Among all of these otherwise alien cultures the people had at least one interest in common, their predilection for the adventures of Tom Sawyer and Huckleberry Finn and Twain's historical romance *The Prince and the Pauper.*

By the mid-twentieth century Mark Twain's boyhood idyls had reached India and Southeast Asia. In the Indian subcontinent during 1896 the American humorist, already well known throughout the British Empire,

had made a strong personal impact on English and Anglo-Indian lecture audiences, but his writings had been limited to the same circles in English-
language editions. After Indian independence in 1947 native publishers
issued the Tom Sawyer/Huck Finn adventures in at least eight languages to
reach as many ethnic readers: Assamese, Bengali, Hindi, Malayalam,
Marathi, Oriya, Tamil, and Telugu; and a Singhalese edition brought Tom
Sawyer to Ceylon. Further editions of Mark Twain began to appear in
Southeast Asian translations: Burmese, Filipino, Indonesian, Malay, and
Thai. The thirteen Mark Twain editions published in this region of the
world arrived belatedly and were thin coverage by Western publishing stan-
dards, but they provided many native peoples at least some insight into
American civilization, as interpreted by one of its most sympathetic critics.

In the Far East during the period 1936-1969 some sixty-three Chinese-
language editions of twelve major works by Mark Twain as well as collections of his stories and sketches were published in Hong Kong, in Taiwan,
and on the Chinese mainland. Most of these editions were undertaken in
Hong Kong and Taipei, but at least ten major works became available on
the mainland, where seventeen editions were published behind the Bamboo
Curtain at a time when anything Western was supposed to be anathema to
the Communist regime. These editions may have had little effect on the
masses much beyond Shanghai and Peking, where they were issued, but the
appearance of ten Mark Twain titles within the six years of 1953-1958 is
noteworthy. Ideologically, the collections of Mark Twain's short stories
and the editions of his *Huckleberry Finn*, *Joan of Arc*, and the Tom Sawyer
trilogy might have seemed innocuous enough to approving censors,
although the first two works contained religious or social implications that
could have served the party line. The 1957 Peking edition of *The Gilded
Age*, a work otherwise unpublished in the Far East, was prefaced with the
information that this novel was "a full panorama of American politics,
laws, and social life boasted of by the American capitalists" and an exposé
of "the origin of the American autocracy in politics and economy of
to-day." The 1958 translator of *Life on the Mississippi*, also published in
Peking, extolled that work as "an ode in praise of the power of the working
class. . . ." The Communist press did not publish *A Connecticut Yankee*, in
spite of its strong social import.

Meanwhile, the Japanese were rapidly becoming one of Mark Twain's
largest audiences after World War II. At least five collections of Twain's
stories and sketches had reached Japanese readers in translation prior to
that time; a translation of *The Prince and the Pauper* had appeared as early
as 1899; and two translations of *Huckleberry Finn* had been published
before the war years. In the postwar decades most of Twain's major works
were rendered into Japanese. At least sixty-eight editions of eleven Mark
Twain titles came from the Japanese press during the years 1950-1976.

Ethnically speaking, it can be said at this juncture that Mark Twain's writings have made a greater impact on Japanese readers than they have on any other single Asian audience.

In the 1960s Mark Twain's worldwide audience came full circle with several South Korean translations and several Africaan editions for South African readers. If literary success can be converted into geolinguistic terms, the conclusion is inescapable that Mark Twain's ethnic outreach eventually encompassed every culture with a level of literacy adequate to support the domestic production of books.

At this point a word of caution is needed in order to avoid any hasty conclusions about the dimensions of Mark Twain's worldwide audience. The foregoing observations, embracing, as they do, 110 years of publication, could lead to some broad but misleading generalizations. If complete demographic data could be taken into account, estimates of the international popularity of Mark Twain or of any other writer would need to be qualified by several historical and linguistic factors. For one, it should be kept in mind that countries of small population do not need as many editions of a given publication as large countries do to meet the demands of their readers (for example, Denmark vis-à-vis Germany). Another factor is that of distribution. The large supply of English-language editions published in the United States and Great Britain have been available to other English-speaking peoples, whose own infrequent domestic editions of the same books are not realistic indicators of their popularity among overseas audiences. Conversely, the limitations imposed on publishers in certain countries by multilingual populations can distort the real extent of a writer's popularity in such areas. The problems of rendering an American writer as idiomatic as Mark Twain into satisfactory translation are especially compounded by the ethnic diversity of such countries as Russia, Czechoslovakia, Yugoslavia, and India (some of the title translations in the Bibliography reflect these difficulties). The factor of literacy levels, both in time and in place, should also be taken into account. In the nineteenth century literacy, and consequently the reading public, were much more limited than in the twentieth century. Large mass markets of readers were out of reach to writers and their publishers until literacy levels rose and publishers could convert to the paperback trade in the mid-twentieth century.

For the above reasons, rather than basing any final assessment of Mark Twain's worldwide popularity on any set of gross publication figures, it would be a sounder approach to trace the growth of his international popularity through five periods comprising five successive generations of readers. Interpretation of Twain's popular acceptance during each stage should make allowance for several conditioning factors. First, during his earlier career Twain was handicapped in his more serious efforts by a preconceived image of the man as a literary comedian, a stereotype that persisted in the public mind and even among many critics well into the twentieth century. Secondly, each generation of readers had to be introduced to Mark Twain in its own time and in its own country. Third, each generation's impression of Twain's writings was circumscribed by the totality of his output at a given point of time and the availability of his works not only in English-language editions but in foreign translations as well. A fourth factor that conditioned his popular reception to some degree was the social and moral attitudes of the time and certain intervening historical events.

4. TRENDS IN THE GROWTH OF MARK TWAIN'S POPULARITY

In examining the trends in Mark Twain's international popularity from one period to another, it is well to keep in mind that Twain gradually changed from a realistic but essentially optimistic outlook on the world during his early years to a pessimistic and finally a futilitarian view of the human enterprise, and that his literary mood and purpose frequently shifted as well. Both the philosophical and literary changes are well demonstrated by the contrast in tone between *Roughing It* of 1872, *A Connecticut Yankee* of 1889, and *The Mysterious Stranger* composed sporadically during the closing years of Mark Twain's life. This transition paralleled the trend toward literary naturalism among serious American writers during the last three decades of the nineteenth century. By the turn of the century Twain had a much closer kinship with Stephen Crane, Theodore Dreiser, and Frank Norris, for example, than with the belated romancers and local colorists of that time. However, the most pessimistic of Mark Twain's writings published after 1899 reached very few foreign readers outside of Great Britain until the mid-twentieth century, and the popular conception of Twain as a professional humorist, anecdotist, and entertaining storyteller persisted well past his death in 1910.[4] This divergence between Twain's literary intentions and his readers' expectations could partially explain the relatively meager reception of what he wrote after 1890 and his suppression of his bleakest writings to await posthumous publication for later generations.

1867-1889

Mark Twain's first book, *The Celebrated Jumping Frog of Calaveras County, and Other Sketches*, published in 1867 in both the United States and Great Britain and followed shortly by Canadian and Australian editions, immediately captured an international audience with its droll and colloquial title story. During these earliest years as a free-lance writer and traveling correspondent, Twain turned out many "sketches" and anecdotal short stories in successive editions that rapidly won him popularity among Anglo-American readers. At least eleven American and Canadian editions and twenty-six British editions appeared before 1880. By 1889 these collections multiplied to some seventy-three editions since 1867, certainly among the best-sellers of that period. Their popularity spread to the Continent with translations into Danish, German, and Swedish in 1874, followed by nine editions in each of these languages by 1889. Twain's stories were further translated into Polish in 1881 and Russian in 1888. Unfortunately for his popular image during these first decades, these early pieces prompted many critics to stereotype Mark Twain as a "professional humorist," entertaining, to be sure, but essentially subliterary. In spite of his production of more substantial works during this period, Twain could not live down this first impression or the expectation that all of his writing would be comical or at least droll.

Meanwhile Twain added another dimension to his reputation in 1869 with the publication of *The Innocents Abroad, or the New Pilgrims' Progress*. British critics, to whom many Americans looked for literary judgments, were dismayed and even shocked by Twain's unorthodox rejection of Old World institutions, his "facetious" treatment of traditional attitudes toward European culture, and his "irreverent" account of the Holy Land, and some critics condemned the book as "irritating" and "offensive." In spite of the critics, readers on both sides of the Atlantic found Twain's first travel work highly entertaining and refreshingly original. Thirty-three English-language editions of *The Innocents Abroad* were published during the 1870s alone to satisfy the popular demand. By 1889 *The Innocents* had run to over fifty such editions; and so sustained was its popularity, especially among British readers, that by the end of the century the book had sold close to one million copies, a literary phenomenon unsurpassed in those times. Within a decade of its first appearance, translated editions became available in Germany (1875), in Sweden (1876), in Denmark (1878), and in the Netherlands (1879). Such a sustained reception can be largely accounted for by a widespread interest in travel literature among Victorians, by the unexpected novelty of Twain's contribution, and by his buoyancy and spontaneity, qualities that he rarely recaptured in his later travel accounts.

In the next few years Mark Twain produced several other works that gave added dimensions to his stature. In 1872 he capitalized on the growing popularity of *The Innocents Abroad* with the publication of *Roughing It*, drawing upon his experience of the Far Western frontier and his explorations of the Sandwich (Hawaiian) Islands. His dynamic portrayals of western characters, his amusing anecdotes, and his colorful descriptions of his Pacific paradise appealed to an extroverted American audience through some thirteen editions during this period, although this work had only a modest reception in England and the British Dominions. Twain's lectures to

British audiences in the early 1870s on "My Fellow Savages of the Sandwich Islands" probably stimulated their interest in the book. Translations of *Roughing It* appeared in Germany and Sweden in 1874.

The Gilded Age (1873) was Mark Twain's first attempt at social satire, intended as an exposure of political corruption and the get-rich-quick fever that he considered as rampant in American life of the time. Viewed by the critics as a literary miscarriage because of his collaboration with Charles Dudley Warner, this novel nonetheless interested enough American readers to sustain fifteen domestic editions until 1890, but it attracted very little attention in Great Britain. Translations made the novel available to Russian readers (1874), German and Hungarian readers (1876), Swedish readers (1877), and Danish readers (1886).

Three years after his first experiment with a novel designed for adult readers, Mark Twain discovered and developed a new literary vein that proved to be the most rewarding one in terms of personal satisfaction and worldwide popularity. *The Adventures of Tom Sawyer* (1876) failed at first to bring him and his publishing house the sales that they anticipated, owing in part to pirated Canadian editions that flooded the American market. For a decade and a half this idyl of boyhood escapades and fantasies produced only seven American and three British editions, although its appeal to foreign readers is evidenced by its translations into French and German (1876), Dutch and Swedish (1877), and Hungarian and Russian (1886). Contrary to Twain's disappointment over the early reception of his story, *Tom Sawyer* was destined to become his most popular novel after his death and the best-seller among all of his works after 1930.

In 1879 Mark Twain published a third account of his travels recently extended to Europe. *A Tramp Abroad* recounted his experiences and observations of the Rhineland and Switzerland in a chronological but rambling format intended to please readers of *The Innocents Abroad*. Perhaps because it lacked the scope and the verve of *The Innocents*, this newest travel work attracted a meager audience in America with only four editions during the next ten years, although it became popular among British readers (ten editions) and among Canadians (seven editions). The first publication of *A Tramp Abroad* was followed very shortly by its translation into Danish and German (1880), Dutch (1881), and Swedish (1882). At this stage of his career Twain apparently found a readier response to his travel writings among Europeans when he met them on their own ground rather than in the American West.

During the 1880s Mark Twain enlarged his international audience by the publication of three major works. *The Prince and the Pauper* (1881), later to become a worldwide favorite, quickly found a domestic and European audience. Its appeal to American, British, and Canadian readers sustained fourteen English-language editions during the decade. The story's attraction to Anglo-American readers can be attributed, in part, to the strong popularity of historical romances among Victorian readers at this time, and more particularly to the fact that it was written as "A Tale for Young People of All Ages," as Twain subtitled it. Twain's underlying protest against social injustice was rendered palatable enough for contemporary readers by its projection back into sixteenth-century England, by a colorful overlay of pageantry, and by an intriguing plot. An English-language edition issued by the German publisher Bernard Tauchnitz in 1881 helped to prepare the way for the novel's European reception. On the strength of Twain's growing international reputation, foreign editors published translations of *The Prince and the Pauper* for readers in Denmark and the Netherlands (1882), France (1883), Russia (1884), Sweden and Hungary (1885), and Germany (1887). The novel had an especially strong popularity in France, where five editions appeared before 1890.

Two years later Mark Twain produced *Life on the Mississippi* (1883). This vivid account of the Mississippi Valley culture and steamboating era of Twain's early years, recalled with a striking admixture of nostalgia and realism, had an instant response among British and Canadian readers, even though they had already enjoyed an earlier and shorter version of the book as *Old Times on the Mississippi* (1876). The completed version was quickly translated into Danish and Swedish and issued in the Tauchnitz series, and a German-language edition appeared in 1888. Americans, who had read the early version in serialized form in 1875, encouraged only two domestic editions before 1890. Unique among all of his works, *Life on the Mississippi* was to become Mark Twain's most widely read nonfictional book after the turn of the century (see Table 2).

The Adventures of Huckleberry Finn, finally completed and published in 1884, was Mark Twain's most uninhibited and self-gratifying creation. Pigeonholed for years to make way for more pressing projects, this episodic novel had gradually developed during Twain's sporadic impulses to recreate the world of his boyhood as seen through the eyes and experiences of a young vagabond. *Huckleberry Finn* eventually was to be acknowledged by most critics as a masterpiece of its kind and to become its author's second most popular work among worldwide readers. Twain himself minimized the novel's literary merits in the belief that it would never have the stature of his other major works. During its first five years of publication, *Huckleberry Finn* had only a modest popular reception with five American and three British editions. Picaresque novels had been a favorite literary genre in Europe for centuries, but Victorian readers were reluctant to accept as a hero such an uncouth character as Huck Finn. They were even more reluctant to expose their children to Huck's colloquial and ungrammatical language. It was not until well after Mark Twain's death and the revolution in social standards and literary taste of the 1920s that the complexity, the pathos, and the literary art of *Huckelberry Finn* were recognized by readers at large. It is significant, however, that in the 1880s the novel was translated within five years into seven foreign languages: Danish, Dutch, and Swedish (1885), French (1886), Hungarian (1887), Russian (1888), and Norwegian (1889). This cosmopolitan response was at least a foreshadowing of the recognition to come.

On balance it can be said that by 1889 Mark Twain had reached the peak of his literary career and his publishing enterprise. He had produced almost all of his most creative works, and at the end of that year was ready to launch one of his most ambitious undertakings. His writings had been published in eleven European countries in more than two hundred editions of various single works, and a substantial part of his work had been translated into nine foreign languages. His greatest popularity during these first two decades had been in Great Britain, where more editions had appeared than in the United States itself. On the European continent he had become very popular in Germany, France, Sweden, and Denmark, with twenty or more editions in each of those countries, and he had a strong following in the Netherlands. Through several translated editions he had become familiar to readers in Hungary and Russia, and had found his way with at least one translation to Swiss, Polish, and Norwegian readers. Internationally, at least 380 editions of his writings had been published during the preceding twenty-three years, more than two-thirds of them abroad. If Mark Twain in 1889 had been fully aware that he had won such a large-scale audience, the knowledge might have allayed his concern about the durability of his work. It might even have tempered his growing pessimism about "the damned human race."

1890–1909

During the last two decades of his life Mark Twain produced nine more works that attracted international attention: three novels, a fictionalized biography, another travel work, and four major stories.

A Connecticut Yankee in King Arthur's Court, published almost simultaneously in the United States and England at the close of 1889, was Twain's all-out attempt, through satire and heavy-handed ridicule, to expose what he believed to be fourteen centuries of social injustice in Great Britain. In the guise of an ingenious Yankee projected back into the sixth century, Twain attacked monarchy, the church, chivalric traditions, and a hierarchical society. Twain's hero and the science-fiction treatment of his adventures captivated readers in America, where the novel ran to thirteen editions during its first two decades. Eventually *A Connecticut Yankee* became one of Twain's best-selling works not only at home but in Europe and Latin America as well. However, it offended British sensibilities through a whole generation of English critics who continued to pronounce it "in bad taste," "not for the cultivated class," "a coarse and clumsy burlesque," and "that mad travesty." Whether the British reading public at large reacted in the same fashion is questionable, but they found only five British editions in the book stalls during these twenty years, and *A Connecticut Yankee* was rarely republished in England after 1902. During this period only two translations were published on the Continent, one each in Danish and Swedish in 1890.

Mark Twain's other works produced during this period did little to enhance his reputation abroad. *The American Claimant* (1892) and *Pudd'nhead Wilson* (1894) were popular with American readers; but with the exception of nine editions of *Pudd'nhead Wilson* in Germany, these two works reached European readers in single editions only. *The American Claimant* was translated into Danish, French, German, Dutch, Hungarian, and Swedish, and *Pudd'nhead Wilson* into Danish and German. *The Personal Recollections of Joan of Arc* (1896) was the closest thing to an inspired labor of love in Twain's literary experience. This fictionalized autobiography did well in America with nine editions before 1910, but after its title was revealed as a literary hoax, Twain's English publisher issued only three editions before that date. It was translated abroad in 1897 into one Dutch edition and three successive Russian editions. A French translation was published in the United States in 1906, but *Joan of Arc* was never published in France as of 1976.

In 1897 Mark Twain published a voluminous account of his year's lecture tour around the British Empire. *Following the Equator*, although packed with information about the countries he had visited, was largely a pedestrian work with only flashes of the verve that had animated his earlier travel works. Lagging interest prompted only five American and three British editions and a single Swedish translation by 1907. Thereafter this work suffered comparative obscurity with only three American and three British editions during the next forty years. After World War II it was introduced to some foreign readers through single translations in Sweden, Hungary, and Germany and was extracted in several English-language editions in India and Pakistan. Mark Twain had intended *Following the Equator* for an international audience of English-speaking people, but it is doubtful whether it ever reached many readers in Australia, New Zealand, India, and South Africa.

In this same decade of the 1890s Mark Twain capitalized on the popularity of his earlier adventures of Tom Sawyer and Huckleberry Finn with two sequels, *Tom Sawyer Abroad* (1894) and *Tom Sawyer, Detective* (1896). Although these new adventures fell short of their predecessors, the two stories had such favorable response that they were issued in a combined total of forty international editions before 1910. Most of the English-language editions were published in the United States. Both titles were soon translated into Dutch and Swedish, another edition of *Tom Sawyer Abroad* into Finnish, and further editions of *Tom Sawyer, Detective* into Danish, French, German, and Spanish. Designed for young readers, these stories sustained their popularity both at home and abroad during subsequent decades, and their readership increased most substantially in Spain, Germany, Sweden, France, Italy, and Argentina. The universal appeal of these Tom Sawyer sequels is demonstrated by further translations of one or the other into Chinese, Czech, Icelandic, Italian, Greek, Hebrew, Japanese, Magyar, Portuguese, Romanian, Russian, Serbo-Croatian, and Slovenian.

During the final decade of his life Mark Twain produced only two works that had any significant bearing on his international popularity: a moralistic satire under the title *The Man That Corrupted Hadleyburg* (1900), and his long-nurtured fantasy, *Captain Stormfield's Visit to Heaven* (1907). Neither found much of an international audience. *The Man That Corrupted Hadleyburg* was probably too mordant and *Captain Stormfield's Visit to Heaven* too irreverent to suit the taste of belated Victorians or even readers of the Edwardian era. During these ten years the Hadleyburg story appeared in five American, two British, and three German editions, but usually as the title story of various collections of Twain's stories and essays. The Stormfield extravaganza came out in only two American editions and one French translation during this period. Later in the twentieth century, when Mark Twain was reassessed as a serious and even profound writer, Captain Stormfield's disenchantment with heaven found an appreciative European audience through translated editions in Belgium, France, Germany, Italy, Spain, Switzerland, Hungary, and Poland, and its antireligious bias stimulated nine editions in Russia.

Although most of these late works had far less appeal than the earlier works of Mark Twain, his world audience expanded and his popularity increased substantially during these last two decades of his life. Between 1890 and 1910 his stories and sketches were translated for Colombian, Czech, Dutch, Hungarian, Italian, and Romanian readers. *The Prince and the Pauper* was introduced to Finnish, Italian, Marathi, Polish, and Spanish readers. *Tom Sawyer* was translated into Finnish, Italian, and Spanish; *Huckleberry Finn* into Czech and Polish; and *Life on the Mississippi* into Finnish. Among all of his writings these five perennial favorites accounted for one-half of some 543 Mark Twain editions published in America and abroad during these twenty years. Mark Twain himself might have been astonished to know that his literary labors, in one form or another, were producing an average of twenty-seven editions per year before he finally gave up the enterprise.

At this point another dimension of Mark Twain's international publication should be noted. Most of Twain's single works were included in the many editions of his collected works in addition to their publication as separate editions. Although these limited and often expensive collected editions would not add substantially to his mass audience, they were a contributing factor toward enhancing Twain's reputation at the end of the century. In Germany, for example, his well-established popularity prompted the Stuttgart publisher Robert Lutz to publish in 1892 a six-volume German-language edition of Mark Twain's "selected humorous writings," which was reissued five times before 1910. This earliest Lutz collection was supplemented by a cheaper "railway edition" of the same writings in 1899-1900, and a new series of Twain's "humorous writings" followed in 1903, reissued in 1907. The Lutz collected editions were republished in revised editions or new issues at least eleven times before 1940, a circumstance that could account for the infrequent appearance in Germany of certain titles as single editions during various periods of the twentieth century.

In the United States during the 1890s most of Mark Twain's writings were brought together as collected works on at least ten occasions, published by two of Twain's own publishing enterprises, Charles L. Webster and Company and The American Publishing Company, and also by Harper & Brothers. Five additional collected editions were undertaken before 1910, and later generations of Americans were supplied with at least seventeen further collections before 1976. Along with sets of Longfellow and Emerson, American households were well stocked with a humorist whose name had become a national byword.

In England, where Mark Twain always enjoyed a tremendous personal popularity as well as a sustained readership,[5] Chatto & Windus were encouraged to publish a collected edition of his works in 1899 and further editions in 1925 and 1931.

Several European and Latin American publishers followed the trend. A modest Russian-language edition of Twain's "collected works" appeared in St. Petersburg in 1898-1899, followed by five, more expansive editions under both the Tsarist and Communist regimes. Foreign-language editions were published in other countries where Twain's popularity rapidly increased after World War II: in Portugal his "complete works"; in Spain his "entire novels" in eight various editions and his "five best works" in two successive editions; in Argentina his "novels and stories" in one edition and his "works" in a later edition; and in Romania a four-volume collection of his major works. All such collections undoubtedly had limited markets, but they give evidence of a large readership already established in each country.

1910-1929

It might be assumed that Mark Twain's international audience would decline after 1910, the year that brought his death and the threshold of a new era. Although *The Mysterious Stranger* and a collection of Twain's letters appeared a few years later, readers could expect little more from his pen until his literary executors began to discover and release unpublished materials. Most important, however, is the context of the times. For at least the next twenty years people throughout the Western world were engrossed in national hostilities and social upheavals that disrupted their lives and left little room for their pursuit of arts and letters. Publication in most European countries was drastically curtailed during the war years of 1914-1918 and the postwar recovery and readjustment of the 1920s. Along with the cultural and philosophical reorientation of the period, literary taste itself was undergoing radical changes. A new generation of writers, who were largely committed to renouncing Victorian values and literary traditions, were beginning to displace the standard authors. What could a nineteenth-century writer, especially an American humorist, have to solace the war generation and help them to cope with their modern problems? Many nineteenth-century literary idols inevitably lost interest for postwar readers. Among the few exceptions was Mark Twain, whose modernity of spirit and concern about the human condition projected him into the twentieth century. The man as a personality was gone, but his works still found a large and ready audience both at home and abroad.

Oddly enough, hostilities between the European powers did not discourage some of their publishers from issuing Mark Twain editions. During the war years six editions of various Mark Twain titles were published in Germany, three editions in England, and several editions in Italy. In Russia, shortly after the Bolshevik Revolution and in the midst of the civil war in that country, five Mark Twain editions appeared in Petrograd and Moscow (1918-1919). During the following decade of the 1920s Soviet presses turned out thirty editions of Twain's various works, including eight editions of *Tom Sawyer* alone, seven collections of his stories, and four editions each of *Huckleberry Finn* and *Connecticut Yankee*. This phenomenal surge of Mark Twain's popularity among the Russian masses, surpassed only by that of Jack London,[6] led to a six-volume Russian edition of Twain's collected works (1927-1929). Such a response, in a country whose ideology was diametrically opposed to Twain's capitalistic background, was to continue unabated for the next fifty years. These wartime publications of an American writer in antagonistic European countries and the subsequent appropriation of many of his works by the Soviet press point up a cultural phenomenon that Mark Twain probably never anticipated: the universal appeal of his humor and storytelling art that could transcend, if it could not reconcile, cultural antipathies and nationalistic rivalries.

Meanwhile, further translations of his writings gave Mark Twain new entrees into Mexico (1919), Yugoslavia (1921), Uruguay (1921), and Chile (1927). His already well-established popularity increased in Germany,

Great Britain, and Sweden; and his following in Denmark and Hungary was well sustained. In France, where he had had only a modest audience prior to 1910, readers were now well supplied with a wide variety of his stories and novels. Spanish readers, who previously had been barely acquainted with Twain, were buying numerous translated editions during the 1920s. And the mass of readers in Italy were beginning to discover Tom Sawyer and Huckleberry Finn, the young prince and pauper, and even Captain Stormfield, as well as a variety of Twain's stories and sketches. All told, during this twenty-year period at least 533 international editions of Mark Twain's various writings were published in some twenty-five countries. This output, large as it was, turned out to be only a prelude to the spreading circles of Twain's international audience in the decades to come.

1930–1949

The publishing trade fell upon hard times in the Great Depression of the 1930s, and American writers had especially lean opportunities in the international market. Even such leading American authors as Ernest Hemingway, John Steinbeck, and William Faulkner, who had begun their careers in the 1920s, did not find large audiences abroad until the late 1940s (see Table 5). During the 1930s Mark Twain was the only nineteenth-century American writer to have a well-sustained international following among Americans and Europeans preoccupied with economic adversity, ideological conflict, and the gathering threat of war. Certain early twentieth-century writers were still highly popular at this time, but among them Jack London and Zane Grey were the only two who outpublished Mark Twain abroad. Sinclair Lewis, James Oliver Curwood, and Edgar Rice Burroughs were close competitors. Pearl Buck, who was just emerging on the literary scene, was the only other American to command a larger share of international attention than Twain.

During this prewar decade Mark Twain's work sold very well in foreign countries. His writings averaged eleven editions per year in the United States and increased to about five editions per year in Russia and three per year in Italy and Great Britain. His popularity declined slightly in Germany, fell off markedly in Spain, and was barely sustained in France. The political turmoil and eventual loss of a free press in Germany and Spain might explain the decline in those countries, although the resurgence of Twain's German and Spanish publication in the 1940s would indicate that he suffered a loss of exposure rather than popularity. In 1939 Edgar Hemminghaus concluded his invaluable study of Mark Twain's reception in Germany with the following observation: "Under the present material, political, and spiritual conditions in the national life of Greater Germany today, it is extremely questionable whether Mark Twain's books will continue to find a market."[7] Hemminghaus, of course, could not foresee the changed conditions of postwar Germany, and his forecast was based on the tenor of German literary criticism rather than the temper of the German people.

The 1930s also broadened the circle of Mark Twain's Latin American audience with the introduction of *Tom Sawyer* to Brazil (1933) and Argentina (1938), and brought Twain to mainland China with a translation of *Tom Sawyer* (1936). Overall during this decade the overwhelming favorite among both American and foreign readers was *Tom Sawyer*, followed by Twain's stories and sketches and *Huckleberry Finn*, and more distantly by *The Prince and the Pauper*, preferences that continued through the 1940s.

The Second World War again drastically reduced publication in European countries and even imposed restrictions in the United States. Despite these circumstances Mark Twain, along with some other writers, was an anomaly in the publishing world. At least fifty-six editions of his various works were issued in the United States, many of them as special editions for the armed services. At the height of the war Russian presses turned out nine editions, and between 1940 and 1945 German publishers produced six editions, and British and Italian publishers five each. Readers in occupied Denmark found time and opportunity to consume ten new editions. During these few years an extraordinary total of thirty-five editions of Mark Twain titles appeared in Spain and thirteen editions in Sweden. Both countries, of course, enjoyed a neutrality that encouraged their own enterprises. During these war years translations of Mark Twain began to be published in Belgium (1944) and appeared for the first time in the Middle East with *Tom Sawyer* in Palestine (1940) and collections of Twain's stories in Turkey (1940).

In the closing years of this decade, after the war, Mark Twain's popularity rebounded in Europe and Russia. At midcentury his publications demonstrated a tremendous popularity continuing in the United States at the rate of nine editions per year, a strong popularity in Germany demanding six editions per year, and a very substantial popularity in Sweden, Spain, France, and Italy. At this point his following was well sustained in Great Britain and Russia and had become established in Poland and Yugoslavia. His Latin American audience was expanding with a huge output of six Spanish-language editions per year in Argentina and frequent Portuguese-language editions in Brazil. By 1950 a new generation was ready to discover Mark Twain not only in America, Europe, and Latin America but literally around the world.

1950–1969

Mark Twain once remarked to a close friend, "My interest in my work dies a sudden and violent death when the work is done."[8] This assertion may have been expressed in a fit of pique toward reviewers and critics, whom he often accused of deliberately misunderstanding his literary intentions. Such an attitude toward the fate of his own books is contradicted by his constant efforts to goad his early publishers into marketing his books more profitably for their author as well as themselves. There is also his bitter denunciation of the pirating of his earliest works in England and Canada, and his long campaign to establish international copyright and lengthier protection in the United States. Mark Twain constantly had an eye on domestic royalties for his cumulative works. He probably had no illusions about foreign royalties other than from British publishers, and we know that he was pleasantly surprised to receive a modest return from Bernard Tauchnitz in Germany.[9] Whatever his thoughts may have been about the possibilities of foreign markets, he apparently did not anticipate widespread European translations and certainly did not envision the worldwide audience that his writings would attract by the mid-twentieth century. If he had lived and published half a century later than he did and had had the protection of twentieth-century international copyright agreements, he would have realized a return from his enterprise far beyond his aspirations. At the same time, it was fortunate for readers abroad that the limited copyright protection of his time did not restrict translation and international reproduction of his works.[10]

The two decades following World War II brought an unprecedented outpouring of Mark Twain editions. It would be confusing and almost meaningless to translate the phenomenon into mere statistics. What emerges from the record is a shifting kaleidoscope of nationalities and races that enlarged Twain's audience among the postwar generation to the point where almost two thousand editions of his various works were published in fifty-four countries to satisfy the demand. This kind of audience did not develop spontaneously, of course. It was the outcome of many things: national liberations and rising expectations, increasing literacy, the advent of inexpensive paperback editions and a book trade that sought out the masses, unsung translators and enterprising publishers—and perhaps most fruitful of all, the discovery that Mark Twain offered all peoples an account of life that turned out to be a common denominator of human experience.

In America by the 1960s domestic editions of Mark Twain were averaging twenty per year. In England production of his works doubled that of the prewar years. The resurgence of his popularity in Germany required an average of nine editions per year to satisfy the demand. In Spain and Italy, where Twain's works had made a belated appearance, the new generation consumed six and seven editions per year during these postwar decades. In France, where his readership had been barely sustained during the previous seventy-five years, publishers began to disregard the judgment of earlier French critics that Twain's humor was not suitable to the Gallic taste. Interest in Twain so increased that his editions quadrupled their prewar output in that country. During these postwar decades his popularity in the Netherlands increased tenfold, it doubled in Denmark and Sweden, and it became well established in Austria, Switzerland, Belgium, Portugal, and Norway.

In eastern Europe, a region where sporadic editions of his works had reached limited audiences before the war, Mark Twain gained a large readership among the Iron Curtain countries. Whether state censors found that some of his writings served their ideological purpose or whether they simply acceded to a growing popular demand for Americana in general and Mark Twain in particular, most of Twain's writings became accessible to the socialist masses. Their author had already established a strong following in Yugoslavia before the war, but during the postwar decades editions of his works increased to an average of four per year during the 1950s and six per year during the 1960s to satisfy the many ethnic groups of that country. Elsewhere Mark Twain titles attracted large readerships in Czechoslovakia, Hungary, and Poland, and had sustained readerships in Romania and Bulgaria. Twain's audience in Finland more than doubled during these years. His already well-established popularity among Russian readers became so enormous after the war that between 1950 and 1970 Soviet presses published an average of seven editions per year, many of them in minority languages. Ten were in Ukrainian alone.

Latin American readers continued to absorb a steady output of Spanish and Portuguese editions of Mark Twain.[11] His popularity remained strong in Argentina and increased substantially in Brazil and Mexico.

In the Middle East, where he had been virtually unknown before 1950, Twain acquired a well-sustained audience in Turkey and Israel. He was introduced to readers in Iran (1958), and Egyptian presses published several more Arabic editions of his titles in the 1960s.

In India, where Mark Twain had been known by only one English-language edition of *Following the Equator* and one early Marathi translation of *The Prince and the Pauper* (1908), many editions of several of his major works reached the mass of native readers after national independence in 1947. During the following two decades at least thirty-four editions were published in nine native languages as well as English. *Tom Sawyer* became the favorite among the Indian peoples, followed by *Huckleberry Finn* and *The Prince and the Pauper*.

Mark Twain's account of the American scene also appeared in India during this period in the form of extracts from *Roughing It* and several editions of *Life on the Mississippi*. Publishers in Southeast Asia, however, apparently considered most of Mark Twain too alien to the cultures of their region to undertake much translation. In the 1960s two editions of *Huckleberry Finn* were published for native readers in Malaysia, and translations of *The Prince and the Pauper* brought their author to Thailand (1963) and to Burma (1969).

In 1889, when Mark Twain and young Rudyard Kipling first met, Twain had been much amused by the opening line of one of Kipling's recent ballads: "Oh, East is East, and West is West, and never the twain shall meet. . . ." Kipling's inadvertent play upon words occasioned little more than banter between the two at the time, but seven years later when Twain lectured his way through India he must have been struck by the fact that his travels had indeed closed the gap between East and West. If he had foreseen the migration that his literary works would make to the Orient half a century later, his satisfaction over his role as a roving ambassador might have been complete.

Mark Twain's lecture tour of the British Empire in 1895-1896 bypassed East Asia, but his literary odyssey became virtually worldwide by the 1950s with the publication of almost all of his major works in Chinese and Japanese, followed by several Korean translations in the 1960s. By the mid-1950s he had been imported to mainland China through Peking and Shanghai editons of *Tom Sawyer*, *Huckleberry Finn*, *Life on the Mississippi*, *The Gilded Age*, *Pudd'nhead Wilson*, and *Joan of Arc* as well as various collections of his short stories. Communist translators took a sympathetic attitude toward the American author, although in their zeal for the party line they felt compelled to distort Twain's role in American life and to telescope American history in some of their prefatory comments (discussed above in Section 3). In the meantime, other Chinese readers were exposed to Mark Twain during these two decades by a spate of at least twenty-two translated editions in Hong Kong and seventeen such editions in Taiwan. Publication of Mark Twain virtually ceased in mainland China during the 1960s, a decline that might be attributed to the Cultural Revolution in Red China.

It was in Japan that Mark Twain acquired his largest Far Eastern audience. An earlier generation of Japanese readers had been introduced to Twain by an 1899 translation of *The Prince and the Pauper*, and at least five Japanese-language editions of his various stories and sketches had been published during the early twentieth century; but it was the mass audience of the 1950s and 1960s that encouraged the production of twelve major works by Mark Twain in at least forty-six Japanese editions.

During this same period Twain's international audience was further extended to South Africa with Akfrikaans translations of *Huckleberry Finn* and two of the Tom Sawyer stories.

1970–

Although comprehensive information about Mark Twain's international editions beyond the year 1976 is not available as of this writing, it is safe to say that the high degree of interest in Mark Twain among worldwide readers continued unabated throughout the 1970s. During the brief period

1970-1976 almost 650 editions of various Mark Twain titles were published in forty-two countries. In addition, Twain was introduced for the first time to native Philippine readers with a Filipino translation of *Tom Sawyer* (1974); Russian publishers rendered Twain into two more languages with a Belorussian edition of his stories (1971) and a Tadzhik edition of *The Prince and the Pauper* (1975); and six more editions of Twain's collected works appeared at home and abroad, two in the United States, two in Germany, and one each in Spain and Switzerland. If the country editions published during these years are measured by the aforementioned popularity scale (see Section 2), Mark Twain's international popularity at this time, more than a century after his writing was first introduced to foreign readers, can be described as follows:

> Enormous popularity in the United States, Germany, Spain, and Russia.
>
> Very strong popularity in Yugoslavia.
>
> Strong popularity in Austria, Denmark, Sweden, Czechoslovakia, Finland, and Japan.
>
> Sustained popularity in Great Britain, France, Italy, Netherlands, Switzerland, Hungary, Poland, Romania, Turkey, and India.

Although publication of his works during these seven years declined somewhat below the level of the 1960s, his output of ninety-two editions per year augurs well for Mark Twain's continued standing as an international best-seller.

In full perspective, it had taken a century, from the 1870 British edition of the *Innocents Abroad* to the 1974 Philippine edition of *Tom Sawyer*, for Mark Twain's audience to expand to its worldwide scope. His universal appeal to the common reader inevitably spread the circles of his readership from the United States and the British Commonwealth to Western Europe, Eastern Europe, and Russia, thence to Latin America, the Middle East, and India, and finally to the Far East and Southeast Asia. Such international coverage was impelled mainly by the popular appeal of his stories and-sketches, *Tom Sawyer*, *Huckleberry Finn*, and *The Prince and the Pauper*, reinforced by the widespread attraction of *A Connecticut Yankee* and *Life on the Mississippi*. The statistics of Mark Twain's publication reveal the same phenomenon. By 1976 *Tom Sawyer* alone had marketed more than eleven hundred foreign editions translated into some fifty-seven languages; and Twain's various works taken collectively had appeared in more than forty-one hundred foreign editions translated into seventy-two languages and issued in fifty-four foreign countries. His foreign audience had grown to the point where it more than tripled his American audience. Enterprising and ambitous as he was, Mark Twain could hardly have aspired to such success or have foreseen the time when he would become probably the most widely known writer to come out of America.

5. COMPARATIVE POPULARITY OF MARK TWAIN'S MAJOR WORKS

Just as writers themselves compete with each other for popular favor, a writer's individual works compete with each other and cannot be expected to be equally successful with all generations of readers or with all nationalities. Mark Twain was no exception. The comparative popularity of his individual works varied considerably in point of time and place. Ths variability becomes apparent when three factors are taken into account: the number of languages into which his various works were translated, the geographical extent of their publication, and their production in terms of average editions per year. These factors become especially significant when after 1900 all of Twain's major works had appeared and competed with each other on an equal basis. From the record (see Tables 1 and 2) it is evident that his stories and sketches were his most popular writings during the Victorian decades up to 1910, and that *The Prince and the Pauper* was the overwhelming favorite among all of his novels and *The Innocents Abroad* by far his most popular travel work during this same period. In the 1910s and especially the 1920s, readers still preferred the stories and sketches but turned increasingly to *The Adventures of Tom Sawyer* and *The Adventures of Huckleberry Finn*, both of which gained ascendancy over *The Prince and the Pauper*. After 1930 *Tom Sawyer* became Twain's international bestseller, followed by *Huckleberry Finn* and the stories and sketches respectively. *The Prince and the Pauper* still attracted a strongly sustained audience during these later four decades from 1930 to 1970; *A Connecticut Yankee in King Arthur's Court* gained a wide popularity; and *Life on the Mississippi* emerged as Twain's most popular travel work, displacing *The Innocents Abroad*, which lapsed into comparative obscurity.

Viewed from the perspective of a full century, the totality of Mark Twain's work made an impressive impact on the world book market. His novels, taken collectively, were published in more than thirty-four hundred international editions, his stories and sketches in more than nine hundred editions, and his travel works in approximately five hundred editions. It is safe to say that by the mid-twentieth century readers of almost all nationalities and cultures had been exposed to something from Mark Twain. However, a closer look at the fortunes of his various works reveals that the main thrust of his international popularity came from a few major works, and that the popular appeal of those works fluctuated within certain countries and from one period to another in many instances. For the purpose of evaluating various degrees of popularity of a given work in a given country, it is assumed that popularity was "enormous" if the work was issued at an average rate of one or more editions per year, "very strong" if issued at the rate of one editon every two years, "strong" if issued at the rate of one edition every three years, and "sustained" if issued every four to five years over an extended period of time. The following offers a chronological summary of the popular trends of each major work:

Stories and *Sketches* (1867-) were translated into forty-two languages and published in various collections under various titles in forty countries to a total of more than nine hundred editions. They were the most popular of Mark Twain's writings from 1867 to 1930. Their popularity until 1940 was enormous in the United States, Great Britain, and Germany; strong in France, Spain, Sweden, and Russia; and sustained in Denmark, Italy, and Romania. After World War II their popularity was enormous in the United States, Germany, Spain, and Russia; very strong in Denmark, France, Italy, Switzerland, Yugoslavia, and Argentina; strong in Sweden, Hungary, and Poland; and sustained in Mexico, Turkey, and Japan.

The Innocents Abroad (1869) was translated into fifteen languages and published in twenty-one countries in a total of 144 editions. The most popular travel work of its time, especially among British and American readers, it out-produced all of Twain's other works except his stories and sketches during the 1870s and 1880s. Its Anglo-American popularity declined after 1890 and was surpassed by that of *Life on the Mississippi* after 1930. Virtually unknown elsewhere after 1890 except for a few sporadic editions in Spain and Russia, there were two editions each of this work in Austria, Italy, Czechoslovakia, and Japan, and a resurgence of publication in Germany in the 1960s.

Roughing It (1872) was translated into thirteen languages and published in seventeen countries in 102 editions. Its popularity in the United States was very strong until 1934 when publication ceased until there began a very strong revival for two decades after 1950. Its popularity in Great Britain was strong until 1903, but there were virtually no editions after that date. It enjoyed strong popularity in Spain for three decades following 1943. Except for Australia, Canada, France, the Netherlands, and Sweden, it was a work unknown to other countries until after World War II.

The Gilded Age (1873) was translated into ten languages and published in twelve countries in sixty-one editions. Publication was limited largely to the United States and Great Britain. American popularity was very strong for three decades but lapsed after 1903 until a revival in the 1960s. British interest was sustained for twenty-five years but lapsed thereafter until republication in the 1960s. There was no appreciable interest elsewhere except for two editions each in Italy, Sweden, Hungary, and Russia.

The Adventures of Tom Sawyer (1876) was translated into fifty-six languages and published in forty-six countries in almost thirteen hundred editions by 1976. Slow to win favor both at home and abroad until 1920, it had a phenomenal rise in popularity thereafter, becoming the most popular of all Mark Twain works after 1930. Before 1930 its popularity was enormous in the United States, very strong in Germany, and sustained in Great Britain and Sweden. After 1930 its popularity was enormous in the United States, Great Britain, France, Germany, Italy, Spain, Sweden, Yugoslavia, and Russia; very strong in the Netherlands, Czechoslovakia, and Argentina; strong in Austria, Belgium, Denmark, Finland, Poland, Brazil, Turkey, India, and Japan; and sustained in Switzerland, Hungary, Romania, and Mexico. This work also had a strong reception in Taiwan after 1950.

A Tramp Abroad (1879) was translated into five languages and published in ten countries in sixty-six editions. Its popularity was very strong in Great Britain until 1912 and strong in the United States until 1907. There was no further publication in Great Britain and only a few sporadic editions in the United States. It had very strong popularity in Germany in the 1960s and 1970s during a revival in twelve editions. It was translated into Danish, Dutch, Spanish, and Swedish.

The Prince and the Pauper (1881) was translated into forty-eight languages and published in forty-four countries in 551 editions. Universally popular among readers of all ages and nationalities, it was an instant success in the United States with a very strong popularity sustained for almost a century until 1976. Its popularity was very strong in Germany throughout the entire period; strong in Great Britain until 1910 and again after 1950; very strong in Russia after 1918 and enormous after 1950; strong in France until 1938 and enormous after 1945; and very strong in Italy after 1930 and enormous after 1945. Its postwar popularity after 1945 was enormous in Yugoslavia; very strong in Argentina, Brazil, Japan, Poland, and Spain; strong in Finland, Mexico, Romania, Turkey, and Israel; and well sustained in India and Sweden.

Life on the Mississippi (1876, 1883) was translated into twenty-three languages and published in twenty-seven countries in 139 editions. The most widely published, most frequently translated, and most popular of Mark Twain's travel works, it enjoyed very strong popularity in the United States from 1883 to 1976. It was very strong in popularity in Great Britain until 1904, but had very little publication thereafter. It enjoyed strong popularity in Germany in the postwar decades after 1945, and several editions each were published sporadically in Sweden, Czechoslovakia, Finland, Yugoslavia, Russia, and India. Widespread international interest between 1960 and 1976 resulted in forty-five editions during those recent years.

The Adventures of Huckleberry Finn (1884) was translated into fifty-two languages and published in forty-seven countries in 841 editions. It is second only to *Tom Sawyer* in international popularity among all of Mark Twain's works. Its popularity in the United States was very strong from 1885 to 1930 and enormous thereafter. It was slow to gain popular acceptance elsewhere until the 1920s. Its popularity in Great Britain, Germany, and Russia was very strong during the 1920s and 1930s and enormous during the postwar period 1948-1976. In the 1950s its popularity became enormous in Czechoslovakia; very strong in Italy, Spain, Sweden, and Argentina; strong in Denmark, the Netherlands, and Japan; and well sustained in Norway, Hungary, Romania, and Yugoslavia. In the 1960s its popularity strengthened to enormous in France, Italy, Spain, and Yugoslavia; was very strong in India; and was strong in Switzerland and Hong Kong.

A Connecticut Yankee in King Arthur's Court (1889) was translated into twenty-one languages and published in twenty-seven countries in two hundred editions. It became an instant success in the United States with very strong popularity maintained until 1950. Publication lapsed during the 1950s but revived with enormous popularity during the 1960s. Strong popularity in Great Britain until 1902 despite adverse criticism was followed by virtual obscurity until a revival of interest occurred during the years 1957-1976. Its popularity in Russia was enormous in the late 1920s and very strong from 1950 to 1976; strong in Spain during the 1950s and 1960s and enormous in the 1970s; very strong in Germany between 1948 and 1961, followed by an enormous popularity in the early 1970s. Elsewhere its popularity was enormous in Argentina 1945-1951, strong in Brazil 1945-1960, very strong in Italy 1952-1972, strong in Czechoslovakia 1954-1976, and sustained in Japan 1951-1976 and in Romania 1961-1976.

The American Claimant (1892), translated into eleven languages and published in fifteen countries in forty-three editions, had a very minor international reception. It had strong popularity in the United States until 1903, which was followed by brief revivals from 1912 to 1924 until lapse of publication in 1972. Several editions were published in the Netherlands and Romania and two each in France, Germany, Portugal, Spain, Sweden, and Czechoslovakia.

Pudd'nhead Wilson (1894), translated into twelve languages and published in nineteen countries in ninety-four editions, had minor international reception. Its popularity was very strong in the United States 1894-1922 and 1955-1976 and in Germany 1895-1909. There were sporadic editions in Hungary, Great Britain, and Sweden, but there was no sustained interest in the latter two countries until the 1960s. Two editions each were published in Denmark, Italy, Spain, and Finland.

Tom Sawyer Abroad (1894) was translated into eighteen languages and published in twenty-three countries in 130 editions. A fairly popular successor to the original Tom Sawyer adventures, its popularity was very strong in the United States 1894-1935 and 1961-1967, in Spain 1946-1976, and in Germany 1959-1976. Popularity was strong in Sweden 1940-1948 and enormous in Argentina 1943-1953. Several editions were published sporadically in Italy, Finland, Hungary, Russia, Brazil, Mexico, and Great Britain, and two editions each in Portugal, Czechoslovakia, Israel, and Japan.

Tom Sawyer, Detective (1896), translated into nineteen languages and published in twenty-five countries in 188 editions, was a highly popular sequel to the preceding Tom Sawyer stories. Popularity in the United States was very strong 1896-1906 and 1917-1935 followed by a strong revival in the 1960s. Popularity in Germany was very strong 1897-1918 and 1958-1976; enormous in Spain 1948-1976; strong in Sweden 1939-1950; strong in Finland 1950-1957; strong in Italy 1951-1966; very strong in France 1958-1967; and strong in Belgium 1961-1968. There were a few editions in Great Britain after 1896 and several sporadic editions in Denmark, Czechoslovakia, Hungary, Yugoslavia, Russia, Argentina, Brazil, and Japan.

Personal Recollections of Joan of Arc (1896) was translated into twelve languages and published in thirteen countries in fifty-two editions. Its popularity in the United States was very strong 1896-1906 and strong 1912-1926; publication lapsed thereafter until a brief revival in the 1960s. Readership was barely sustained in Great Britain 1896-1922. It was briefly popular in Russia 1897-1902, and in Czechoslovakia 1951-1957, and had very strong popularity in Spain 1949-1956. There were a few sporadic editions in Sweden after 1944.

Following the Equator (1897) was translated into four languages and published in seven countries in twenty-six editions. Its popularity in the United States was strong but brief 1897-1903 and barely sustained 1912-1925; publication lapsed thereafter until 1971. Its popularity was barely sustained in Great Britain 1897-1907 and 1922-1931. Two editions each were published in Germany, Sweden, India, and Pakistan.

The Man That Corrupted Hadleyburg (1900) was translated into ten languages and published in fourteen countries in forty-four editions, and was usually issued as the title of Twain's story and essay collections. It had strong popularity in the United States 1900-1936 and 1957-1970 with revived publication. There were a few sporadic editions in Great Britain, Germany, Spain, Hungary, Romania, Russia, and Argentina.

Captain Stormfield's Visit to Heaven (1907), which was later included in *Report from Paradise* (1952), was translated into eleven languages and published in ten countries in twenty-seven editions. Its popularity in Russia was strong 1935-1944 and very strong 1955-1964; there was sustained interest in Italy 1945-1965; and brief interest in the United States before 1910, in the early 1930s, and in the early 1950s. Several sporadic editions were published in Germany, as were two each in Italy and Poland.

The Mysterious Stranger (1916) was translated into eight languages and published in eleven countries in twenty-eight editions. Its popularity in the United States was barely sustained 1916-1935 but revived strongly with republications in the 1960s. There was no appreciable popularity in other countries, although two editions each were published in Germany, Czechoslovakia, Yugoslavia, and Chile.

Letters from the Earth (1962), a posthumous collection of unpublished materials, was translated into twelve languages and published in eleven countries in eighteen editions. Its popularity was barely sustained in the United States 1962-1974 but was briefly very strong in Russia 1963-1966. It attracted widespread European attention with two editions each in Bulgaria and Finland and one edition each in France, Germany, Iceland, Italy, Sweden, Czechoslovakia, and Poland.

The comparative popularity of Mark Twain's various works can hardly be measured in absolute terms because of the variable factors involved. The publication spans of his works varied from as many as 110 years in the case of his stories and sketches to as few as fifteen years for his *Letters from the Earth* as of 1976. Other variables involve the numbers of languages into which they were translated, the numbers of countries in which they were published, and their total international, total domestic, and total foreign editions (see Table 1). Popularity ratings would vary somewhat, of course, if certain factors were unduly weighted against the others. If anything, the domestic editions factor should be discounted because it weights the international balance of editions disproportionately. In spite of the variables, however, a close estimate of comparative popularity can be made. By taking into account all of these factors and measuring the performance of the major works in each of five categories—total international editions, total foreign editions, average foreign editions published per year following first foreign publication, total countries, and total languages—the popularity of Mark Twain's major works relative to each other can be described as follows:

	MAJOR WORK	SCALE OF RELATIVE POPULARITY
1.	The Adventures of Tom Sawyer	100
2.	The Adventures of Huckleberry Finn	55+
3.	Stories and Sketches	40
4.	The Prince and the Pauper	33+
5.	A Connecticut Yankee in King Arthur's Court	21+
6.	Tom Sawyer, Detective	20+
7.	Life on the Mississippi	17
8.	The Innocents Abroad	15+
9.	Tom Sawyer Abroad	14+
10.	Pudd'nhead Wilson	12
11.	Roughing It	11+
12.	Personal Recollections of Joan of Arc	9+
13.	A Tramp Abroad	9
14.	The American Claimant	9
15.	The Man That Corrupted Hadleyburg	8+
16.	The Gilded Age	8
17.	Captain Stormfield's Visit to Heaven	7+
18.	The Mysterious Stranger	7+
19.	Following the Equator	6+

The placement of several works relative to each other is debatable (for example, numbers 13, 14, and 15, and numbers 17 and 18), depending on the evaluative criteria one chooses to emphasize. However, it is evident that more than a century of Mark Twain's worldwide popularity was due mainly to the combined appeal of his five major fictional works: *Tom Sawyer*, *Huckleberry Finn*, the stories and sketches, *The Prince and the Pauper*, and *A Connecticut Yankee*. Closer inspection indicates that his eight lesser fictional works contributed substantially to his popularity, and that his five travel works contributed the least over such an extensive time. This collective judgment of five generations of readers may be altered during another century, but it is very doubtful that Tom Sawyer and Huckleberry Finn will lose their preeminence among Mark Twain's creations.

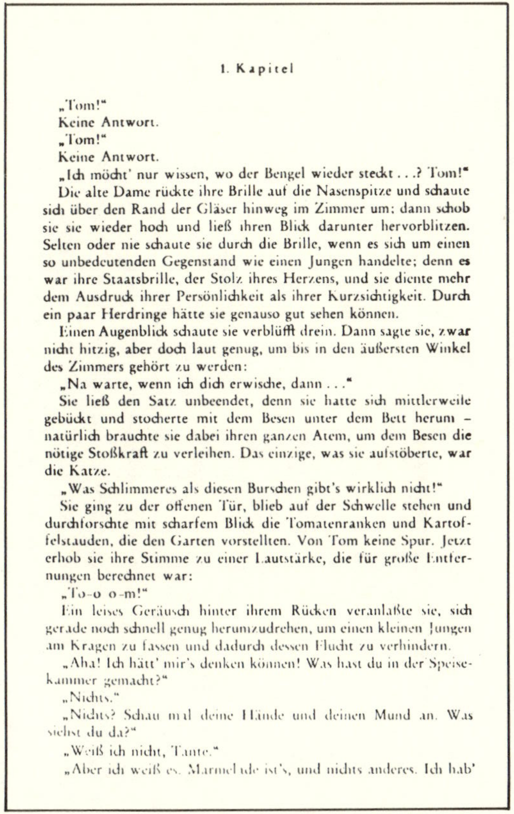

Fig. 1. Page from a German edition of *The Adventures of Tom Sawyer* (Courtesy Goldmann Publisher [Munich])

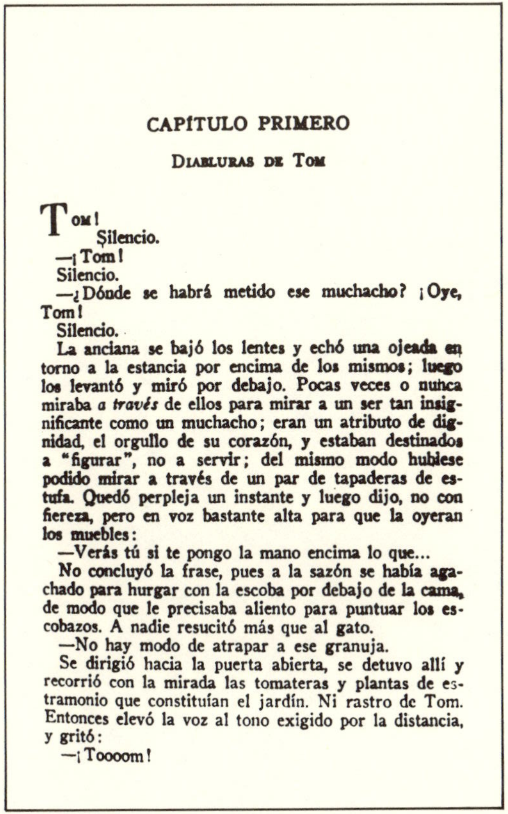

Fig. 2. Page from a Spanish edition of *The Adventures of Tom Sawyer* (Courtesy Plaza & Janes, S.A. [Barcelona])

I. Kapitel

„Tom!"

Keine Antwort.

„Tom!"

Keine Antwort.

„Ich möcht' nur wissen, wo der Bengel wieder steckt...? Tom!"

Die alte Dame rückte ihre Brille auf die Nasenspitze und schaute sich über den Rand der Gläser hinweg im Zimmer um; dann schob sie sie wieder hoch und ließ ihren Blick darunter hervorblitzen. Selten oder nie schaute sie durch die Brille, wenn es sich um einen so unbedeutenden Gegenstand wie einen Jungen handelte; denn es war ihre Staatsbrille, der Stolz ihres Herzens, und sie diente mehr dem Ausdruck ihrer Persönlichkeit als ihrer Kurzsichtigkeit. Durch ein paar Herdringe hätte sie genauso gut sehen können.

Einen Augenblick schaute sie verblüfft drein. Dann sagte sie, zwar nicht hitzig, aber doch laut genug, um bis in den äußersten Winkel des Zimmers gehört zu werden:

„Na warte, wenn ich dich erwische, dann..."

Sie ließ den Satz unbeendet, denn sie hatte sich mittlerweile gebückt und stocherte mit dem Besen unter dem Bett herum – natürlich brauchte sie dabei ihren ganzen Atem, um dem Besen die nötige Stoßkraft zu verleihen. Das einzige, was sie aufstöberte, war die Katze.

„Was Schlimmeres als diesen Burschen gibt's wirklich nicht!"

Sie ging zu der offenen Tür, blieb auf der Schwelle stehen und durchforschte mit scharfem Blick die Tomatenranken und Kartoffelstauden, die den Garten vorstellten. Von Tom keine Spur. Jetzt erhob sie ihre Stimme zu einer Lautstärke, die für große Entfernungen berechnet war:

„To-o-o-m!"

Ein leises Geräusch hinter ihrem Rücken veranlaßte sie, sich gerade noch schnell genug herumzudrehen, um einen kleinen Jungen am Kragen zu fassen und dadurch dessen Flucht zu verhindern.

„Aha! Ich hätt' mir's denken können! Was hast du in der Speisekammer gemacht?"

„Nichts."

„Nichts? Schau mal deine Hände und deinen Mund an. Was sehet du da?"

„Weiß ich nicht, Tante."

„Aber ich weiß es. Marmelade ist's, und nichts anderes. Ich hab'"

CAPÍTULO PRIMERO

DIABLURAS DE TOM

Tom!

   Silencio.

—Tom!

Silencio.

—¿Dónde se habrá metido ese muchacho? ¡Oye, Tom!

Silencio.

La anciana se bajó los lentes y echó una ojeada en torno a la estancia por encima de los mismos; luego los levantó y miró por debajo. Pocas veces o nunca miraba a través de ellos para mirar a un ser tan insignificante como un muchacho; eran un atributo de dignidad, el orgullo de su corazón, y estaban destinados a "figurar", no a servir; del mismo modo hubiese podido mirar a través de un par de tapaderas de estufa. Quedó perpleja un instante y luego dijo, no con fiereza, pero en voz bastante alta para que la oyeran los muebles:

—Verás tú si te pongo la mano encima lo que...

No concluyó la frase, pues a la sazón se había agachado para hurgar con la escoba por debajo de la cama, de modo que le precisaba aliento para puntuar los estacobazos. A nadie resucitó más que al gato.

—No hay modo de atrapar a ese granuja.

Se dirigió hacia la puerta abierta, se detuvo allí y recorrió con la mirada las tomateras y plantas de estramonio que constituían el jardín. Ni rastro de Tom. Entonces elevó la voz al tono exigido por la distancia, y gritó:

—¡Tooom!

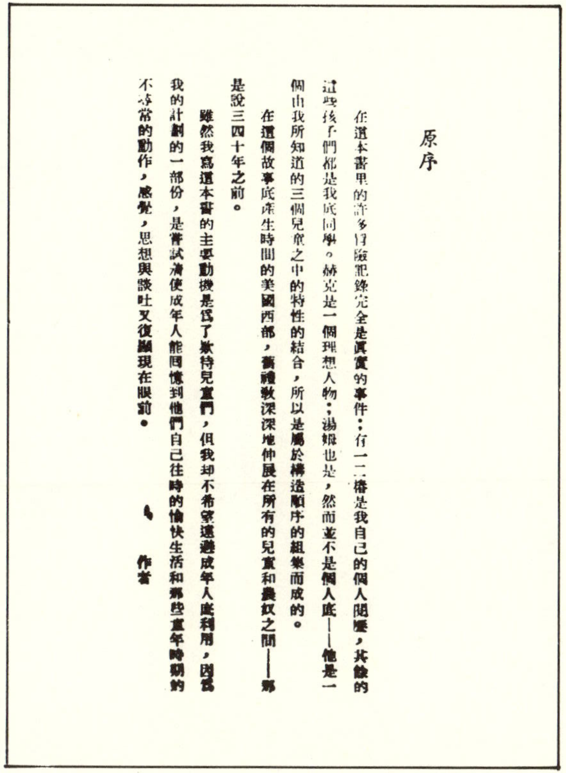

原序

　在這本書裏的許多冒險記完全是真實的事件；有一二件是我自己的個人經歷，其餘的都是我所知道的孩童們的經驗。哈克·芬是確有其人；湯姆·莎耶也是，然而並不是屬於一個個人，他是我所認識的三個兒童的性格的結合，所以是屬於構造順序的組集而成的。

　在這兒所開的故事裏先生時間的美國西部的奇異習俗，深深地分在兒童和奴隸之間——那是發生在三四十年之前。

　雖然我這本書的主要動機是為了娛樂兒童們，但我卻不希望成年人因此而將它拋開，因為我的計劃的一部份，是嘗試使成年人愉快地想起他們自己往時的生活和希望與思想與談話與又復調現在又可以去做的那種奇異的圖謀。

作者

Fig. 3. Page from a Japanese edition of *The Adventures of Tom Sawyer* (Courtesy Shinchosha Company [Tokyo])

6. MARK TWAIN'S COMPETITION WITH OTHER LEADING AMERICAN WRITERS IN THE MID-TWENTIETH CENTURY

A writer's success can be inferred from a consensus of literary critics, or from his sheer output of publication (so often the highly touted publicity for today's "best-sellers"), or from his popular reception compared with that of other writers. Each criterion has its inherent difficulties.

Literary critics rarely reach a point of unanimity in their judgments. To do a writer justice they must evaluate each of his works according to its particular merits or defects. The task is further complicated by the writer's literary role and by the medium in which he works. Critics can hardly compare novelists with poets, short story writers with dramatists, or biographers with humorists. Each genre imposes its own criteria and demands comparison of a novelist with other novelists, a humorist with other humorists, etc. If the writer engages in several literary genres, he compounds the difficulties of literary criticism by overriding convenient categories and resists attempts to judge his work as a whole. Mark Twain is a notable example of a literary maverick who often confounded the critics.

A writer's productivity in terms of his total publications might appear to be a more objective, and therefore more reliable, means of measuring his success relative to that of other writers. However, totality of publication does not, in itself, reveal the writer's scope or depth or his merits and limitations. Some writers have made a reputation from a single work, and others have become temporary best-sellers with works that last less than a decade.

Strongly sustained popularity, on the other hand, is a measure of success that transcends literary vogues, bridges the gap between literary genres, and sometimes even runs counter to professional criticism. The reading public respond to writers whom they enjoy, whatever the reason for their enjoyment, and they return to such writers uncritically but with spontaneous appreciation. For example, Jack London, Pearl Buck, Vicki Baum, Zane Grey, Edgar Allan Poe, Arthur Miller, T. S. Eliot, and Irving Stone each has his or her special appeal that seeks out and enlarges a special audience. Popularity renders a verdict of its own. It may not be the highest court of appeal, but popular success can be measured by how much of a readership a writer sustains over an appreciable period of time.

Large as he has loomed as a major American writer, Mark Twain had many rivals during his time and especially after 1920. He competed for public favor, both at home and abroad, with a dozen nineteenth-century American writers and at least two dozen other American writers who emerged as international best-sellers by the 1930s (see Table 5). James Fenimore Cooper, Edgar Allan Poe, and Louisa May Alcott had firmly established their foreign reputations in the nineteenth century, and each maintained a strong popularity into the mid-twentieth century. Cooper had a tremendous following in Germany and France, Poe in Great Britain, France, and Italy, and Alcott in Great Britain and Denmark. These three, however, were the only early American writers who shared a large measure of popularity with Mark Twain after the turn of the century.

1930–1939

Among twentieth-century American writers Twain's closest competitors for European favor were Pearl Buck and Jack London. By the 1930s London had gained tremendous popularity in Russia[12] and Italy and a strong, continuing popularity in France, Norway, Poland, Czechoslovakia, Germany, and Great Britain. His best-selling *Call of the Wild* and other novels and tales were translated and published in almost every European country by the midcentury.

Pearl Buck, emerging from the late 1920s, quickly became a best-seller in the United States, attracted very large audiences in Germany and Great Britain, and enjoyed a well-sustained popularity in France, Czechoslovakia, Italy, Norway, Poland, and Hungary. Her novel *The Good Earth* ran to at least twenty-eight international editions during the 1930s and by 1960 had been translated into almost every written language.

Mystery stories, which had fascinated American and European readers since the eighteenth century, captured a large share of the growing market after 1920. Erle Stanley Gardner and Ellery Queen, who introduced their detective series early in the 1930s, rapidly gained a tremendous following in the United States and Great Britain and a well-established popularity in certain European countries, Gardner in Hungary and Italy and Queen in France and Germany. Both of these writers were among the top seven bestselling American writers after 1945, Gardner topping all competitors during the late 1950s (see Table 5). In the field of American "westerns," Zane Grey, a longstanding favorite among American readers, maintained his tremendous popularity in both the United States and Great Britain in the 1930s and attracted very large audiences in Spain, Czechoslovakia, and Italy and well-sustained audiences in Poland, Hungary, and Germany. During this same decade Edgar Rice Burroughs and Vicki Baum were also high on the list of international favorites, Burroughs particularly in Great Britain, Norway, Denmark, France, and Hungary, and Baum particularly in Poland, Great Britain, Italy, France, Sweden, and Hungary.

In the midst of this competition of the 1930s Mark Twain outproduced all of the foregoing writers in total international editions. As might be expected, his largest readership remained in the United States, where domestic editions of his works were more than double those of his closest competitor, Louisa May Alcott, and far exceeded those of all other leading American writers. In Great Britain his popularity gave way to that of Sinclair, Grey, Burroughs, Alcott, Gardner, Queen, and T. S. Eliot. On the European continent, however, Jack London was the only American writer to outpublish Twain. In Russia, where the Soviet press had introduced Twain to the masses during the 1920s, his popularity grew enormously during the 1930s with an output of thirty-eight editions in less than ten years. During this decade Italian readers consumed twenty-six editions of his various writings, British readers twenty-three editions, and interest in his works increased in Germany, Poland, and Spain.

Despite the Great Depression, ideological conflicts, and international preoccupation with the gathering threat of war, American writers, collectively speaking, made impressive inroads on the European market during these prewar years. Their individual popularity varied so much from one country to another that broad generalizations cannot be made about the European-wide impact of specific writers. Mark Twain, more than thirty years after the publication of his last major work, was still outperforming all American writers in the European and American book trade of the 1930s. Such formidable writers as Ernest Hemingway, William Faulkner, and John Steinbeck, who became best-sellers abroad after World War II, had already appeared on the American scene in the 1920s but were just beginning to reach European readers in the 1930s.

1940–1947

It would seem inevitable that international publication, especially among the warring nations, would diminish almost to the vanishing point during the years 1940-1945. Yet there are indications that in spite of hostilities and consuming war efforts, the publication of some writers was uninterrupted in many European countries as well as in the United States. Information on this matter was not available to the League-of-Nations sponsored *Index Translationum*, which ceased publication in 1940 and did not resume until 1948. However, the continued publication of Mark Twain during this period is a case in point that indicates widespread enterprise among publishers during those years. In actuality, the output of Mark Twain editions increased over that of the 1930s and all prewar decades. Over two hundred wartime editions of his various works were issued, more than half of them in Europe. The larger number appeared in neutral countries, notably Spain and Sweden, and a substantial number were published in Latin America; but many editions were published in occupied countries, and even the Russian press found opportunity to produce nine editions, the German press six editions, and the Italian press five editions of Twain's major works during the most desperate years of the war. Once again, as had happened during World War I, the popular appeal of Mark Twain's writings transcended cultural and nationalistic barriers.

1948–1976

The postwar years of 1948-1976 brought a veritable outpouring of domestic and foreign editions of American writers. Some thirty-eight of these writers, whose works most frequently appeared during the decades from 1931 to 1976 (see Table 5), had already made a considerable impact during the 1930s through a combined publication of 2,800 editions. Following the war and postwar recovery of the 1940s, international editions of these same writers more than doubled to over seven thousand in the 1950s and burgeoned to nine thousand editions in the 1960s. This massive output peaked at more than one thousand editions in the single year of 1966.

Foreign publication of Americn writers became so widespread during these two decades that the result of any attempt to differentiate their comparative popularity among so many countries (more than one hundred by 1970) would have little meaning. From midcentury to 1970 Mark Twain, Pearl Buck, Jack London, Erle Stanley Gardner, Ernest Hemingway, and John Steinbeck led the field with an international audience worldwide in its scope.[13] International editions of Twain, Buck, and London were so closely matched from 1948 to 1970 that, in effect, they shared the international market on equal terms. To do them full justice, it would be more accurate to say that by 1976 Jack London achieved the greatest international popularity by a thin margin, followed closely by Pearl Buck and more distantly by Mark Twain. What is most significant, of course, is that Mark Twain, a product of the mid-nineteenth century, still held a commanding position among the most popular American writers at the middle of the twentieth century.

7. MARK TWAIN AND THE MODERN BEST-SELLERS

In view of his sustained and constantly increasing popularity among foreign as well as domestic readers, it would be surprising not to find something of Mark Twain's work among the best-sellers of the twentieth century. During the four decades after 1930, when American writers had unprecedented publication at home and abroad, their international audiences affirmed a few titles as their favorite reading. It would be misleading to call these books "universal" best-sellers, because of the time span involved and the enormous scope of the international book market. However, sixteen titles can be identified as the best-selling works in terms of their total international editions and the number of countries in which they were published. The total output of each was weighted with domestic editions, but with few exceptions foreign editions equaled or exceeded American editions. It will be noted that the list includes titles by several nineteenth-century authors whose works as a whole otherwise placed them well down the list of leading American writers during the mid-twentieth century (see Table 5). Also notable is the fact that Mark Twain reoccurs with three best-sellers, as compared with two by Erskine Caldwell and one by each of the other writers.

American Best-Sellers, 1930-1969

	FOREIGN EDITIONS	AMERICAN EDITIONS	PUBLISHING COUNTRIES
Edgar Allan Poe's *Tales*	157	101	31
Mark Twain's *Adventures of Tom Sawyer*	85	84	21
Harriet Beecher Stowe's *Uncle Tom's Cabin*	69	30	23
Herman Melville's *Moby Dick*	61	70	22
Mark Twain's *Adventures of Huckleberry Finn*	58	71	21
Louisa May Alcott's *Little Women*	52	51	16
Erskine Caldwell's *Tobacco Road*	44	11	21
Pearl Buck's *The Good Earth*	43	25	20
Sinclair Lewis's *Babbitt*	45	10	19
John Steinbeck's *The Grapes of Wrath*	41	26	20
Theodore Dreiser's *An American Tragedy*	42	21	19
Erskine Caldwell's *God's Little Acre*	40	15	19
William Faulkner's *Sanctuary*	40	22	17
Lew Wallace's *Ben Hur*	37	25	21
Ernest Hemingway's *A Farewell to Arms*	37	16	20
Mark Twain's *The Prince and the Pauper*	35	26	19

NOTE: Publication data in the table are not absolute figures. They are based on entries in the *Cumulative Book Index* and the *National Union Catalog* and subject to more extensive investigation in European and other bibliographical sources, but they are comparable enough with each other to indicate the relative popularity of the various titles.

Other titles, such as Irving Stone's *Lust for Life*, Sinclair Lewis's *Arrowsmith*, and Ernest Hemingway's *The Sun Also Rises*, were fairly close competitors with the above titles but fell appreciably short of the sixteen leaders.

At first glance it might seem that these international best-sellers had little in common with each other except for the fact that they were all fiction, the most popular literary genre, and the fact that they were exceptionally well written. Five of the novels obviously were well adapted to young readers. Eight had strong moral or sociological import. Ten were deeply rooted in the American experience. Only a few were set against non-American backgrounds. And all of them exhibit different outlooks on life and distinctly different literary modes. Disparate as they may be, the author of each addressed some important aspect of the human problem with which readers everywhere could identify. Or it may be that their universal appeal lies simply in the fact that the reading masses could understand, enjoy, and respond to such works.

Mark Twain could not match Edgar Allan Poe's international popularity, but the appearance of *Tom Sawyer*, *Huckleberry Finn*, and *The Prince and the Pauper* in such select company indicates that the best of Twain's writing had a vitality and a modernity that sustained it through at least four generations.

8. MARK TWAIN'S INTERNATIONAL ROLE

In 1907 when Mark Twain made his last trip abroad to receive an honorary degree from Oxford University, British speakers strove to outdo each other with superlatives in their tributes to the man and his literary accomplishment. Their praises on this occasion and the testimonials of those who eulogized him after his death three years later would seem to have put a capstone on Mark Twain's reputation and popularity. It was Augustine Birrell, however, who made the most sensible and astute observation: "I am not going to say what the world a thousand years hence will think of Mark Twain. Posterity will take care of itself, will read what it wants to read, will forget what it chooses to forget, and will pay no attention whatsoever to our critical mumblings and jumblings."[14] Birrell might have added that five decades later it would become superfluous to recite the judgments of those who had commended or condemned Twain and fruitless to echo those who had extolled him. Time has erased many earlier judgments, and new generations are forming their own opinions. The purpose of the present work is not to evaluate Twain's literary achievement, but rather to provide a survey of his extensive publication and offer an interpretation of its significance. The bibliographical record that follows yields no hard and fast conclusions about Twain's literary stature, but it calls forth a few observations about his historical role in shaping the American image abroad. Seen from the perspective of the late twentieth century, that role was a major contribution—and perhaps the most important one—that this writer made to the world at large.

In his own time, whether consciously or subconsciously, Mark Twain served America as an unofficial ambassador of goodwill. Through his lectures, speeches, personal contacts, extensive travels, and protracted residences abroad, he encountered more people in England, on the Continent, and throughout the British Empire than any American of his own or preceding generations. Almost inevitably the man's presence, his personality, and his attitudes became, in these peoples' minds, a prototype of the American character. Whether he was actually archetypical or even fairly representative of his fellow countrymen is beside the point. People abroad who heard him or read about him or merely saw him identified America with Mark Twain, and their impression left an imprint on the international consciousness that outlasted the man himself. Eventually the living personality faded from memory, but the prototype image persisted among later generations, to whom the name Mark Twain became synonymous with the cross section of American life portrayed in his most widely read works.

In 1855 Walt Whitman had described his America in the vivid panoramic and kaleidoscopic passages of "Song of Myself." A generation later Mark Twain portrayed his own America, less exultantly but just as graphically, in his sketches and anecdotes of western life, and in *Roughing It*, *The Gilded Age*, *Tom Sawyer*, *Huckleberry Finn*, and *Life on the Mississippi*. What impression of American life and American character these portraits made on his thousands of foreign readers is speculative at best. Whether those readers were Europeans or Latin Americans or Asians, their vision of the American scene must have been a conglomeration of images such as the following: a vast expanse of virgin prairies, impassive mountains, alkali deserts, pristine lakes, and mammoth rivers, waiting to be civilized and exploited by an unconquerable people; rugged prospectors pursuing elusive gold; lashing pony express riders, swaying stagecoaches, bucking broncos, and garrulous storytellers; sleepy villages and boys who never grow up adventuring on a mighty river that silently flows to a fabulous world somewhere beyond; roaring raftsmen, palatial steamboats, and imperturbable riverboat pilots spinning their wheels around countless disasters; gamblers, confidence men, lynch mobs, runaway slaves, feuding plantation owners, Bible-thumping revivalists, and temperance crusaders; horse races, minstrel shows, and murder trials; shabby cabins and ornate mansions; charming women and scheming politicians; visions of wealth; spectacular parades and golden-tongued orators; and somewhere in the background a new breed of people, unsophisticated but ingenious, industrious, self-righteous, patriotic, exuberant, emancipated from the past, ready to reform the world, and foreshadowing the millennium. These and countless other images embedded in Mark Twain's best known works made up a montage from which many non-Americans could have formed their only conception of America. The montage is exaggerated, incomplete, and an over-simplification of the reality. But the average reader is not a student of history or sociology. His vision of unfamiliar times and places comes to him adventitiously through popular literature and other mass media.

Whether or not Mark Twain was a great writer, he at least gave the outside world many insights into his own country and its culture. His international role in this respect can be characterized most succinctly by a paraphrase of historian George Trevelyan: "Mark Twain did more than any other man to make plain people in England [and abroad] understand plain people in America."[15] Therein, perhaps, lies Mark Twain's real significance and greatest achievement.

NOTES

1. Mark Twain to Andrew Lang, undated letter (1890?). *Mark Twain's Letters*, ed. Albert Bigelow Paine, New York and London, Harper & Brothers, 1917. p. 528.

2. For sources and contexts of these and other similar quotations, *see* Edgar H. Hemminghaus, *Mark Twain in Germany*, New York, Columbia University Press, 1939; Roger Asselineau, *The Literary Reputation of Mark Twain from 1910 to 1950*, Paris, Librarie Marcel Didier, 1954 (reprinted Westport, Conn., Greenwood Press, 1971); Frederick Anderson, *Mark Twain: The Critical Heritage*, New York, Barnes & Noble, 1971; and Robert M. Rodney, "Mark Twain in England," unpublished thesis, University of Wisconsin, 1946.

3. M. M. Brasher, *Mark Twain Son of Missouri*. Chapel Hill, University of North Carolina Press, 1934. p. 263.

4. *The Man That Corrupted Hadleyburg* (1900) and *Captain Stormfield's Visit to Heaven* (1907) found limited international audiences through ten foreign-language translations each, published after World War I. The sardonic *King Leopold's Solilo-quy* (1905) belatedly reached small audiences in five translations during the 1960s. Mark Twain's "darker" writings *What Is Man?* (1906), *The Mysterious Stranger* (1916), and *Letters from the Earth* (1962) eventually appeared in three, nine, and ten foreign languages respectively, but publication of the first two works abroad was delayed largely until after World War II. *The War Prayer*, one of Twain's most excoriating attacks against human folly, first appeared in the United States in 1923 but was not reissued there until 1968 and was exported abroad in a single German translation in 1923. Between 1940 and 1973 various collections of Mark Twain diatribes on man were published in the United States: *Mark Twain in Eruption* (1940), *Mark Twain on the Damned Human Race* (1962), *Mark Twain's "Which Was the Dream?"* . . . (1967), *Fables of Man* (1972), *A Pen Warmed-up in Hell* . . . (1972), and *Mark Twain and the Three R's: Race, Religion, Revolution—and Related Matters* (1973). Only the last two of these provocative titles were translated abroad, the first for Japanese and the latter for Spanish readers. All of the

above works appeared too late to change appreciably the popular image of their writer.

5. Dennis Welland in his *Mark Twain in England* (p. 231) estimates that the three English publishers Routledge, Hotten, and Chatto & Windus issued at least 1,150,000 copies of Mark Twain's books by the year 1910. Taking into account all of the British editions issued by other English publishers as well, and using a conservative average of eighty-five hundred copies per edition, British editions of Mark Twain's writings would have totaled at least 1,900,000 copies during his lifetime and probably exceeded 3,685,000 by the year 1976. The probability that twentieth-century editions were issued in greater numbers of copies than those of the earlier editions makes impossible a close approximation of the total output during the full century, but the above estimates indicate the enormity of Mark Twain's popularity among British readers both during and subsequent to his lifetime.

6. Cf. Glenora W. Brown and Deming B. Brown, *A Guide to Soviet Russian Translations of American Literature*. Their research into the comparative popularity of American writers in Soviet Russia revealed that Mark Twain's various writings sold more than 2,500,000 copies in that country between 1918 and 1946.

7. Edgar H. Hemminghaus, *Mark Twain in Germany*, p. 146. Hemminghaus made a conservative estimate that by 1937 Mark Twain's various works had sold almost 1,300,000 copies in Germany.

8. Letter to Joseph Twichell, Jan. 5, 1874. *Mark Twain's Letters*. New York and London, Harper & Brothers, 1917. p. 225.

9. Cf. *Mark Twain—Howells Letters*, ed. Henry Nash Smith and Wiliam M. Gibson. Cambridge, Mass., Belnap Press of Harvard University, 1960. p. 262.

10. Mark Twain's ineffectual efforts to protect his writings against early piracy by unauthorized British and Canadian publishers, his later arrangements with his English publishers Chatto & Windus to control foreign translations of his works, and his long-continued campaign for some kind of effective international copyright law are treated in Howard G. Baetzhold's *Mark Twain and John Bull: The British Connection* (Indiana University Press, 1970) and more extensively in Dennis Welland's *Mark Twain in England* (Humanities Press, 1978).

11. Mark Twain's popularity among readers of Spanish and Portuguese descent is reflected in the publication of forty-three Spanish- and twenty Portuguese-language editions during the brief period 1955-1962. Cf. *Spanish and Portuguese Translations of United States Books 1955-1962. A Bibliography*. U.S. Library of Congress, 1963.

12. London's phenomenal popularity in Russia produced four hundred editions of his various works in that country between 1917 and 1947, followed by Upton Sinclair with almost two hundred editions and Mark Twain with almost one hundred. Cf. Glenora W. and Deming B. Brown, *A Guide to Soviet Russian Translations of American Literature*. New York, King's Crown Press, Columbia University, 1954.

13. The above comparison is based on data from the *Index Translationum*. The *Index* in 1950 had a broad coverage of some thirty-six countries but did not report on eight major publishing countries until later dates. *Index* entries indicate approximately twelve hundred Mark Twain editions from 1948 to 1970, whereas sources consulted for the bibliography that follows reveal more than two thousand editions for the same period.

14. Testimonial to Mark Twain at a London Pilgrim's Club Luncheon, June 25, 1907. London *Times*, June 26, 1907. 3:2.

15. George M. Trevelyan in the *Overland Monthly*, 87, April 1929. p. 108.

Bibliographical Sources

The following bibliographies, catalogs, special studies, and libraries yielded information for the Bibliography of Mark Twain's International Editions. Many Mark Twain entries in these sources are duplicative of each other, and many others are unique. In any case, each source listed below was indispensable to a comprehensive coverage of the country involved. The code abbreviations are keyed to the source abbreviations indicated under each country in the Bibliography.

CODE	SOURCE AND COVERAGE
ABC	Fermin Peraza Sarassa, ed. *Anuario Bibliografico Cubano*. 1937-66. Gainesville, Fla., 1938-67. Habana, 1960. CUBA
ABL	W. Heinsius. *Algemeines Bucher-Lexikon*. 1700-1892. Leipzig, Gledisch: Brockhaus, 1812-94. Reprinted: Graz, Akademische Druck-und Verlagsaustalt, 1962. AUSTRIA/GERMANY/SWITZERLAND
ABM	Rudolph H. Gjelsness. *The American Book in Mexico. A Bibliography of Books by Authors of the United States of America Published in Mexico, 1952-55*. University of Michigan: Dept. of Library Science: Studies (no. 4). Ann Arbor, 1957. MEXICO
ACAP	*Annual Catalogue of Australian Publications*. 1936-60. Canberra, Commonwealth National Library. AUSTRALIA
ACB	*The American Catalogue of Books, 1876-1900*. New York, Publishers Weekly, 1876-1910. CANADA/UNITED STATES
AEHA	*Anuario Espanol e Hispano-Americano*. . . . 1945-59. Madrid, Ed. del Anuario Maritimo Espanol. ARGENTINA/SPAIN
ALRT	B. A. Libman, comp. *American Literature in Russian Translation and Criticism. Bibliography 1776-1975*. Moscow, Publishing House "Science," 1977. RUSSIA

CODE   SOURCE AND COVERAGE

ANB   *Australian National Bibliography*. 1961-. Canberra, National Library
         of Australia.   AUSTRALIA

ASB   *Aarskatalog for Svenska Bokhandeln*. 1861-1952. Stockholm, Bibli-
         ographical Institute of the Royal Library.   SWEDEN

BA   *Bibliography of Australia*. 1781-1900. J. A. Ferguson, 1963. Sydney,
         Angus & Robertson, 1941-70.   AUSTRALIA

BAL   Jacob Blanck, comp. *Bibliography of American Literature*. Biblio-
         graphical Society of America. New Haven, Yale University Press; Lon-
         don, Oxford University Press, 1957.
                     CANADA/GERMANY/GREAT BRITAIN/UNITED STATES

BB   *Bibliografia Brasileira*. 1938/1939-55/1963-. Rio de Janeiro, Ministerio
         da Educacao e Cultura. Instituto Nacional do Livros.   BRAZIL

BBA   *Boletin Bibiografico Argentino*. 1937-63. Buenos Aires, Publicacion
         Oficial.   ARGENTINA/BRAZIL

BBel   *Bibliographie de Belgique*. 1875-. Brussels, Bibliotheque Royale.
                                                                   BELGIUM

BBP   *British Books in Print*. 1965-. London, Whitaker.   GREAT BRITAIN
BBPo   Henryk Sawoniak. *Bibliografia Bibliografij Polskich*. 1951-60.
         Wroclaw, Zaklad Narodowy im. Ossolinskich, 1967.   POLAND

BC   *Bibliografia Cubana*. 1959/1962-. Habana, Biblioteca Nacional "Jose
         Marti."   CUBA

BCB   *Brinkman's Catalogus van Boeken, Plaat-En Kaartwerken . . . 1850-*.
         Amsterdam, Brinkman, 1883-93. Leiden, Sitjhoff, 1903-.
                                                   BELGIUM/NETHERLANDS

BCCB   *Brinkman's Cumulatieve Catalogus van Boeken. . . .* Amsterdam,
         Brinkman, 1846-80. Leiden, Sijthoff, 1881-.
                                                   BELGIUM/NETHERLANDS

BE   *Bibliografia Espanola*. 1958-. Servicio Nacional de Informacion Biblio-
         grafica. Madrid, Direccion General de Archivos Bibliotecas, 1959-.
                                             ARGENTINA/MOROCCO/SPAIN

BF   *Bibliographie de la France; ou, Journal General de l'Imprimerie et
         de la Librairie*. Paris, Cercle de la Librairie. 1811-.   FRANCE

Bib   *Biblio. Catalogue des Ouvrages Parus en Langue Francaise dans le
         Monde Entier, Octobre 1933-71*. Paris, Hachette.
                                             BELGIUM/FRANCE/SWITZERLAND

BJ   *Bibliografija Jugoslavije: Knjige, Brosure i Muskikalije*. 1950-. Belgrade,
         Bibliografski Inst. FNRJ.   YUGOSLAVIA

BM   British Museum, London.   GREAT BRITAIN

BMC   *British Museum General Catalogue of Printed Books* and supplements.
         1881-1900, 1900-05, 1931-54, 1956-65, 1966-70. London. British
         Museum Department of Printed Bcoks.   GREAT BRITAIN

CODE	SOURCE AND COVERAGE

BMT Merle Johnson. *A Bibliography of the Works of Mark Twain, Samuel Langhorne Clemens. . . .* New York and London, Harper & Brothers, 1910. Rev. 1935.   CANADA/UNITED STATES

BN Bibliotheque Nationale, Paris.
EGYPT/FRANCE/GERMANY/RUSSIA

BNF Biblioteca Nazionale Centrala, Firenze.   ITALY

BNI *Bibliografia Nazionale Italiana.* 1958-. [continuation of *Bollettino-delle Publicazioni Italiane. . . .* 1886-1957]. Firenze, Biblioteca Nazionale Centrale.   ITALY

BNR Biblioteca Nazionale, Roma.   ITALY

BON John E. Englekirk. *Bibliografia de Obras Norteamericanas en Traduccion Espanola.* Mexico, "Solvetiro de la Revista Iberoamericana," 1944.
SPAIN/SPANISH AMERICA

BP K. Estreicher. *Bibliografia Polska.* 1870-1939/1951-. Cracow, Czionkami Drukarni Universytetu Jagiellonskiego.   POLAND

CABCT Donald Murray, Chan Wai-Hueng, Samuel Huang, "A Checklist of American Books in Chinese Translation," *American Book Collector* (Chicago), 22 (March-April 1972), 28-29.   FAR EAST

Can *Canadiana.* 1950-. Ottawa, National Library of Canada, 1951-.
CANADA

CBI *The Cumulative Book Index: A World List of Books in the English Language.* New York, Wilson, 1928, 1932-. AUSTRALIA/CANADA/
GREAT BRITAIN/NEW ZEALAND/UNITED STATES

CC *Catalogo Cumulativo 1886-1957.* Nendeln, Liechtenstein, Kraus Reprint, 1968.   ITALY

CGBN *Catalogue General des Livres Imprimes de la Bibliotheque Nationale (Ouvrages Publies avant 1960).* 1897-. Paris, Imprimerie Nationale.
BELGIUM/CANADA/EGYPT/FRANCE/GERMANY/
GREAT BRITAIN/RUSSIA

CGLE *Catalogo General de la Libreria Espanola, 1931-50.* Madrid, Instituto Nacional del Libro Espanol, 1957-65.   SPAIN

CGLEH *Catalogo General de la Libreria Espanola e Hispano-americana, 1901-30.* Madrid, Instituto Nacional del Libro Espanol, 1932-51.
ARGENTINA/SPAIN

CGLEs *Catalogue General des Livres Estoniens (Eesti Raamatute Uldnimestik).* 1924-36. Tartus, Eesti Kirjanduse Seltsi Kirjastus.   ESTONIA/RUSSIA

CGLF *Catalogue General de la Librairie Francaise.* 1867-1945. Paris, Lorenz.
FRANCE/SWITZERLAND

CLIM *Catalogo de Libros Impresos en Mexico.* Mexico, Instituto Mexicano del Libro, 1956.   MEXICO

CPL Chicago Public Library.   ARGENTINA/EASTERN EUROPE/
GERMANY/POLAND/RUSSIA

CODE	SOURCE AND COVERAGE

DB *Deutsche Bibliographie.* 1947-. Frankfurt am Main, Buchhandler-Vereinigung.   AUSTRIA/GERMANY/SWITZERLAND

DBA *Dansk Bogfortegnelse: Aarskatalog.* 1851-. Copenhagen, Gads.
                   DENMARK

ECB *The English Catalogue of Books.* . . . London, Sampson Low, 1864-1901. London, Croyden, Surrey: Publishers' Circular, 1906-59, 1968.   GERMANY/GREAT BRITAIN/SWITZERLAND

GSRT Glenora W. Brown and Deming B. Brown, eds. *A Guide to Soviet Russian Translations of American Literature.* New York, King's Crown Press, Columbia University, 1954.   RUSSIA

HKL Hong Kong City Hall Library. Published bibliography.
          CHINA/HONG KONG/TAIWAN

HV *Halbjahresverzeichnis in der deutschen Buchhandel erscheinenen Bucher.* Leipzig, Borsenverein der Deutschen Buchhandler, 1798-1944. [becomes *Jahresverzeichnis des deutschen Schrifttums*]
         AUSTRIA/GERMANY/SWITZERLAND

INB *The Indian National Bibliography.* 1957-. Calcutta, Central Reference Library, 1958-.   INDIA

IRC *Impex Reference Catalogue of Indian Books* and supplement. 1960-, 1960-62. New Delhi, Indian Book Export and Import Co. INDIA

IT *Index Translationum. Repertoire International des Traductions.* Paris, International Institute of Intellectual Cooperation, 1932-40. Paris, Unesco, 1949-.   INTERNATIONAL

JDS *Jahresverzeichnis des deutschen Schrifttums.* 1945/1946-67. Leipzig, Borsenverein, 1948-. AUSTRIA/GERMANY/SWITZERLAND

KSLF *Katalog ofver den Svenska Litteraturen i Finland.* . . . 1886-1900/1892-1924. Helsingfors.   FINLAND

LB *La Librairie Belge: Ouvrages d'Expression Francaise Edites en Belge,* 1945/1955-. Bruxelles, Cercle Belge de la Librairie. BELGIUM

LC U.S. Library of Congress. BULGARIA/FRANCE/GERMANY/GREAT BRITAIN/ISRAEL/RUSSIA/SWITZERLAND/UNITED STATES

LE *Libros Espanolis, Catalogo ISBN.* Madrid, Instituto Nacional del Libro Espanol. . . , 1973.   SPAIN

LEV Mary C. Turner. *Libros en Venta en 20 Paises de las Americas y Espana.* New York, R. R. Bowker Co., 1964. *Supplemento.* 1964-66.
     ARGENTINA/CHILE/COLOMBIA/MEXICO/SPAIN

LF *La Librairie Francaise. Catalogue General.* 1931. Also 1946, 1956, 1968. Paris, Cercle de la Librairie.
        BELGIUM/FRANCE/SWITZERLAND

MB Josefina Berroa. *Mexico Bibliographico, 1957-1960; Catalogo General de Libros Impresos en Mexico.* Mexico, J. Berroa, 1961. MEXICO

CODE	SOURCE AND COVERAGE

MK Petrik Geza, ed. *Magyar Konyveszet*. Budapest, Orszagos Szechenyi Konyvtar. 1936-41, 1946-.   HUNGARY

MLH A. Palau y Dulcet. *Manual del Librero Hispanoamericano. . . .* 1948-. Barcelona, Libreria Palau. Oxford, Dolphin Book Co.   SPAIN

MTE Dennis Welland. *Mark Twain in England*. Atlantic Park, N.J., Humanities Press, 1978.   GREAT BRITAIN

MTG Edgar H. Hemminghaus. *Mark Twain in Germany*. New York, Columbia University Press, 1939.   AUSTRIA/GERMANY/SWITZERLAND

MTI Keshav Mutalik. *Mark Twain in India*. Bombay, Noble Publishing House, 1978.   INDIA

MTJ Shunsuke Kamei, "Mark Twain in Japan," *Mark Twain Journal*," 12 (Spring 1963), pp. 10-11, 20.   JAPAN

MTR *Mark Twain in Romania: Bibliography of the Romanian Translations Published in Volumes and in Magazines (1888-1966)*. Bucharest, Romanian Institute for Cultural Relations with Foreign Countries, 1967.   ROMANIA

MTRG Thomas A. Tenney. *Mark Twain: A Reference Guide*. Boston, Mass., G. K. Hall & Co., 1977.   UNITED STATES

MTRT Inna Mikhailovna Levidova. *Mark Tven* [Mark Twain: Bibliography. Index. Russian Translations and Critical Literature in the Russian Language. 1867-1972]. Moskva, Knita, 1974.   RUSSIA

NB *Norsk Bokfortegnelse*. 1814/1847-. Christiana, 1848-1924. Oslo, Norske Bokhandlerforening, 1928-.   NORWAY

NBIL *The National Bibliography of Indian Literature: 1901-1953*. New Delhi, Sahitya Akademi, 1962.   INDIA

NL Newberry Library, Chicago.   GREAT BRITAIN/SWEDEN

NUC *The National Union Catalog: Pre-1956 Imprints*. 1968. Annual, 1956-. London and Chicago, Mansell. Chicago, American Library Association.   INTERNATIONAL

PB *Przewodnik Bibliograficzny*. Warszawa, Biblioteka Narodowa, 1946-.   POLAND

PBP *A Provisional Bibliography of United States Books Translated into Portuguese*. Library of Congress Reference Department. Washington, U.S. Library of Congress, 1957.   BRAZIL/PORTUGAL

PBS Ilo Remer et al. *A Provisional Bibliography of United States Books Translated into Spanish*. Hispanic Foundation: Bibliographical Series No. 3. Washington, U.S. Library of Congress, 1957.   ARGENTINA/CHILE/MEXICO/SPAIN

RSAL Valentina A. Libman, comp. Robert V. Allen, trans. Clarence Gohdes, ed. *Russian Studies of American Literature: A Bibliography*. University

CODE	SOURCE AND COVERAGE
	of North Carolina Studies in Comparative Literature, no. 46. Chapel Hill, University of North Carolina Press, 1969. RUSSIA
SB	*Das Schweizer Buch. Le Livre Suisse. Il Libro Svizzero.* 1901-. Bibliogaphisches Bulletin der Schweizerischen Landes-bibliothek in Bern. Berne-Bumpliz, Benteli. GERMANY/SWITZERLAND
SBF	*Svensk Bokforteckning Aarskatalog.* 1953-. Stockholm, Tidnings-aktiebolaget Svensk Bokhandel. SWEDEN
SBK	*Svensk Bok-Katalog.* 1866-. Stockholm, Tidnings-aktiebolaget Svensk Bokhandel. SWEDEN
SBV	*Schweizer Bucherverzeichnis. Repertoire du Livre Suisse. Repertorio del Libro Svizzero. Elenco del Llbro Svizzero.* 1948/1951-. Zurich, Schweizerischer Buchhandler- und Verlegerverein. GERMANY
SF	*Svenskt Forfattarlexikon. Register.* 1900-. Stockholm, Raben & Sjogren, 1942, 1953, 1959, 1963. SWEDEN
SK	Pakarinen. *Suomalainen Kirjallisuus.* 1544-1939/1943. Helsinki, Helsinki University Library, 1912-52. FINLAND/RUSSIA
SKFL	*Suomen Kirjallisuus. Finlands Literatur.* 1944/1948-. Helsinki, Yliopiston Kirjasto. FINLAND
SLVS	*Die Schone Literatur der Vereinigten Staaten von Amerika in deutschen Ubersetzungen; eine Bibliographie.* Bonn, Bouvier. Charlottesville, Bibliographical Society of the University of Virginia, 1961. AUSTRIA/GERMANY/SWITZERLAND
SPT	*Spanish and Portuguese Translations of United States Books 1955-1962. A Bibliography.* Hispanic Foundation: Bibliographical Series No. 8. Washington, U.S. Library of Congress, 1963. ARGENTINA/BRAZIL/MEXICO/MOROCCO/PORTUGAL/SPAIN
SWPP	Ewa Korzeniewska. *Slownik Wspolczesnych Pisarzy Polskich.* Warszawa, Panstwowe Wydawnictwo Nankowe, 1963-66. POLAND
TB	*Turkiye Bibliyografyasi.* 1928/1938-. Istanbul, Devlet Basimevi. TURKEY
UnC	University of California/Berkeley. RUSSIA
UnG	University and National Library, Geneva. FRANCE/GERMANY
UnI	Universitat Bibliotek, Innsbruck. AUSTRIA/GERMANY
UnP	Universita Perugia Biblioteca, Perugia. ITALY
UnS	Universitats Salzburg Bibliotek, Salzburg. AUSTRIA/GERMANY
USC	*The United States Catalog: Books in Print. . . .* New York, H. W. Wilson Co., 1912, 1928. CANADA/GREAT BRITAIN/NEW ZEALAND/UNITED STATES
VBL	Christian Gottlob Kayser. *Vollstandiges Bucherlexikon. . . .* 1750-1910. Leipzig, Tauchnitz, 1834-1911. GERMANY

CODE	SOURCE AND COVERAGE
ZBZ	Zentral Bibliotek, Zurich.
	AUSTRIA/GERMANY/FRANCE/SWITZERLAND

Explanatory Note

The following provisional bibliography is designed to serve as a survey of more than five thousand editions of Mark Twain's single and collected works published internationally during more than a century following the appearance of Twain's first foreign edition in 1867. The editions are listed chronologically under each title of Mark Twain's various works as those works were published within countries located in the following world regions: the United States, the British Commonwealth, Western Europe, Eastern Europe, European and Asiatic Russia, Latin America, the Near East, the Indian subcontinent, Southeast Asia, and the Far East. The bibliography comprises all editions that could be identified from the preceding bibliographical sources by date and title and by place of publication and/or name of publisher. In most instances the citations have been cross-checked against entries that have appeared in two or more bibliogaphical sources. The bibliogaphy is "provisional" to the extent that many other editions, largely foreign ones, have had to be omitted for lack of sufficient identifying information, and to the extent that numerous editions have undoubtedly escaped discovery by even the most assiduous bibliographers. However, it is probable that Mark Twain's international editions would not have exceeded six thousand during the period covered, so that present entries are complete enough for reliable comparisons of Twain's popularity between various countries and between various periods. The full extent and the various dimensions of Mark Twain's worldwide popularity may be observed more readily in the tables that follow the Bibliography.

The source abbreviations indicated with each country are keyed to the list of Bibliographical Sources on page lxiii.

THE BIBLIOGRAPHY

1

Domestic (American) Editions 1867–1980

Sources: ACB/BAL/BMT/CBI/LC/MTRG/NUC/USC

American Claimant

1892 The American Claimant, New York: Charles L. Webster. Subsequent
edition: 1903.

1896 The American Claimant and Other Stories and Sketches, New York:
Harper & Brothers. Subsequent editions: 1897, 1898, 1899, 1900,
1902, 1912, 1915, 1917, 1924.

1899 Same. New York: P.F. Collier & Son. Subsequent edition: 1924.

1971 Same. New York: AMS Press.

Autobiography

1924 Mark Twain's Autobiography. Ed. Albert Bigelow Paine. 2 vols.
New York and London: Harper & Brothers.

1925 Same. Ed. Albert Bigelow Paine. 2 vols. New York: P.F.Collier
& Son.

1959 The Autobiography of Mark Twain including chapters now published
for the first time. Ed. Charles Neider. New York: Harper &
Brothers. Subsequent editions: 1960 and 1966.

1961 The Autobiography of Mark Twain. With An Introduction, Notes, and
A Special Essay by Charles Neider, New York: Washington Square Press.

Captain Stormfield

1907 Extract from Captain Stormfield's Visit to Heaven, New York: Harper
& Brothers. Subsequent edition: 1909.

1932 Extracts from Captain Stormfield's Visit to Heaven. In The Complete
     Short Stories and Famous Essays of Mark Twain, New York: P.F.
     Collier & Son.

1935 Same. In The Family Mark Twain, New York and London: Harper &
     Brothers.

1952 Captain Stormfield's Visit to Heaven. In Report from Paradise,
     New York: Harper & Brothers.

1970 Mark Twain's Quarrel with Heaven; Captain Stormfield's Visit to
     Heaven, and Other Sketches. Ed. Ray B. Browne. The Masterworks
     of Literature Series. New Haven, Conn.: College and University
     Press Services.

                          Christian Science

1907 Christian Science, with Notes Containing Corrections to Date, New
     York and London: Harper & Brothers. Subsequent editions: 1907,
     1907, 191-?, 1915, 1917.

                          Connecticut Yankee

1889 A Connecticut Yankee in King Arthur's Court: A Satire, New York:
     Charles L. Webster. Subsequent editions: 1890, 1891.

1889 A Connecticut Yankee in King Arthur's Court, New York & London:
     Harper & Brothers. Subsequent editions: 1896, 1897, 1899, 1900,
     1901, 1902, 1903, 1904, 1906, 1912, 1917, 1925, 1925, 1930, 1960,
     1965.

1915 A Connecticut Yankee at the Court of King Arthur, New York: Harper
     & Brothers.

1917 A Connecticut Yankee in King Arthur's Court, New York: Editions
     for the Armed Services.

1917 Same. Modern Library of the World's Best Books, No. 162. New York:
     Modern Library. Subsequent editions: 1949, 1970.

1917 Same. New York: P.F. Collier.

1935 Same. In The Family Mark Twain, New York and London: Harper &
     Brothers.

1939 Same. In The Favorite Works of Mark Twain, New York: Garden City
     Publishing Co.

1942 Same. New York: The Heritage Press. Subsequent editions: 1948,1968.

1945 Same. New York: Grosset & Dunlap. Subsequent editions: 1945, 1961.

1948 Same. Adaptation Series. New York: Globe Books.

Fig. 4. *The American Claimant*, cover of 1892 American edition published by Charles L. Webster & Co.

THE

AMERICAN CLAIMANT

BY

MARK TWAIN

NEW YORK
CHARLES L. WEBSTER & CO.
1892

Fig. 5. *The American Claimant*, title page of 1892 American edition published by Charles L. Webster & Co.

YOU don't know about me, without you have read a book by the name of "The Adventures of Tom Sawyer," but that ain't no matter. That book was made by Mr. Mark Twain, and he told the truth, mainly. There was things which he stretched, but mainly he told the truth. That is nothing. I never seen anybody but lied, one time or another, without it was Aunt Polly, or the widow, or maybe Mary. Aunt Polly—Tom's Aunt Polly, she is—and Mary, and the Widow Douglas, is all told about in that book—which is mostly a true book; with some stretchers, as I said before.

THE WIDOW.

Now the way that the book winds up, is this: Tom and me found the money that the robbers hid in the cave, and it made us rich. We got six thousand dollars apiece—all gold. It was an awful sight of money when it was piled up. Well, Judge Thatcher, he took it and put it out at interest, and it fetched us a dollar a day apiece, all the year round—more than a body could tell what to do with. The Widow Douglas, she took me for her son, and allowed she would sivilize me; but it was rough living in the house all the time, considering how dismal regular and decent the widow was in all her ways; and so when I couldn't stand it no longer, I lit out. I got into my old rags, and my sugar-hogshead again, and was free and satisfied. But

2

Fig. 7. *Adventures of Huckleberry Finn,* page 17 of 1885 American first edition published by Charles L. Webster and Company

ADVENTURES

OF

HUCKLEBERRY FINN

(TOM SAWYER'S COMRADE,)

SCENE: THE MISSISSIPPI VALLEY.
TIME: FORTY TO FIFTY YEARS AGO.

BY

MARK TWAIN.

WITH ONE HUNDRED AND SEVENTY-FOUR ILLUSTRATIONS.

NEW YORK:
CHARLES L. WEBSTER AND COMPANY.
1885.

Fig. 6. *Adventures of Huckleberry Finn,* title page of 1855 American first edition published by Charles L. Webster and Company

Chapter the Last

OUT OF BONDAGE.

The first time I catched Tom, private, I asked him what was his idea, time of the evasion?—what it was he'd planned to do if the evasion worked all right and he managed to set a nigger free that was already free before? And he said, what he had planned in his head, from the start, if we got Jim out all safe, was for us to run him down the river, on the raft, and have adventures plumb to the mouth of the river, and then tell him about his being free, and take him back up home on a steamboat, in style, and pay him for his lost time, and write word ahead and get out all the niggers around, and have them waltz him into town with a torchlight procession and a brass band, and then he would be a hero, and so would we. But I reckoned it was about as well the way it was.

We had Jim out of the chains in no time, and when Aunt Polly and Uncle Silas and Aunt Sally found out how good he helped the doctor nurse Tom, they made a heap of fuss over him, and fixed him up prime, and give him all he wanted to eat, and a good time, and nothing to do. And we had him up to the

Fig. 8. *Adventures of Huckleberry Finn,* page 364 of 1885 American first edition published by Charles L. Webster and Company

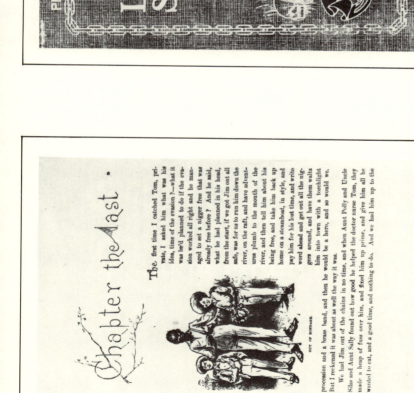

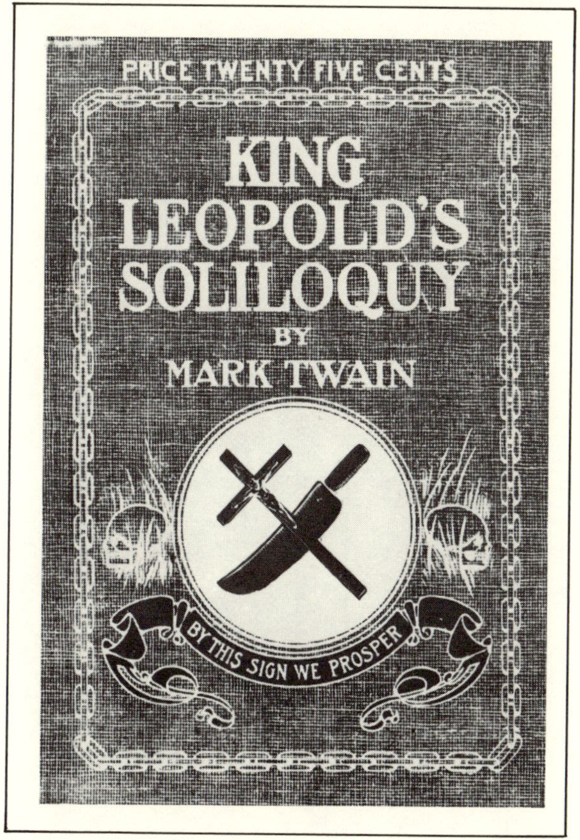

Fig. 9. *King Leopold's Soliloquy,* cover of 1905 American edition published by P. R. Warren Co.

Fig. 10. *Mark Twain's (Burlesque) Autobiography and First Romance*, cover/title page of 1871 American edition published by Sheldon & Company

1949 Same. New York: Limited Editions Club.

1957 <u>A Yankee at the Court of King Arthur</u>, New York: Grove Press.

1960 <u>A Connecticut Yankee in King Arthur's Court</u>. Ed. E. Hudson Long.
Great Illustrated Classics. New York: Dodd, Mead.

1960 Same. American Century Series. AC30. New York: Hill & Wang.

1962 Same. Harcourt Library of English and American Classics. New York:
Harcourt, Brace & World.

1963 Same. Prepared by Hamlin Hill. San Francisco: Chandler Publishing
Company. [facsimile of the 1st (1889) edition]

1963 Same. Signet Classic, CP 315. New York: New American Library.

1966 Same. A Legacy Library Facsimile. Ann Arbor, Mich.: University
Microfilms.

1970 Same. New York: Amsco School Publications.

1970 Same. New York: Random House.

Essays

1897 <u>How To Tell A Story and Other Essays</u>, New York: Harper & Brothers.
Subsequent editions: 1898, 1902, 1905, 1912, 1916.

1899 <u>In Defense of Harriet Shelley</u>, New York: Harper & Brothers. Subsequent edition: 1918.

1900 <u>The Complete Short Stories and Famous Essays of Mark Twain</u>, New
York: P.F. Collier & Son.

1900 <u>How To Tell A Story and Other Essays</u>, Hartford, Conn.: American
Publishing Company.

1903 <u>My Debut as a Literary Person with Other Essays and Stories</u>,
Hartford, Conn.: American Publishing Company.

1907 <u>How To Tell A Story</u>, New York: P.F. Collier & Son. Subsequent
edition: 1921.

1915 <u>The Man That Corrupted Hadleyburg, and Other Stories and Essays</u>,
New York: Harper & Brothers.

1917 <u>What Is Man? and Other Essays</u>, New York and London: Harper &
Brothers.

1918 <u>Literary Essays</u>, New York: P.F. Collier & Sons.

1963 <u>The Complete Essays of Mark Twain</u>. Ed. Charles Neider. Garden
City, N.Y.: Doubleday.

1972 What Is Man? and Other Essays, Freeport, N.Y.: Books for Libraries
     Press.

Following the Equator

1897 Following the Equator, A Journey around the World, Hartford, Conn.:
     American Publishing Company. Subsequent editions: 1898, 1902.

1899 Same. New York and London: Harper & Brothers. Subsequent editions:
     1903, 1912, 1915, 1925.

1971 Same. New York: AMS Press.

Gilded Age

1873 The Gilded Age. A Tale of Today, Hartford, Conn.: American Pub-
     lishing Company. Subsequent editions: 1873, 1874, 1874, 1874,
     1874, 1874, 1874, 1874, 1876, 1879, 1880, 1884, 1887, 1888, 1890,
     1892, 1898, 1901, 1902, 1903.

1901 Same. New York: Harper & Brothers. Subsequent editions: 1903,
     1912, 1915, 1920, 1922, 1924.

1915 Same. New York: Grosset & Dunlap. Subsequent editions: 1928, 1938,
     1948.

1964 Same. Trident Press Book. New York: Simon & Schuster.

1965 The Adventures of Colonel Sellers: Being Mark Twain's Share of
     "The Gilded Age." Ed. Charles Neider. Garden City, N.Y.: Doubleday.

1968 The Gilded Age; A Tale of Today, Seattle: University of Washington
     Press.

1969 Same. Signet Classic. New York: New American Library of World
     Literature.

1972 Same. Ed. Bryant Morey French. Indianapolis: Bobbs-Merrill.

Huckleberry Finn

1885 The Adventures of Huckleberry Finn (Tom Sawyer's Comrade), New
     York: Charles L. Webster. Subsequent editions: 1885, 1886, 1888,
     1891, 1892, 1893.

1896 Same. New York and London: Harper & Brothers. Subsequent editions:
     1896, 1898, 1899, 1901, 1902, 1904, 1906, 1912, 1912, 1915, 1917,
     1918, 1923, 1923, 1923, 1927, 1931, 1931, 1938, 1939, 1948, 1951,
     1951.

1902 Same. Hartford, Conn.: American Publishing Company.

1912 Huckleberry Finnas Apysaka [Adventures of Huckleberry Finn], Chicago: Draugas. [Lithuanian]

1918 The Adventures of Huckleberry Finn (Tom Sawyer's Comrade). Authorized Edition. New York: P.F. Collier & Son. Subsequent edition:
1963.

1922 The Adventures of Tom Sawyer and The Adventures of Huckleberry
Finn, New York: Modern Library. Subsequent editions: 1940, 195-?,
1966.

193-? The Adventures of Huckleberry Finn (Tom Sawyer's Comrade). Chicago:
Goldsmith.

1933? The Adventures of Huckleberry Finn, n.p.: Standard Fiction Library.

1933 The Adventures of Huckleberry Finn (Tom Sawyer's Comrade). Ed.
Bernard DeVoto. New York: Limited Editions Club. Subsequent edition: 1942.

1935 The Adventures of Huckleberry Finn. In The Family Mark Twain. New
York and London: Harper & Brothers.

1938 Same. The World's Popular Classics. New York: Books, Inc. Subsequent editions: 1942, 1942, 1942.

1939 Same. Authorized Edition. New York: Grosset & Dunlap. Subsequent
editions: 1940, 1948, 1948, 1960, 1962, 1963.

1939 Same. In The Favorite Works of Mark Twain, New York: Garden City.

194-? The Adventures of Huckleberry Finn (Tom Sawyer's Comrade). Armed
Service Editions. New York: Council on Books in Wartime.

1940 The Adventures of Huckleberry Finn (condensed). Popular Classics.
Springfield, Mass.: McLoughlin Brothers.

1940 The Adventures of Tom Sawyer [and] The Adventures of Huckleberry
Finn, New York: Heritage Press. Subsequent editions: 1952, 1956,
1960.

1941 The Adventures of Huckleberry Finn (Tom Sawyer's Comrade), Akron,
Ohio: New York: Saalfield.

1941 Same. Whitman Classic. Racine, Wis.: Whitman. Subsequent editions:
1955, 1965.

1941 The Adventures of Huckleberry Finn. World Juvenile Library. Cleveland: World. Subsequent edition: 1947.

1942 Same. The New Library of Living Literature. New York: The New
Library.

1943 Same. New York: Heritage Press. Subsequent edition: 1948.

1944   Tom Sawyer; and, Huckleberry Finn. Everyman's Library. New York:
       E.P. Dutton. Subsequent edition: 1954.

1946   The Adventures of Huckleberry Finn. In Four Great American Novels.
       Ed. Raymond W. Short. New York: Henry Holt.

1946   Same. In The Portable Mark Twain. Ed. Bernard DeVoto. New York:
       Viking Press.

1948   Same. Rinehart Editions. New York: Rinehart. Subsequent edi-
       tions: 1951, 1955.

1950   Same. Heirloom Library. New York: Lothrop, Lee & Shepard.

1950   Same. Heirloom Library. New York: Chanticleer Press. Subsequent
       edition: 1950.

1950   Same. Chester Springs, Penn.: Dufour.

1951   Same. Globe Adapted Classics. New York: Globe Book Co.

1951   Huckleberry Finn. Adapted. Chicago: Scott, Foresman.

1953   The Adventures of Huckleberry Finn. Great Illustrated Classics.
       New York: Dodd, Mead.

1953   The Adventures of Tom Sawyer and the Adventures of Huckleberry
       Finn. Chicago: Spencer Press.

1954   The Adventures of Huckleberry Finn. Doubleday Classics. New York:
       Garden City Books.

1954   The Adventures of Huckleberry Finn, simplified and adapted. Ameri-
       can Classics. New York: Regents Publishing Co.

1955   The Adventures of Huckleberry Finn. Children's Illustrated Classics.
       New York: E.P. Dutton.

1955   Same. New York, London: Thomas Nelson.

1955   Same. Chicago: Great Books Foundation.

1956   Same. Golden Picture Classics. New York: Simon & Schuster.

1958   Adventures of Huckleberry Finn. Ed. Henry Nash Smith. Riverside
       Editions. Boston: Houghton Mifflin. Subsequent editions: 1962,
       1962.

1959   The Adventures of Huckleberry Finn (Tom Sawyer's Comrade), New York:
       Harper & Row. Subsequent editions: 1965, 1969.

1959   Mark Twain's Huckleberry Finn, Boston: D.C. Heath.

1960   The Adventures of Huckleberry Finn. Ed. Wallace Stegner. Laurel
       Edition. New York: Dell. Subsequent edition: 1965.

1960 Tom Sawyer; and, Huckleberry Finn. New Collins Classics. New York:
      W.W. Norton.

1960 The Adventures of Tom Sawyer; and, The Adventures of Huckleberry
      Finn. Platt & Munk Great Writers Collection. New York: Platt &
      Munk.

1960 Mark Twain and Huck Finn. Ed. Walter Blair. Berkeley, Calif.:
      University of California Press.

1960 The Adventures of Huckleberry Finn. Ed. Harold Minton. New York:
      Washington Square Press.

1961 Same. Dolphin Books. New York: Doubleday.

1961 Same. New York: Macmillan. Subsequent editions: 1961, 1962,
      1962.

1961 Same. Shorter Classics. Boston: Ginn. Subsequent editions: 1964,
      1965.

1961 Huckleberry Finn; Text, Sources, and Criticism. Ed. Kenneth L.
      Lynn. New York: Harcourt, Brace & World.

1961 Samuel Langhorne Clemens: The Adventures of Huckleberry Finn: An
      Annotated Text. Backgrounds and Sources, Essays in Criticism. Ed.
      Sculley Bradley at al. New York: Norton.

1962 The Art of Huckleberry Finn: Texts, Sources, Criticism. Ed.
      Hamlin Hill [and] Walter Blair. 2nd edition. San Francisco:
      Chandler. Subsequent edition: 1969.

1962 The Adventures of Huckleberry Finn, San Francisco: Chandler.
      [facsimile of the first edition]

1962 Same. New York: Collier Books. Subsequent editions: 1962, 1963.

1962 Same. Norton Critical Editions. New York: Norton. Subsequent
      edition: 1965.

1962 The Adventures of Huckleberry Finn, Tom Sawyer's Comrade. Signet
      Classics. New York: New American Library.

1962 Huck Finn and His Critics. Ed. Richard Lettis et al. New York:
      Macmillan.

1962 J.B. Scholes, Samuel L. Clemens' "The Adventures of Huckleberry
      Finn." A Study Guide, Bound Brook, N.J.: Shelley.

1965 The Adventures of Huckleberry Finn, New York: F. Watts. Subse-
      quent editions: 1966, 1969.

1965 Raymond J. Pflug, The Adventures of Huckleberry Finn: The
      Evolution of A Classic, Boston: Ginn.

1967 Adventures of Huckleberry Finn, Indianapolis: Bobbs-Merrill.

1967 Same. New York: St. Martins.

1967 Huckleberry Finn, New York: Bantam Books.

1968 Same. Camden, N.J.: Nelson.

1968 The Adventures of Huckleberry Finn. Cambridge Classics Library.
      Bronxville, N.Y.: Cambridge Book Co.

1969 Same. New York: Amsco School Publications.

1969 Adventures of Huckleberry Finn. In 4 Classic American Novels, New
      York: New American Library.

1969 Mark Twain's Hannibal, Huck & Tom. Ed. Walter Blair. The Mark
      Twain Papers. Berkeley: University of California Press.

1970 The Adventures of Huckleberry Finn, Glenview, Ill.: Scott,
      Foresman.

1970 John D. Seelye, The True Adventures of Huckleberry Finn, Evanston:
      Northwestern University Press.

1971 Huck Finn. Ed. Paul Brady. Carbondale, Ill.: Southern Illinois
      University Press.

1971 Adventures of Huckleberry Finn. New Edition. Lincoln, Neb.:
      Cliffs' Notes.

1972 The Adventures of Huckleberry Finn, New York: Amsco School Publi-
      cations.

1973 Same. In Walter Blair, Mark Twain & Huck Finn, Berkeley: Uni-
      versity of California Press.

1975 The Adventures of Huckleberry Finn (Tom Sawyer's Comrade),
      Franklin Center, Pa.: Franklin Library.

1976 The Adventures of Huckleberry Finn. In G.C. Carrington, The
      Dramatic Unity of Huckleberry Finn, Columbus, Ohio: Ohio State
      University Press.

1977 Same. 100 Greatest Masterpieces of American Literature. Franklin
      Center, Pa.: Franklin Library.

c1977 The Adventures of Huckleberry Finn: An Authoritative Text.... Ed.
      Sculley Bradley et al. [2nd edition] New York: Norton.

c1978 The Complete Adventures of Tom Sawyer and Huckleberry Finn, New
      York: Harper & Row.

1978 Same. Centennial Edition. New York: Harper & Row.

1979? The Adventures of Huckleberry Finn. Tempo Books. New York:
      Grosset & Dunlap.

1979 Same. In Illustrated Works of Mark Twain: Selections.... New York:
      Avenel Books.

c1980 June Edwards, Huckleberry Finn; Adapted, Milwaukee: Raintree.

Innocents Abroad

1869 The Innocents Abroad, or the New Pilgrims' Progress, Hartford,
      Conn.: American Publishing Company. Subsequent editions: 1870,
      1871, 1872, 1873, 1874, 1875, 1876, 1877, 1878, 1879, 1880, 1881,
      1884, 1885, 1886, 1888, 1889, 1890, 1891, 1892, 1893, 1895, 1897,
      1901.

1870 Same. Clifton & Detroit: W.E. Tunis.

1894 Same. Boston: Joseph Knight.

190-? The Innocents Abroad, New York: Harper & Brothers. [micro-form]

1902 Same. Boston: L.C. Page.

1903 The Innocents Abroad; or, The New Pilgrims' Progress, New York and
      London: Harper & Brothers. Subsequent editions: 1904, 1905, 1906,
      1909, 1911, 1912, 1915, 1935, 1956?

1911 Same. New York: Grosset & Dunlap. Subsequent editions: 1924, 1936.

1927 Same. Modern Readers' Series. New York: Macmillan. Subsequent
      editions: 1928, 1929.

1929 Same. New York: The Book League of America.

1960? The Innocents Abroad. New Collins Classics. New York: W.W. Norton.

1962 The Innocents Abroad; or, The New Pilgrims' Progress, New York:
      Limited Editions Club. Thistle Press.

1962 Same. New York: Heritage Press.

1964 Same. Bantam Classics. New York: Bantam Books.

1966 Same. New American Library: New English Library. Signet Classic.
      New York: Signet Books.

Joan of Arc

1896 Personal Recollections of Joan of Arc..., New York: Harper & Bro-
      thers. Subsequent editions: 1896, 1897, 1899, 1900, 1902, 1906,
      1912, 1915, 1917?, 1919, 1924, 1926.

1897 Saint Joan of Arc. [extract] New York: Harper & Brothers. Subse-
      quent edition: 1919.

1906 Joan of Arc, New York: Harper & Brothers. [French translation]

196-? Personal Recollections of Joan of Arc..., New York: Harper & Row.

1965? Same. Garden City, N.Y.: Doubleday.

1980 Same. Hartford, Conn.: Stowe-Day Foundation.

King Leopold's Soliloquy

1905 King Leopold's Solilquy: A Defense of His Congo Rule. By Mark
      Twain, Boston, Mass.: P.R. Warren. Subsequent edition: 1905.

1970 King Leopold's Soliloquy, New York: International Publishers.

Letters

1917 Mark Twain's Letters. 2 vols. Ed. Albert Bigelow Paine. New York
      and London: Harper & Brothers. Subsequent edition: 1927. [See
      also 1975 entry]

1932 Mark Twain, The letter Writer. Ed. Cyril Clemens. Boston: Meador.

1938 Mark Twain's Letter to William Bowen. Limited Edition. San
      Francisco: Book Club of California. [See also 1975 entry]

1941 Mark Twain's Letters to Will Bowen; "My First, & Oldest & Dearest
      Friend." Ed. Theodore Hornberger. Privately printed. Austin,
      Texas: University of Texas. [See also 1976, 1977, 1978 entries]

1946 Mark Twain, Business Man. Ed. Charles Webster. Boston: Little,
      Brown.

1949 The Love Letters of Mark Twain. Limited Edition. Ed. Dixon
      Wecter. New York: Harper & Brothers. [See also 1976 entry]

1949 Mark Twain to Mrs. Fairbanks. Ed. Dixon Wecter. Huntington
      Library Publications. San Marino, Calif.: Huntington Library.

1953 Mark Twain to Uncle Remus [Joel Chandler Harris]; 1881-1885. Ed.
      Thomas H. English. Emory University Publications: Sources and
      Reprints, Series VII, No. 3. Atlanta: The Library, Emory Uni-
      versity.

1953 Letters in Guy A. Cardwell, Twins of Genius, East Lansing, Mich.:
      Michigan State College Press. [correspondence between Mark Twain
      and George Washington Cable]

1960 Mark Twain [and] George Washington Cable: A Record of a Literary
      Friendship. Ed. Arlin Turner. East Lansing, Mich.: Michigan
      State University Press. [correspondence between Mark Twain and
      Cable]

1960 Mark Twain--Howells Letters; the Correspondence of Samuel L. Clem-
      ens and William Dean Howells, 1872-1910. Ed. Henry Nash Smith and
      William M. Gibson. 2 vols. Cambridge, Mass.: Belnap Press of
      Harvard University.

1961 Mark Twain's Letters to Mary [Benjamin Rogers]. Ed. Lewis Leary.
New York: Columbia University Press. Subsequent edition: 1963.

1961 "My Dear Bro": A Letter from Samuel Clemens to His Brother Orion.
Foreword by Frederick Anderson. Berkeley, California: The
"Berkeley Albion."

1961 The Pattern for Mark Twain's Roughing It; Letters from Nevada by
Samuel and Orion Clemens, 1861-1862. Ed. Franklin R. Rogers. Uni-
versity of California Publications. English Studies, 23. Berkeley:
University of California Press.

1966 Mark Twain's Letters from Hawaii. Ed. A. Grove Day. New York:
Appleton-Century. [See also 1975 entry]

1967 Mark Twain's Letters to His Publishers, 1867-1894. Ed. Hamlin Hill.
The Mark Twain Papers. Berkeley, Calif.: University of California
Press.

1967 Selected Mark Twain--Howells Letters, 1872-1910. Ed. Frederick
Anderson et al. Cambridge, Mass.: Belnap Press of Harvard University.

1969 Mark Twain's Correspondence with Henry Huttleston Rogers, 1893-
1909. Ed. Lewis Leary. The Mark Twain Papers. Berkeley, Calif.:
University of California Press.

c1970 Mark Twain's Letters to the Rogers Family (The Millicent Library
Collection). Ed. Earl J. Dias. New Bedford, Mass.: Reynolds-
Dewalt Printing.

1975 Mark Twain's Letter to Will Bowen; Buffalo, February Sixth, 1870,
New York: Haskell House.

1975 Mark Twain's Letters. Arranged by Albert Bigelow Paine. 2 vols.
New York: AMS Press. [reprint of the 1917 edition]

1975 Mark Twain's Letters from Hawaii. Ed. A. Grove Day. Honolulu:
University of Hawaii Press. [See also 1966 entry]

1976 The Love Letters of Mark Twain. Ed. Dixon Wecter. Westport, Ct.:
Greenwood Press. [See also 1949 entry]

1976 Mark Twain's Letters to Will Bowen; my first, & oldest & dearest
friend, Folcroft, Pa.: Folcroft Library Editions. [See also
1941, 1977, 1978 entries]

1977 Same. Norwood, Pa.: Norwood Editions. [See also 1941, 1976, 1978
entries]

1978 Same. Philadelphia: R. West. [See also 1941, 1976, 1977 entries]

1978 Mark Twain's Collected Correspondence. Vols. I-III. In The Mark
Twain Papers. Ed. Frederick Anderson et al. Berkeley: University of California Press.

Letters from the Earth

1962 Letters from the Earth. Ed. Bernard DeVoto. New York and Evanston:
      Harper & Row. Subsequent edition: 1974.

1969 Same. Ed. Bernard DeVoto. Fawcett World Library. Greenwich,
      Conn.: Fawcett. [See also 1962 entry]

Life on the Mississippi

1883 Life on the Mississippi, Boston: James R. Osgood.

1888 Same. New York: Charles L. Webster. Subsequent edition: 1891.

1896 Same. New York: Harper & Brothers. Subsequent editions: 1898,
      1899, 1900, 1901, 1902, 1903, 1903, 1905, 1905, 1906, 1911, 1911,
      1912, 1915, 1917, 1917, 1923, 1927, 1931, 1935, 1938, 1948, 1950,
      1951.

1899 Same. Hartford, Conn.: American Publishing Co.

1917 Same. Authorized Edition. New York: P.F. Collier & Son.

1917 Same. New York: Grosset and Dunlap. Subsequent edition: 1938.

1931 Same. In The Chief American Prose Writers. Ed. Norman Foerster.
      New York: Houghton, Mifflin.

1935 Same. In The Family Mark Twain, New York and London: Harper &
      Brothers.

1939 Same. In The Favorite Works of Mark Twain, New York: Garden City.

194-? Same. New York: Editions for the Armed Services.

1942 A Critical Edition of the Morgan Manuscript of Mark Twain's Life
      on the Mississippi. Ed. Willis J. Wager. Microfilm. New York: n.pub.

1944 Life on the Mississippi, New York: Heritage Press. Subsequent
      edition: 1959.

1944 Same. New York: Limited Editions Club.

1945 Same. Authorized Edition. New York: Bantam Books. Subsequent
      edition: 1963.

1957 Same. American Century Series. New York: Sagamore Press.

196-? Same. New York: Harper & Row. Subsequent edition: 1965.

1961 Same. Signet Classic. New York: New American Library.

1965 Same. Classic Series. New York: Airmont.

1967 Same. Minneapolis: Dillon Press.

1968 Same. Washington Square Press Collateral Classic. New York: Washington Square Press.

1969 Same. New York: Amsco School Publications.

1969 Same. Great Illustrated Classics. New York: Dodd, Mead.

1969 Same. Grosse Pointe, Mich.: Scholarly Press.

1973 Same. Skokie, Ill.: National Textbook.

1974 Life on the Mississippi. Selections. Ed. Tom H. Walker. Palo Alto, Calif.: American West.

Man That Corrupted Hadleyburg

1900 The Man That Corrupted Hadleyburg and Other Stories and Essays, New York: Harper & Brothers. Subsequent editions: 1901, 1902, 1904, 1906, 1915, 1917, 1918.

1917 The Man That Corrupted Hadleyburg and Other Essays and Stories, New York: P.F. Collier & Son.

1928 The Man That Corrupted Hadleyburg and Other Stories and Essays. Authorized Edition. New York: P.F. Collier.

1932 The Man That Corrupted Hadleyburg and Other Stories. In The Complete Short Stories and Famous Essays of Mark Twain, New York: P.F. Collier.

1933 The Man That Corrupted Hadleyburg. In The College Omnibus. Ed. J.D. McCallum. New York: Harcourt, Brace.

1935 Same. In The Family Mark Twain, New York and London: Harper & Brothers.

1936 Same. In The Bedside Book of Famous American Stories. Ed. J.A. Burrell and B.A. Cerf. New York: Random House.

1957 Same. In The Complete Short Stories of Mark Twain. Ed. Charles Neider. Garden City, N.Y.: Hanover House.

1962 Same. In Selected Shorter Writings of Mark Twain. Ed. Walter Blair. Riverside Editions. Boston: Houghton, Mifflin.

1964 Pudd'nhead Wilson, and The Man That Corrupted Hadleyburg, Evanston, Ill.: Harper & Row.

1968 The Celebrated Jumping Frog of Calaveras County, and The Man That Corrupted Hadleyburg, New York: F. Watts.

1970 The Man That Corrupted Hadleyburg. In The Notorious Jumping Frog
      & Other Stories. Ed. Edward Wagenknecht. New York: Limited
      Editions Club.

                        Mysterious Stranger

1916 The Mysterious Stranger. A Romance, New York and London: Harper
      & Brothers.

1922 The Mysterious Stranger and Other Stories, New York and London:
      Harper & Brothers. Subsequent edition: 1950.

1932 The Mysterious Stranger. In The Complete Short Stories and Famous
      Essays of Mark Twain, New York: P.F. Collier.

1935 Same. In The Family Mark Twain, New York and London: Harper &
      Brothers.

1944 Same. New York: Editions for the Armed Services.

1946 Same. In The Portable Mark Twain. Ed. Bernard DeVoto. New York:
      Viking Press.

1957 Same. In The Complete Short Stories of Mark Twain. Ed. Charles
      Neider. Garden City, N.Y.: Hanover House.

1962 Same. In Selected Shorter Writings of Mark Twain. Ed. Walter
      Blair. Riverside Editions. Boston: Houghton Mifflin.

1962 The Mysterious Stranger and Other Stories. Signet Classic. New
      York: New American Library.

1968 Mark Twain's "The Mysterious Stranger" and the Critics. Ed. John
      S. Tuckey. Belmont, Calif.: Wadsworth. Subsequent edition: 1970.

1969 Mark Twain's Mysterious Stranger Manuscripts. Ed. William M.
      Gibson. The Mark Twain Papers. Berkeley and Los Angeles: Uni-
      versity of California Press.

1970 The Mysterious Stranger. Ed. William M. Gibson. The Mark Twain
      Papers. Berkeley, Calif.: University of California Press.

1978 S.J. Kahn. Mark Twain's Mysterious Stranger, Columbia, Mo.:
      University of Missouri Press.

                            Notebook

1935 Mark Twain's Notebook. Ed. Albert Bigelow Paine. New York and
      London: Harper & Brothers. Subsequent edition: 1935.

1967 Same. Ed. Albert Bigelow Paine. Ann Arbor, Mich.: University
      Microfilms. [photocopy positive of "Second Edition"]

1971 Same. 2nd edition. St. Clair Shores, Mich.: Scholarly Press.

1972 Same. New York: Cooper Square Publishers.

1975 <u>Mark Twain's Notebooks and Journals</u>. Vols. I-II. In <u>The Mark</u>
      <u>Twains Papers</u>. Ed. Frederick Anderson et al. Berkeley: Univer-
      sity of California Press.

1979 Same. Vol. III. In <u>The Mark Twain Papers</u>. Ed. Frederick Anderson
      et al. Berkeley: University of California Press.

Prince and the Pauper

1882 <u>The Prince and the Pauper: A Tale for Young People of All Ages</u>.
      Boston: James R. Osgood.

1882 Same. New York: Charles L. Webster. Subsequent editions: 1885,
      1887, 1888, 1889, 1890, 1891, 1892, 1894.

1891 Same. Hartford, Conn.: American Publishing Company.

1896 Same. New York: Harper & Brothers. Subsequent editions: 1896,
      1900, 1901, 1902, 1903, 1904, 1905, 1906, 1909, 1909, 1909, 1909,
      1909, 1912, 1915, 1917, 1920, 1921, 1931, 1931, 1931, 1936, 1936,
      1940, 1956.

1909 Same. New York: Grosset & Dunlap. Subsequent editions: 1937,
      1961, 1965.

1921 Same. Authorized Edition. New York: P.F. Collier.

1937 <u>The Prince and the Pauper</u>. Children's Bookshelf. Philadelphia,
      Chicago: John C. Winston.

1940 Same. World Juvenile Library. Cleveland: World Publishing Co.
      Subsequent edition: 1948.

1942? Same. Red Star Classics. Chicago, Ill.: Donohue.

1942 <u>The Prince and the Pauper; A Tale for Young People of All Ages</u>.
      <u>Mark Twain Every Child Should Know</u>. Library. 4th Series. New York:
      Doubleday, Doran.

1946 <u>The Prince and the Pauper</u>. New York: City of New York, Board of
      Education.

1946 Same. Classic Comics. New York: Gilberton.

1948? Same. Junior Book Room Edition. Boston: Houghton, Mifflin.

1953 Same. New York: Globe Book Co.

1953 Same. Adapted and Retold. Syracuse, N.Y.: Sanborn.

1954 The Prince and the Pauper; A Tale for Young People of All Ages,
      Garden City, N.Y.: Junior Deluxe Editions.

1956 The Prince and the Pauper. Adapted. Chicago: Scott, Foresman.

196-? The Prince and the Pauper; A Tale for Young People of All Ages,
      New York: Books Incorporated.

1961 The Prince and the Pauper. Dolphin Books. Garden City, N.Y.:
      Doubleday, Doran.

1962 The Prince and the Pauper; A Tale for Young People of All Ages,
      New York: Collier Books. Subsequent edition: 1963.

1962 Same. New York: Harper & Row. Subsequent editions: 1965, 1969?

1964 The Prince and the Pauper. New American Library: New English
      Library. New York: Signet Books.

1965 Same. New York: Doubleday, Doran.

1965 The Prince and the Pauper; A Tale for Young People of All Ages,
      and Other Stories. Great Illustrated Classics. New York: Dodd,
      Mead.

1965 The Prince and the Pauper; A Tale for Young People of All Ages,
      New York: Heritage Press.

1967 The Prince and the Pauper. Phoenix, Ariz.: Frank E. Richards.

1967 Same (abridged). New York: Scholastic Book Services.

1968 The Prince and the Pauper; A Tale for Young People of All Ages.
      Children's Illustrated Classics. New York: E.P. Dutton.

1968 The Prince and the Pauper. Magnum Easy Eye Book. New York:
      Lancer Books.

1969 Same. Chicago: Children's Press.

Pudd'nhead Wilson

1894 The Tragedy of Pudd'nhead Wilson, and the Comedy, Those Extra-
      ordinary Twins, Hartford, Conn.: American Publishing Company.
      Subsequent editions: 1895, 1897, 1899, 1900. 1902.

1899 Pudd'nhead Wilson and Those Extraordinary Twins, New York: Harper
      & Brothers. Subsequent editions: 1899, 1903, 1905, 191-?, 1915,
      1920, 1922, 195-?

1912? The Tragedy of Pudd'nhead Wilson and Comedy of Those Extraordinary
      Twins, New York: Harper & Brothers.

1922   Pudd'nhead Wilson and Those Extraordinary Twins. Authorized
        Edition. New York: P.F. Collier.

1932   Pudd'nhead Wilson. In The Complete Short Stories and Famous Essays
        of Mark Twain, New York: P.F. Collier.

1935   Same. In The Mark Twain Omnibus, New York and London: Harper &
        Brothers.

1948   Same. New York: Grosset.

1955   Pudd'nhead Wilson; A Tale by Mark Twain, New York: Grove Press.
        Subsequent edition: 1955.

1959   Pudd'nhead Wilson. Bantam Classic. New York: Bantam Books. Sub-
        sequent edition: 1964.

1961   The Morgan Manuscript of Mark Twain's Pudd'nhead Wilson, Cambridge,
        Mass.: Harvard University Press.

1962   Pudd'nhead Wilson, A Tale. Harcourt Library of English & American
        Classics. New York: Harcourt, Brace & World.

1964   Pudd'nhead Wilson, and The Man That Corrupted Hadleyburg, Evanston,
        Ill.: Harper & Row.

1964   The Tragedy of Pudd'nhead Wilson. Signet Classic. New York: New
        American Library.

1966   Same. Harper Perennial Classic. New York: Harper & Row.

1966   Pudd'nhead Wilson. Airmont Classic. New York: Airmont Publish-
        ing Co.

1968   Pudd'nhead Wilson; and, Those Extraordinary Twins. Ed. Frederick
        Anderson. Chandler Facsimile Editions in American Literature.
        San Francisco: Chandler Publishing Co. [facsimile of 1st edition
        of 1894]

1974?   Same. Grosse Pointe, Mich.: Scholarly Press.

1974   Pudd'nhead Wilson, Avon, Conn.: Limited Editions Club.

Report from Paradise

1952   Report from Paradise, New York: Harper & Brothers. [Captain
        Stormfield's Visit to Heaven and Letter from the Recording Angel]

Roughing It

1872   Roughing It, Hartford, Conn.: American Publishing Company. Subse-
        quent editions: 1872, 1873, 1874, 1875, 1876, 1878, 1879, 1880,
        1883, 1884, 1886, 1888, 1890, 1891, 1892, 1395, 1899, 1900, 1901
        1902, 1903.

1899   Same. New York and London: Harper & Brothers. Subsequent editions:
       1903, 1904, 1912, 1913, 1915, 1934, 195-?, 1957, 1959.

1913   Same. New York: Grosset & Dunlap. Subsequent edition: 1927.

1927   Mark Twain in Nevada. Reno, Nev. Branch of the American Associa-
       tion of University Women. [selections]

1953   Roughing It in California, Kentfield, Calif.: L-D Allen Press.
       [selections]

1953   Roughing It. Rinehart Editions. New York: Rinehart. Subsequent
       edition: 1965.

1962   Same. Signet Classic. New American Library. New York: Signet
       Books.

1963   Same. New English Library. New York: Signet Books.

c1972 Same. Avon, Conn.: Heritage Press.

1972   Same. Ed. Franklin R. Rogers. Berkeley: University of California
       Press.

1972   Same. New York: Limited Editions Club.

"1601"

1880   Conversation, As It Was By the Social Fireside, in the Times of
       the Tudors. n.p. n.pub.

       [This fugitive sketch, commonly known as "1601," was written
       in 1876 and first printed in Japan and England (cf. Albert
       Bigelow Paine, Mark Twain: A Biography, p. 580). At least
       sixty-two printings appeared in the United States between
       1880 and 1980. Most of them were privately printed without
       indication of place or date or sponsor, and therefore are
       unidentifiable for the purpose of this bibliography. Some
       of the issues printed abroad are entered under "Stories and
       Sketches" in the Foreign Editions section of the bibliography.
       A checklist of various printings issued prior to 1936 is
       provided by Irvin Hass in his 1601; or, Conversation by the
       Social Fireside as It Was in the Time of the Tudors, Chicago:
       Black Cat Press, 1936]

Speeches

1910   Mark Twain's Speeches, New York and London: Harper & Brothers.
       Subsequent edition: 1923.

1970? Same. New York: Greystone Press. [facsimile of the edition in-
       cluded in The Complete Writings of Mark Twain, Definitive Edi-
       tion, 1922-25]

Stories and Sketches

1866   "Jim Smiley's Frog." In Beadle's Dime Book of Fun, no. 3, New
       York: Beadle and Company. [abbreviated version of the original
       1865 newspaper version; see 1940 entry]

1867   The Celebrated Jumping Frog of Calaveras County, and Other
       Sketches, New York: C.H. Webb. Subsequent editions: 1868, 1869,
       1870. [see also 1959, 1969, and 1973 entries]

1871   Mark Twain's (Burlesque) Autobiography and First Romance, New
       York: Sheldon [see also 1910, 1930, 1970, 197-?, 1975, and 1977
       entries]

1874   Mark Twain's Sketches. Authorized Edition. New York: American
       News Company.

1875   Mark Twain's Sketches, New and Old, Hartford, Conn.: American
       Publishing Company. Subsequent editions: 1876?, 1879, 1880,
       1881, 1883, 1887, 1890, 1892, 1895, 1902, 1903. [see also 1905
       entry]

1877   A True Story, and The Recent Carnival of Crime. Vest-pocket
       Series of Standard and Popular Authors. Boston: James R. Osgood.

1878   Punch, Brothers, Punch! and Other Sketches, New York: Slote,
       Woodman. [see also 1906 entry]

1882   The Stolen White Elephant, etc., Boston: James R. Osgood. Subse-
       quent editions: 1882, 1883, [see also 1888, 1967, and 1970 en-
       tries]

1888   The Stolen White Elephant, and Other Stories, New York: Charles
       L. Webster. Subsequent editions: 1891, 1894. [see also 1882,
       1967, and 1970 entries]

1892   Merry Tales, by Mark Twain. Fiction, Fact, and Fancy Series. New
       York: Charles L. Webster. [see also 1970 entry]

1893   The £1,000,000 Bank-note, and Other New Stories, by Mark Twain,
       New York: Charles L. Webster. [see also 1917, 1947, and 1970
       entries]

1895   A True Story. In Capital Stories by American Authors. New York:
       The Christian Herald.

1896   Tom Sawyer Abroad; Tom Sawyer, Detective; and Other Stories; etc.,
       etc., New York: Harper & Brothers. Subsequent editions: 1900,
       1901, 1904, 1905, 1906, 1917, 1919, 1924, 1924, 1924. [see also
       1917 entry]

1896   The American Claimant, and Other Stories, and Sketches, New York:
       Harper & Brothers. Subsequent edtions: 1897, 1898, 1899, 1900,
       1912?, 1917, 1924. [see also 1899 and 1971 entries]

1898   The Loves of Alonzo Fitz Clarence and Rosannah Ethelton.... Chimney Corner Series. New York: F.M. Lupton.

1899   The American Claimant, and Other Stories, and Sketches, New York: P.F. Collier & Son. Subsequent edition: 1924. [see also 1896 and 1971 entries]

1900   The Complete Short Stories and Famous Essays of Mark Twain, New York: P.F. Collier & Son. Subsequent edition: 1932.

1902   A Double-Barrelled Detective Story by Mark Twain, New York and London: Harper & Brothers. [see also 1955 entry]

1903   Jumping Frog, New York: Harper & Brothers. [see also 1866, 1867, 1909, 1924?, 1940, 1949, 1959, 1965, 1968, 1969, 1970, and 1973 entries]

1903   The $30,000 Bequest, and Other Stories by Mark Twain, New York and London: Harper & Brothers. Subsequent editions: 1906, 1906, 1915, 1917, 1917. [see also 1917 entry]

1903   The Jumping Frog, in English, then in French, then clawed back into a civilized language once more by patient, unremunerated toil, by Mark Twain, New York and London: Harper & Brothers. Subsequent edition: 1904. [see also 1932 and 1971 entries]

1903   A Dog's Tale...by Mark Twain. Printed for the National Anti-Vivisection Society. pamphlet [see also 1904 entry]

1904   A Dog's Tale, New York and London: Harper & Brothers. Subsequent edition: 1905 [see also 1903 entry]

1904   An Unexpected Acquaintance, New York and London: Harper & Brothers. [reprinted from A Tramp Abroad, Chap. XXV]

1904   Extracts from Adam's Diary Translated from the Original Ms. by Mark Twain, New York and London: Harper & Brothers. Subsequent edition: 1906.

1905   Sketches, New and Old, by Mark Twain, New York and London: Harper & Brothers. Subsequent editions: 1912?, 1914, 1915, 1917, 1922, 1922. [see also 1875 entry]

1906   Eve's Diary. In Their Husbands' Wives. Ed. William Dean Howells and Henry Mills Alden. New York and London: Harper & Brothers.

1906   Eve's Diary Translated from the Original Ms. by Mark Twain, London and New York: Harper & Brothers.

1906   The Private Life of Adam and Eve; being extracts from their diaries, translated from the original mss. by Mark Twain, New York: Harper & Brothers. Subsequent edition: 1931. [see also 1962, 1967, and 1975 entries]

1906   Punch, Brothers, Punch! and Other Sketches. By Mark Twain. n.p. n. pub. [see also 1878 entry]

1906 A Horse's Tale, New York: Harper & Brothers. Subsequent edition: 1907.

1909 Is Shakespeare Dead? from My Autobiography by Mark Twain, New York and London: Harper & Brothers.

1909 The Jumping Frog, New York: Beecher Ogden.

1910 Mark Twain's (Burlesque) Autobiography, Cleveland: Ormeril. [see also 1871, 1930, 1970, 197-?, 1975, and 1977 entries]

1915 The Man That Corrupted Hadleyburg, and Other Stories and Essays, New York: Harper & Brothers.

1917 The£1,000,000 Bank-note, New York and London: Harper & Brothers. [see also 1893, 1947, and 1970 entries]

1917 The $30,000 Bequest, and Other Stories by Mark Twain. Authorized Edition. New York: P.F. Collier & Son. [see also 1903 entry]

1917 Tom Sawyer Abroad, Tom Sawyer, Detective, and Other Stories, etc., etc., New York: P.F. Collier & Son. [see also 1896 entry].

1919 The Curious Republic of Gondour and Other Whimsical Sketches. Penguin Series. New York: Boni and Liveright. [see also 1969, 1974, 1975, and 1977 entries]

192-? Humorous Fables [by] Mark Twain. Little Blue Book, no. 668. Girard, Kan.: Haldeman-Julius.

1920 The Celebrated Jumping Frog of Calaveras County. In The Great Modern American Stories. Ed. William Dean Howells. New York: Boni & Liveright.

1920 Same. In The Best American Humorous Short Stories. Ed. Alexander Jessup. New York: Boni & Liveright.

1922 The Mysterious Stranger and Other Stories, New York and London: Harper & Brothers. [see also 1962 entry]

1923 The Celebrated Jumping Frog of Calaveras County. In Representative American Short Stories. Ed. Alexander Jessup. Boston, New York: Allyn and Bacon.

1924? A Curious Experience and Other Amusing Pieces. Little Blue Book, no. 932. Girard, Kan.: Haldeman-Julius.

1924? Eight Humorous Sketches, Girard, Kan.: Haldeman-Julius.

1924? Jumping Frog and Other Humorous Tales. Ten Cent Pocket Series, no. 291. Girard, Kan.: Haldeman-Julius.

1924 Tom Sawyer Abroad, and Other Stories by Mark Twain, New York: Grosset and Dunlap. Subsequent editions: 1935, 1961.

1924 Tom Sawyer, Detective, and Other Stories, New York: Grosset and
      Dunlap. Subsequent edition: 1961.

1926 Sketches of the Sixties by Bret Harte and Mark Twain. Being For-
      gotten Material Now Collected for the First Time from "The Cali-
      fornian," 1864-68. Ed. John Howell. San Francisco: John Howell.
      Subsequent edition: 1927. [see also 1970 entry]

1927 The Celebrated Jumping Frog of Calaveras County. In Great Stories
      of All Nations. Ed. Maxim Lieber. n.p. Tudor.

1928 The Adventures of Thomas Jefferson Snodgrass. Ed. Charles Honce.
      Chicago: Covici, Friede. [see also 1969 and 1973 entries]

1930 Mark Twain's Burlesque Autobiography, Larchmont, N.Y.: Peter
      Pauper Press. [see also 1871, 1970, 197-?, 1975, and 1977 entries]

1930 Same. New York: Random House.

1931 The Celebrated Jumping Frog of Calaveras County. In The Twenty-
      five Finest Short Stories. Ed. Edward J. O'Brien. New York:
      R.R. Smith.

1932 The Jumping Frog and Other Stories. In The Complete Short Stories
      and Famous Essays of Mark Twain, New York: P.F. Collier.

1932 The Notorious Jumping Frog of Calaveras County; the original story
      in English, the retranslation clawed back from the French into a
      civilized language once more, by patient and unremunerated toil,
      by Mark Twain. Privately printed. New York: P.C. Duschnes.
      [see also 1903 and 1971 entries]

1933 1601 and Sketches Old and New, New York: Golden Hind Press.

1933 Tom Sawyer, Whitewasher, New York and London: Harper & Brothers.
      [extract from The Adventures of Tom Sawyer]

1935 The Complete Short Stories and Humorous Sketches of Mark Twain.
      Centennial Edition. New York: W.H. Wise. [see also 1957, 1958,
      and 1961 entries]

1936 The Celebrated Jumping Frog of Calaveras County. In The Bedside
      Book of Famous American Stories. Ed. J.A. Burrell and B.A. Cerf.
      New York: Random House.

1936 Same. In Orton Lowe, Our Land and Its Literature, New York and
      London: Harper and Brothers.

1937 Selected Short Stories of Mark Twain. Ed. Bernard DeVoto. New
      York: Editions for the Armed Services.

1937 The Adventures of Tom Sawyer; The Celebrated Jumping Frog of Cal-
      averas County and Other Tales. Immortal Masterpieces of Litera-
      ture, Vol. 2. New York: Consolidated Book Publishers. [see also
      1940 and 1949 entries]

1938 The Washoe Giant in San Francisco, being heretofore unpublished
      sketches by Mark Twain published in the Golden Era in the sixties
      .... Limited Edition. Ed. Franklin D. Walker. San Francisco:
      George Fields. [see also 1973, 1976, and 1977 entries]

1939 Dos Royte Kaylkhele [The Red Globe: The Death Disk], New York:
      Idishe Shul. [Yiddish]

1940 The Adventures of Tom Sawyer, together with The Celebrated
      Jumping Frog of Calaveras County and Other Tales, New York: Book
      League of America.

1940 Jim Smiley and His Jumping Frog. By Mark Twain, Chicago: Pocahon-
      tas Press. [reproduction of the earliest version that appeared
      in the New York Saturday Press, November 18, 1865]

1942 The Great Dark. In Bernard DeVoto, Mark Twain at Work, Cambridge,
      Mass.: Harvard University Press.

1946 The Letters of Quintus Curtius Snodgrass. Ed. Ernest E. Leisy.
      Dallas, Tex.: University Press, Southern Methodist University.

1946 Three Sketches by Mark Twain, Stamford, Conn.: Overbrook Press.

1947 The $1,000,000 Bank-note, New York: Comet Press. [see also 1893,
      1917, and 1970 entries]

1949 The Adventures of Tom Sawyer, together with the Celebrated Jump-
      ing Frog of Calaveras County, and Other Tales. World's Greatest
      Literature. Chicago: Fountain Press.

1949 The Jumping Frog, and Other Stories and Sketches from the Exqui-
      site Pen of Samuel L. Clemens, Mount Vernon, N.Y.: Peter Pauper
      Press.

1952 Mark Twain's First Story ["The Dandy Frightening the Squatter"].
      Ed. Franklin J. Meine. Iowa City: Prairie Press. [see also
      1973 entry]

1952? Short Stories, By Mark Twain, New York: P.F. Collier.

1955 Mark Twain's A Double Barrelled Detective Story; A Mystery-Comedy
      in Three Acts, Evanston, Ill.: Row, Peterson. [see also 1902
      entry]

1957 The Complete Short Stories of Mark Twain. Now Collected for the
      First Time. Ed. Charles Neider. Hanover House Books. Garden
      City, N.Y.: Doubleday.

1958 Same. Ed. Charles Neider. Bantam Classic. New York: Bantam
      Books.

1959 The Celebrated Jumping Frog of Calaveras County, and Other
      Sketches. Limited Edition. New York: West Virginia Pulp and
      Paper Company. [see also 1867, 1969, and 1973 entries]

1959 Concerning Cats: Two Tales by Mark Twain. Ed. Frederick Anderson.
      San Francisco: Book Club of California.

1961 The Complete Humorous Sketches and Tales of Mark Twain. Ed.
      Charles Neider. Garden City, N.Y.: Hanover House.

1961 Contributions to "The Galaxy," 1868-1871 by Mark Twain (Samuel
      Langhorne Clemens). Ed. Bruce R. McElderry, Jr. Gainesville, Fla.:
      Scholars' Facsimiles and Reprints.

1962 Diaries of Adam and Eve. Coronado Library. Sandoval, N.M.: Coro-
      nado Press. [see also 1906, 1967, 1971, and 1975 entries]

1962 The Mysterious Stranger and Other Stories. Signet Classic. New
      York: New American Library.

1963 Jim Baker's Bluejay Yarn, New York: Orion Press.

1963 Simon Wheeler, Detective. Ed. Franklin R. Rogers. New York: New
      York Public Library.

1965 The Celebrated Jumping Frog of Calaveras County. Centennial
      Edition. Palmer Lake, Colo.: Filter Press. [facsimile of the
      1865 edition]

1965 The Prince and the Pauper; A Tale for Young People of All Ages,
      and Other Stories. Great Illustrated Classics. New York: Dodd,
      Mead.

1967 The Private Life of Adam and Eve; being extracts from their diar-
      ies, translated from the original mss. by Mark Twain, Ann Arbor,
      Mich.: University Microfilms. [photocopy positive of the 1931
      Harper & Brothers edition] [see also 1906, 1962, 1971, and 1975
      entries]

1967 Short Stories of Mark Twain. Funk & Wagnalls Paperbook. New York:
      Funks & Wagnalls.

1967 The Stolen White Elephant, etc., by Mark Twain, Ann Arbor, Mich.:
      University Microfilms. [photocopy positive of the 1882 James R.
      Osgood edition]

1968 The Celebrated Jumping Frog of Calaveras County, and The Man That
      Corrupted Hadleyburg, New York: F. Watts.

1969 The Celebrated Jumping Frog of Calaveras County, and Other Sketches.
      American Humorists Series. Literature House Book. Upper Saddle
      River, N.J.: Gregg Press. [facsimile of the 1867 C.H. Webb
      edition] [see also 1867, 1959, and 1973 entries]

1969 The Adventures of Thomas Jefferson Snodgrass. Ed. Charles Honce.
      Folcroft, Pa.: Folcroft Press. [see also 1928 and 1973 entries]

1969 Clemens of the Call; Mark Twain in San Francisco. Ed. Edgar M.
      Branch. Berkeley, Calif.: University of California Press.

1969   The Curious Republic of Gondour, and Other Whimsical Sketches,
       Folcroft, Pa.: Folcroft Press. Subsequent edition: 1974 [see
       also 1919, 1974, 1975, and 1977 entries]

197-? A Curious Experience, and Other Amusing Pieces. Little Blue Book
       no. 932. Girard, Kan.: Haldeman-Julius.

197-? Mark Twain's (burlesque) Autobiography, Larchmont, N.Y.: Peter
       Pauper Press. [see also 1871, 1930, 1970, 1975, and 1977 entries]

1970   Mark Twain's (burlesque) Autobiography and First Romance, New
       York: Haskell House. [see also 1871, 1930, 197-?, 1975, and 1977
       entries]

1970   Mark Twain's Quarrel with Heaven: "Captain Stormfield's Visit to
       Heaven" and Other Sketches, New Haven, Conn.: College & Univer-
       sity Press Services.

1970   Merry Tales, by Mark Twain. Fiction, Fact, and Fancy Series.
       Folcroft, Pa.: Folcroft Press. [see also 1892 entry]

1970   The Notorious Jumping Frog & Other Stories. Ed. Edward Wagenknecht.
       New York: Limited Editions Club. Avon, Conn.: Heritage Press.

1970   The £1,000,000 Bank-Note, and Other New Stories, Freeport, L.I.,
       N.Y.: Books for Libraries Press. [see also 1893, 1917, and 1947
       entries]

1970   Sketches of the Sixties by Bret Harte and Mark Twain. Being For-
       gotten Material Now Collected for the First Time from "The
       Californian," 1864-67, St. Clair Shores, Mich. Scholarly Press.
       [see also 1926 entry]

1970   The Stolen White Elephant, etc. Short Story Index Reprint Series.
       Freeport, L.I., N.Y.: Books for Libraries Press. [see also 1882,
       1888, and 1967 entries]

1971   The American Claimant, and Other Stories and Sketches, New York:
       AMS Press. [see also 1896 and 1899 entries]

1971   The Diaries of Adam and Eve, New York: American Heritage Press.
       [see also 1906, 1962, 1967, and 1975 entries]

1971   Same. New edition. Lawrence, Kan.: Coronado Press. [see also
       1906, 1962, 1967, and 1975 entries]

1971   The Jumping Frog in English, then in French, then clawed back into
       a civilized language once more by patient, unremunerated toil, by
       Mark Twain, New York: Dover Publications. [see also 1903 and
       1932 entries]

1973   The Adventures of Thomas Jefferson Snodgrass. Ed. Charles Honce.
       Folcroft, Pa.: Folcroft Library Editions. [see also 1928 and
       1969 entries]

1973 The Celebrated Jumping Frog of Calaveras County, and Other
      Sketches. Ed. John Paul. Boston: Gregg Press. [see also 1867,
      1959, and 1969 entries]

1973 Mark Twain's First Story ["The Dandy Frightening the Squatter"].
      Ed. Franklin J. Meine. Folcroft, Pa.: Folcroft Library Editions.
      [see also 1952 entry]

1973 The Washoe Giant in San Francisco.... Ed. Franklin Walker. Fol-
      croft, Pa.: Folcroft Library Editions. [see also 1938, 1976, and
      1977 entries]

1974 The Curious Republic of Gondour, and Other Whimsical Sketches,
      Folcroft, Pa.: Folcroft Library Editions. [see also 1919, 1969,
      1975, 1975, and 1977 entries]

1974 Same. New York: Haskell House. [see also 1919, 1969, 1974, 1975,
      1975, and 1977 entries]

1975 Same. Norwood, Pa.: Norwood Editions. [see also 1919, 1969, 1974,
      1974, and 1977 entries]

1975 The Diary of Adam and Eve. Hallmark Crown Edition. Kansas City,
      Mo.: Hallmark Cards. [see also 1906, 1962, 1967, and 1971 entries]

1975 Mark Twain's Burlesque Autobiography, Norwood, Pa.: Norwood Edi-
      tions. [see also 1871, 1930, 1970, 197-?, and 1977 entries]

1976 The Washoe Giant in San Francisco.... Ed. Franklin Walker. Nor-
      wood, Pa.: Norwood Editions. [see also 1938, 1973, and 1977 en-
      tries]

1977 Same. Philadelphia: R. West. [see also 1938, 1973, and 1976 en-
      tries]

1977 The Curious Republic of Gondour, and Other Whimsical Sketches,
      Philadelphia: R. West. [see also 1919, 1969, 1974, 1974, and
      1975 entries]

1977 Mark Twain's Burlesque Autobiography, Folcroft, Pa.: Folcroft
      Library Editions. [see also 1871, 1930, 1970, 197-?, and 1975
      entries]

                              Tom Sawyer

1876 The Adventures of Tom Sawyer, Hartford, Conn.: American Publish-
      ing Co. Subsequent editions: 1877, 1880, 1885, 1886, 1887, 1888,
      1891, 1892, 1893, 1894, 1895, 1897, 1898, 1899, 1900, 1901, 1903.

19-- Same. New York: Gordon & Payne.

1903 Same. New York and London: Harper & Brothers. Subsequent edi-
      tions: 1903, 1910, 1912?, 1915, 1917, 1917, 1920, 1920, 1920,
      1923, 1926, 1931, 1932, 1932, 1938, 1938, 1950.

192-? Same.   Chicago: Donohue.

1920 Same.   Authorized Edition. New York: P.F. Collier.

1920 Same.   New York: Grosset & Dunlap. Subsequent editions: 1922,
      1931, 1933, 1933, 194-?, 1944?, 1946, 1946, 1946, 1946, 1948, 1963.

1922 The Adventures of Tom Sawyer and The Adventures of Huckleberry
      Finn, New York: The Modern Library. Subsequent editions: 1940,
      195-?, 1966?

1930? The Adventures of Tom Sawyer, Chicago: Goldsmith. Subsequent edi-
      tion: 1934.

1930 Same.   New York: Random House.

1931 Same.   Akron, Ohio: Saalfield. Subsequent edition: 1937?

1931 Same.   Boston, New York: Ginn. Subsequent edition: 1966.

1931 Same.   Complete Authorized Edition. New York: A.L. Burt.

1931 Same.   Philadelphia, Chicago: John C. Winston. Subsequent edi-
      tions: 1931, 1937?, 1942, 1952, 1957.

1931 Same.   Racine, Wis.: Whitman. Subsequent editions: 1944, 1965?

1932 Same.   New York: Blue Ribbon Books.

1932 Same.   Washington, D.C.: National Home Library Foundation. Subse-
      quent edition: 1936.

1933 Same.   New York: Three Sirens Press. Illustrated Editions Co.

1935 Same.   In The Family Mark Twain, New York and London: Harper &
      Brothers.

1936 Same.   New York: Heritage Press. Subsequent editions: 1936, 1937,
      1943?, 1948?, 1963.

1936 Same.   New York: Noble and Noble.

1937 The Adventures of Tom Sawyer; together with The Celebrated Jumping
      Frog of Calaveras County and Other Tales. Immortal Masterpieces of
      Literature, Vol. 2. New York: Consolidated Book Publishers. [see
      also 1940, 1949 entries]

1937 The Adventures of Tom Sawyer, New York: Book League of America.

1937 Same.   Reading, Pa.: The Spencer Press.

1938 Same.   New York: Books, Inc. Subsequent editions: 1942?, 1942?,
      196-?

1938 Same.   Nelson Classics. Camden, N.J.: Nelson.

1938 Same. Abridged Edition. Chicago: Rand McNally.

1939 <u>Tom Sawyer</u>. Limited Editions Club. Cambridge, Mass.: University Press.

194-? <u>The Adventures of Tom Sawyer</u>, New York: Editions for the Armed Services.

1940? Same. Springfield, Mass.: McLoughlin Bros.

1940 <u>The Adventures of Tom Sawyer, retold in 96 pages by Bennett Kline</u>, Racine, Wis.: Whitman.

1940 <u>The Adventures of Tom Sawyer, together with The Celebrated Jumping Frog of Calaveras County, and Other Tales</u>, New York: Book League of America. [see also 1937, 1949 entries]

1940 <u>The Adventures of Tom Sawyer [and] The Adventures of Huckleberry Finn</u>, New York: Heritage Press. Subsequent editions: 1952, 1956, 1960.

1940 <u>The Adventures of Tom Sawyer</u>. Young Moderns Bookshelf. New York: Sun Dial Press.

1942? Same. Best Books. Boston, New York: Bruce, Humphries.

1942? Same. Duo-tone Classics. n.p. Library Edition Books.

1942 Same. Cleveland, Ohio: World. Subsequent editions: 1942?, 1946.

1943 Same. Mount Vernon, N.Y.: Peter Pauper Press. Subsequent edition: 1943.

1944 <u>The Adventures of Tom Sawyer; and, Huckleberry Finn</u>. Everyman's Library. New York: E.P. Dutton. Subsequent editions: 1954, 1955.

1946 <u>The Adventures of Tom Sawyer</u>, New York: Hartsdale House.

1949 <u>The Adventures of Tom Sawyer; together with The Celebrated Jumping Frog of Calaveras County, and Other Tales</u>. World's Greatest Literature. Chicago: Fountain Press. [see also 1937, 1940 entries]

1949 <u>The Adventures of Tom Sawyer</u>, Chicago: Scott, Foresman.

1950 Same. Heirloom Library. New York: Chanticleer Press.

1951 Same. New York: Globe Book Co. Subsequent edition: 1963.

1953 <u>The Adventures of Tom Sawyer and The Adventures of Huckleberry Finn</u>, Chicago: Spencer Press.

1954 <u>The Adventures of Tom Sawyer</u>, Garden City, N.Y.: Junior De Luxe Editions.

1956 Same. Chicago: Coach House Press.

1956   Same. Golden Picture Classics. New York: Simon & Schuster.

1958   Same. Great Illustrated Classics. New York: Dodd, Mead.

1959   Same. Signet Classic. New York: New American Library.

1960?   Tom Sawyer; and, Huckleberry Finn. New Collins Classics. New
        York: W.W. Norton.

1960   The Adventures of Tom Sawyer; and, The Adventures of Huckleberry
        Finn. Platt & Munk Great Writers Collection. New York: Platt &
        Munk.

1961   The Adventures of Tom Sawyer, New York: Doubleday. Subsequent
        edition: 1965.

1961   Same. New York: Macmillan. Subsequent edition: 1962.

1962   Same. New York: Airmont Books.

1962   Same. New York: Collier Books. Subsequent edition: 1963.

1962   Same. New York: Harcourt, Brace & World.

1962   Same. Riverside Literature Series. Boston: Houghton Mifflin.

1963   Same. New York: Washington Square Press.

1965   Same. New York: Harper & Row.

1966   Tom Sawyer. Bantam Pathfinder Edition. New York: Bantam Books.

1967   The Adventures of Tom Sawyer. Laurel-leaf Library. New York: Dell.

1967   Same. In Reading the Novel. Ed. E.J. Gordon and V.T. Wilkinson.
        Boston: Ginn.

1967   Same. Phoenix, Ariz.: Frank E. Richards.

1967   Same. Ultratype Edition. New York: F. Watts.

1968   Same. Cambridge Classics Library. Bronxville, N.Y.: Cambridge
        Book Co.

1969   Same. New York: Amsco School Publications.

1969   Same. Chicago: Children's Press.

1969   Mark Twain's Hannibal, Huck and Tom. Ed. Walter Blair. The Mark
        Twain Papers. Berkeley, Calif.: University of California Press.

1970   Tom Sawyer. Lifetime Library. Middletown, Conn.: American
        Education Publications.

1970?   The Adventures of Tom Sawyer, New York: Books.

197-? <u>The Adventures of Tom Sawyer; Tom Sawyer Abroad; Tom Sawyer, Detec-tive</u>, Garden City, N.Y.: Doubleday.

1970 <u>The Adventures of Tom Sawyer</u>. In A. Serrano-Plaja, <u>Magic Realism in Cervantes</u>. Berkeley: University of California Press.

1972 Same. Pocket Books. New York: Washington Square Press.

1972 Same. Cleveland and New York: World.

c1975 Same. World Books Limited Edition. Chicago: Field Enterprises Educational Corporation.

1977 Same. Franklin Center, Pa.: Franklin Library.

1978 Same. The Collector's Library of the World's Best-loved Books. Limited Edition. Franklin Center, Pa.: Franklin Library.

c1978 <u>The Complete Adventures of Tom Sawyer and Huckleberry Finn</u>, New York: Harper & Row.

1978 Same. Centennial Edition. New York: Harper & Row.

1979 <u>The Adventures of Tom Sawyer</u>. In <u>Illustrated Works of Mark Twain</u>: <u>Selections....</u> Avenel Books. New York: Crown.

Tom Sawyer Abroad

1894 <u>Tom Sawyer Abroad by Huck Finn</u>, New York: Charles L. Webster. Sub-sequent edition: 1894.

1896 <u>Tom Sawyer Abroad; Tom Sawyer, Detective; and Other Stories; Etc., Etc.</u> New York: Harper & Brothers. Subsequent editions: 1900, 1901, 1902, 1904, 1905, 1906, 1915, 1917, 1919, 1924, 1924.

1917 Same. New York: P.F. Collier. Subsequent edition: 1924.

1928 <u>Tom Sawyer Abroad</u>. Special Aviation Edition. New York: Harper & Brothers.

1932 <u>Tom Sawyer Abroad and Other Stories</u>. In <u>The Complete Short Stories and Famous Essays of Mark Twain</u>, New York: P.F. Collier.

1935 Same. New York: Grosset and Dunlap. Subsequent edition: 1961.

1935 <u>Tom Sawyer Abroad</u>. In <u>The Family Mark Twain</u>, New York and London: Harper & Brothers.

1962 <u>Tom Sawyer Abroad; and, Tom Sawyer, Detective,</u> New York: Collier Books. Subsequent edition: 1963.

1965 <u>Tom Sawyer Abroad</u>, New York: Grosset and Dunlap.

1967 Same. Golden Press Classics Library. New York: Golden Press.

197-? The Adventures of Tom Sawyer; Tom Sawyer Abroad; Tom Sawyer, Detec-
      tive, Garden City, N.Y.: Doubleday.

Tom Sawyer, Detective

1896 Tom Sawyer Abroad; Tom Sawyer, Detective; and Other Stories; Etc.,
      Etc., New York: Harper & Brothers. Subsequent editions: 1900, 1901,
      1904, 1905, 1906, 1917, 1919, 1924, 1924.

1917 Same. New York: P.F. Collier. Subsequent edition: 1924.

1924 Tom Sawyer, Detective and Other Stories, New York: Grosset and
      Dunlap. Subsequent editions: 1935, 1961.

1962 Tom Sawyer Abroad; and, Tom Sawyer, Detective, New York: Collier
      Books. Subsequent edition: 1963.

1965 Tom Sawyer, Detective. Companion Library. New York: Grosset and
      Dunlap.

197-? The Adventures of Tom Sawyer; Tom Sawyer Abroad; Tom Sawyer, Detec-
      tive, Garden City, N.Y.: Doubleday.

Tramp Abroad

1879 A Tramp Abroad, Hartford, Conn.: American Publishing Co. Subse-
      quent editions: 1880, 1880, 1889, 1891, 1899, 1902.

1903 Same. New York and London: Harper & Brothers. Subsequent editions:
      1907, 1915, 1921.

1966 Same. New York: Limited Editions Club.

1967 Same. New York: Heritage Press.

c1977 Same. Abridged. Ed. Charles Neider. New York: Harper & Row.

1978 Same. Abridged. Ed. Charles Neider. Perennial Library. New
      York: Harper & Row.

Travel Sketches

1910 Travels at Home; Selected from the Works of Mark Twain.... Ed.
      Percival Chubb. New York and London: Harper & Brothers.

1923 Europe and Elsewhere, New York and London: Harper & Brothers.

1937 Letters from the Sandwich Islands, Written for the Sacramento
      "Union" by Mark Twain, San Francisco: Grabhorn Press.

1938 Same. Stanford, Calif.: Stanford University Press. [See also
      1972 entry]

1939 Letters from Honolulu, Written for the Sacramento "Union" by Mark
      Twain. Limited Edition. Ed. John W. Vandercook. Honolulu:
      Thomas Nickerson.

1940 Mark Twain's Travels with Mr. Brown; Being Heretofore Uncollected
      Sketches Written by Mark Twain for the San Francisco "Alta Cali-
      fornia" in 1866 & 1867.... Ed. Franklin D. Walker and Ezra Dane.
      Limited Edition. New York: Knopf. [See also 1971 entry]

1943 Washington in 1868, by Samuel L. Clemens. Ed. Cyril Clemens. Bio-
      graphical Series, No. 12. Webster Groves, Mo.: International
      Mark Twain Society.

1957 Mark Twain of the "Enterprise"; Newspaper Arts & Other Documents,
      1862-1864. Ed. Henry Nash Smith. Berkeley, Calif.: University
      of California Press.

1957 Mark Twain: San Francisco Virginia City Territorial Enterprise
      Correspondent; Selections from His Letters to the Territorial
      Enterprise, 1865-1866. Ed. Henry Nash Smith and Frederick Ander-
      son. San Francisco: Book Club of California.

1958 Travelling with the Innocents Abroad; Mark Twain's Original Reports
      from Europe and the Holy Land. Ed. Daniel Morley McKeithan. Norman,
      Okla.: University of Oklahoma Press.

1961 The Pattern for Mark Twain's "Roughing It": Letters from Nevada
      by Samuel and Orion Clemens 1861-1862. Ed. Franklin B. Rogers.
      Berkeley and Los Angeles: University of California Press.

1961 The Travels of Mark Twain. Ed. Charles Neider. New York: Coward-
      McCann.

1963 Mark Twain's San Francisco. Ed. Bernard Taper. New York: McGraw-
      Hill. [See also 1978 entry]

1969 Clemens of the "Call"; Mark Twain in San Francisco. Ed. Edgar M.
      Branch. Berkeley and Los Angeles: University of California Press.

1971 Mark Twain's Travels with Mr. Brown.... Ed. Franklin Walker and
      G. Ezra Dane. New York: Russell & Russell. [See also 1940 entry]

1972 Letters from the Sandwich Islands, written for the "Sacramento
      Union" by Mark Twain. Ed. G. Ezra Dane. New York: Haskell House.
      [See also 1938 entry]

1978 Mark Twain's San Francisco. Ed. Bernard Taper. Westport, Ct.:
      Greenwood Press. [See also 1963 entry]

What Is Man?

1906 What Is Man? Privately printed. New York: De Vinne Press.

1917 What Is Man? and Other Essays, New York and London: Harper & Bro-
      thers.

1972 What Is Man? Freeport, N.Y.: Books for Libraries Press.

                        Miscellenous Writings

1870 Memoranda. In The Galaxy, June-December 1870. New York: Sheldon.

1883 English As She Is Spoke: or, A Jest in Sober Earnest, New York:
      D. Appleton. [See also 1924 entry]

1883 Wit and Humor of the Age...by Mark Twain, Josh Billings, Robt. J.
      Burdette, Alex. Sweet, Eli Perkins..., Chicago: Western Publish-
      ing House. [See also 1902 entry]

1888 Mark Twain's Library of Humor, New York: Charles L. Webster. [See
      also 1902, 1906, 1969, 1975 entries]

1893 Pudd'nhead Wilson's Calendar for 1894, New York: Century. [See
      also 1937, 1974 entries]

1898 Library of Wit and Humor, by Mark Twain and Others, Chicago:
      Thompson & Thomas. [See also 1902, 1906, 1969, 1975 entries]

1900 English as She Is Taught, Boston, Mass.: Mutual Book Co. [See
      also 1917 entry]

1901? To the Person Sitting in Darkness by Mark Twain, New York. [pamph-
      let reprinted from The North American Review, February 1901, and
      distributed by the Anti-Imperialist League of New York]

1902? Gen. Grant's English and Other Recitations, New York: E.S. Werner
      Publishing and Supply Co.

1902? Hot Stuff. Mark Twain and Others, Chicago, New York: George M.
      Hill. [See also 1912 entry]

1902? Library of Wit and Humor, Chicago: M.A. Donohue. [See also 1888,
      1906, 1969, 1975 entries]

1902? Wit and Humor of the Age, Philadelphia: People's Publishing Co.
      [See also 1883 entry]

1903 Editorial Wild Oats, New York and London: Harper & Brothers. Subse-
      quent editions: 1905, 1908, [See also 1970, 1971 entries]

1903 The Literary Guillotine, by Mark Twain. Ed. C.B. Loomis Herford.
      New York and London: J. Lane.

1906 Mark Twain's Library of Humor. 4 vols. New York and London: Har-
      per & Brothers. [See also 1888, 1902, 1969, 1975 entries]

1906 Mark Twain on Simplified Spelling. n.p. Simplified Spelling Board.

1909   Queen Victoria's Jubilee: The Great Procession of June 22, 1897,
       in The Queen's Honor, Reported Both in the Light of History, and
       as a Spectacle, by Mark Twain. Privately printed from the "New
       York Journal," June 22-23, 1897.

1911   Mark Twain's Letter to the California Pioneers, Oakland, Calif.:
       DeWitt & Snelling.   [reprinted from the "Buffalo Express," Oct.
       19, 1869]

1912? Hot Stuff. Mark Twain and Others, Chicago: Reilly & Britton [See
       also 1902 entry]

1913   Loyalty of Friendship. Gems of Thought Series. New York: Barse
       & Hopkins.

1917   English As She Is Taught, Boston: A.M. Davis. [See also 1900 entry]

1918   The Mark Twain Calendar, New York: n. pub. [See also 1919 entry]

1919   Same. New York: George Sully. Subsequent edition: 1923. [See
       also 1918 entry]

192-? Amusing Answers to Correspondents, and Other Pieces [by] Mark Twain,
       Little Blue Book No. 662. Girard, Kan.: Haldeman-Julius.

1921? My Watch: An Instructive Little Tale, Waltham, Mass.: Waltham
       Watch Co.

1923   The War Prayer. In Europe and Elsewhere, New York and London:
       Harper & Brothers. [See also 1968, 1971, 1975 entries]

1924? English As She Is Spoke, Girard, Kan.: Haldeman-Julius. [See also
       1883 entry]

1929   Mark Twain Anecdotes, Webster Groves, Mo.: The Mark Twain Society.

1934   Concerning the Jews, New York: Harper & Brothers.

1935   Coley B. Taylor, Mark Twain's Margins on Thackeray's "Swift," New
       York: Gotham House.

1935   Slovenly Peter [Der Struwwelpeter] Translated into English Jingles
       from the Original German of Dr. Heinrich Hoffman by Mark Twain,
       New York: Limited Editions Club. Marchbanks Press.

1935   Slovenly Peter; or, Happy Tales and Funny Pictures, freely trans-
       lated by Mark Twain [from Heinrich Hoffman's Struwwelpeter], New
       York and London: Harper & Brothers.

1937   Extracts from Pudd'nhead Wilson's Calendar, Madison, N.J.: Golden
       Hind Press. [See also 1893, 1974 entries]

1937   How To Cure A Cold, San Francisco: Cloister Press.

1940 Mark Twain in Eruption: Hitherto Unpublished Pages about Men and Events, by Mark Twain. Ed. Bernard DeVoto. New York and London: Harper & Brothers. Subsequent editions: 1940, 1940. [See also 1940, 1968 entries]

1940 Same. Ed. Bernard DeVoto. New York: Grosset and Dunlap. Subsequent edition: 1947. [See also 1968 entry]

1941 Republican Letters, by Samuel L. Clemens. Ed. Cyril Clemens. Biographical Series, No. 10. Webster Groves, Mo.: International Mark Twain Society. [articles reprinted from the "Chicago Republican" in 1868] [See also 1970 entry]

1942 Mark Twain's Letters in the Muscatine Journal. Ed. Edgar M. Branch. Limited Edition. Chicago: The Mark Twain Association of America. [See also 1970, 1975, 1977 entries]

1942 Mark Twain at Work. Ed. Bernard DeVoto. Cambridge, Mass.: Harvard University Press.

1948 Mark Twain in Three Moods: Three New Items of Twainiana. Ed. Dixon Wecter. San Marino, Calif.: Friends of the Huntington Library. [See also 1970, 1976, 1977 entries]

1952 Richard Brown and the Dragon; Retold from An Anecdote by Samuel Langhorne Clemens' A Tramp Abroad, Garden City, N.Y.: Doubleday.

1957 Mark Twain Jest Book. Ed. Cyril Clemens. Kirkwood, Mo.: Mark Twain Journal.

1958 Mark Twain Speaks Out: Four Pieces - Never Before Published - from One of the World's Oldest, and Most Neglected, Classics. Ed. Charles Neider. New York: n. pub.

1960 Mark Twain and the Government; Selected and Arranged by Svend Petersen. Caldwell, Ida.: Caxton Printers.

1961 Mark Twain on the Art of Writing. Ed. M.B. Fried. Buffalo: The Salisbury Club. [See also 1970, 1976, 1977 entries]

1961 "Ah Sin," A Dramatic Work by Mark Twain and Bret Harte. Ed. Frederick Anderson. San Francisco: The Book Club of California.

1964 A Cure for the Blues [by] Mark Twain, with The Enemy Conquered; or, Love Triumphant, by G. Ragsdale McClintock. Rutland, Vt.: C.E. Tuttle.

1968 Huck Finn & Tom Sawyer among the Indians. In "Life" magazine, Vol. 65, No. 25, December 20, 1968. Chicago: Time, Inc. [from an unpublished manuscript, c1889] [See also 1969 entry]

1968 Mark Twain in Eruption: Hitherto Unpublished Pages about Men and Events. Ed. Bernard DeVoto. Capricorn Book. New York: Capricorn Books. [See also 1940 entries]

1968 The War Prayer, New York: Harper & Row. St. Crispin Press. Subsequent edition: 1970. [See also 1923, 1971, 1975 entries]

1969 Mark Twain's Hannibal, Huck & Tom. Ed. Walter Blair. Berkeley, Cal.: University of California Press. [includes Huck Finn and Tom Sawyer Among the Indians, and Tom Sawyer, A Play] [See also 1968 entry]

1969 Mark Twain's Library of Humor, New York: Garrett Press. [See also 1888, 1902, 1906, 1975 entries]

1970 Mark Twain's Letters in the Muscatine Journal. Ed. Edgar M. Branch. Folcroft Library Editions. Folcroft, Pa.: Folcroft Press. Subsequent edition: 1973. [See also 1942, 1975, 1977 entries]

1970 Republican Letters, by Samuel L. Clemens. Ed. Cyril Clemens. Folcroft, Pa.: Folcroft Press. Subsequent edition: 1977. [See also 1941 entry]

1970 Mark Twain in Three Moods. Ed. Dixon Wecter. Folcroft, Pa.: Folcroft Library Editions. Subsequent edition: 1975. [See also 1948, 1976, 1977 entries]

1970 Mark Twain on the Art of Writing. Ed. M.B. Fried. Folcroft, Pa.: Folcroft Press. Subsequent edition: 1973. [See also 1961, 1976, 1977 entries]

1970 Editorial Wild Oats. American Journalists. New York: Arno Press; New York Times Co. [See also 1903, 1971 entries]

1970 Same. Freeport, Long Island, N.Y.: Books for Libraries Press. [See also 1903, 1970, 1971 entries]

1971 Editorial Wild Oats, by Samuel Langhorne Clemens. Complete and unabridged. New York: Books for Libraries Press. [See also 1903, 1970 entries]

1971 The War Prayer. Perennial Library. New York: Harper & Row. [See also 1923, 1968, 1975 entries]

1972 Advice for Good Little Girls by Mark Twain, New Britain, Conn.: Robert E. Mussman.

1972 The Great Landslide Case, by Mark Twain, Berkeley: Friends of the Bancroft Library.

1972 Fables of Man [by] Mark Twain. Ed. John C. Tuckey. Berkeley: University of California Press. [See also 1980 entry]

1974 Pudd'nhead Wilson's Calendar, Avon, Conn.: Limited Editions Club. [See also 1893, 1937 entries]

1975 Mark Twain's Letters in the Muscatine Journal. Ed. Edgar M. Branch. Norwood, Pa.: Norwood Editions. [See also 1942, 1970, 1977 entries]

1975 Mark Twain's Library of Humor, New York: Hart. [See also 1888, 1902, 1906, 1969 entries]

1975 The War Prayer, Ithaca, N.Y.: Lindenfield. [See also 1923, 1968, 1971 entries]

1976 The Mammoth Cod, and, Address to the Stomach Club [by] Mark Twain. 1st edition. Waukesha, Wis.: Maledicta Press.

1976 Mark Twain on the Art of Writing. Ed. M.R. Fried. Norwood, Pa.: Norwood Editions. [See also 1961, 1970, 1977 entries]

1976 Mark Twain in Three Moods: Three New Items of Twainiana. Ed. Dixon Wecter. Norwood, Pa.: Norwood Editions. [See also 1948, 1970, 1977 entries]

1977 Same. Ed. Dixon Wecter. Philadelphia: R. West. [See also 1948, 1970, 1976 entries]

1977 Interviews with Samuel L. Clemens, 1874-1910.... Ed. L.J. Budd. American Literary Realism. Arlington, Tex.: University of Texas.

1977 Mark Twain on the Art of Writing. Ed. M.B. Fried. Philadelphia: R. West. [See also 1961, 1970, 1976 entries]

1977 Mark Twain's Letters in the Muscatine Journal. Philadelphia: R. West. [See also 1942, 1970, 1975 entries]

c1980 The Devil's Race-track: Mark Twain's Great Dark Writings; the Best from "Which Was the Dream?" and "Fables of Man." Ed. John D. Tuckey. Berkeley: University of California Press. [See also 1972 entry]

Selections

1873 A Book for An Hour, containing choice reading and character sketches. A Curious Dream and Other Sketches, revised and selected for this work by the author, Mark Twain, New York: B.J. Such. Subsequent editions: 1873, 1873.

1900 Comical Hits by Famous Wits...., Chicago: Thompson & Thomas.

1910 Travels in History, by Mark Twain. Ed. C.N. Kendall. New York and London: Harper & Brothers. [selections from The Prince and the Pauper, A Connecticut Yankee, and Joan of Arc]

1920 Moments with Mark Twain: Selected by Albert Bigelow Paine, New York and London: Harper & Brothers.

1935 The Family Mark Twain, New York and London: Harper & Brothers. [See also 1972 entry]

1935 The Mark Twain Omnibus. Ed. Max J. Herzberg. New York and London: Harper & Brothers.

1935   Mark Twain Wit and Wisdom. Ed. Cyril Clemens. Philadelphia:
       Frederick A. Stokes. [See also 1969 and 1978 entries]

1935   Mark Twain. Representative Selections. Ed. Fred Lewis Pattee.
       American Writers Series. New York, Cincinnati: American Book Co.

1939   The Favorite Works of Mark Twain. Ed. Owen Wister. De luxe edi-
       tion. New York: Garden City Publishing Co.

1946   The Portable Mark Twain. Ed. Bernard DeVoto. Viking Portable
       Library. New York: Viking Press. Subsequent editions: 1950,
       1963.

1946   Mark Twain at Your Finger Tips. Ed. Caroline Thomas Harnsberger.
       Chicago: Cloud, Inc. [See also 1948 entry]

1948   Same. Ed. Caroline Thomas Harnsberger. New York: Beechhurst
       Press. [See also 1946 entry]

1949   An Evening with Mark Twain. The Nutshell Library. Rochester,
       N.Y.: Sherwin Cody Course in English.

1958   Mark Twain. Ed. Edward Fuller. Laurel Reader. New York: Dell
       Publishing Co.

1959   The Art, Humor, and Humanity of Mark Twain. Ed. Minnie M. Brashear
       and Robert M. Rodney. Norman, Okla.: University of Oklahoma Press.

1959   Mark Twain Tonight; An Actor's Portrait: Selections from Mark
       Twain, edited, adapted, and arranged, with a prologue, by Hal
       Holbrook. New York: Ives, Washburn.

1960   Mark Twain's Picture of His America: Selected Source Materials for
       College Research Papers. Ed. Neal Frank Doubleday. Boston: D.C.
       Heath.

1961   Life As I Find It: Essays, Sketches, Tales, and Other Material....
       Ed. Charles Neider. Hanover House Books. Garden City, N.Y.:
       Doubleday. [See also 1977 entry]

1961   Mark Twain. Wit and Wisecracks. Selected by Doris Bernadete.
       Mount Vernon, N.Y.: Peter Pauper Press.

1962   Mark Twain on the Damned Human Race. Ed. Janet Smith. American
       Century Series. New York: Hill and Wang.

1962   Selected Shorter Writings of Mark Twain. Ed. Walter Blair. River-
       side Editions. Boston: Houghton Mifflin.

1963   The Forgotten Writings of Mark Twain. Ed. Henry Duskis. Philo-
       sophical Library. New York: Citadel Press.

1963   Mark Twain's Frontier: A Textbook of Primary Source Materials for
       Student Research and Writing. Ed. James E. Camp and X.J. Kennedy.
       New York: Holt, Rinehart and Winston.

1966   The Birds and Beasts of Mark Twain. Ed. Robert M. Rodney and Min-
       nie M. Brashear. Norman: University of Oklahoma Press.

1966   On the Poetry of Mark Twain; with Selections from His Verse. Ed.
       Arthur L. Scott. Urbana: University of Illinois Press.

1967   Great Short Works of Mark Twain. Ed. Justin Kaplan. Perennial
       Classic. New York: Harper & Row.

1967   Mark Twain's Satires and Burlesques. Ed. Franklin R. Rogers. The
       Mark Twain Papers. Berkeley and Los Angeles: University of Cali-
       fornia Press.

1967   Mark Twain's "Which Was the Dream?" and Other Symbolic Writings of
       the Later Years. Ed. John S. Tuckey. The Mark Twain Papers. Ber-
       keley and Los Angeles: University of California Press.

1967   A Treasury of Mark Twain, the Wit and Wisdom of A Great American
       Writer. Ed. Edward Lewis and Robert Myers. Kansas City, Mo.:
       Hallmark Editions.

1969   Mark Twain Wit and Wisdom. Ed. Cyril Clemens. Folcroft, Pa.:
       Folcroft Press. Subsequent edition: 1977. [See also 1935, 1978
       entries]

1969   Readings from Samuel Clemens. Ed. Shigeo Imamura and J.W. Ney.
       Waltham, Mass.: Blaisdell.

1969   Your Personal Twain.... New World Paperbacks. New York: Interna-
       tional Publishers Co.

1970   Man Is The Only Animal That Blushes... or Needs To; the Wisdom of
       Mark Twain. Selected by Michael Joseph. A Stanyan Book. Los
       Angeles: Stanyan Books. New York: Random House.

1972   Everyone's Mark Twain. Comp. Caroline Thomas Harnsberger. South
       Brunswick: A.S. Barnes.

1972   The Family Mark Twain, New York: Harper & Row. Subsequent edi-
       tion: 1975. [See also 1935 entry]

1972   Mark Twain on Man and Beast. Ed. Janet Smith. New York: Lawrence
       Hill.

1972   A Pen Warmed-up in Hell; Mark Twain in Protest. Ed. Frederick
       Anderson. New York and London: Harper & Row. [See also 1973,
       1979 entries]

1973   Same. Ed. Frederick Anderson. Perennial Library. New York and
       London: Harper & Row. [See also 1972, 1979 entries]

1973   Mark Twain and the Three R's: Race, Religion, Revolution - and
       Related Matters. Ed. Maxwell Geismar. Indianapolis: Bobbs-
       Merrill.

1975 The Boys' Ambition: [from] Life on the Mississippi. Seedling
      Book. Minneapolis: Lerner Publications.

c1976 The Unabridged Mark Twain. Ed. Lawrence Teacher. Philadelphia:
      Running Press.

1976 Mark Twain Speaking. Ed. Paul Fatout. Iowa City: University of
      Iowa Press.

1976 The Higher Animals: A Mark Twain Bestiary. Ed. Maxwell Geismar.
      New York: Crowell.

1977 The Comic Mark Twain Reader; the Most Humorous Selections from
      His Stories, Sketches, Novels, Travel Books and Speeches. Ed.
      Charles Neider. Garden City, N.Y.: Doubleday.

1977 Life As I Find It: Essays, Sketches, Tales, and Other Material....
      Ed. Charles Neider. Perennial Library. New York: Harper & Row.
      [See also 1961 entry]

1978 Mark Twain Wit and Wisdom. Ed. Cyril Clemens. Norwood, Pa.:
      Norwood Editions. [See also 1935, 1969 entries]

1978 Mark Twain Speaks for Himself. Ed. Paul Fatout. West Lafayette,
      Ind.: Purdue University Press.

1979 Illustrated Works of Mark Twain: Selections.... Selected by
      Michael Patrick Hearn. Avenel Books. New York: Crown.

1979 A Pen Warmed-up in Hell: Mark Twain in Protest. Ed. Frederick
      Anderson. Colophon Books. New York and London: Harper & Row.
      [See also 1972, 1973 entries]

Collected Works

    Any estimate of Mark Twain's popularity in the United
States should take into account that most of Mark Twain's major
writings were included in his collected works, which ran to at
least thirty-two editions between 1890 and 1980. The following
list of his collected works includes only those editions that
can be identified by date, title, and publisher. No attempt is
made here to distinguish between various revisions or reissues
of the same edition. The appearance of Twain's writings in
collected editions would be a far less accurate measure of the
popularity of individual titles than their appearance as separate
editions, already identified in the preceding bibliography. The
collected works were published in limited editions which seldom
reached a large audience, and some titles (for example, Christian
Science, Joan of Arc, and Literary Essays) that were included in
the collected editions did not sell readily as separate editions.
On the other hand, it is notable that American interest in Mark
Twain persisted so strongly into the 20th Century that at least
twenty-five editions of his collected works were published between 1890 and 1930. The lapse of such publication between 1930
and the 1960's can be attributed to the intervening Great De-

pression and World War II and to the influx of inexpensive
paper-back editions that made books more readily available
to mass audiences by the mid-20th Century.

1891   Mark Twain's Works.   New Holiday Edition.   3 vols.   New York:
       Charles L. Webster.

1899   Mark Twain's Works in Uniform Edition.   25? vols.   Hartford, Conn.:
       American Publishing Co.

1899   The Writings of Mark Twain.   Edition de luxe.   25 vols.   Hartford,
       Conn.:   American Publishing Co.

1899   The Writings of Mark Twain.   Japan Edition.   23 vols.   Hartford,
       Conn.:   American Publishing Co.

1899   The Writings of Mark Twain.   Biographical Edition.   New York and
       London: Harper & Brothers.

1899-1900   The Writings of Mark Twain.   Royal Edition.   22 vols.   Hart-
       ford, Conn.:   American Publishing Co.   Subsequent edition
       1899-1907 in 25 volumes.

1899-1907   The Writings of Mark Twain.   Autograph Edition.   22 vols.
       Hartford, Conn.:   American Publishing Co.   Subsequent edi-
       tion 1899-1907 in 25 volumes.

1899-1918   The Writings of Mark Twain.   Uniform Edition.   20 vols.   New
       York: Harper & Brothers.

1899-1918   The Writings of Mark Twain.   Author's National Edition.   25
       vols.   New York and London: Harper & Brothers.

1899-1922   The Writings of Mark Twain.   Author's National Edition.   25
       vols.   New York: P.F. Collier & Son.   Harper & Brothers ed.

1901   The Writings of Mark Twain.   Riverdale Edition.   25 vols.   Hart-
       ford, Conn.:   American Publishing Co.

1901-1907   The Writings of Mark Twain.   Underwood Edition.   25 vols.
       Hartford, Conn.:   American Publishing Co.   New York: N.C.
       Newbegin Co.

1903   The Writings of Mark Twain.   Hillcrest Edition.   23 vols.   Hart-
       ford, Conn.:   American Publishing Co.

1906-1907   The Writings of Mark Twain.   Hillcrest Edition.   25 vols.
       New York and London: Harper & Brothers.

1907-1935   The Complete Works of Mark Twain.   Authorized Edition.   24
       vols.   New York: Harper & Brothers.

1910   The Writings of Mark Twain.   Library Edition.   25 vols.   New York:
       Harper & Brothers.

1913-1928 Mark Twain's Works. 29 vols. in 23. New York and London: Harper & Brothers. Subsequent edition: 1933.

1917 Mark Twain's Works. 26 vols. New York and London: Harper & Brothers.

1917-1925 The Complete Works of Mark Twain. American Artist's Edition. 24 vols. New York: Harper & Brothers.

1918 The Writings of Mark Twain. Limp Leather. New York and London: Harper & Brothers.

1921 The Writings of Mark Twain. Uniform Trade Edition. 20 vols. New York: Harper & Brothers.

1922-1925 The Complete Writings of Mark Twain. Definitive Edition. 37 vols. New York: Gabriel Wells.

1923-1924 Mark Twain's Works. Mississippi Edition. 23 vols. New York and London: Harper & Brothers.

1923-1925 The Writings of Mark Twain. Memorial Edition. 37 vols. New York: Harper & Brothers.

1929 The Writings of Mark Twain. Stormfield Edition. 37 vols. New York: Harper & Brothers.

1964 The Complete Novels of Mark Twain. 2 vols. Ed. Charles Neider. Garden City, N.Y.: Doubleday. Subsequent edition: 1969.

1966 The Complete Travel Books of Mark Twain. The Early Works: "The Innocents Abroad" and "Roughing It." 2 vols. Ed. Charles Neider. Garden City, N.Y.: Doubleday.

1967 The Complete Travel Books of Mark Twain. The Later Works: "A Tramp Abroad," "Life on the Mississippi," "Following the Equator." 2 vols. Ed. Charles Neider. Garden City, N.Y.: Doubleday, Doran.

1967 Mark Twain's Letters to His Publishers, 1867-1894. Ed. Hamlin Hill. Berkeley and Los Angeles: University of California Press. [The first of fourteen volumes projected by The Mark Twain Papers, University of California, to include Mark Twain's Notebooks and Journals and his Collected Correspondence]

1968-1969 The Writings of Mark Twain. Author's National Edition. 25 vols. Grosse Pointe, Mich.: Scholarly Press. New York: Harper & Brothers.

1972-1980 The Works of Mark Twain. Published for the Iowa Center for Textual Studies by the University of California Press. Berkeley.

1975- The Mark Twain Papers. Frederick Anderson, General Editor. Berkeley: University of California Press. [Projected to approximately twenty volumes, volume numbers arbitrarily assigned, embodying Mark Twain's Notebooks and Journals and Mark Twain's Collected Correspondence]

2

Foreign Editions
1867–1976

BRITISH COMMONWEALTH

Australia

Sources: ACAP/ANB/BA/CBI/NUC

Gilded Age

1874 The Gilded Age. A Novel. Australian Edition. Melbourne: Robertson.

Huckleberry Finn

1946 Huckleberry Finn. John Mystery Pocket Books. Sydney: Publicity Press.

1946 The Adventures of Huckleberry Finn, Sydney: Shakespeare Head Press.

1950 Same. Sydney: Shakespeare Head Press.

Innocents Abroad

1870 The Innocents Abroad; or New Pilgrim's Progress. Australian Edition. Melbourne: Robertson.

1870 The Innocents Abroad; or, The New Pilgrim's Progress. Australian Edition. Melbourne: Robertson.

1871 Same. Australian Edition. Melbourne: Robertson.

Letters

1964 A Letter from Mark Twain, Brisbane: Shopcott.

Life on the Mississippi

1877 The Mississippi Pilot. Australian Edition. Melbourne, Sydney, & Adelaide: Robertson.

Roughing It

1872 The Innocents at Home. Australian Edition. Melbourne: Robertson.

1873 Same. Australian Edition. Melbourne: Robertson.

Stories and Sketches

1868 The Celebrated Jumping Frog of Calaveras County, and Other Sketches.
      Australian Edition. Melbourne: Robertson.

Tramp Abroad

1880 A Tramp Abroad. New Edition. Melbourne, Sydney, Adelaide, &
      Brisbane: Robertson.

Travel Sketches

c1975 Letters from the Sandwich Islands. Ed. Joan Abramson.   An Island
      Heritage Limited Edition. The Hawaiian Bicentennial Library, v.
      1. Norfolk Island, Australia: Island Heritage.

Canada

Sources: ACB/BAL/BMT/Can/CBI/CGBN/NUC/USC

Connecticut Yankee

1890 A Connecticut Yankee in King Arthur's Court, Toronto: Rose.

1957 A Yankee at the Court of King Arthur. Zodiac Press Books. Toronto:
      Clarke, Irwin.

Huckleberry Finn

1885 The Adventures of Huckleberry Finn. (Tom Sawyer's Comrade),
      Toronto: Musson.

1947 The Adventures of Huckleberry Finn. Rainbow Classics. Toronto:
      McClelland & Stewart.

1963 Same. Toronto: Macmillan.

1966 Same. Toronto: Oxford University Press.

1969 Same. Toronto: Clarke, Irwin.

Innocents Abroad

1869? The Innocents Abroad. Canadian Edition. Home Series, no. 256.
      Toronto: Bryce.

1870? The Innocents Abroad, A Book of Travel in Pursuit of Pleasure...
      The Voyage Out, Montreal: Chisholm & Bros.

1870 The Innocents Abroad, or The New Pilgrims' Progress, Montreal and
      Toronto: Chisholm.

1870   Same. Toronto: Irving.

1871   Same. Toronto: Irving.

1880   The Innocents Abroad; or, The New Pilgrim's Progress. Robertson's
       Cheap Series. Toronto: Robertson.

1966   Innocents Abroad or The New Pilgrim's Progress, Toronto: New
       American Library of Canada.

Joan of Arc

1896? Personal Recollections of Joan of Arc, Toronto: n.pub.

Life on the Mississippi

1876   Old Times on the Mississippi, Toronto: Belford Brothers.

1876   Same. Toronto: Belford.

1878   Same. Toronto: Rose-Belford.

1883   Life on the Mississippi, Montreal: Dawson Brothers.

1926   Old Times on the Mississippi, Toronto: Belford Brothers.

Prince and the Pauper

1881   The Prince and the Pauper; A Tale for Young People of All Ages,
       Montreal: Dawson Bros.

1882   Same. Toronto: Rose-Belford.

1882   Same. Toronto: Robertson.

1951   Prints ja Kerjus, Toronto: Ortoprint. [Esthonian]

1959   Prynts 1 Slydar, Winnipeg: Trident Press. [Ukrainian]

1960   Le Prince et le Pauvre, Montreal: Editions de l'Iris. [French]

1964   The Prince and the Pauper, A Tale for Young People of All Ages,
       Toronto: New American Library of Canada.

Pudd'nhead Wilson

1964   The Tragedy of Pudd'nhead Wilson. Signet Classic. Toronto: New
       American Library of Canada.

Roughing It

n.d. The Innocents at Home, Toronto: Musson.

1880 Roughing It. Toronto: Belford.

1882 Same. Toronto: Rose.

1899 Same. Toronto: Rose.

1901 Same. Toronto: Rose-Belford.

Stories and Sketches

n.d. The Celebrated Jumping Frog of Calaveras County, and Other Sketches, Toronto: Musson.

1871 Mark Twain's (Burlesque), Autobiography and First Romance, Toronto: Canadian News and Publishing Company.

1871 Mark Twain's Autobiography, (Burlesque), First Romance, and Memoranda, Toronto: Campbell & Son.

1879 Sketches by Mark Twain, Toronto: Belford, Clarke.

1880 Sketches by Mark Twain. Now First Published in Complete Form, Toronto: Slemin & Higgins.

1881 A Curious Experience, By Mark Twain, Toronto: Gibson.

1881 Mark Twain's Sketches...Complete. Robertson's Cheap Series. Toronto: Robertson.

1882? A Curious Experience, Toronto: Robertson.

1926 "1601" by Mark Twain, Montreal: [privately printed]

1961 The Complete Humorous Sketches and Tales of Mark Twain..., Toronto: Hanover House Books. Doubleday.

1963 Jim Baker's Bluejay Yarn, Toronto: Orion, Ambassador.

1973 A Conversation As It Was at the Social Fireside in the Time of the Tudors; or, "1601" [by] Mark Twain, Willowdale, Ont.: Avondale Press.

Tom Sawyer

1876 The Adventures of Tom Sawyer, Toronto: Belford Brothers.

1877 Same. Toronto: Belford Brothers.

1878 Same. Toronto: Rose-Belford.

1879 Same. The Rose Library No. 1. Toronto: Rose-Belford.

1910? Same. Toronto: Musson.

1920 Same. Toronto: Rose-Belford.

1942 Same. Toronto: Oxford University Press.

1946 Same. Toronto: Ambassador.

1946 Same. Rainbow Classics. Toronto: McClelland & Stewart.

1950 Same. Rainbow Classics. Toronto: McClelland & Stewart.

1952? Same. Toronto: Musson.

1957 Same. Heirloom Library. Toronto: Ambassador.

Tramp Abroad

n.d. A Tramp Abroad, Toronto: Musson.

188-? Same. London, Ont.: R.R. News Co.

1880? Same. Toronto: Rose.

1880 Same. Toronto: Belford.

1880 Same. Toronto and Montreal: Dominion News Co.

1880 Same. Toronto: Slemin & Higgins.

1880 A Tramp Abroad...Complete, Toronto: Robertson.

1899 A Tramp Abroad. Collection of British Authors. Toronto: Tauch-
      nitz.

Travel Sketches

1878 An Idle Excursion, Toronto: Rose-Belford.

1878 Rambling Notes of An Idle Excursion, Toronto: Rose-Belford.

1882 Same. Toronto: Rose-Belford.

Miscellaneous Writings

1871 Memoranda, from the Galaxy [by] Mark Twain, Toronto: Canadian
      News and Publishing Co.

1888 Mark Twain's Library of Humour, Montreal: Dawson Brothers.

1926 1601. Conversation by the Social Fireside, Montreal: [privately printed.]

1940 Mark Twain in Eruption; Hitherto Unpublished Pages about Men and Events, by Mark Twain. Edited Bernard DeVoto. Toronto: Musson.

Great Britain

Sources: BAL/BBP/BM/BMC/CBI/CGBN/ECB/LC/MTE/NL/NUC/USC

American Claimant

1892 The American Claimant, London: Chatto & Windus.

Autobiography

1960 The Autobiography of Mark Twain. Edited Charles Neider. London: Chatto & Windus.

Connecticut Yankee

1889 A Connecticut Yankee in King Arthur's Court, London: Chatto & Windus.

1889 A Yankee at the Court of King Arthur, London: Chatto & Windus.

1893 Same. London: Chatto & Windus.

1897 Same. London: Chatto & Windus.

1902 Same. New Edition. London: Chatto & Windus.

1912 A Connecticut Yankee in King Arthur's Court, London: Chatto & Windus.

1957 Same. Zodiac Series. London: Chatto & Windus.

1960 A Connecticut Yankee in King Arthur's Court. American Century Series. London: Mark Peterson.

1963 Same. Seven Seas Books. London: Collet's.

1971 A Connecticut Yankee at King Arthur's Court, Harmondsworth: Penguin Books.

1976 Same. Harmondsworth: Penguin Books.

Following the Equator

1897 More Tramps Abroad, London: Chatto & Windus.

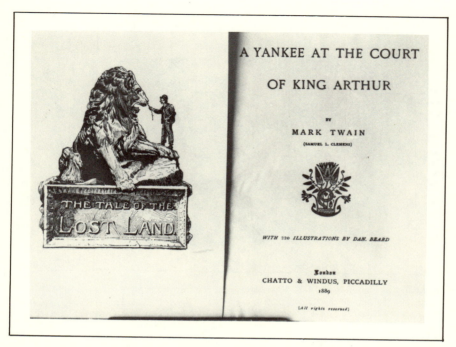

Fig. 11. *A Yankee at the Court of King Arthur,* title page and facing page of 1889 British edition published by Chatto & Windus

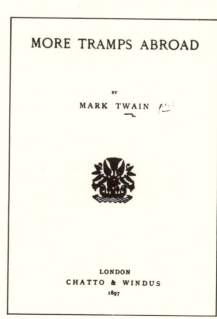

Fig. 12. *More Tramps Abroad,* title page of 1897 British edition published by Chatto & Windus

Fig. 14. *Mark Twain's Mississippi Pilot*, cover of 1877 British edition published by Ward, Lock, and Tyler

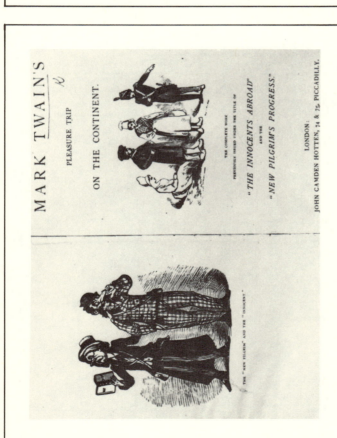

Fig. 13. *Mark Twain's Pleasure Trip on the Continent*, title page and facing page of 1871 British edition published by John Camden Hotten

EYE OPENERS

GOOD THINGS,

IMMENSELY FUNNY SAYINGS & STORIES
THAT WILL BRING A SMILE
UPON THE GRUFFEST COUNTENANCE,

BY

MARK TWAIN,

*Author of "A Pleasure Trip on the Continent" ("The Innocents Abroad"
and "The New Pilgrim's Progress"), "The Jumping Frog,"
"Screamers, a Gathering of Delicious Bits."*

LONDON: JOHN CAMDEN HOTTEN, 74, PICCADILLY.

(All Rights Reserved.)

ORTHODOX.—A speaker at a juvenile pic-nic
is said to have delivered an address of which the
following is a sample:—"You ought to be very kind to your
little sisters. I once knew a bad boy who struck his sister a blow
over the eye. Although she didn't fade and die in the summer-
time when the June roses were blowing, with sweet words of
kindness on her pallid lips, she rose up and hit him over the head
with a rolling-pin, so that he couldn't go to school for over a
month on account of not being able to put on his hat."

Fig. 16. *Eye Openers*, title page and facing page of 1871 British edition published by John Camden Hotten

Fig. 15. *The Celebrated Jumping Frog*, cover of 1867 British edition published by George Routledge and Sons

SCREAMERS,

A GATHERING OF

SCRAPS OF HUMOUR,

DELICIOUS BITS, AND SHORT STORIES.

BY

MARK TWAIN,

AUTHOR OF

"*Sketches Fresh in the Continental*," ("*The Innocents Abroad*" and
"*The New Pilgrims' Progress*"); "*The Jumping Frog*";
"*Eye Openers, a Collection of Good Things*"

LONDON:

WARD, LOCK, & TYLER, WARWICK HOUSE,
PATERNOSTER ROW, E.C.

Fig. 18. *Screamers*, title page of 1872 British edition
published by Ward, Lock, & Tyler

Fig. 17. *Screamers*, cover of 1872 British edition published
by Ward, Lock, & Tyler

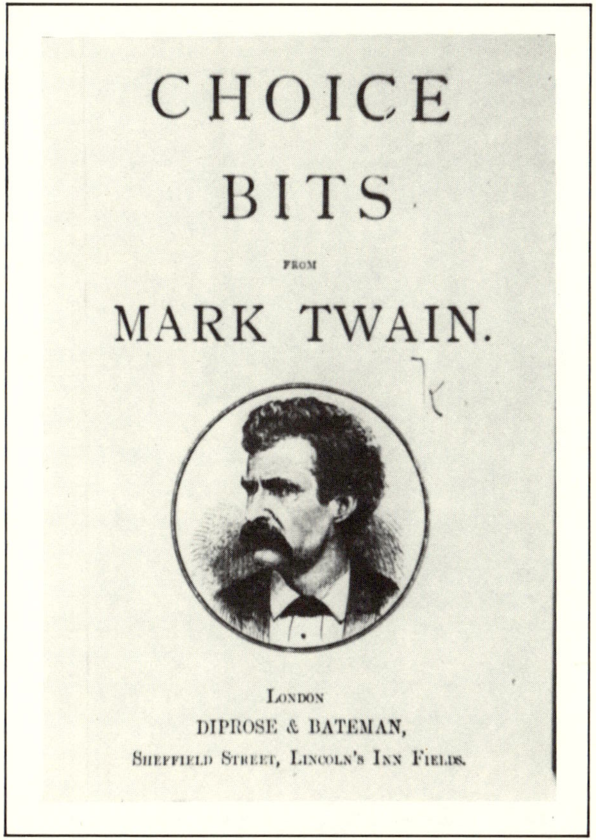

Fig. 20. *Choice Bits from Mark Twain,* title page of 1885 British edition published by Diprose & Bateman

Fig. 19. *Mark Twain's American Drolleries,* cover of 1875 British edition published by Ward, Lock, & Tyler

Fig. 22. *Funny Stories and Humourous Poems* by Mark Twain and Oliver Wendell Holmes, cover of 1875 British edition published by Ward, Lock, & Tyler

PRACTICAL JOKES

WITH

ARTEMUS WARD

INCLUDING THE STORY OF

THE MAN WHO FOUGHT CATS

BY MARK TWAIN
AND OTHER HUMOURISTS

LONDON
John Camden Hotten, 74, PICCADILLY
(All Rights Reserved)

Fig. 21. *Practical Jokes with Artemus Ward*, title page of 1872 British edition published by John Camden Hotten

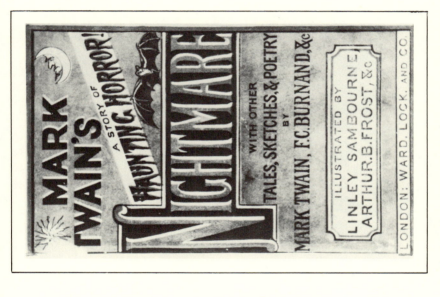

Fig. 23. *Mark Twain's Nightmare. A Story of Haunting Horror!* Cover of 1878 British edition published by Ward, Lock, and Co.

1898 Same. London: Chatto & Windus.

1907 Same. London: Chatto & Windus.

1922 Same. Uniform Library Edition. London: Chatto & Windus.

1927 Same. London: Chatto & Windus.

1931 Same. New Edition. London: Chatto & Windus.

1973 Mark Twain in Australia and New Zealand. Penguin Colonial Facsimiles. Harmondsworth: Penguin Books. [extracts from Following the Equator]

Gilded Age

1873 The Gilded Age, A Novel, London: Routledge & Sons.

1874 The Gilded Age. 3 vols. London, New York: Routledge & Sons.

1883 The Gilded Age, A Novel, London, New York: Routledge & Sons.

1885 The Gilded Age, London: Chatto & Windus.

1892 Same. London: Chatto & Windus.

1895? The Gilded Age, A Novel, London: Routledge & Sons.

1897 The Gilded Age, London: Chatto & Windus.

1922 Same. London: Chatto & Windus.

1966 The Adventures of Colonel Sellers; being Mark Twain's share of "The Gilded Age." Ed. Charles Neider. London: Chatto & Windus.

1967 The Gilded Age. First Novel Library. FN8. London: Cassell.

Huckleberry Finn

1884 The Adventures of Huckleberry Finn (Tom Sawyer's Comrade), London: Chatto & Windus.

1886 Same. London: Chatto & Windus.

1887 Same. London: Chatto & Windus.

1897 Same. London: Chatto & Windus.

1909 The Adventures of Huckleberry Finn, London: Chatto & Windus.

1912 Same. London: Nelson.

1920 The Adventures of Huckleberry Finn, Tom Sawyer's Comrade, London:

1920 The Adventures of Huckleberry Finn, London: Chatto & Windus.

1923 The Adventures of Huckleberry Finn (Tom Sawyer's Comrade), London:
      Nash & Co.

1924 Same. Popular Edition. London: Harrap.

1924 Same. London, Edinburgh, New York: Nelson & Sons.

1929 Same. Cheap Edition. London: Nelson & Sons.

1930 Same. London: Eveleigh & Nash.

1933 Same. Standard Fiction Library. London: Harrap.

1935 Same. Cheap Edition. London: Nelson.

1937 Same. Cheaper Edition. London: Grayson and Grayson.

1937 Same. Nelson Classics. London: Nelson.

1937 Same. London: Virtue.

1939 Huckleberry Finn, London: Nelson.

1943 Tom Sawyer; and, Huckleberry Finn. Everyman's Library. 2 vols.
      in 1. London, Toronto: Dent & Sons.

1944 Same. Everyman's Library. 2 vols. in 1. London, Toronto: Dent
      Sons.

1946 The Adventures of Huckleberry Finn. Pocket Classics. London:
      Langdon.

1948 Huckleberry Finn. Ingram Library. London: Ingram.

1949 Same. Camden Illustrated Classics. London: Elek.

1950 Same. Cresset Library Series. London: Cresset.

1950 Tom Sawyer and Huckleberry Finn. Everyman's Library. London:
      Dent & Sons.

1951 Huckleberry Finn, London: Blackie.

1953 Same. School Classics Series. London: Nelson.

1953 Same. Winchester Classics Series. London: Nelson.

1953 Same. Puffin Story Books. London: Penguin.

1953 Tom Sawyer and Huckleberry Finn, London: Collins.

1954 Huckleberry Finn. Library of Famous Books. London: Blackie.

1954 The Adventures of Tom Sawyer, and, Huckleberry Finn. Everyman's
      Library. 2 vols. in 1. London: Dent.

1954 Tom Sawyer and Huckleberry Finn. Everyman's Library. New Edition.
      London: Dent.

1954 Huckleberry Finn. Classics Series. London: Nelson.

1954 Same. Hamlyn Classics. London: Planned Bookselling.

1954 Same. London: Rylee.

1955 Adventures of Huckleberry Finn. Children's Illustrated Classics.
      London: Dent & Son.

1956 The Adventures of Huckleberry Finn. Longmans Simplified English
      Series: London. Longmans.

1958 Same. Children's Illustrated Classics. London: Dent.

1958? Huckleberry Finn. Heirloom Library. London: Weidenfeld & N.

1960 The Adventures of Huckleberry Finn. Fontana Books. London:Collins.

1960 Mark Twain's Huckleberry Finn, London: Harrap.

1961 The Adventures of Huckleberry Finn. New Windmill Series. London:
      Heinemann.

1961 Same. School Edition. New Windmill Series. London: Heinemann.

1961 Huck Finn. Unicorn Series. London: Hutchinson.

1963 Adventures of Tom Sawyer; and, Huckleberry Finn. 2 vols. in 1.
      London: Dent.

1963 Tom Sawyer; and, Huckleberry Finn. School Edition. Literature of
      Yesterday Series. London: Dent.

1963 The Adventures of Huckleberry Finn (Tom Sawyer's Comrade), London:
      Zodiak Press: Chatto.

1964 Huckleberry Finn, London: Everyman Publishers. Dent.

1964 Adventures of Tom Sawyer and Huckleberry Finn, London: Everyman
      Publishers. Dent.

1964 The Adventures of Huckleberry Finn. Shorter Classics. London:
      Ginn.

1964 Same. London, Toronto: Oxford University Press.

1965 Same. Chosen Books. Glasgow: Blackie & Son.

1965   Same. Retold Classics. London: Collins.

1965   Same. Shorter Classics. London: Ginn.

1966   Same. Penguin English Library. Harmondsworth: Penguin.

1966   Huckleberry Finn, London: Hamlyn.

1967   Same. Classics Series. London: Dean.

1967   Adventures of Huckleberry Finn, London: Hamlyn.

1967   The Adventures of Huckleberry Finn. Puffin Book. Harmondsworth:
       Penguin.

1968   Same. Harmondsworth: Penguin.

1973   Same. Longman Simplified English Series. London: Longman.

1974   Same. Longman Simplified English Series. London: Longman.

Innocents Abroad

1869? The Innocents Abroad, London: Ward, Lock Co. Toronto: W. Bryce.

1870   The Innocents Abroad. A Book of Travel in Pursuit of Pleasure.
       The Voyage Out. 2 vols. London: Hotten.

1870   The New Pilgrim's Progress. A Book of Travel in Pursuit of
       Pleasure. By Mark Twain. The Journey Home, London: Hotten.

187-? The Innocents Abroad, and The New Pilgrims' Progress from the New
       World to the Old, London: Ward, Lock & Bowden.

1871? The New Pilgrim's Progress. A Book of Travel in Pursuit of Pleasure.
       The Journey Home, London: Hotten.

1871   Mark Twain's Pleasure Trip on the Continent. Companion to Murray's
       Guide. London: Hotten.

1872   The New Pilgrim's Progress. Author's English edition. London:
       Routledge & Sons.

1872   The Innocents Abroad. Abridged edition. London: Routledge &
       Sons.

1872   Same. London: Ward & Lock.

1873   The Travelling Innocents, London: Ward, Lock, & Tyler.

1873   The Yankee Pilgrims' Progress, London: Ward, Lock & Tyler.

1873   Mark Twain's Pleasure Trip on the Continent, London: Hotten.

1874   Same. London: Hotten.

1875 The New Pilgrim's Progress. New edition. London: Ward & Lock.

1879 The Innocents Abroad, London: Routledge & Sons.

1879 Same. London: Ward & Lock.

1881 The Innocents Abroad; or, the New Pilgrim's Progress, London: Chatto & Windus.

1882 Same. London: Chatto & Windus.

1884 Same. London: Ward & Lock.

1884 The New Pilgrim's Progress, London: Haweis.

1884 The Innocents Abroad; or, The New Pilgrim's Progress, London: Routledge & Sons.

1886 The New Pilgrim's Progress, London: George Routledge and Sons.

1886 The New Pilgrim's Progress from the New World to the Old, London: Ward & Locke.

1886 The Innocents Abroad; or, the New Pilgrim's Progress, London: George Routledge and Sons.

1887 The New Pilgrim's Progress, London: Routledge.

1887 The Innocents Abroad; or, the New Pilgrim's Progress. Routledge's World Library. London: Routledge & Sons.

189-? The New Pilgrim's Progress. Abridged. London: "Review of Reviews" Office.

189-? The Innocents Abroad, and The New Pilgrims' Progress, London, New York and Melbourne: Ward, Lock, & Bowden.

1890 The Innocents Abroad and the New Pilgrim's Progress. A new edition. London: Chatto & Windus.

1891 Same. New Edition. London: Chatto & Windus.

1897 The Innocents Abroad; or, The New Pilgrim's Progress. New Edition. London: Chatto & Windus.

1898 The Innocents Abroad. Humorous Books. London: Routledge & Sons.

1899 The New Pilgrim's Progress. New Edition. London: Routledge & Sons.

1905 The Innocents Abroad, London: Ward & Locke.

1905? The New Pilgrims' Progress from the New World to the Old. Beston's Humorous Series. London: Ward, Locke & Tyler.

1910 <u>The Innocents Abroad</u>. World Library. London: Ward, Lock.

1914 Same. The Wayfarer's Library. London: Dent.

1916 Same. London: Chatto & Windus.

1917 Same. Cheap Edition. London: Kelly.

1921 <u>The Innocents Abroad; and, The New Pilgrim's Progress</u>. New impression. London: Chatto & Windus.

1922 <u>The Innocents Abroad</u>. Pocket Classics. London: Collins.

1922 Same. London: Hayes.

1930 Same. Canterbury Classics. London: Collins.

1937 Same. Collins' Classics. London: Collins.

1954 Same. Collins' Classics. New Edition. London: Collins.

1961 Same. London: Collins.

Joan of Arc

1896 <u>Personal Recollections of Joan of Arc...</u>, London: Chatto & Windus.

1902 Same. New Edition. London: Chatto & Windus.

1907 Same. London: Chatto & Windus.

1912 Same. London: Chatto & Windus.

1921 Same. London: Chatto & Windus.

1922 Same. London: Chatto & Windus.

King Leopold's Soliloquy

1907 <u>King Leopold's Soliloquy, A Defense of His Congo Rule</u>, London: Unwin.

Letters

1920 <u>The Letters of Mark Twain...</u>, London: Chatto & Windus.

1960 <u>Mark Twain - Howells Letters, 1872-1910</u>. Ed. Henry Nash Smith. 2 vols. London: Oxford University Press.

1961 <u>Mark Twain's Letters to Mary</u>. Ed. Lewis Leary. London: Oxford University Press.

1967   Mark Twain's Letters from Hawaii. Ed. A. Grove Day. London:
       Chatto & Windus.

Life on the Mississippi

1877   The Mississippi Pilot, London: Routledge & Sons.

1877   The Mississippi Pilot, by Mark Twain. Two Men of Sandy Bar and
       Poems by Bret Harte, London: Croome.

1877   The Mississippi Pilot, London: Ward, Lock, and Tyler.

1877? Same. Glasgow: Grand Colosseum Warehouse Co.

1878   An Idle Excursion, and Other Papers. [including "Old Times on the
       Mississippi"], London: Chatto & Windus.

1881? The Mississippi Pilot. Humorous Books, no. 53. London: Ward,
       Ward, Lock.

1883   Life on the Mississippi, London: Chatto & Windus.

1883   Same. New Edition. London: Chatto & Windus.

1883   The Mississippi Pilot. By Mark Twain. And Two Men of Sandy Bar.
       By Bret Harte, London: Ward, Lock.

1887   Life on the Mississippi. New Edition. London: Chatto & Windus.

189-? The Mississippi Pilot, London: Ward, Lock & Bowden.

1897   Life on the Mississippi. New Edition. London: Chatto & Windus.

1899   Same. New Edition. London: Chatto & Windus.

1901   Same. New Edition. London: Chatto & Windus.

1904   Same. London: Chatto & Windus.

1914   Same. London: Chatto & Windus.

1921   Same. London: Chatto & Windus.

1962   Same. World Classics. London, New York: Oxford University Press.

Man That Corrupted Hadleyburg

1900   The Man That Corrupted Hadleyburg and Other Stories and Sketches.
       Uniform Library Edition. London: Chatto & Windus.

1907   The Man That Corrupted Hadleyburg, Other Stories, Sketches,
       London: Chatto & Windus. .

1921 The Man That Corrupted Hadleyburg, and Other Stories and Sketches,
      London: Chatto & Windus.

                      Prince and the Pauper

1881 The Prince and the Pauper: A Tale for Young People of All Ages,
      London: Chatto & Windus.

1881 The Prince and the Pauper: A Tale. New Edition. London: Chatto
      & Windus.

1882 The Prince and the Pauper; A Tale for Young People of All Ages,
      London: Chatto & Windus.

1888 The Prince and the Pauper: A Tale, London: Chatto & Windus.

1888 Same. New Edition. London: Chatto & Windus.

1892 The Prince and the Pauper, A Tale for Young People of All Ages,
      London: Chatto & Windus.

1897 The Prince and the Pauper: a Tale for the Young of all Ages,
      London: Chatto & Windus.

1901 The Prince and the Pauper; A Tale for Young People of All Ages.
      New Edition. London: Chatto & Windus.

1904 Same. New Edition. London: Chatto & Windus.

1908 The Prince and the Pauper, London: Chatto & Windus.

1920 The Prince and the Pauper: a Tale for Young People of all Ages,
      London: Chatto & Windus.

1923 The Prince and the Pauper, London: Dent.

1954 Same. Queen's Classics. New Edition. London: Chatto & Windus.

1957 Same. New Method Supplementary Readers. London: Longmans.

1963 Prince and the Pauper. A Tale for Young People of All Ages.
      Rainbow Series. London: Ward, Lock.

1964 The Prince and the Pauper, Westerham: Westerham Press.

1968 The Prince and the Pauper. After the Story by Mark Twain. A Ward
      Lock Classic in Color. London: Ward Lock. Bologna: STEB.

1974 The Prince and the Pauper. Retold..., London: Longman.

1976 The Prince and the Pauper: A Tale for Young People of All Ages,
      London: Dent.

Pudd'nhead Wilson

1894 Pudd'nhead Wilson: A Tale, London: Chatto & Windus.

1911 Same. London: Chatto & Windus.

1921 Same. London: Chatto & Windus.

1955 Pudd'nhead Wilson: A Tale by Mark Twain, London: Zodiac Press.
      Chatto. Clarke, Irwin.

1963 Pudd'nhead Wilson. The Queen's Classics. London: Chatto &
      Windus.

1965 Same. Broadstream Books. London: Cambridge University Press.

1969 Pudd'nhead Wilson; and, Those Extraordinary Twins. Penguin English
      Library. Harmondsworth: Penguin.

Roughing It

1872 "Roughing It." The Innocents at Home. Author's English Edition...
      Copyright Edition. 2 vols. London: Routledge and Sons.

1872 The Innocents at Home: A Sequel to "Roughing It," London:
      Routledge and Sons. [Vol. II, Chaps. 5-38 of Roughing It]

1882 Roughing It, and the Innocents at Home, London: Routledge and
      Sons.

1883 Same. London: Routledge and Sons.

1885 Same. New Edition. London: Chatto & Windus.

189-? Roughing It, London: Routledge and Sons.

1897 Roughing It; and Innocents at Home, London: Chatto & Windus.

1899 The Innocents at Home. New Edition. London: Routledge and Sons.

1901 Roughing It and The Innocents at Home, London: Chatto & Windus.

1903 Roughing It, London: Routledge and Sons.

1965 Roughing It. [abridged] Broadstream Books. London: Cambridge
      University Press.

Stories and Sketches

1867 The Celebrated Jumping Frog of Calaveras County, and other Sketches,
      London: Routledge and Sons.

1867? The Jumping Frog and Other Humorous Sketches...from the Original Edition, London: Hotten. Melbourne: George Robertson.

1870   The Jumping Frog and Other Humorous Sketches, London: Hotten.

1870   The Celebrated Jumping Frog of Calaveras County, and Other Sketches, London: Routledge & Sons.

1871   The Jumping Frog, & other Humorous Sketches, London: Hotten.

1871? Mark Twain's (Burlesque) 1. Autobiography. 2. Medieval Romance. 3. On Children. Author's Edition. London: Hotten [an unauthorized edition]

1871   Mark Twain's (Burlesque) Autobiography and First Romance, London: Routledge & Sons.

1871? Eye Openers, Good Things, Immensely Funny Sayings & Stories that Will Bring A Smile upon the Gruffest Countenance...by Mark Twain, London: Hotten. [pirated edition]

1871   Eye Openers, London: Ward, Lock & Tyler.

1871   Screamers; A Gathering of Scraps of Humour, Delicious Bits, & Short Stories by Mark Twain, London: Hotten.

1872   Same. London: Ward, Lock & Tyler.

1872   A Curious Dream; and other Sketches. (Selected and revised by the author), London: Routledge & Sons.

1872   Mark Twain's Sketches, Selected and Revised by the Author. Copyright Edition. London: Routledge & Sons.

1873   Mark Twain's The Celebrated Jumping Frog of Calaveras County and Other Sketches with the Burlesque Autobiography and First Romance, London: Routledge & Sons.

1873   The Choice Humorous Works of Mark Twain. Now First Collected. With Extra Passages to the "Innocents Abroad," now first reprinted and a life of the author..., London: Hotten.

1874   The Choice Humorous Works of Mark Twain...Revised and Corrected by the Author, London: Chatto & Windus.

1874   The Jumping Frog, and Other Humorous Sketches, London: Ward & Lock.

1875   Same. Beeton's Humorous Books. London: Ward, Lock, and Tyler.

1875   Eye Openers: Good Things, Immensely Funny Sayings, & Stories That Will Bring A Smile upon the Gruffest Countenance. by Mark Twain. Beeton's Humorous Books. London, New York: Ward, Lock & Tyler.

1875 Screamers; A Gathering of Scraps of Humour, Delicious Bits, & Stories by Mark Twain, London, New York: Ward, Lock.

1876 Information Wanted, and Other Sketches by Mark Twain. 2nd ed. London: Routledge and Sons.

1876 The Jumping Frog, and Other Humorous Sketches, London: Ward & Lock.

1877? "1601." [privately printed]

1877? Choice Bits from Mark Twain, London: n.pub.

1878 Punch, Brothers, Punch! and Other Sketches, London: Chatto & Windus.

1878 Same. Edinburgh: Livingstone.

1878 Same. London: Simpkin.

1878 An Idle Excursion, and Other Papers, London: Chatto & Windus.

1878 The Choice Humorous Works of Mark Twain, London: Chatto & Windus.

1880 Same. London: Chatto & Windus.

1881 Same. London: Chatto & Windus.

1882 The Celebrated Jumping Frog of Calaveras County and Other Sketches with the Burlesque Autobiography and First Romance, London: Routledge and Sons.

1882 The Celebrated Jumping Frog, & other Humorous Sketches, London: Routledge & Sons.

1882 The Stolen White Elephant, Etc., London: Chatto & Windus.

1882 Same. New edition. London: Chatto & Windus.

1883 Same. London: Chatto & Windus.

1883 English As She Is Spoke; or, A Jest in Sober Earnest. The Vellum-parchment Shilling Series of Miscellaneous Literature no. 1. [4th edition] London: Field & Tuer.

1884 The Jumping Frog and other Humorous Sketches, London: Ward & Locke.

1884 The Stolen White Elephant. New edition. London: Chatto & Windus.

1885 Choice Bits from Mark Twain, London: Diprose & Bateman.

1885 Eye Openers, Good Things, Funny Sayings, & Stories, London: Ward & Lock.

1885 Mark Twain's Funniest Fiction..., London: Maxwell.

1886 The Jumping Frog, London: Routledge.

1887 English As She Is Taught..., London: Unwin.

1888 The Choice Humorous Works of Mark Twain, London: Chatto & Windus.

1888 The Stolen White Elephant, Etc. New Edition. London: Chatto & Windus.

189-? Mark Twain's Celebrated Jumping Frog of Calaveras County, and Other Sketches with the Burlesque Autobiography and First Romance, London: Routledge.

1892 A Curious Dream and other Sketches, London: Routledge.

1892 Information Wanted, and other Sketches, London: Routledge.

1892 Sketches: selected and revised by the author, London: Chatto & Windus.

1893 The £1,000,000 Bank-Note, and Other New Stories, by Mark Twain, London: Chatto & Windus.

1895 Same. London: Chatto & Windus.

1896 Tom Sawyer, Detective...Other Tales, London: Chatto & Windus.

1897 Choice Humorous Works. Revised and Corrected by Author. New edition. London: Chatto & Windus.

1897 Mark Twain's Sketches. Selected and Revised by the Author. A New Edition. London: Chatto & Windus.

1897 The Stolen White Elephant &c. New edition. London: Chatto & Windus.

1897 Tom Sawyer Abroad; Tom Sawyer, Detective and Other Stories; Etc., Etc., London: Chatto & Windus.

1897 Tom Sawyer Detective...and Other Tales, London: Chatto & Windus.

1899 The Choice Humorous Works of Mark Twain. New edition. London: Chatto & Windus.

1899 A Curious Dream, and Other Sketches. Selected and revised by the Author. London: Routledge.

1899 Information Wanted, and other Sketches. New edition. London: Routledge.

1900 The Man That Corrupted Hadleyburg and other Stories and Sketches. Uniform Library Edition. London: Chatto & Windus.

1901 Tom Sawyer Detective...and Other Tales, London: Chatto & Windus.

1902   The Choice Humorous Works of Mark Twain. New edition. London: Chatto & Windus.

1902   A Double-barrelled Detective Story, London: Chatto & Windus.

1903   Sketches. Selected and revised by the Author. St. Martin's Library. London: Chatto & Windus.

1903   A Dog's Tale, London: Antivivisection Society.

1906   The Jumping Frog, and other Sketches. Carlton Classics. London: Long.

1907   The Man That Corrupted Hadleyburg, Other Stories, Sketches, London: Chatto & Windus.

1909   The Stolen White Elephant, Etc., London: Chatto & Windus.

1911   Same. London: Chatto & Windus.

1912   The Stolen White Elephant, London: Everett.

1918   The Stolen White Elephant, etc., London: Chatto & Windus.

1920   A Double-Barrelled Detective Story, London: Chatto & Windus.

1921   The Man That Corrupted Hadleyburg, and Other Stories and Sketches, London: Chatto & Windus.

1921   The Stolen White Elephant, Etc., London: Chatto & Windus.

1921   Tom Sawyer, Detective...and Other Tales, London: Chatto & Windus.

1922   The Choice Humorous Works of Mark Twain, London: Chatto & Windus.

1924   The Jumping Frog, and Other Sketches. Carlton Classics. London: Long.

1926   The Stolen White Elephant. Cheap Edition. London: Newnes.

1931   Burlesque Autobiography, London: Simpkin, Marshal, Hamilton, Kent.

1936   "1601"; A Tudor Fireside Conversation, As Written by the Ingenuous Virtuous and Learned Mark Twain, London: n.pub.

1937   Mark Twain's 1601. Conversation As It Was by the Social Fireside in the Time of the Tudors, London: [privately printed]

1941   Jumping Frog. Services Library. London: Chatto & Windus.

1949   The Jumping Frog, and Other Stories and Sketches, London: Mayflower.

1963   Six Stories, by Mark Twain. The Queen's Classics. London: Chatto & Windus.

1969   "1601"; A Tudor Fireside Conversation, As Written by the Ingenuous
       Virtuous and Learned Mark Twain, London: Land's End Press.

                              Tom Sawyer

1876   The Adventures of Tom Sawyer, London: Chatto & Windus.

1877   Same. New Edition. London: Chatto & Windus.

1885   Tom Sawyer. New Edition. London: Chatto & Windus.

1897   The Adventures of Tom Sawyer. New Edition. London: Chatto &
       Windus.

1908   Same. London: Chatto & Windus.

1911   Same. London: Chatto & Windus.

1912   Same. London: Chatto & Windus.

1920   Same. New Impression. London: Chatto & Windus.

1923   Same. London: Nash & G.

1924   Same. Popular Edition. London: Harrap.

1924   Same. Cheap Edition. London: Nelson.

1929   Same. London: Nelson.

1930   Same. London: Nash.

1931   Same. Limited Edition. London: Rodker.

1933   Same. Standard Fiction Library. London: Harrap.

1936   Same. Famous Books for Boys and Girls. London: Nelson

1936   Same. London: Nonesuch Press.

1937   Same. Nelson Classics. London: Nelson.

1937? Same. London: Virtue.

1938   Same. London: Chatto & Windus.

1938   Same. Nelson Classics. London: Nelson.

1939   Tom Sawyer, London: Nelson.

1939   The Adventures of Tom Sawyer. Teaching of English Series.
       London: Nelson

1943   Tom Sawyer and Huckleberry Finn. Everyman's Library, No. 976.
       London: Dent.

1944 Same. Everyman's Library. London, Toronto: Dent.

1947 Tom Sawyer. Camden Illustrated Classics. London: Elek.

1947 The Adventures of Tom Sawyer. Library Edition. London: Ingram.

1947 Same. The Albatross Modern Continental Library, Vol. 1622. London, Paris, Verona: Mondadori.

1948? Same. Pocket Classics. London: Langdon.

1949 Tom Sawyer, London: Ingram.

1949 Same. Simplified English Series. London: Longmans.

1950 Tom Sawyer and Huckleberry Finn. Everyman's Library. London: Dent.

1950 The Adventures of Tom Sawyer. Puffin Story Books. London: Penguin.

1951 Tom Sawyer. New edition. London: Blackie.

1953 Tom Sawyer and Huckleberry Finn, London: Collins.

1953 Tom Sawyer. School Classics. London: Nelson.

1953 Same. Winchester Classics. London: Nelson.

1953 Same. Hamlyn Classics. New Edition. London: Planned Bookselling.

1953 Same. London: Rylee.

1954 Same. Library of Famous Books. New Edition. London: Blackie.

1954 Same. Classics Series. London: Nelson.

1954 The Adventures of Tom Sawyer, and, Huckleberry Finn. Everyman's Library. London: Dent.

1954 Tom Sawyer and Huckleberry Finn. Everyman's Library. New Edition. London: Dent.

1955 The Adventures of Tom Sawyer. Children's Illustrated Classics. London: Dent.

1956 Same. Shortened Classics. London: Schofield and S.

1957 Same. Heirloom Library. London: Weidenfeld & Nicolson.

1959 Same. London: Harrap.

1959 Tom Sawyer & Huckleberry Finn. Everyman's Library, 976. London: Dent.

1959 Adventures of Tom Sawyer. Queen's Classics. London: Chatto & Windus.

1961 Same. New Windmill Series. London: Heinemann.

1961 The Adventures of Tom Sawyer. School Edition. New Windmill Ser-
      ies. London: Heinemann.

1962 Tom Sawyer. Retold.... Kennett Library. London: Blackie.

1962 Adventures of Tom Sawyer. Zodiac Series. London: Chatto & Windus.

1963 Same. Boys and Girls Library. London: Collins.

1963 Same. Laurel & Gold Series. London: Collins.

1963 Adventures of Tom Sawyer and Huckleberry Finn, London: Dent.

1963 Tom Sawyer; and, Huckleberry Finn. School Edition. Literature
      of Yesterday Series. London: Dent.

1964 Adventures of Tom Sawyer and Huckleberry Finn, London: Dent.

1964 Tom Sawyer, London: Collins.

1965 Same. Laurel & Gold Series. London: Collins.

1965 The Adventures of Tom Sawyer. Longman Structural Readers. London:
      Longmans.

1965 Same. Shorter Classics. London: Ginn.

1966 Adventures of Tom Sawyer. Classics Series. London: Nelson.

1966 Same. Streamline Books. London: Nelson.

1966 Same. Clear Print Classics. London: Rylee.

1967 The Adventures of Tom Sawyer, London: Hamlyn.

1968 Same. Abridged. London: Oldhams.

1970 Same. London: Rylee.

1970 Tom Sawyer, London: Collins.

1975 The Adventures of Tom Sawyer, Maidenhead, Berkshire: Purnell Books.

1976 Same. Children's Illustrated Classics. London: Dent.

1976 The Adventures of Tom Sawyer [by] Mark Twain; Retold, London:
      Dean & Son.

Tom Sawyer Abroad

1894 Tom Sawyer Abroad, London: Chatto & Windus.

1896   Tom Sawyer; Tom Sawyer, Detective and Other Stories; Etc.,
       Etc., London: Chatto & Windus.

1920   Tom Sawyer Abroad, London: Chatto & Windus.

Tom Sawyer, Detective

1896   Tom Sawyer, Detective. Told by Huck Finn. Other Tales, London:
       Chatto & Windus.

1896   Tom Sawyer Abroad; Tom Sawyer, Detective and Other Stories; Etc.,
       Etc. London: Chatto & Windus.

1897   Tom Sawyer Detective As Told by Huck Finn, and Other Tales, London:
       Chatto & Windus.

1901   Same. New Edition. London: Chatto & Windus.

1921   Same. London: Chatto & Windus.

1966   Tom Sawyer Detective. Colour Classics. n.p.: Golden Pleasure.

Tramp Abroad

1879   A Tramp Abroad. Hartford, Conn.: American Publishing Company.
       London: Chatto & Windus.

1880   Same. London: Chatto & Windus.

1880   Same. 2 vols. London: Chatto & Windus.

1880   Same. New Edition in 1 vol. London: Chatto & Windus.

1881   Same. London: Chatto & Windus.

1882   Same. London: Chatto & Windus.

1884   Same. New Edition. London: Chatto & Windus.

1885   Same. New Edition. London: Chatto & Windus.

1877   Same. London: Chatto & Windus.

1888   Same. London: Chatto & Windus.

1889   Same. New Edition. London: Chatto & Windus.

1890   Same. London: Chatto & Windus.

1891   Same. London: Chatto & Windus.

1896   The Tramp Abroad, London: Chatto & Windus.

1898   A Tramp Abroad. New Edition. London: Chatto & Windus.

1907   Same. London: Chatto & Windus.

1909   Same. London: Chatto & Windus.

1912   Same. Everett's Library. London: Everett.

Travel Sketches

1878   An Idle Excursion, and Other Papers, London: Chatto & Windus.

1938   Letters from the Sandwich Islands; Written for the Sacramento
       Union, by Mark Twain, London: Oxford University Press.

1957   Mark Twain of the Enterprise; Newspaper Articles & Other Documents,
       1862-1864. Ed. Henry Nash Smith. Berkeley, California. Univer-
       sity of California Press. London: Cambridge University Press.

What Is Man?

1910   What Is Man?, London: Watts.

1919   What Is Man? and Other Essays, London: Chatto & Windus.

1936   What Is Man? Thinkers' Library. London: Watts.

Miscellaneous Writings

1885   The Mark Twain Birthday Book, London: Remington.

1885? Same. London: Ward, Lock.

1888   Same. London: Remington.

1888   Mark Twain's Library of Humour, London: Chatto & Windus.

1896   The Mark Twain Birthday Book, London: Ward, Lock.

1897   Mark Twain's Library of Humour. New Edition. London: Chatto
       & Windus.

1906   Doloy Tsara! [Down with the Tsar!] [The Tsar's Soliloquy].
       Marka [Mark], Londn [London]. [pamphlet] [Russian]

1917   Who Was Sarah Findlay? By Mark Twain. With A Suggested Solution
       of the Mystery by J.M. Barrie, London: [privately printed]

1943   Washington in 1868. Ed. Cyril Clemens. London: Laurie.

1963   The Forgotten Writings of Mark Twain. Ed. Henry Duskis. New York:
       Citadel Press. London: Owen.

Selections (collections with reprinted material from Mark Twain)

1869 Tom Hood's Comic Readings in Prose and Verse, London: Frederick Warne and Co.

1870 A Third Supply of Yankee Drolleries. The Most Recent Works of the Best American Humourists..., London: Hotten. Melbourne: Robertson.

1872 Practical Jokes with Artemus Ward, London: Hotten.

1872 The World of Wit and Humour, London, Paris and New York: Cassell, Petter & Galpin.

1873 Fun for the Million..., London: Hotten.

1873 Tom Hood's Comic Annual for 1874..., London: Published at the Fun Office.

1874 Practical Jokes with Artemus Ward, London: Hotten.

1875 American Drolleries; Containing the Jumping Frog and Screamers. By Mark Twain, London: Ward, Lock, & Tyler.

1875? American Drolleries, by Mark Twain, Glasgow: Grand Colosseum Warehouse.

1875 Funny Stories and Humorous Poems by Mark Twain and Oliver Wendell Holmes. Household and Railway Novels. London: Ward, Lock, & Tyler.

1878 Mark Twain's Nightmare [Punch, Brothers, Punch! or A Literary Nightmare. A Story of Haunting Horror] with Tales, Sketches, and Poetry, by Mark Twain, F.C. Burnand, H.S. Leigh, etc., etc., London: Ward, Lock.

1885 Same. London: Ward & Locke.

1886 Practical Jokes with Artemus Ward, London: Ward & Lock.

189-? Bret Harte's Deadwood Mystery and Mark Twain's Nightmare..., London: Croome.

189-? American Drolleries, London: Ward, Lock & Bowden.

1892 Modern Humour for Reading or Recitation, London: Hutchinson.

1895 American Drolleries. By Mark Twain, Glasgow: Grand Colosseum Warehouse Co.

1904 Mark Twain and Others. Literary Guillotine, London: Lane.

1930 Pages from Mark Twain. Junior Modern English Series. London: Harrap.

1946 Viking Portable Mark Twain. Edited Bernard DeVoto. London: Mayflower. New York: Viking Press.

1965 Afloat and Ashore with Mark Twain. World of English. London: Arnold.

Collected Works

1899-1903 The Writings of Mark Twain. Author's Edition de luxe. 23 vols. London: Chatto & Windus.

1925-1928 The Writings of Mark Twain. Florida Edition. 17 vols. London: Chatto & Windus.

1931 Mark Twain's Works. Popular Edition. 17 vols. London: Chatto & Windus.

New Zealand

Sources: CBI/USC

1948? The Adventures of Huckleberry Finn, Christchurch: Whitcombe & Tombs.

1948? The Adventures of Tom Sawyer, Christchurch: Whitcombe & Tombs.

WESTERN EUROPE

Austria

Sources: ABL/DB/HV/IT/JDS/MTG/NUC/SLVS/UnI/UnS/ZBZ

Connecticut Yankee

1923 Ein Yankee am Hofe des Konigs Artus [A Yankee at the Court of King Arthur]. Die Phantastischen Bucher. Wien: Stein.

1948 Ein Yenkee am Hofe des Konigs Artus. Satirischer Roman. Wien: W. Verkauf.

1956 Ein Yankee am Hofe des Konigs Artus. (Roman), Wien: Forum.

Huckleberry Finn

1947 Huckleberry Finn, Linz, Wien, Pittsburgh: Ibis.

1949 Same. Wien: Obelisk.

1952 Same. Linz, Wien: Ibis.

1954 Same. Wien: Kremayr & Scheriau.

1954 Wir Befreien Jim [We Liberate Jim], Wien-Modling: St. Gabriel.

1955 Huckleberry Finn, Wien: Buchgemeinschaft Jung-Donauland.

1955 Die Abenteuer des Tom Sawyer und Huckleberry Finn [The Adventures of Tom Sawyer and Huckleberry Finn], Wien, Heidelberg: Ueberreuter.

1964 Huckleberry Finn, Linz: Trauner.

1966 Die Abenteuer des Tom Sawyer und Huckleberry Finn, Wien: Kremayr und Scheriau.

1972 Tom Sawyer. Huckleberry Finn, Klagenfurt: Kaiser; Buchgemeinde Alpenland.

1974 Tom Sahyeri/Huckleberry Finn. Sonderausgabe [Special Edition]. Wien: Tosa; ABC-Buchclub.

1975 Tom Sawyer. Huckleberry Finn. Sonderausgabe [Special Edition]. Wien: Salzer-Ueberreuter.

1975 Same. Salzburg: Spectrum.

1975 Die Abenteuer des Huckleberry Finn, Wien: Buchgemeinschaft Donauland.

Innocents Abroad

1924   Bummel durch das Mittelmeer [Spree through the Mediterranean],
       Wien: Amerikanischer.

1948   Komisches Altes Europa! [Comical Old Europe!]. Die neue lustige
       Bucher. Wien: Stephenson.

Life on the Mississippi

1950   Auf dem Mississippi [On the Mississippi], Wien: Obelisk.

1973   Als Lotse auf dem Mississippi [As Pilot on the Mississippi], Wien:
       Ueberreuter.

Prince and the Pauper

1901   Konig und Betteljunge [King and Young Beggar]. Bucherei fur die
       Jugend. Wien: Witwe & Sohn.

1913   The Prince and the Pauper. Abridged school edition. Vienna:
       Tempsky.

1966   Prinz und Bettelknabe [Prince and Beggar Boy]. Wien: Buchgemein-
       schaft Donauland.

1966   Prinz und Bettelknabe. Roman, Wien: Kremayr und Scheriau.

Stories and Sketches

1969   Adams Tagebuch und Andere Heitere Geschichten [Adam's Diary and
       Other Cheerful Stories], Wien: Herder.

1971   Der Gestohlene Weisse Elefant [The Stolen White Elephant], Wien:
       Ueberreuter.

1975   Schone Geschichten: 28 Ausgewahlte Skizzen und Erzahlungen [Fine
       Stories: 28 Selected Sketches and Stories]. Neuauflage [New
       Edition]. Wels: Welsermiehl.

Tom Sawyer

1945   Tom Sawyers Abenteuer [Tom Sawyer's Adventures], Linz: Ibis.

1947   Same. Wien: Die Lesergilde.

1952   Zeuge Tom [Witness Tom], Wien-Modling: St. Gabriel.

1953   Tom Sawyers Lustige Streiche [Tom Sawyer's Merry Pranks], Wien:
       Kremayr & Scheriau.

1955 Die Abenteuer des Tom Sawyer und Huckleberry Finn [The Adventures of Tom Sawyer and Huckleberry Finn], Wien, Heidelberg: Ueberreuter.

1957 Tom Sawyers Abenteuer, Wien: Osterr. Bundesverlegen.

1964 Same. Linz: Trauner.

1966 Die Abenteuer des Tom Sawyer und Huckleberry Finn, Wien: Kremayr und Scheriau.

1972 Tom Sawyer. Huckleberry Finn, Klagenfurt: Kaiser; Buchgemeinde Alpenland.

1974 Tom Sawyers Abenteuer, Wien: Jugend & Volk; Halder-Pichler-Tempsky; Osterr Bundesverlag.

1974 Tom Sahyeri/Huckleberry Finn. Sonderausgabe [Special Edition]. Wien: Tosa; ABC-Buchclub.

1975 Tom Sawyer. Huckleberry Finn. Sonderausgabe [Special Edition]. Wien: Salzer-Ueberreuter.

1975 Same. Salzburg: Spectrum.

1975 Tom Sawyer, Wien: Ueberreuter.

Tom Sawyer Abroad

1970 Tom Sawyer auf Weltreise [Tom Sawyer on World Trip], Wien: Ueber-reuter.

Tramp Abroad

1901 A Tramp Abroad. School edition. Vienna: Tempsky.[English]

Miscellaneous Writings

1946 Zeitungsgeschichten [Newspaper Stories], Bregenz: "Homonuculous."

Belgium

Sources: BBel/BCB/BCCB/Bib/CGBN/IT/LB/LF

Captain Stormfield's Visit to Heaven

1944 Le Capitaine Tempete et Autres Contes [Captain Tempest and Other Stories]. Collection Les Libertes Belges. Bruxelles: G.I.G.

Connecticut Yankee

1949 Un Yankee a la Cour du Roi Arthur. Roman [A Yankee at the Court of King Arthur. Novel], Paris-Bruxelles: Editions de la Paix.

Huckleberry Finn

1947 De Lotgevallen van Huckleberry Finn [The Adventures of Huckleberry Finn], Antwerp: De Sleutel.

1952 Same. Antwerpen: Van Gelder.

1955 Same. Brussel: Reinaert-junior.

1963 Les Aventures de Tom Sawyer et Huckleberry Finn [The Adventures of Tom Sawyer and Huckleberry Finn]. Collection "Marabout-Geant." Verviers: Gerard.

1967 De Avonturen van Huckleberry Finn [The Adventures of Huckleberry Finn]. Heroica-bibliotheek. Brussel: Reinaert.

Life on the Mississippi

1966 Sur le Grand Fleuve [On the Great River]. Nouveaux Horizons. n.p.: Seghers.

Prince and the Pauper

1968 Prins en Bedelaar [Prince and Beggar]. Heroica-bibliotheek. Brussel: De Arbeiderspers. Reinaert.

1969 Prins en Bedelknaap [Prince and Beggar Boy], Schelde: De Goudvink.

Stories and Sketches

1944 Exploits de Tom Sawyer, Detective et Autres Nouvelles [Exploits of Tom Sawyer, Detective and Other Stories]. Collection "Les Libertes Belge." Bruxelles: Edition G.I.G.

1944 Les Peterkins et Autres Contes [The Peterkins and Other Stories]. Collection "Les Libertes Belges." Bruxelles: Edition G.I.G.

1945 Plus fort que Sherlock Holmes [More Clever than Sherlock Holmes], Bruxelles: N.R.B.

1970 De Verstrooide Speurder [The Absent-minded Detective], Brussel: Reinaert.

Tom Sawyer

n.d. Les Aventures de Tom Sawyer [The Adventures of Tom Sawyer], Liege: Desoer.

n.d. The Adventures of Tom Sawyer, Antwerp: Mertens. [English]

1934 Tom Sawyer, Oude-God: Boekengilde Die Poorte.

1947 Die Avonturen van Tom Sawyer [The Adventures of Tom Sawyer], Antwerp:
De Sleutel.

1955 Same. Brussel: Reinaert-junior.

1957 Tom Sawyer, Antwerp: Zuid-Nederlandse.

1957 De Avonturen van Tom Sawyer, Antwerp: DeSleutel.

1958 Same. Antwerp: Gottmer.

1958 Tom Sawyer, Berchem-Antwerp: De Internationale Pers.

1963? Les Aventures de Tom Sawyer. Editions Hemma. Chevron: Hemma.

1963 Les Aventures de Tom Sawyer et Huckleberry Finn. Collection "Marabout-Geant." Verviers: Gerard.

1965 Tom Sawyer. Heroica-bibliotheek. Brussel: Reinaert.

1968 De Avonturen van Tom Sawyer, Schelde: De Goudvink.

1970 Tom Sawyer. Europa-selectie. Antwerpen: Beckers.

1970 De Avonturen van Tom Sawyer, Schelde: De Goudvink.

Tom Sawyer, Detective

1944 Exploits de Tom Sawyer, Detective et Autres Nouvelles [Exploits of
Tom Sawyer, Detective and Other Short Stories]. Collection "Les
Libertes Belge." Bruxelles: Edition G.I.G.

1961 Omnibus. Tom Sawyer als Kwajongen; Tom Sawyer als Zeerover; Tom
Sawyer als Speurder [Tom Sawyer as Mischievous Boy; Tom Sawyer as
Pirate; Tom Sawyer as Tracker], Antwerp: Mertens & Stappaerts.

1965 Tom Sawyers als Detective, Antwerp: Zuid-Nederlandse.

1966 Tom Sawyer als Detective, Antwerpen: Zuid-Nederlandse.

1968 Omnibus. Tom Sawyer als Kwajongen. Tom Sawyer als Zeerover.
Tom Sawyer als Speurder, Schelde: De Goudvink.

Denmark

Sources: DBA/IT/NUC

American Claimant

1894 Arvingerne fra Amerika. Roman. [Heir from America. Novel],
      Kjobenhavn: Schubothes.

Connecticut Yankee

1890 En Yankee hos Ridderne om det Runde Bord [A Yankee with Knights
      about the Round Table], Kjobenhavn: Schubothes.

1961 En Yankee ved Kong Arthurs Hof [A Yankee at King Arthur's Court],
      Kjobenhavn: Skrifola.

Gilded Age

1886 Forgyldt [Gilt], Kjobenhavn: Schubothes.

Huckleberry Finn

1885 Huck Finns Haendelser [Huck Finn's Accidents], Kjobenhavn: Schu-
      bothes.

190-? Same. Kobenhavn: Forlaget Danmark.

1910 Same. Kobenhavn: Dansk-norsk.

1913 Same. Kobenhavn: Kunstforlaget Danmark.

1939 Huck Finn. Huckleberri Finn's Haendelser, Kobenhavn: Pedersen.

1945 Negerfangen [The Negro Captive]. Forkortet Overs. af [Abridged
      from] The Adventures of Huckleberry Finn. Krone-Serien. Koben-
      havn: Forlagshuset.

1950 Huck Finn, Kobenhavn: Samleren.

1951 Same. Kobenhavn: Ungdommens Forlag.

1952 Same. Kobenhavn: Ungdommens Forlag.

1962 Huckleberry Finn, Kobenhavn: Gyldendal.

1964 Huck Finn, Kobenhavn: Samleren.

1966? Huckleberry Finn, Kobenhavn: Gyldendal.

1971 Huck Finn. [6th edition] Kobenhavn: Ungdommens Forlag.

1971 Huck Finn's Eventyrlige Oplevelser [Huck Finn's Adventurous Exper-
      iences], Kobenhavn: Fremad.

1973 Huckleberry Finn, Kobenhavn: Gyldendal.

1974 Same. Kobenhavn: Skandinavisk.

Innocents Abroad

1878   Naive Reisende [Naive Travellers], Kobenhavn: Schubothes.

1884   Same. Kobenhavn: Schubothes.

1904   Skore H'der Udenlands [Simpletons Abroad]. In Udvalg [Selection],
       Vol. I. Kobenhavn: Gyldendal.

Life on the Mississippi

1883   Fra Mississipifloden. Skildringer. [From the Mississippi River.
       Pictures], Kjobenhavn: Schubothes.

1961   Livet pa Mississippi [Life on the Mississippi], Kobenhavn: Fischer
       og Hertz.

Prince and the Pauper

1882   Fyrsten og Tiggeren. Roman [The Prince and the Beggar. Novel],
       Kobenhavn: Schubothes.

1975   Prinsen og Tiggerdrengen, Kobenhavn: Lademann.

Pudd'nhead Wilson

1909   Fjolle-Wilson [Foolish Wilson], Kobenhavn: Langhoff.

1968? En Drabe Negerblod [One Drop Negro Blood], Kobenhavn: Host.

Report from Paradise

1955   Kaptajnen i Paradis...[Captain in Paradise], Kobenhavn: Grafisk.

1971   Same. Kobenhavn: Grafisk Forlag.

Stories and Sketches

1874   Udvalgte Skitser [Selected Sketches]. Esquisses Choisies.
       Kjevenhaven: Jorgensens.

1879   4 Smaa Skizzer [Four Small Sketches], Kobenhavn: Hartwig.

1881   Paa Reiser. To Skitser [Upon Travels. Two Sketches], Kjobenhavn:
       Schubothes.

1881   Skildringer og Skitser [Pictures and Sketches], Kobenhavn: Reitzel,
       Gron.

1882   Den Stjaalne Hvide Elefant og Andere Nye Skizzer [The Stolen White
       Elephant and Other New Sketches], Kjobenhavn: Mackeprang.

1882 Same. Kjobenhavn: Schubothes.

1884 Lost og Fast [Loose and Fast]. Smaaskitser [Little Sketches],
      Kobenhavn: Schubothes.

1888 Udvalgte Skitser. Dansk Folkebibliothek. Kjobenhavn: Mackeprang.

1889 Nye Skitser [New Sketches]. [2nd edition] Kjobenhavn: Nyt Dansk
      Forlagskonsortium.

1890? Udvalgte Skitser, Kjobenhavn: Hanberg og Gjellerup.

1893 Million-Sedlen med Flere Skitser [Million-Note with More Sketches],
      Kjobenhavn: Schubothes.

1911 Lystige Historier. Skildringer og Skitser. [Merry Tales. Pictures
      and Sketches], Kobenhavn: Fergo.

1912 Udvalgte Fortaellinger [Selected Tales], Kobenhavn: Kunstforlaget
      Danmark.

1913 For Lud og Koldt Vand. Lystige Historier [To Be Neglected. Merry
      Tales], Kobenhavn: Fergo.

1914 Million-Pund-Sedlen og Andre Nye Fortaellinger [Million Pound Bank-
      note and Other New Stories]. In Udvalg af Amerikansk Humor [Selec-
      tion of American Humor], Vol. II. Kobenhavn: Fredericksberg Biblio-
      teka.

1914 Adams Dagbog og Andre Fortaellinger [Adam's Diary and Other Stories].
      In Udvalg af Amerikansk, Vol. III. Kobenhavn: Fredericksberg
      Biblioteka.

1914 En Indviklet Detektivhistorie og Andre Fortaellinger [A Complicated
      Detective Story and Other Stories]. In Udvalg af Amerikansk, Vol.
      IV. Kobenhavn: Fredericksberg Biblioteka.

1914 Skitser og Fortaellinger [Sketches and Stories]. In Udvalg af
      Amerikansk, Vol. V. Kobenhavn: Fredericksberg Biblioteka.

1916 Lystige Historier, Kjobenhavn: Kjobenhavns Bogforlag.

1941 Den Stjaalne Hvide Elefant; og Andere Fortaellinger, Kobenhavn:
      Thaning & Appel.

1943 Civiliserede Menneskealdere og Andre Fortaellinger [Civilized
      Generations and Other Stories], Kobenhavn: Carit Andersen.

1943 Den Store Franske Duel og Andre Historier [The Great French Duel and
      Other Stories], Kobenhavn: Thaning & Appel.

1944 Den Stjaalne Hvide Elefant og Andere Fortaellinger. Verdenslittera-
      turens Humor, Kobenhavn: Thaning & Appel.

1944 Evas Dagbog [Eve's Diary], Kobenhavn: Hernov.

1945   Civiliserede Menneskealdere og Andre Fortaellinger, Kobenhavn:
       Carit Andersen.

1945   30.000 Dollars og Andre Fortaellinger [$30,000 and Other Stories],
       Kobenhavn: Carit Andersen.

1945   Ude i Nevada og Andre Fortaellinger [Out in Nevada and Other Sto-
       ries], Kobenhavn: Carit Andersen.

1946   Blandt Mormoner og Andre Historier [Among the Mormons and Other
       Stories]. Verdenslitteraturens Humor. Kobenhavn: Thaning &
       Appel.

1953   Mark Twains Bedste [Mark Twain's Best], Kobenhavn: Carit Andersen.

1956   Same. Omnibus Bogerne. [2nd Edition] Kobenhavn: Carit
       Andersen.

1956   Mark Twain Fortaeller [Mark Twain Tales]. Omnibus Bogerne. Koben-
       havn: Carit Andersen.

1961   Den Artige Dreng [The Good Boy], Kobenhavn: Grafisk Cirkel.

1961   Muntre Historier [Merry Stories], Kobenhavn: Carit Andersen.

1961   Den Stjaalne Hvide Elefant og Andre Fortaellinger. Humorist
       Serien. Kobenhavn: Thaning & Appel.

1963   Mark Twains Bedste. En Begravelse i Nevada og Andre Muntre
       Historier [Mark Twain's Best. A Funeral in Nevada and Other
       Merry Tales], Kobenhavn: Carit Andersen.

1963   Den Store Franske Duel og Andre Historier, Kobenhavn: Thaning &
       Appel.

1965   Mark Twain Fortaeller. Millionpundsedlen og Andre Muntre Historier
       [Mark Twain Stories. Million Pound Bank-note and Other Merry Sto-
       ries], Kobenhavn: Carit Andersen.

1969   Jagten Pa Den Svigefulde Kalkun og Andre Historier [Hunting the
       Deceitful Turkey and Other Stories], Kobenhavn: Gyldendal.

1971   Festlige Fortaellinger [Festive Tales], Kobenhavn: Thanning
       & Appel.

1971   Same. Nyt Udgave [New edition]. Virum: Edito.

1975   Milliopundssedlen og Andre Fortaellinger [Million Pounds Bank-
       note and Other Stories], Kobenhavn: Carit Andersen.

Tom Sawyer

1879   Lille Toms Eventyr [Little Tom's Adventures], Kjobenhavn: Schu-
       bothes.

1906   Toms Eventyr, Kobenhavn: Langhoff.

1911   Lille Toms Eventyr, Kobenhavn: Kunstforlaget Danmark.

1916   Toms Eventyr, Kobenhavn: Langhoff.

1923   Same. Kobenhavn: Gyldendal.

1938   Same. Kobenhavn: Pedersen.

1945   Tom Sawyer. Krone Serien. Kobenhavn: Forlagshuset.

1949   Toms Eventyr, Kobenhavn: Korch.

1951   Same. Kobenhavn: Samleren.

1951   Same. Kobenhavn: Ungdommens Forlag.

1952   Same. [2nd edition]   Kobenhavn: Ungdommens Forlag.

1957   Same. Kobenhavn: Ungdommens Forlag.

1961   Tom Sawyer. Kobenhavn: Fremad.

1961   Toms Eventyr. Kobenhavn: Gyldendal.

1963   Same. Nyt opl. [New edition]. Kobenhavn: Ungdommens Forlag.

1964   Same. Kobenhavn: Samleren.

1965   Tom Sawyers Eventyr, Kobenhavn: Andreasen & Lachmann.

1967? Toms Eventyr, Kobenhavn: Gyldendal.

1974   Tom Sawyer, Kobenhavn: Skandinavisk Litografisk Forlag.

1975   Same. Nyt Udgave [New Edition]. Kobenhavn: Lademann.

1975   Toms Eventyr. [3rd edition]   Kobenhavn: Gyldendal.

Tom Sawyer Abroad

1954   Tom Paa Reise [Tom Abroad], Kobenhavn: Ungdommens Forlag.

Tom Sawyer, Detective

1908   Tom som Opdager [Tom as Detective], Kobenhavn: Langhoff.

1931   Same. Kobenhavn: Erichsen.

1953   Tom som Detektiv, Kobenhavn: Ungdommens Forlag.

Tramp Abroad

1880 Erindringer fra en Fodtour i Europa [Reminiscences from a Walking Tour in Europe], Kobenhavn: Schubothes.

1881 En Landstryger paa Reise. Skitser fra en Reise i Europa [A Tramp Abroad. Sketches from A Trip in Europe], Kjobenhavn: Nyt Dansk Forlagskonsortium.

1887 Same. Kobenhavn?: Skandinavens Boghandel.

1889 En Landstryger paa Reise, Kobenhavn: Mackeprang.

1912? Same. Kobenhavn?: J. Anderson.

Selections

1875 Udvalgte Arbejder [Selected Works]. 2 vols. Kobenhavn: Wulff.

1880 Udvalgte Arbejder. Ny Raekke [Selected Works. New Series], Kobenhavn: Nyt Dansk Forlagskonsortium.

1904 Udvalg [Selection], Kobenhavn: Gyldendal.

1914 Udvalg af Amerikansk Humor [Selection of American Humor], Kobenhavn: Fredericksberg Biblioteks.

c1978 Mark Twain's Verden: Historier og Artikler [Mark Twain's World: Stories and Articles], Kobenhavn: Lademann.

France

Sources: BF/Bib/BN/CGBN/CGLF/IT/LC/LF/NUC/UnG/ZBZ

American Claimant

1906 Le Pretendant Americain, Roman [The American Claimant, Novel]. Collection d'Auteurs Etrangers. [3rd edition] Paris: Mercure de France.

1911? Le Cochon dans les Trefles [The Pig in the Clover]. In Extenso. Ser. 1, no. 18. [abridged] Paris: La Renaissance du Livre. Gillequin.

Captain Stormfield's Visit to Heaven

1909 Le Capitaine Tempete et Autres Contes [Captain Storm and Other Stories]. Collection d'Auteurs Etrangers. Paris: Mercure de France.

Connecticut Yankee

1950 Un Yankee a la Cour du Roi Arthur, Roman [A Yankee at the Court
      of King Arthur, Novel], Paris, Bruxelles: Editions de la Paix.

1959 Un Americain a la Cour du Roi Arthur. Collection Un Livre J.
      Paris: O.D.E.J.

Huckleberry Finn

1886 Les Aventures de Huck Finn, l'Ami de Tom Sawyer [The Adventures of
      Huckleberry Finn, the Friend of Tom Sawyer], Paris: Hennuyer.

1914 Same. Paris: Hennuyer.

1926 Huck Finn. Collection La Joie de Nos Enfants. Paris: Georges-
      Celestin Cres.

1927? Les Aventures de Huck Finn, l'Ami de Tom Sawyer. Collection La
      Joie de Nos Enfants. Paris: Les Arts et le Livre.

1948 Les Aventures d'Huckleberry Finn, Paris: Editions d'Hier et
      d'Aujourd'hui.

1948 Les Aventures de Huck Finn. Bibliotheque Verte. Paris: Hachette.

1950 Same. [abridged] Collection Charme des Jeunes. Paris: Istra.

1951 Same. Bibliotheque Verte. Paris: Hachette.

1960 Les Aventures d'Huckleberry Finn, Paris: Club des Jeunes Amis
      du Livre.

1960 Same. Paris: Livre-Club du Librairie.

1960 Same. Paris: Les Editeurs Francais Reunis.

1961 Same. Le Livre Club du Librairie. Paris: Livre Club du Librairie.

1961 Les Aventures de Huck Finn. Collection Super Club. Paris: O.D.E.J.

1961 Les Aventures d'Huckleberry Finn, Paris: Stock.

1962 Les Aventures de Huckleberry Finn, Paris: Delagrave.

1963 Same. Bibliotheque Juventa. Paris: Delagrave.

1965 Same. Sommets du Roman Americain. Paris, Lausanne: Hachette.

1965 Les Aventures de Tom Sawyer; Le Prince et le Pauvre; Les Aventures
      de Huck Finn. Pour la Jeunesse. Collection Trois en Un. Paris:
      Hachette.

1966 Les Aventures de Huck Finn. Collection Un Livre-Club Junior.
      Paris: O.D.E.J.

1968 Les Aventures de Huckleberry Finn, Paris: Nouvel Office d'Edition.

1969 Same. Paris: Selection du Reader's Digest [condensation].

1970 Same. Evreux: Le Circle du Bibliophile.

1973 Les Aventures d'Huckleberry Finn, Paris: Editions la Farandole.

1976 Same. Paris: Editions la Farandole.

1976 Les Aventures de Huck Finn, Neuilly-sur-Seine: Editions de Saint-Clair.

Letters from the Earth

1965 Quand Satan Raconte la Terre au Bon Dieu, suivi de Papiers de la Famille Adam et d'Autres Documents Essentiels. [When Satan Told About the Earth to the Good God, followed by Papers of the Adam Family and Other Essential Documents], Paris: Grasset.

Life on the Mississippi

1949 Life on the Mississippi. Collection Bantam en Langue Anglaise. Paris: Presses de la Cite. [English]

1966 Sur le Grand Fleuve [On the Great River]. Collection Nouveaux Horizons: Paris. Seghers.

Prince and the Pauper

1883 Le Prince et le Pauvre [The Prince and the Pauper]. Nouvelle Bibliotheque a 3 Francs. Poitiers-Paris: Oudin.

1886 Same. Paris: Lecene et Oudin.

1887 Same. Paris: Lecene et Oudin.

1888 Same. Paris: Lecene et Oudin.

1889 Same. Paris: Lecene et Oudin.

1891 Same. Paris: Lecene et Oudin.

1894 Same. Paris: Lecene et Oudin.

1909 Same. Paris: Societe Francaise d'Imprimerie et de Librairie.

1924 Same. Paris: Charpentier.

1924 Same. Paris: Fasquelle.

1929 Same. Collection Joie de Nos Enfants de Huit a Seize Ans. Paris: Georges-Celestin Cres.

1936   Same.   Elbeuf-Paris: Duval.

1938   Same.   Collection Les Loisirs de la Jeunesse.   Paris: Gedalge.

1938   Same.   Bibliotheque Nelson Illustree. Paris-Londres-Edinbourg-
New York: Nelson.

1946   Same.   Poitiers: Ste. Francaise d'Imprimerie et de Libraire.

1947   Same.   Bibliotheque Juventa. Paris: Delagrave.

1950   Same.   Collection Charme des Jeunes. Paris, Strasbourg: Istra.

1953   Same.   Bibliotheque Verte. Paris: Hachette.

1954   Same.   Collection Les Loisirs de la Jeunesse. [4th edition]
Paris: Gedalge.

1956   Same.   Collection Anemones. Paris: Bias.

1957   Same.   Collection Anemones. Paris: Bias.

1959   Same.   Bibliotheque Juventa. Paris: Delagrave.

1960   Same.   Collection Junior. Paris: O.D.E.J.

1964   Same.   Collection Junior. Paris: O.D.E.J.

1964   Same.   [adaptation]   Collection Les Grands Classiques Illustres.
Paris?: Del Duca.

1964   Same.   Jeunesse Selection. Cadets. Saint Germain-en-Laye: M.D.I.

1965   Les Aventures de Tom Sawyer; Le Prince et le Pauvre; Les Aventures
de Huck Finn. Collection Trois en Un. Pour la Jeunesse. Paris:
Hachette.

1966   Le Prince et le Pauvre. Collection Super-1000. Paris: Editions
G.P.

1969   Same. Paris: Delagrave.

Pudd'nhead Wilson

1920   Wilson Tete-de-mou. Les Jumeaux Extraordinaires [Soft-headed Wilson.
The Extraordinary Twins]. Collection Litteraire des Romans
Fantaisistes. Paris: L'Edition Francaise Illustree.

Roughing It

1902   A la Dure, Roman [The Hard Mode, Novel]. Editions de la Revue
Blanche. Paris: Fasquelle.

1959   Mes Folles Annees [My Mad Years], Paris: Les Editeurs Francais
Reunis.

1959 Same. Paris: Club des Amis du Livre Progressiste.

Stories and Sketches

1881 Esquisses Americaines de Mark Twain [American Sketches of Mark Twain], Paris: Ollendorff.

1888 Selections from American Humor, Paris: Reinwald. [English]

1888 Esquisses Humoristiques [Humorous Sketches]. Nouvelle Bibliotheque Populaire. Paris: Gauthier.

189-? La Grenouille Sauteuse [The Jumping Frog]. Nouvelle Bibliotheque Populaire. Paris: Gauthier.

1893 Le Vol de l'Elephant Blanc, Comedie en Cinq Tableaux d'apres Mark Twain [The Theft of the White Elephant, Comedy in Five Scenes, after Mark Twain], n.p.: Delhomme et Briguet.

1894 Le Vol de l'Elephant Blanc, Comedie, n.p.: Beauchesne.

1900 Contes Choisis [Selected Stories]. Collection d'Auteurs Etrangers. Paris: Mercure de France.

1900 Same. Collection d'Auteurs Etrangers. [2nd edition] Paris: Mercure de France.

1903 Le Vol de l'Elephant Blanc, Piece en Un Acte, d'apres le Conte de Marc Twain [The Theft of the White Elephant, Play in One Act, after the Story by Mark Twain], n.p.: Levy.

1904 Exploits de Tom Sawyer, Detective, et Autres Nouvelles [Exploits of Tom Sawyer, Detective, and Other Short Stories]. Collection d' Auteurs Etrangers. Paris: Mercure de France.

1905 Un Pari de Milliardaires et Autres Nouvelles [A Bet of Billions and Other Short Stories]. Collection d'Auteurs Etrangers. [4th edition] Paris: Mercure de France.

1907 Plus Fort que Sherlock Holmes, Suivi de 7 Contes [More Clever than Sherlock Holmes, followed by 7 Stories], Paris: Mercure de France.

1907 Same. Collection d'Auteurs Etrangers. [2nd edition] Paris: Mercure de France.

1909 Le Capitaine Tempete et Autres Contes [Captain Storm and Other Stories]. Collection d'Auteurs Etrangers. Paris: Mercure de France.

1910 Le Cultivateur de Chicago, ou How I Became the Editor of Un [sic] Agricultural Paper, Comedie en Deux Actes Tiree d'Une Nouvelle de Mark Twain [The Farmer of Chicago, or How I Became the Editor of An Agricultural Paper, Comedy in Two Acts Drawn from a Short Story by Mark Twain], n.p.: Ondet.

1910? Contes Choisis, Paris, N.Y.: Nelson.

1910 Le Legs de 30.000 Dollars, et Autres Contes [The 30,000 Dollar
      Bequest, and Other Stories], Paris: Mercure de France.

1910 Les Peterkins, et Autres Contes [The Peterkins, and Other Stories].
      Collection d'Auteurs Etrangers. [13th edition] Paris: Mercure
      de France.

1919 Le Legs de 30.000 Dollars, et Autres Contes. [5th edition] Paris:
      Mercure de France.

1922 Le Journal d'Eve, suivi du Journal d'Adam [The Diary of Eve, follow-
      ed by the Diary of Adam], n.p.: Delachaux et Niestle.

1922 Contes Choisis, Paris, N.Y.: Nelson.

1924 Plus Fort que Sherlock Holmes. Collection d'Auteurs Etrangers.
      [14th edition]. Paris: Mercure de France.

1925 Exploits de Tom Sawyer, Detective, et Autres Nouvelles. Collection
      d'Auteurs Etrangers. [11th edition] Paris: Mercure de France.

1925 Contes Choisis. Collection Nelson. Paris-Londres-Edinbourg-New
      York: Nelson.

1930 Le Legs de 30.000 Dollars, et Autres Contes. Collection d'Auteurs
      Etrangers. [8th edition] Paris: Mercure de France.

1932 Mark Twain's 1601; or, Fireside Conversation in the Time of Queen
      Elizabeth, Paris: W.L. Root. [English]

1938 Le Vol de l'Elephant Blanc, Piece en 2 Actes de'apres Une Nouvelle
      du Celebre Humoriste Americain Mark Twain [The Theft of the White
      Elephant, Play in 2 Acts after A Short Story of the Celebrated
      American Humorist Mark Twain], Paris: Vaubaillon.

1945 Plus Fort que Sherlock Holmes. Editions N.R.B. Paris: Mercure de
      France.

1946 Contes Choisis, Paris: Mercure de France.

1946 Douze Contes [Twelve Stories], Paris: Editions du Pavois.

1947 Un Pari de Milliardaires et Autres Nouvelles, Paris: Mercure de
      France.

1949 Contes Choisis, Paris: Societe Francaise d'Imprimerie et de
      Librairie.

1954 Un Pari de Milliardaire, Paris: Mercure de France.

1955 Contes de Mark Twain. Collection Oeuvres Celebres pour la Jeunesse.
      Paris: Nathan.

1955 Dix-Neuf Contes de Mark Twain [Nineteen Stories of Mark Twain].
      Collection Fiction,28. Paris: Club des Librairies de France.

1958 Six Comic Tales. Collection Anglo-Americaine. Paris: Hatier.
      [English]

1958 The Stolen White Elephant and Other Comic Tales. Collection Anglo-
      Americaine. Paris: Hatier. [English]

1958 Tom Sawyer Detective, suivi de: Le Rapt de l'Elephant Blanc [Tom
      Sawyer Detective, followed by: The Abduction of the White Ele-
      phant]. Collection Vogue. Paris: Editions de la Rue des Carmes.

1958 Same. Collection Cristal. Paris: Fabbri.

1959 Same. Collection Vogue. Paris: Editions de la Rue des Carmes.

1960 The Stolen White Elephant and Other Comic Tales. Collection Anglo-
      Americaine. Paris: Hatier. [English]

1962 Un Pari de Milliardaire [adaptation]. Theatre de la Jeunesse Claude
      Santelli. Paris: Radiodiffusion Television Francaise. Edition
      Les Yeux Ouverts.

1962 "1601." Conversation, As It Was by the Social Fireside in the Time
      of the Tudors, Paris: Brentano's. [English]

1962 Contes Choisis, Paris: Mercure de France.

1963 Same. Paris: Mercure de France.

1966 La Celebre Grenouille Sauteuse et Autres Contes [The Celebrated
      Jumping Frog and Other Stories]. Collection Nouveaux Horizons.
      Paris: Seghers.

1967 Tom Sawyers [sic] Detective, suivi de Le Rapt de l'Elephant Blanc.
      Collection Livre-club J. Paris: O.D.E.G.E.

1969 Contes Choisis, Paris: Le Livre de Poche.

1970 Andree Philippe, Contes Humoristiques Anglo-Saxons, Paris: Editions
      de l'Erable.

Tom Sawyer

1876? Les Aventures de Tom Sawyer [The Adventures of Tom Sawyer]. Biblio-
      theque Nouvelle de la Jeunesse. Paris: Hennuyer.

1884 Same. Paris: Hennuyer.

1926 Same. Elbeuf: Duval.

1926 Tom Sawyer. La Joie de Nos Enfants. Paris: Les Oeuvres Repre-
      sentatives.

1927? Les Aventures de Tom Sawyer. Collection La Joie de Nos Enfants.
      Paris: Les Arts et le Livre.

1936 Same. Elbeuf-Paris: Duval.

1938 Tom Sawyer. Bibliotheque de la Jeunesse. Paris: Hachette.

1946 Les Aventures de Tom Sawyer, Paris: Editions Hier et Aujourd'hui.

1947 Same. Collection Charmes de Jeunes. Paris: Istra.

1947 The Adventures of Tom Sawyer. The Albatross Continental Library,
      Vol. 1622. London, Paris, Verona: Mondadori. [English]

1948 Tom Sawyer. Collection Bibliotheque Verte. Paris: Hachette.

1948 Same. Bibliotheque de la Jeunesse. Paris: Hachette.

1948 Les Aventures de Tom Sawyer. Collection Les Heures Claires. Paris:
      Hazan.

1949 Same. Paris: Hazan.

1950 Same. Paris: Hazan.

1950 Same. Elbeuf-Paris: Duval.

1950 Tom Sawyer. Le Club Francais du Livre. Aventures. Paris: Le Club
      Francais du Livre.

1950 Same. Paris: Le Club Francais du Livre.

1953 Same. Collection Juventa. Paris: Delagrave.

1953 Same. [Tom Sawyer's School Days]. Bibliotheque Juventa. Paris:
      Delagrave.

1953 Some Adventures of Tom Sawyer. The Rainbow Library. Paris: Didier.
      [English]

1955 Les Aventures de Tom Sawyer. Collection Mille Episodes. Paris:
      Editions La Farandole.

1958 Tom Sawyer. Collection Excellence. Paris: Bias.

1960 Les Aventures de Tom Sawyer, Paris: Mercure de France.

1960 Same. Club des Jeunes Amis du Livre. Paris: Compagnie des
      Librairies et Editeurs Associes.

1961 Same. Les Ecrivains Celebres. Le Realisme. Mark Twain. Edi-
      tions d'Art. Paris: Mazenod.

1962 Tom Sawyer. Bibliotheque Juventa. Paris: Delagrave.

1962   Les Aventures de Tom Sawyer. Bibliotheque Rouge et Or. Serie Sou-
       veraine. Paris: Editions G.P.

1963   Same. Collection Nouveaux Horizons. Paris-Strasbourg: Istra.

1963   Same. Collection Les Ecrivains Celebres. Paris: Mazenod.

1965   Same. Les Amis du Club International du Livre. Paris: Ambassade
       du Livre.

1965   Les Aventures de Tom Sawyer; Le Prince et le Pauvre; Les Aventures
       de Hick Finn. Collection Trois en Un. Pour la Jeunesse. Paris:
       Hachette.

1966   Les Aventures de Tom Sawyer. Les Grands Classiques Illustres.
       Paris: Editions Mondiales. Bologne: Steb.

1966   Same. [adaptation]   Collection Les Grands Classiques Illustres.
n.p.: Del Duca.

1968   Same. Paris: Nouvel Office d'Edition.

1968? Same. Paris: O.D.E.G.E.

1969   Same. Paris: Hachette.

1969   Same. Paris: Editions G.P.

1969   Same. Le Medallion. Paris: Mercure de France.

1970   Tom Sawyer, Paris: Delagrave.

1972   Tom Sawyer [abridged],Paris: Charpentier.

1973   Les Aventures de Tom Sawyer, Paris: Galliward.

1973   Same. Paris: Hachette.

1975   Same. Paris: Diffusion F. Beauval. Neuilly-sur-Seine: Saint-Clair.

1975   Tom Sawyer, Paris: Charpentier.

Tom Sawyer Abroad

1935   Tom Sawyer a Travers le Monde [Tom Sawyer through the World].
       Collection des Maitres de la Litterature Etrangere. Paris:
       Michel.

Tom Sawyer, Detective

1904   Exploits de Tom Sawyer, Detective, et Autres Nouvelles [Exploits
       of Tom Sawyer, Detective, and Other Short Stories]. Collection
       d'Auteurs Etrangers. Paris: Mercure de France.

1925 Same. Collection d'Auteurs Etrangers. [11th edition] Paris: Mercure de France.

1958 Tom Sawyer Detective, suivi de: Le Rapt de l'Elephant Blanc [Tom Sawyer Detective, followed by: The Abduction of the White Elephant]. Collection Vogue. Paris: Editions de la Rue des Carmes.

1958 Same. Collection Cristal. Paris: Fabbri.

1959 Same. Collection Vogue. Paris: Editions de la Rue des Carmes.

1959 Tom Sawyer Detective. Collection Cristal. Paris: Fabbri.

1964 Same. [adaptation]. Collection Les Romans du Livre d'Or. Paris: Editions des Deux Coqs d'Or.

1967 Same. (Dans: Scott, S.W., Ivanhoe). Paris: Editions des Deux Coqs d'Or.

1967 Tom Sawyers [sic] Detective, suivi de Le Rapt de l'Elephant Blanc. Collection Livre-club J. Paris: Odegepresse.

Germany

Sources: ABL/BAL/BN/CGBN/CPL/DB/ECB/HV/IT/JDS/LC/MTG/NUC/SB/SBV/SLVS/UnG/ UnI/UnS/VBL/ZBZ

American Claimant

1892 The American Claimant. Collection of British Authors, Nr. 2863. Leipsic: Tauchnitz. [English]

1892 Der Amerikanische Pratendent. Roman, Stuttgart: Anstalt.

Autobiography

1969 Autobiographie. Edited Charles Neider. Fischer-Bucherei, Nr. 1021. Frankfurt: Fischer.

Captain Stormfield

1910 Extract from Captain Stormfield's Visit to Heaven and Is Shakespeare Dead? Collection of British Authors, Nr. 4209. Copyright Edition. Leipsic: Tauchnitz. [English]

1954 Kapitan Stormfields Besuch im Himmel, Berlin: Aufbau.

1963 Same. In Tot oder Lebendig. Siebzehn Erzahlungen. Fischer-Bucherei. Frankfurt: Fischer.

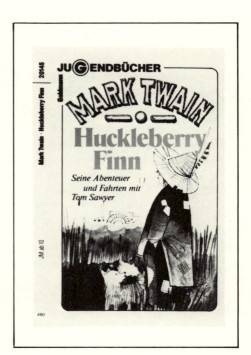

Fig. 24. *Huckleberry Finn. Seine Abenteuer und Fahrten mit Tom Sawyer*, cover of 1962 German edition published by Goldmann (Courtesy Goldmann Publisher [Munich])

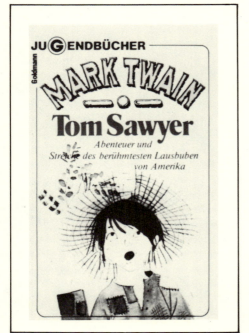

Fig. 25. *Tom Sawyer. Abenteuer und Streiche des berühmtesten Lausbuben von Amerika.* Cover of 1961 German edition published by Goldmann (Courtesy Goldmann Publisher [Munich])

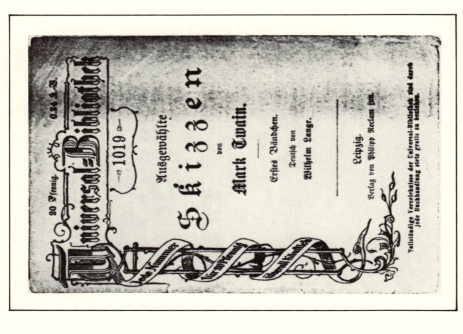

Fig. 27. *Ausgewählte Skizzen von Mark Twain,* title page of 1878 German edition published by Philipp Reclam (Courtesy Philipp Reclam Jun [Leipzig])

Mark Twain

Der berühmte
Springfrosch
der Provinz Calaveras

Reclam

Fig. 26. *Der berühmte Springfrosch der Provinz Calaveras,* cover of 1962 German edition published by Philipp Reclam Jun (Courtesy Philipp Reclam Jun [Stuttgart])

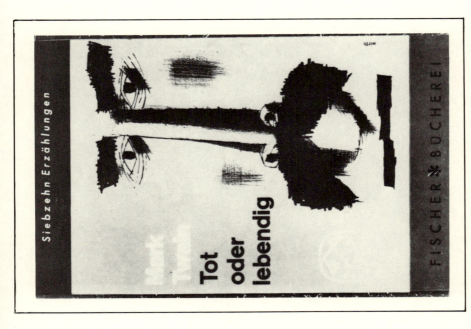

Fig. 28. *Tot oder Lebendig*, cover of 1961 German edition published by Fischer (Courtesy of S. Fischer Publisher [Frankfurt and Hamburg])

Christian Science

1907   Christian Science. With Notes Containing Corrections to Date.
        Collection of British Authors, Nr. 3979. Leipsic: Tauchnitz.
        [English]

Connecticut Yankee

1890   A Yankee at the Court of King Arthur. Collection of British
        Authors, Nr. 2638-39. Leipsic: Tauchnitz. [English]

1948   Ein Yankee am Hofe des Konigs Artus. Satirischer Roman [A Yankee
        at the Court of King Arthur. Satirical Novel]. Janus-Bibliotek
        der Weltliteratur. Stuttgart: Hatje.

1952   Ein Yankee an Konig Artus' Hof [A Yankee at King Arthur's Court].
        Romane der Weltliteratur. Berlin: Aufbau.

1953   Same. Romane der Weltliteratur. [2nd edition]. Berlin: Aufbau.

1954   Same. Romane der Weltliteratur. [3rd edition]. Berlin: Aufbau.

1954   Same. Dusseldorf: Progress.

1956   Same. Dusseldorf. Progress.

1956   Ein Yankee am Hofe des Konigs Artus. Roman, Frankfurt, Wien:
        Forum.

1957   Ein Yankee an Konig Artus' Hof. Romane der Weltliteratur. Berlin:
        Aufbau.

1957   Same. Dusseldorf: Progress.

1958   A Connecticut Yankee in King Arthur's Court, Berlin. Seven Seas.
        [English]

1961   Ein Yankee an Konig Artus' Hof, Munchen: Heyne.

1961   Ein Yankee am Hofe des Konigs Artus, Koln: Phaidon.

1970   Ein Yankee aus Connecticut an Konig Artus' Hof. [A Yankee from
        Connecticut at King Arthur's Court]. Fischer-Bucherei, nr. 1087.
        Frankfurt: Fischer.

1971   Same. Frankfurt-am-Main: Fischer-Bucherei.

1973   Same. Frankfurt-am-Main: Fischer-Taschenbuch.

1974   Same. Frankfurt-am-Main: Fischer-Taschenbuch.

1974   Ein Yankee an Konig Artus' Hof, Berlin: Neues Leben.

1974   Ramon de La Fuente, Hank Morgan am Hofe Konig Arthurs. [from the
        Spanish Un Yanqui en la Corte del Rey Arturo].Nurnberg: Schwager &
        Steinlein.

1975   Ein Yankee aus Connecticut an Konig Artus' Hof, Frankfurt-am-Main:
       Fischer-Taschenbuch.

Following the Equator

1897   More Tramps Abroad. Collection of British Authors, nr. 3252-3253.
       Leipsic: Tauchnitz. [English]

1965   Dem Aquator Nach [Past the Equator], Hamburg: Hoffman und Campe.

Gilded Age

1876   Das Vergoldete Zeitalter. Roman [The Gilded Age. Novel]. In
       Amerikanische Humoristen, Bd. 6-7. Leipzig: Grunow.

Huckleberry Finn

1885   The Adventures of Huckleberry Finn (Tom Sawyer's Comrade). Collec-
       tion of British Authors, Nr. 2307-2308. Authorized Edition.
       Leipsic: Tauchnitz. [English]

1890   Die Abenteuer und Fahrten des Huckleberry Finn [The Adventures
       and Journeys of Huckleberry Finn]. Sternbanner-Serie, Bd. 8.
       Amerikanische Humoristen und Novellisten. Stuttgart: Lutz.

1899   Same. Eisenbahn-Ausgabe [Railroad Edition]. Stuttgart: Lutz.

1902   Die Abenteuer Huckleberry Finns (des Kamaraden von Tom Sawyer)
       [The Adventures of Huckleberry Finn (the Comrade of Tom Sawyer)].
       Bibliothek der Gesamtliteratur des In-und-Auslandes [Library of
       All Literature of Home and Abroad], Nr. 1577-1579. Halle: Hendel.

1904   Huckleberry Finns Fahrten und Abenteuer. Jugendausgabe [Youth Edi-
       tion]. Mark Twains Humoristische Schriften fur die Jugend [Mark
       Twain's Humorous Writings for the Young]. Stuttgart: Lutz.

1909   Die Abenteuer Huckleberry Finns, des Kameraden von Tom Sawyer,
       Berlin: Weichert.

1913   Die Abenteuer des Tom Sawyer und Huckleberry Finn, Strassburg and
       Leipzig: Singer.

1914   Tom Sawyers Abenteuer und Streiche. Huckleberry Finns Abenteuer
       und Fahrten [Tom Sawyer's Adventures and Pranks. Huckleberry Finn's
       Adventures and Travels]. Romane der Weltliteratur. Leipzig:
       Hesse & Becker.

1920   Huckleberry Finns Abenteuer und Fahrten. Romane der Weltliteratur.
       Leipzig: Hesse & Becker.

1921   Huckleberry Finns Fahrten und Abenteuer, Berlin: Ullstein.

1922 Die Abenteuer Tom Sawyers und Huckleberry Finns (des Kameraden von
      Tom Sawyer). Meistererzahler der Weltliteratur, Bd. 12. Berlin:
      Lehmann & Fink.

1925 Die Streiche Tom Sawyers und Huckleberry Finns [The Pranks of Tom
      Sawyer and Huckleberry Finn]. Veroffentlichungen der Deutschen
      Buchgemeinschaft [Publications of the German Book Community], Bd.
      79. Berlin: Deutsche Buchgemeinschaft.

1925 Die Abenteuer Huckleberry Finns (des Kameraden von Tom Sawyer),
      Berlin: Maschler.

192-? Die Abenteuer des Huckleberry Finn, Berlin: Maschler.

1926 Huckleberry Finns Abenteuer und Fahrten. Die Schatzkammer [The
      Treasury series], Bd. 47. Leipzig: Hesse & Becker.

1927 Die Abenteuer des Tom Sawyer und Huckleberry Finn. Zenith-Bucherei.
      Leipzig: Zenith.

1930? Same. Berlin: Dressler.

1930 Same. Leipzig: Hesse & Becker.

1931 Huck Finns Fahrten und Abenteuer. Jugendausgabe [Youth Edition].
      Mark Twains Humoristische Schriften fur die Jugend. [6th edition]
      Stuttgart: Lutz.

1936 Die Abenteuer des Tom Sawyer und Huckleberry Finn, Berlin: Williams.

1938 [Huckleberry Finn], Berlin: Deutscher Verlagsbuchhandlung.

1939 [Huckleberry Finn], Potsdam: Voggenreiter.

1940 [Huckleberry Finn], Stuttgart: Lutz.

1940? Huckleberry Finn, Ein Mississippi-roman [Huckleberry Finn, A
      Mississippi Novel], Potsdam: Voggenreiter.

1943 Die Abenteuer des Huckleberry Finn, Baden-Baden: Hebel.

1943 [Huckleberry Finn], n.p.: Volk und Reich.

1948 Die Abenteuer des Huckleberry Finn, Baden-Baden: Hebel.

1949 Same. Baden-Baden: Hebel.

1950 Huckleberry Finn. Seine Fahrten und Abenteuer [Huckleberry Finn.
      His Journeys and Adventures], Worpswede: Reitze.

1951 Huckleberry Finn. Fahrten und Abenteuer, Heidelberg: Kemper.

1951 Huckleberry Finn. Eine Mississippi-Erzahlung [Huckleberry Finn.
      A Mississippi Story], Reutlingen: Ensslin & Laiblin.

1951 Tom Sawyer und Huckleberry Finn. Abenteuer am Mississippi [Tom Sawyer and Huckleberry Finn. Adventure on the Mississippi], Reutlingen: Ensslin & Laiblin.

1952 Die Abenteuer des Huckleberry Finn, Rudolstadt: Greifen.

1952 Same. Trier, Munchen: Droemer.

1952 Huckleberry Finn. Ill. Klassiker [Illustrated Classics]. 3. Rudolstadt, Frankfurt: T.I.

1953 Same. Ill. Klassiker. 4. Rudolstadt, Frankfurt: T.I.

1954 Wir Befreien Jim [We Liberate Jim]. [extracted from Huckleberry Finn]. Frische: Saat.

1954 Tom Sawyer und Huckleberry Finn. Fahrten und Abenteuer, Hamburg: Reitze.

1954 Huckleberry Finn, Koln: Agrippina.

1955 Same. Koln: Kolner Jugendbuchverleger.

1955 Same. Hamburg, Berlin: Hausberei.

1955 Die Abenteuer des Huckleberry Finn, Berlin: Neues Leben.

1956 Huckleberry Finn. [extract] Koln: Atlas.

1956 Die Abenteuer des Tom Sawyer und Huckleberry Finn, Berlin: Deutsche Buch-Gemeinschaft.

1956 Huckleberry Finns Abenteuer. Sammlung Dieterich, Bd.194. Leipzig: Dieterich.

1956 Die Abenteuer des Huckleberry Finn, Stuttgart: Bluchert.

1957 Same. [3rd edition] Berlin: Neues Leben.

1958 Same. [7th edition] Munchen: Droemer/Knaur.

1958 Tom Sawyers Abenteuer. Die Abenteuer des Huckleberry Finn. [extracts] Gottingen: Fischer.

1958 The Adventures of Huckleberry Finn, Berlin: Seven Seas. [English]

1959 Huckleberry Finns Abenteuer. [2nd edition] Leipzig: Dieterich.

1959 Die Abenteuer des Huckleberry Finn, Wiesbaden: Agrippina.

1960 Same. Kompassbucherei, Bd. 11. Berlin: Neues Leben.

1960 Same. Wiesbaden: Agrippina.

1960? Tom Sawyer und Huckleberry Finn, Hamburg: Reitze.

1962 Huckeberry Finns Abenteuer und Fahrten. Goldmanns Gelbe Taschen-
     bucher. Munchen: Goldmann.

1963 Huckleberry Finn, Stuttgart: Boje.

1964? Die Abenteuer des Huckleberry Finn, Gutersloh: Bertelsmann Leser-
      ing.

1964 Same. Buchgemeinschafts-Ausgabe. Gutersloh: Mohn. Bertelsmann.

1964 Die Abenteuer des Tom Sawyer und Huckleberry Finn, Stuttgart:
     Deutsche Bucherbund.

1964 Die Abenteuer von Tom Sawyer und Huckleberry Finn, Hanau: Dausien.

1965 Die Abenteuer des Huckleberry Finn, Gottingen: Fischer.

1965 Tom Sawyers Abenteuer. Die Abenteuer des Huckleberry Finn,
     Gottingen: Fischer.

1966 Tom Sawyer. Huckleberry Finn, Frankfurt: Buchergilde Gutenberg.
     Hannover: Fackeltrager.

1968 Huckleberry Finns Fahrten und Abenteuer, Frankfurt: Ullstein.

1968 Die Abenteuer des Huckleberry Finn. Ravensburger Taschenbucher.
     Bd. 103. [2nd edition] Ravensburg: Maier.

1969 Same. Munchen: Heyne.

1969 Huckleberry Finns Abenteuer, Wurzburg: Arena.

1969 Huckleberry Finn, Stuttgart: Spectrum.

1970 Same. Balve/Westfalen: Engelbert.

1970 Same. [13th edition] Reutlingen: Ensslin & Laiblin.

1970 Die Abenteuer des Huckleberry Finn. [4th edition] Ravensburg:
     Maier.

197-? Die Abenteuer des Huckleberry Finn [von] Mark Twain, Berlin:
      Maschler.

1971 Tom Sawyer und Huckleberry Finn, Balve (Westfallen): Englebert.

1971 Same. Stuttgart: Spectrum.

1971 Die Abenteuer des Huckleberry Finn, Freiburg im Breisgau: Herder.

1971 Die Abenteuer des Tom Sawyer und Huckleberry Finn. Sonderausgabe
     [Special Edition]. Munchen: Sudwest.

1972 Huckleberry Finn: Eine Mississippi-Erzahlung [Huckleberry Finn:
     A Mississippi Tale]. [20th edition] Reutlingen: Ensslin &
     Laiblin.

1972 Die Abenteuer des Huckleberry Finn. Neuausgabe [New Edition]
      Gottingen: Fischer.

1973 Same. [5th edition] Ravensburg: Maier.

1973 Die Abenteuer des Tom Sawyer und Huckleberry Finn, Munchen:
      Droemer-Knaur.

1973 Tom Sawyer und Huckleberry Finn: Abenteuer am Mississippi.
      [14th edition] Reutlingen: Ensslin & Laiblin.

1974 Die Abenteuer des Huckleberry Finn. [extract] [6th edition]
      Ravensburg: Maier.

1974 Tom Sawyer. Huckleberry Finn, Berlin: Neues Leben.

1974 Huckleberry Finns Abenteuer, Berlin: Buchclub 65.

1975 Same. Frankfurt-am-Main: Insel: Suhrkamp-Taschenbuch.

1975 Same. Leipzig: Reclam.

1975 Die Abenteuer des Huckleberry Finn. [7th edition] Ravensburg:
      Maier.

1975 Huckleberry Finn: Seine Abenteuer und Fahrten mit Tom Sawyer
      [Huckleberry Finn: His Adventures and Travels with Tom Sawyer],
      Munchen: Goldmann.

1975 Tom Sawyer. Huckleberry Finn, Freiburg im Breisgau: Herder.

1976 Same. [2nd edition] Freiburg im Breisgau: Herder.

1976 Same. [2nd edition] Berlin: Neues Leben.

1976 Die Abenteuer des Huckleberry Finn. [8th edition] Ravensburg:
      Maier.

1976 Tom Sawyers Abenteuer. Huckleberry Finns Abenteuer, Munchen:
      Deutscher Taschenbuch.

1976 Huckleberry Finn: Eine Mississippi Erzahlung, Reutlingen: Ensslin
      & Laiblin.

1976 Huckleberry Finn, Heidelberg: Ueberreuter.

                        Innocents Abroad

1875 Die Arglosen auf Reisen [The Unsuspecting on A Journey]. In
      Amerikanische Humoristen, Bd. 4. Leipzig: Grunow.

1875 Die Neue Pilgerfahrt [The New Pilgrim Journey]. In Amerikanische
      Humoristen, Bd. 5. Leipzig: Grunow.

1879 The Innocents Abroad, or, The New Pilgrims' Progress. Author's
Edition. Collection of British Authors, Nr. 1812-1813. Leipsic:
Tauchnitz. [English]

1924 Bummel durch das Mittelmeer [Loafing through the Mediterranean].
Die Lustigen Bucher. Bd. VI. Leipzig: Stephenson.

1964? Reise durch die Alte Welt [Journey through the Old World], Hamburg:
Hoffmann und Campe.

1965? Same. [2nd edition]. Hamburg: Hoffmann und Campe.

1968 Same. [3rd edition]. Hamburg: Hoffman und Campe

1972 Die Arglosen im Ausland; Reiseabenteuer in der Alten Welt [The
Unsuspecting Abroad; Travel Adventures in the Old World], Frankfurt-am-Main: Fischer Taschenbuch.

Joan of Arc

1896 Personal Recollections of Joan of Arc... Collection of British
Authors, Nr. 3138-3139. Leipsic: Tauchnitz. [English]

1970 Personliche Errinnerungen an Jeanne d'Arc [Personal Recollections
of Joan of Arc], Munchen: Deutscher Taschenbuch.

King Leopold's Soliloquy

1961 King Leopold's Soliloquy. Seven Seas Books. Berlin: Seven Seas.
[English]

1961 Konig Leopolds Selbstgesprach. Eine Verteidigung Seiner Herrschaft
im Kongo [King Leopold's Soliloquy. A Defense of His Dominion
in the Congo], Berlin: Tribune.

Letters from the Earth

1969 Briefe von der Erde [Letters from the Earth], Munchen: Deutscher
Taschenbuch.

Life on the Mississippi

1883 Life on the Mississippi. Collection of British Authors, Nr. 2143-
2144. Leipsic: Tauchnitz. [English]

1888 Leben auf dem Mississippi [Life on the Mississippi]. Sternbanner-
Serie: Amerikanische Humoristen und Novellisten, Bd.V. Stuttgart:
Lutz.

1948 Auf dem Mississippi [On the Mississippi]. Lux-Jugend-Lesebogen,
33. Murnau-Munchen: Lux.

1949 Leben auf dem Mississippi, Wiesbaden: Kesselringsche Verlagsbuch-
      handlung.

1956 Life on the Mississippi. Englisch-Amerikanische Bibliothek, Bd. 7.
      Halle: Niemeyer. [English]

1957 Leben auf dem Mississippi, Berlin: Aufbau.

1961 Old Times on the Mississippi, Frankfurt, Berlin, Bonn: Diesterweg.
      [English]

1963 Leben auf dem Mississippi - Im Gold-und Silberland [Life on the
      Mississippi-in Gold-and Silver Land]. Goldmanns Gelbe Taschen-
      bucher, Bd. 968. Munchen: Goldmann.

1965? Leben auf dem Mississippi, Balve: Engelbert.

1969 Same. Berlin: Neues Leben.

1969 Same. Recklinghausen: Bitter.

1973 Als Lotse an dem Mississippi [As Pilot on the Mississippi], Heidel-
      berg: Ueberreuter.

Man That Corrupted Hadleyburg

1900 The Man That Corrupted Hadleyburg, and Other Stories and Sketches.
      Copyright Edition. Collection of British Authors, Nr. 3453-3454.
      Leipsic: Tauchnitz. [English]

1900 Querkopf Wilson. Wie die Stadt Hadleyburg Verderbt Wurde. Zwei
      Erzahlungen [Crank Wilson. How the Town of Hadleyburg Was Corrupt-
      ed. Two Stories], Stuttgart: Lutz.

Mysterious Stranger

1921 Der Geheimnisvolle Fremde. Eine Phantasie [The Mysterious Stranger.
      A Phantasy], Leipzig: Insel.

1958 Der Geheimnisvolle Fremde, Berlin: Aufbau.

Prince and the Pauper

1881 The Prince and the Pauper. A Tale for Young People of All Ages.
      Authorized Edition. Collection of British Authors, Nr. 2027-2028.
      Leipsic: Tauchnitz. [English]

1887 Furst und Bettler [Prince and Beggar], Konstanz: Deutschen Heimat.

1890 Der Prinz und der Betteljunge. Eine Erzahlung fur die Jugend jeden
      Alters und Geschlechts [The Prince and the Young Beggar. A Story
      for the Young of Every Age and Sex], Giessen: Ricker.

1895 The Prince and the Pauper. Vocabulary. [school edition] Berlin:
      Gartner. [English]

1895 The Prince and the Pauper, Berlin: Heyfelder. [English]

1901 The Prince and the Pauper. Vocabulary [school edition]. [2nd
      edition] Berlin: Gartner. [English]

1901 The Prince and the Pauper. Vocabulary [school edition]. English
      Library. Vol. 34. Dresden: Kuhtmann. [English]

1905 Prinz und Bettelknabe. Eine Erzahlung fur die Reifere Jugend
      [Prince and Beggar Boy. A Story for the Mature Youth]. Loewes
      Jugend-Bucher. Stuttgart: Loewes.

1905 Prinz und Bettler [Prince and Beggar], Leipzig: Spanner.

1908 Same. [2nd issue] Leipzig: Spanner.

1909 The Prince and the Pauper. Vocabulary [school edition]. [3rd
      edition] Berlin: Gartner. [English]

1910 Prinz und Bettelknabe.... Loewes Jugend-Bucher. [3rd edition].
      Stuttgart: Loewes.

1911 Prinz und Bettler. [3rd issue] Leipzig: Spanner.

1913 The Prince and the Pauper. Abridged edition [school edition].
      Leipsic: Freytag. Vienna: Tempsky. [English]

1914 The Prince and the Pauper [school edition], Bielefeld & Leipsic:
      Velhagen & Klasing. [English]

1919 Same. [2nd edition] Bielefeld & Leipsic: Velhagen & Klasing.
      [English]

1921 Prinz und Bettelknabe. Eine Erzahlung fur die Reifere Jugend.
      [4th edition] Stuttgart: Loewes.

1926 The Prince and the Pauper. Vocabulary [school edition]. [4th
      edition] Berlin: Gartner. [English]

1927 Prinz und Bettelknabe. Eine Erzahlung fur die Reifere Jugend.
      [6th edition] Stuttgart: Loewes.

1937 Same. Loewes Jugend-Bucher. [12th edition] Stuttgart: Loewes.

1948 Der Konig und der Betteljunge [The King and the Young Beggar].
      Internationale Jugendschriften. Meitingen: Kyrios.

1952 Prinz und Bettelknabe. Abenteuer in Vertauschten Rollen. [Prince
      and Beggar Boy. Adventure in Exchanged Roles], Heidelberg: Kemper.

1956 Prinz und Betteljunge, Munchen: Obpacher.

1957 Prinz und Bettelknabe, Stuttgart: Loewes.

1957 Same. Ill. Klassiker. Rudolstadt: T.I.

1957 Prinz und Bettelknabe. Eine Erzahlung fur Grosse und Kleine Leute.
      [Prince and Beggar Boy. A Story for Big and Little People]. [2nd
      edition] Berlin: Kinderbuchverlegen.

1962 The Prince and the Pauper, Dortmund: Lensing. [English]

1963 Der Prinz und der Bettelknabe, Stuttgart: Spectrum.

1964 Der Prinz und Betteljunge, Ravensburg: Maier.

1966 Der Prinz und der Bettlerknabe. [6th edition] Berlin: Kinderbuch-
      verlegen.

1966? Same. Stuttgart, Hamburg: Deutsche Bucherbund.

1968 Prinz und Betteljunge. [3rd edition] Ravensburg: Maier.

1970 Prinz und Bettelknabe, Dusseldorf: Hoch.

1970 Same. Stuttgart: Deutsche Bucherbund.

1971 Der Prinz und der Bettelknabe, Berlin: Aufbau.

1971 Prinz und Betteljunge. [5th edition] Ravensburg: Maier.

1972 Same. [6th edition] Ravensburg: Maier.

1973 Prinz und Bettelknabe, Stuttgart: Boje.

1974 Der Prinz und Bettlerknabe. [2nd Edition] Stuttgart: Spectrum.

1975 Prinz und Bettelknabe, Munchen: Deutscher Taschenbuch.

1976 Same. [2nd Edition] Munchen: Deutscher Taschenbuch.

                              Pudd'nhead Wilson

1895 Pudd'nhead Wilson. A Tale. Collection of British Authors, nr.
      3039. Leipsic: Tauchnitz. [English]

1898 Der Querkopf Wilson. Roman [The Crank Wilson. Novel]. Sammlung
      Ausgewahlter Kriminal-und Detektiv-Romane [Choice Collection of
      Criminal-and Detective-Novels]. Bd. 19. Stuttgart: Lutz.

1899 Same. Stuttgart: Lutz.

1900 Querkopf Wilson. Wie die Stadt Hadleyburg Verderbt Wurde. Zwei
      Erzahlungen [Crank Wilson. How the Town of Hadleyburg Was Corrupted.
      Two Stories], Stuttgart: Lutz.

1901 Der Querkopf Wilson. Roman. Sammlung Ausgewahlter Kriminal- und
      Detektiv-Romane. [2nd edition] Stuttgart: Lutz.

1903 Same. Stuttgart: Lutz.

1906 Same. Stuttgart: Lutz.

1907 Same. Stuttgart: Lutz.

1909 Same. Stuttgart: Lutz.

1935 Same. Stuttgart: Lutz.

1966 Querkopf Wilson, Berlin: Neues Leben.

Roughing It

1874 Jim Smileys Beruhmter Springfrosch und Dergleichen Wunderliche
      Kauze Mehr. Im Silberlande Nevada [Jim Smiley's Celebrated Jump-
      ing Frog and More Such Screech-Owls. In Nevada Silver Land].
      Amerikanische Humoristen, Bd. 2 [American Humorists, Vol. 2].
      Leipzig: Grunow.

1880 Roughing It. Collection of British Authors, Nr. 1929. Leipsic:
      Tauchnitz. [English]

1881 The Innocents at Home. Collection of British Authors, nr. 1948.
      Leipsic: Tauchnitz. [English]

1900 Im Gold-und Silberland [In Gold-and Silver-land]. Eisenbahn-
      Ausgabe [Railroad Edition]. 8. Stuttgart: Lutz.

1900 Leben auf dem Mississippi. Nach dem Fernen Westen [Life on the
      Mississippi. To the Far West]. Eisenbahn-Ausgabe. Stuttgart:
      Lutz.

1922 Durch Dick und Dunn [Through Thick and Thin], Berlin: Ullstein.

1929 Roughing It, Leipsic: Tauchnitz. [English]

1963 Leben auf dem Mississippi. Im Gold- und Silberland. Goldmanns
      Gelbe Taschenbucher. Bd. 968. Munchen: Goldmann.

1973 Durch Dick und Dunn, Berlin: Neues Leben.

Stories and Sketches

1874 Jim Smileys Beruhmter Springfrosch und Dergleichen Wunderliche
      Kauze Mehr. Im Silberlande Nevada [Jim Smiley's Celebrated Jumping
      Frog and More Such Strange Screech-Owls. In Nevada Silver Land].
      In Amerikanische Humoristen, Bd. 2 [American Humorists, Vol.2].
      Leipzig: Grunow.

1877 Skizzenbuch [Sketchbook]. Amerikanische Humoristen, Bd. 12.
      Leipzig: Grunow.

1878 Ausgewahlte Skizzen [Selected Sketches]. Universal-Bibliothek,
      Nr. 1019, 1079, 1149, 2072, 2954, 3749. Leipzig: Reclam.

1882 The Stolen White Elephant and Other Stories. Collection of
      British Authors, nr. 2077. Leipsic: Tauchnitz. [English]

1883 Sketches New and Old. Collection of British Authors, nr. 2162.
      Leipsic: Tauchnitz. [English]

1886 Unterwegs und Daheim. Neue Sammlung Humoristischer Skizzen [On the
      Way and at Home. New Collection of Humorous Sketches]. Stern-
      banner-Serie, Bd. 2. Stuttgart: Lutz.

1886 Selections from American Humour. Authorized Edition. Collection
      of British Authors, nr. 2529. Leipsic: Tauchnitz. [English]

1889 Ausgewahlte Skizzen. Universal-Bibliothek, Nr. 2954. Leipzig:
      Reclam.

1890 Same. Leipzig: Reclam.

1890 Heitere Liebesgeschichten. Von Mark Twain, L. Koelle, etc. [Cheer-
      ful Love Stories. By Mark Twain, L. Koelle, etc.]. Zehnpfennig-
      Bibliothek [Ten-penny Library], Nr. 1. Berlin, Leipzig: Bonnier?

1891 Ausgewahlte Skizzen. Universal-Bibliothek. Leipzig: Reclam.

1892 Same. Universal-Bibliothek. Leipzig: Reclam.

1893 The £1.000.000 Bank-Note, and Other New Stories. Collection of
      British Authors, Nr. 2907. Leipsic: Tauchnitz. [English]

1893 Skizzen [Sketches]. Meyers Volksbucher, Nr. 991-995. Leipzig:
      Bibliographisches Institut.

1897 Ausgewahlte Skizzen. Universal-Bibliothek. [6th edition] Leipzig:
      Reclam.

1897 Tom Sawyer, Detective, As Told by Huck Finn, and Other Tales.
      Collection of British Authors, Nr. 3184. Leipsic: Tauchnitz
      [English]

1897 Die Millionenpfundnote. Humoreske [The Million Pound Bank-note.
      Humorous Pieces]. Buchersammlung fur Gabelsberger Stenographie
      [Book Collection for Gabelsberger Stenography]. Nr. 37. Neustadt:
      n. pub.

1897 Die Million-Pfund-Banknote und Andere Erzahlungen [The Million
      Pound Bank-note and Other Stories]. Kurschners Bucherschatz
      [Kurschner's Book Treasure]. Nr. 49. Berlin-Eisenach-Leipzig:
      Hillger.

1899 Skizzenbuch. Eisenbahn-Ausgabe [Railroad-Edition]. Stuttgart:
      Lutz.

1900 The Man That Corrupted Hadleyburg, and Other Stories and Sketches.
      Copyright Edition. Collection of British Authors, nr. 3453-3454.
      Leipsic: Tauchnitz. [English]

1900 Querkopf Wilson. Wie die Stadt Hadleyburg Verderbt Wurde. Zwei
      Erzahlungen [Crank Wilson. How the Town of Hadleyburg Was Corrupted.
      Two Stories], Stuttgart: Lutz.

1901 Adams Tagebuch und Andere Geschichten [Adam's Diary and Other
      Stories], Stuttgart: Lutz.

1901 Erzahlungen und Plaudereien [Stories and Chatters], Leipzig:
      Meners Volksbucher.

1902 A Double-Barrelled Detective Story, Etc. Collection of British
      Authors, nr. 3591. Copyright Edition. Leipsic: Tauchnitz.
      [English]

1903 Des Treulosen Ende [The Faithless End] [A Double-Barrelled Detective
      Story]. Amerikanische Detektiv-Romane, Bd. 28. Berlin: Jakobsthal.

1903 Kipling and Mark Twain. Five Tales. [Mark Twain's "A Restless
      Night" and "A Trip to the Rigi-Kulm"] [school edition] Halle:
      Gesenius. [English]

1905 Die £1,000,000 Pfundnote und Andere Humoristische Erzahlungen und
      Skizzen [The £1,000,000 Bank-note and other Humorous Stories and
      Sketches]. Hesses Volksbucherei, Nr. 226. Leipzig: Hesse &
      Becker.

1905 Tot oder Lebendig. Erzahlungen und Skizzen [Dead or Living.
      Stories and Sketches]. Hesses Volksbucherei, Nr. 237. Leipzig:
      Hesse & Becker.

1907 The $30,000 Bequest, and Other Stories by Mark Twain. Collection
      of British Authors, nr. 3959. Copyright edition. Leipsic: Tauch-
      nitz. [English]

1907 A Double-Barrelled Detective Story. Two Little Tales. The Death
      Disk. A Defense of General Funston. Collection of British Authors.
      Leipsic: Tauchnitz. [English]

1908 Wie Hadleyburg Verderbt Wurde und Andere Erzahlungen, Stuttgart:
      Lutz.

1910 Die Abenteuer Tom Sawyers. Ausgewahlte Skizzen [The Adventures of
      Tom Sawyer. Selected Sketches]. Vereinfachter Deutscher Steno-
      graphie [Simplified German Stenography], System Stolze-Schrey.
      Berlin: n. pub.

1912 Der Beruchtigte (Springende) Frosch der Grafschaft Calaveras und
      Andere Erzahlungen [The Notorious (Jumping) Frog of Calaveras
      County and Other Stories]. 30-Pfennig-Bucherei [30-Pennies-
      Library]. Bd. 14. Leipzig, Berlin: Bonnier:

1912 American Humor. W. Irving: Rip Van Winkle; Bret Harte: Baby
      Sylvester; Mark Twain: How I Edited An Agricultural Paper. [school
      edition] Sammlung Englischer und Franzosischer Autoren [Collection
      of English and French Authors], Bd. 12. Leipsic: Jaeger. [Eng-
      lish]

1916 Sketches. Series 1. English Textbooks, nr. 32. Leipsic: Tauch-
      nitz. [English]

1918 Sketches. Series 2. Tauchnitz Pocket Library, nr. 88. Leipsic:
      Tauchnitz. [English]

1919 Ausgewahlte Skizzen [Selected Sketches]. Universal-Bibliothek.
      6 vols. Vols. 4,6. Leipzig: Reclam.

1920 Die Geschichte der Kapitolinischen Venus und Andere Skizzen [The
      Story of the Capitoline Venus and Other Sketches]. Reclams Auto-
      maten-Bucher, nr. 33. Leipzig: Reclam.

1920 Der Gestohlene Weisse Elefant. Humoreske [The Stolen White Ele-
      phant. Humorous Pieces]. Reclams Automaten-Bucher, nr. 34.
      Leipzig: Reclam.

1923 Tolle Geschichten von Mark Twain [Mad Stories by Mark Twain].
      Berlin: Ullstein.

1924 Mit Heiteren Augen. Geschichten [With Cheerful Eyes. Stories],
      Leipzig: Buchergilde Gutenberg.

1924 Aus Einem Wanderleben. 9 Skizzen [Out of A Travel Life. 9
      Sketches]. Die Kultur, Jg. 2, H. 9, Juni 1924, s. 1-33.

1925 Mark Twain: Meine Uhr [Mark Twain: My Watch]. In Steongraphischer
      Schrift. Kurzschriftliche Ubungschefte, Heft. 2. Berlin: Apitz.

1926 Humoristische Skizzen [Humorous Sketches]. Weltgeist-Bucher, nr.
      127. Berlin: Weltgeist-Bucher.

1927 Humoresken [Humorous Pieces]. Hafis-Lesebucherei, Bd. 27. Leipzig:
      Fikentscher.

1927 Ausgewahlte Skizzen [Selected Sketches]. Bd. 1. Berlin: Buch-
      handlung des Stenographenverbandes Stolze-Schrey.

1928 Ausgewahlte Skizzen [Selected Sketches]. Reclams Universal-Biblio-
      thek, nr. 3749. 6 vols. Vols. 4,6. Leipzig: Reclam.

1928 Lustige Gefahrten - Tolle Sachen. Erzahlungen und Skizzen [Merry
      Companions - Mad Things. Stories and Sketches]. Die Schatzkammer,
      Bd. 147. Leipzig: Hesse & Becker.

1929 Same. Die Schatzkammer, Bd. 147a. Leipzig: Hesse & Becker.

1930 The Death-Disk. [school edition] Diesterwegs Neusprachliche
      Lesehefte, nr. 181. Frankfurt: Diesterweg. [English]

1933 Das Lacheln des Weisen. (Die Schonsten Humoresken der Guten Alten
      Mark Twain) [The Smile of the Wise. (The Finest Humorous Pieces of
      the Good Old Mark Twain)], Berlin: Deutsche Buch-Gemeinschaft.

1935 The Death-Disk. [school edition] Diesterwegs Neusprachliche
      Lesehefte, nr. 181. [5th edition] Frankfurt: Diesterweg. [Eng-
      lish]

1935 Erzahlungen [Stories]. Neusprachliche Lesebogen, nr. 270. Biele-
      feld: Velhagen & Klasing.

1946 Weisser Elefant Gestohlen! und Andere Skizzen [Stolen White Ele-
      phant! and Other Sketches], Dusseldorf: Merkur.

1946 Same. n.p.: Ermass.

1947 Ein Kannibale auf der Eisenbahn [Cannibalism on the Railroad],
      Berlin: Steuben.

1947 Das Lacheln des Weisen. Die Schonsten Heiteren Erzahlungen [The
      Smile of the Wise. The Finest Cheerful Stories], Berlin: Hori-
      zont.

1948 Humoresken [Humorous Pieces]. Die Kleine Freundesgabe. 15.
      Heidelberg-Waibstadt: Kemper.

1952 Jugendbucher der Weltliteratur: Johanna Spyri, Mark Twain, Robert
      Louis Stevenson [Youth Books of World Literature: Johanna Spyri,
      Mark Twain, Robert Louis Stevenson], Reutlingen: Ensslin & Laiblin.

1952 Erzahlungen [Stories], Berlin: Aufbau.

1953 Same. [2nd edition] Berlin: Aufbau.

1953 Tagebuch von Adam und Eva [Diary of Adam and Eve], n.p.: Barmer-
      lea.

1954 Humoristische Erzahlungen, Berlin: Aufbau.

1958 Same. Berlin: Aufbau.

1959 Die Eine-Million-Pfund-Note. 5 Erzahlungen [The One Million Pound
      Bank-note. 5 Stories], Berlin: Aufbau

1959 Die Eine-Million-Pfund-Note. 12 Humoristische Erzahlungen [The
      One Million Pound Bank-note. 12 Humorous Stories], Munchen:
      Obpacher.

1959 Die Schonsten Geschichten [The Finest Stories]. Verlegen fur Inter-
      national Kultur-Austausch. Frankfurt und Berlin: Erdmann.

1959 Sieben Meister des Literarischen Humors in England und Amerika
      [Seven Masters of Literary Humors in England and America], Heidel-
      berg: Quelle und Meyer.

1959   Schandliche Verfolgung Eines Knaben [Disgraceful Persecution of
       A Boy]. (Ausgewahlte Skizzen). Reclams Universal-Bibliothek.
       [2nd edition] Leipzig: Reclam.

1960   Same. [3rd edition] Leipzig: Reclam.

1960   Die Besten Geschichten [The Best Stories], Bremen: Schunemann.

1960   Wjac Zboza hac Rozuma a Druhe Powedavcka [More Health than Brains
       and Other Stories]. Budysin [East Germany]: VEB. Verlegen.
       Domowina. [Sorbian]

1961   Tot oder Lebendig. Siebzehn Erzahlungen [Dead or Living. Seventeen
       Stories], Frankfurt und Hamburg: Fischer.

1962   Die Besten Geschichten [The Best Stories]. [3rd edition] Bremen:
       Schunemann.

1962   The ₤1,000,000 Bank-Note and Other Pieces of American Humour.
       Schoninghs Englische Lesebogen. 150. Paderborn: Schoningh.
       [English]

1962   Die Millionen-Pfundnote. Humoristische Skizzen [The Million
       Pound Note. Humorous Sketches]. Goldmanns Gelbe Taschenbucher.
       Munchen: Goldmann.

1962   Sechs Erstaunliche Kurzgeschichten [Six Astonishing Short Stories],
       Ebenheusen bei Munchen: Langewiesche-Brandt.

1962   Der Beruhmte Springfrosch der Provinz Calaveras. Sieben Humoresken
       [The Celebrated Jumping Frog of Calaveras Province. Seven Humorous
       Pieces]. Reclams Universal Bibliothek. Nr. 8675. Stuttgart:
       Reclam.

1963   Von Adam bis Vanderbilt. 13 Geschichten aus Amerika [From Adam to
       Vanderbilt. 13 Stories from America]. Goldmanns Gelbe Taschen-
       bucher. Bd. 958. Munchen: Goldmann.

1964   Der Gestohlene Weisse Elefant [The Stolen White Elephant], Leipzig:
       Hochschule fur Grofik & Buchkurst.

1964   Die Geschichte vom Gestohlenen Weissen Elefanten [The Story of the
       Stolen White Elephant], Frankfurt: Kruse.

1964   Der Gestohlene Weisse Elefant und Andere Satirische Geschichten
       von Grossen und Kleinen Tieren [The Stolen White Elephant and
       Other Satirical Stories of Large and Small Animals], Berlin:
       Rutten & Loening.

1964   Rauhe Sitten in Tennessee, und Andere Geschichten [Rough Manners
       in Tennessee, and Other Stories], Stuttgart: Union.

1965   Heitere Geschichten [Cheerful Stories]. Verlegen fur International
       Kultur-Austausch. [2nd edition] Herrenalb/Schwarzwald: Erdmann.

1965 Das Tagebuch von Adam und Eva und Andere Geschichten [The Diary of
      Adam and Eve and Other Stories]. [2nd edition] Weimar:
      Kiepenheuer.

1967 Wilde, O.; Poe, E.A.; Twain, Mark. The Happy Prince und Andere
      Kurzgeschichten [The Happy Prince and Other Short Stories],
      Stuttgart, Berlin, Zurich: Junker.

1968 Die Million-Pfundnote und Andere Erzahlungen [The Million Pound
      Bank-note and Other Stories], Wiesbaden: Vollmer.

1968 Wohltun Tragt Zinsen Erzahlungen [To Give Pleasure Bears Interest
      Stories]. Fischer-Bucherei, 881. Frankfurt: Fischer.

1968 Das Tagebuch von Adam und Eva und Andere Geschichten [The Diary of
      Adam and Eve and Other Stories], Weimar: Kiepenheuer.

1969 Adams Tagebuch und Andere Heitere Geschichten [Adam's Diary and
      Other Cheerful Stories], Freiburg, Basel, Wien: Herder.

1969 Der Beruhmte Springfrosch der Provinz Calaveras. 7 Humoresken
      [The Celebrated Jumping Frog of Calaveras Province. 7 Humor-
      ous Pieces], Stuttgart: Reclam.

1969 Heitere Geschichten [Cheerful Stories]. [3rd edition] Tubingen:
      Erdmann.

1970 Ein Kannibale auf der Eisenbahn und Andere Geschichten [Cannibalism
      on the Railroad and Other Stories], Frankfurt: Ullstein.

1971 Der Beruhmte Springfrosch von Calaveras; Ausgewahlte Erzahlungen
      [The Celebrated Jumping Frog of Calaveras Province; Selected
      Stories], Munchen: Gunther Klotz.

1971 Same. Munchen: Goldmann.

1971 Ein Geheimnisvoller Besuch: Skizzen [A Mysterious Visit: Sketches].
      [5th Edition] Leipzig: Reclam.

1971 Einige Gedanken uber die Wissenschaft der Onanie 1601 oder Kaminge-
      sprache der hohen Gesellschaft in der Zeit der Tudors [Several
      Thoughts about Knowledge of 1601 Onanism or Fireside Conversa-
      tion of high Society in the Time of the Tudors]. In Richard
      Amory, Rote Manner auf Grumen Matten; oder, Winnetous Erben,
      Munchen: Royner & Bernhard.

1971 Der Gestohlene Weisse Elefant, Heidelberg: Ueberreuter.

1971 Six Odd Short Stories. Sechs Erstaunliche Kurzgeschichten.
      [4th Edition] Munchen: Langewiesche-Brandt.

1974 Der Beruhmte Springfrosch der Provinz Calaveras: 7 Humoresken.
      Nachdruck [Reprint]. Stuttgart: Reclam.

1974 Die Grosse Revolution auf Pitcairn und Andere Erzahlungen [The Great
      Revolution on Pitcairn and Other Stories], Munchen: Goldmann.

1974 Sechs Erstaunliche Kurzgeschichten [Six Odd Short Stories]. [Ger-
      man-English] Munchen: Deutscher Taschenbuch.

1975 Same. Munchen: Deutscher Taschenbuch.

1976 Same. Munchen: Deutscher Taschenbuch.

Tom Sawyer

1876 The Adventures of Tom Sawyer. Collection of British Authors, Nr.
      1622. Leipsic: Tauchnitz. [English]

1876 Tom Sawyer. Eine Jugendgeschichte [Tom Sawyer. A Youth Story].
      Amerikanische Humoristen, Bd. 5. Leipzig: Grunow.

1876 Die Abenteuer Tom Sawyers [The Adventures of Tom Sawyer]. Amerikan-
      ische Humoristen, Bd. 11. Leipzig: Grunow.

1899 Tom Sawyers Streiche und Abenteuer [Tom Sawyer's Pranks and Adven-
      tures]. Eisenbahn-Ausgabe [Railroad Edition]. Stuttgart: Lutz.

1900 The Adventures of Tom Sawyer. Abridged [school] edition. Leipsic:
      Freytag: [English]

1900 Die Abenteuer des Tom Sawyer [The Adventures of Tom Sawyer]. Bib-
      liothek der Gesamtliteratur des In- und Auslandes, Nr. 1413-1415.
      Halle: n.pub.

1900 Tom Sawyers Abenteuer [Tom Sawyer's Adventures]. 2 bande [2
      volumes]. Kurschners Bucherschatz, Nr. 176-177. Berlin: Hillger.

1904 Tom Sawyers Abenteuer und Streiche. Jugendausgabe [Youth Edition].
      Mark Twains Humoristische Schriften fur die Jugend. Stuttgart:
      Lutz.

1909 Die Abenteuer Tom Sawyers [The Adventures of Tom Sawyer], Berlin:
      Weichert.

1910 Die Abenteuer Tom Sawyers. Ausgewahlte Skizzen [The Adventures of
      Tom Sawyer. Selected Sketches]. Vereinfachter Deutscher Steno-
      graphie, System Stolze-Schrey. Serie I, Bd. 9. Berlin: Schulze.

1913 Die Abenteuer des Tom Sawyer und Huckleberry Finn [The Adventures
      of Tom Sawyer and Huckleberry Finn], Strassburg und Leipzig: Sing-
      er.

1914 Tom Sawyers Abenteuer und Streiche. Huckleberry Finns Abenteuer
      und Fahrten [Tom Sawyer's Adventures and Pranks. Huckleberry Finn's
      Adventures and Travels]. Romane der Weltliteratur. Leipzig: Hesse
      & Becker.

1914   The Adventures of Tom Sawyer. School Edition. Velhagen & Klasings
       Sammlung Franzoischer und Englischer Schulausgaben. English
       Authors, Nr. 141B. Leipsic: Velhagen & Klasing. [English]

1919   Tom Sawyers Abenteuer und Streiche. Jugendausgabe [Tom Sawyer's
       Adventures and Pranks. Youth Edition]. Mark Twains Humoristische
       Schriften fur die Jugend. [4th edition] Stuttgart: Lutz.

192-? Abenteuer und Streiche Tom Sawyers [Adventures and Pranks of Tom
       Sawyer], Stuttgart: Lutz.

1920   Tom Sawyers Abenteuer und Streiche [Tom Sawyer's Adventures and
       Pranks]. Romane der Weltliteratur. Leipzig: Hesse & Becker.

1921   Tom Sawyers Abenteuer   [Tom Sawyer's Adventures], Berlin:
       Ullstein.

1922   Die Abenteuer Tom Sawyers und Huckleberry Finns (des Kameraden
       von Tom Sawyer)[The Adventures of Tom Sawyer and Huckleberry
       Finn (the Comrade of Tom Sawyer)]. Meisterzahler der Weltliter-
       atur, Bd. 12. Berlin: Mitteldeutsche Verlagsanstalt Lehmann
       & Fink.

1925   Tom Sawyers Abenteuer [Tom Sawyer's Adventures]. Die Bunten Romane
       der Weltliteratur, Bd. 50. Berlin: Schillerbuchhandlung.

1925   Die Streiche Tom Sawyers und Huckleberry Finns [The Pranks of Tom
       Sawyer and Huckleberry Finn]. Veroffentlichungen der Deutschen
       Buchgemeinschaft, Bd. 79. Berlin: Deutsche Buchgemeinschaft.

1925   Die Abenteuer Tom Sawyers [The Adventures of Tom Sawyer], Berlin:
       Maschler.

1925   The Adventures of Tom Sawyer. New [school] edition. Velhagen &
       Klasings Sammlung Franzoischer und Englischer Schulausgaben.
       Ausgabe B. Nr. 141. Bielefeld und Leipsic: Velhagen & Klasing.
       [English]

1926   Tom Sawyers Abenteuer und Streiche [Tom Sawyer's Adventures and
       Pranks]. Die Schatzkammer, Bd. 46. Leipzig: Hesse & Becker.

1927   The Adventures of Tom Sawyer. Abridged [school] edition. Velhagen
       & Klasings Sammlung Franzoischer und Englischer Schulausgaben.
       Reform-Ausgaben, Bd. 57. Bielefeld und Leipsic: Velhagen &
       Klasing. [English]

1927   Die Abenteuer des Tom Sawyer und Huckleberry Finn [The Adventures
       of Tom Sawyer and Huckleberry Finn]. Zenith-Bucherei. Leipzig:
       Zenith.

1928   Tom Sawyers Abenteuer. Roman   [Tom Sawyer's Adventures. Novel].
       Gesellschaft fur Literatur. Hamburg: Leuchtfeuer.

1929   Tom Sawyers Abenteuer [Tom Sawyer's Adventures], Berlin: Die Buch-
       gemeinde.

193-? Same. Berlin: Ullstein.

1930? Die Abenteuer des Tom Sawyer und Huckleberry Finn [The Adventures
of Tom Sawyer and Huckleberry Finn], Berlin: Dressler.

1930 Tom Sawyers Abenteuer und Streiche [Tom Sawyer's Adventures and
Pranks]. Die Schatzkammer, Bd. 46. Leipzig: Hesse & Becker.

1931 Same. Jugendausgabe [Youth Edition]. Mark Twains Humoristische
Schriften fur die Jugend. [7th edition] Stuttgart: Lutz.

1936 Die Abenteuer des Tom Sawyer [The Adventures of Tom Sawyer], Engels:
Deutscher Staatsverlag.

1936 Die Abenteuer des Tom Sawyer und Huckleberry Finn [The Adventures
of Tom Sawyer and Huckleberry Finn], Berlin: Williams.

1938 Tom Sawyers Abenteuer [Tom Sawyer's Adventures], Berlin: Deutscher.

1938 Same. Der Quell. Bd. 53. Leipzig: Janke.

1938 Same. Roman-Sammlung aus Vergangenheit und Gegenwart, Bd. 61.
Leipzig: Rothbarth.

1939 Die Abenteuer Tom Sawyers [Tom Sawyer's Adventures], Potsdam:
Voggenreiter.

1940 Tom Sawyers Abenteuer und Streiche [Tom Sawyer's Adventures and
Pranks], Stuttgart: Lutz.

1943 Die Abenteuer Tom Sawyers [Tom Sawyer's Adventures], Potsdam.
Voggenreiter.

1947 Tom Sawyers Abenteuer und Streiche [Tom Sawyer's Adventures and
Pranks], Berlin: Aufbau.

1947 Die Abenteuer des Tom Sawyer [The Adventures of Tom Sawyer],
Berlin: Williams.

1947 Tom Sawyer, Wiesbaden: Kesselringsche.

1948 Der Mordskerl [The Incredible Tom]. Die Bunte Reibe. Berlin:
Felsen.

1949 Der Lausejunge Tom Sawyer. Seine Abenteuer und Streiche [The Young
Devil Tom Sawyer. His Adventures and Pranks], Heidelberg/Waibstadt:
Kemper.

1949 Tom Sawyers Abenteuer [Tom Sawyer's Adventures], Hamburg: Glabus.

1949 Tom Sawyers Abenteuer. Eine Mississippi-Erzahlung [Tom Sawyer's
Adventures. A Mississippi Story]. Das Ensslin Buch. Reutlingen:
Ensslin und Laiblin.

1949 Tom Sawyers Abenteuer und Streiche [Tom Sawyer's Adventures and
Pranks], Dusseldorf: Merkur.

1949 Same. [2nd edition]. Berlin: Aufbau.

1950 Same. [3rd edition] Berlin: Aufbau.

1950 Tom Sawyer. Simplified from The Adventures of Tom Sawyer. Funda-
      mental English Readers. 3. Berlin, Hamburg, Kiel: Westermann.
      [English]

1951 Tom Sawyers Abenteuer [Tom Sawyer's Adventures], n.p.: Bucher-
      gilde: Bermerlea.

1951 Tom Sawyer. Abenteuer und Streiche [Tom Sawyer. Adventures and
      Pranks]. [2nd edition] Heidelberg: Kemper.

1951 Die Abenteuer des Tom Sawyer [The Adventures of Tom Sawyer]. Volks-
      Ausgabe. Munchen, Trier: Droemer.

1951 Die Abenteuer Tom Sawyers. Eine Lustige Geschichte [The Adventures
      of Tom Sawyer. A Merry Story], Hildesheim: Verlegen Jugend und
      Volk.

1951 Tom Sawyer und Huckleberry Finn; Abenteuer am Mississippi [Tom
      Sawyer and Huckleberry Finn; Adventures on the Mississippi],
      Reutlingen: Ensslin & Laiblin.

1951 Tom Sawyers Abenteuer und Streiche [Tom Sawyer's Adventures and
      Pranks]. [4th edition] Berlin: Aufbau.

1952 Same. [7th edition] Berlin: Aufbau.

1953 Same. [9th edition] Berlin: Aufbau.

1954 Tom Sawyers Abenteuer [Tom Sawyer's Adventures], Berlin: Neues
      Leben.

1954 Die Abenteuer Tom Sawyers [The Adventures of Tom Sawyer], Koln:
      Agrippina.

1954 The Adventures of Tom Sawyer Simplified. Fundamental English
      Readers. Schul- und Erziehungswesens. [3rd edition]. Hamburg:
      Westermann. [English]

1954 Tom Sawyer und Huckleberry Finn. Fahrten und Abenteuer [Tom
      Sawyer and Huckleberry Finn. Travels and Adventures],Hamburg: Reitze.

1955 Die Abenteuer des Tom Sawyer und Huckleberry Finn, Wien, Heidelberg:
      Ueberreuter.

1955 Tom Sawyers Abenteuer und Streiche [Tom Sawyer's Adventures and
      Pranks], Koln: Kolner Jugenbuchverlegen.

1956 Same. Koln: Atlas.

1956 Die Abenteuer des Tom Sawyer und Huckleberry Finn [The Adventures
      Tom Sawyer and Huckleberry Finn], Berlin: Deutsche Buch-Gemein-
      schaft.

1956   Die Abenteuer des Tom Sawyer [The Adventures of Tom Sawyer],
       Stuttgart: Bluchert.

1958   Same. Munchen, Zurich: Droemer/Knaur.

1958   Tom Sawyers Abenteuer. Die Abenteuer des Huckleberry Finn [Tom
       Sawyer's Adventures. The Adventures of Huckleberry Finn].
       [extracts] Gottingen: W. Fischer.

1958   Tom Sawyer. Goldmann's Gelbe Taschenbucher No. 47. Munchen:
       Goldmann.

1958   The Adventures of Tom Sawyer Simplified. Fundamental English
       Readers. No. 3. Braunschweig, Berlin, Hamburg, Munchen, Kiel,
       Darmstad: Westermann. [English]

1959   Same. [English]

1959   Tom Sawyers Abenteuer [Tom Sawyer's Adventures]. Kompass-Bucherei.
       Bd. 4. Berlin: Neues Leben.

1959   Die Abenteuer des Tom Sawyer [The Adventures of Tom Sawyer], Wies-
       baden: Agrippina.

1959   Same. [8th, 9th edition]. Munchen, Zurich: Droemer/Knaur.

1960   Same. Wiesbaden: Agrippina.

1960? Tom Sawyer und Huckleberry Finn, Hamburg: Reitze.

1961   The Adventures of Tom Sawyer Simplified. Fundamental English
       Readers. No. 3. Braunschweig, Berlin, Hamburg, Munchen, Kiel,
       Darmstad: Westermann. [English]

1961   Tom Sawyer. Goldmanns Gelbe Taschenbucher. Munchen: Goldmann.

1962   Same. Stuttgart: Boje.

1963   Tom Sawyers Abenteuer [Tom Sawyer's Adventures], Gutersloh: Mohn.

1963   Same. Gutersloh: Lesering.

1964   Die Abenteuer von Tom Sawyer und Huckleberry Finn [The Adventures
       of Tom Sawyer and Huckleberry Finn], Hanau am Main: Dausien.

1964   Die Abenteuer des Tom Sawyer und Huckleberry Finn [The Adventures
       of Tom Sawyer and Huckleberry Finn], Stuttgart: Deutsche Bucher-
       bund.

1964   Tom Sawyers Abenteuer [Tom Sawyer's Adventures]. [2nd edition]
       Berlin und Weimar: Aufbau.

1965   Tom Sawyers Abenteuer. Die Abenteuer des Huckleberry Finn [Tom
       Sawyer's Adventures. The Adventures of Huckleberry Finn],
       Gottingen: W. Fischer.

1966   Tom Sawyer. Huckleberry Finn, Frankfurt: Buchergilde Gutenberg.
        Hannover: Fackeltrager.

1967   Tom Sawyers Abenteuer [Tom Sawyer's Adventures], Berlin: Kinder-
        buchverlegen.

1967   Same. Ullstein-Buch Nr. 2609: Ullstein-Urlaubsklassiker. Berlin,
        Frankfurt: Ullstein.

1968   Same. [3rd edition] Ravensburg: Maier.

1968   Same. Stuttgart: Spectrum.

1968   Die Abenteuer des Tom Sawyer [The Adventures of Tom Sawyer],
        Munchen: Heyne.

1969   Tom Sawyers Abenteuer [Tom Sawyer's Adventures]. [9th edition]
        Berlin: Neues Leben.

1970   Tom Sawyer, Balve/Westfallen: Engelbert.

1970   Same. [13th edition] Reutlingen: Ensslin & Laiblin.

1970   Tom Sawyers Abenteuer [Tom Sawyer's Adventures], Freiburg: Herder.

1970   Same. Wurzburg: Arena.

1971   Same. Neuausgabe [New Edition].Gottingen: Fischer.

1971   Same. [3rd Edition] Ravensburg: Maier.

1971   Tom Sawyer und Huckleberry Finn, Balve (Westfallen): Engelbert.

1971   Same. Stuttgart: Spectrum.

1971   Die Abenteuer des Tom Sawyer und Huckleberry Finn. Sonderausgabe
        [Special Edition].Munchen: Sudwest.

1971   Tom Sawyer, Aachen: Williams.

1972   Tom Sawyers Abenteuer. [4th Edition] Ravensburg: Maier.

1972   Same. [3rd Edition] Leipzig: Reclam.

1973   Same. Berlin, Weimar: Aufbau.

1973   Tom Sawyers Abenteuer: Eine Mississippi-Erzahlung [Tom Sawyer's
        Adventures: A Mississippi-Story]. [22nd Edition] Reutlingen:
        Ensslin & Laiblin.

1973   Die Abenteuer des Tom Sawyer und Huckleberry Finn, Munchen:
        Droemer-Knaur.

1973   Tom Sawyer und Huckleberry Finn: Abenteuer am Mississippi. [14th
        Edition] Reutlingen: Ensslin & Laiblin.

1974   Tom Sawyers Abenteuer, Frankfurt am Main: Insel-Verlag. Suhrkamp-
       Taschenbuch-Verlag in Koum.

1974   Same. [6th Edition] Ravensburg: Maier.

1974   Tom Sawyers Abenteuer: die Erlebnisse einer Lausbuben am Grossen
       Fluss [The Experiences of A Devilish Boy on the Great River].
       [2nd Edition] Wurzburg: Arena.

1974   Tom Sawyer. Huckleberry Finn, Berlin: Neues Leben.

1975   Same. Freiburg im Breisgau: Herder.

1975   Tom Sawyer, Heidelberg: Ueberreuter.

1975   Tom Sawyers Abenteuer. [7th Edition] Ravensburg: Maier.

1976   Same. Berlin, Weimar: Aufbau.

1976   Same. Guterloh: Bertelsmann. Stuttgart: Europa Bildungsgemein-
       schaft. Berlin, Darmstadt: Deutsche Buchgemeinschaft.

1976   Same. [8th Edition] Ravensburg: Maier.

1976   Tom Sawyer: in einem Gekurtzten Fassung [Tom Sawyer: in A Shortened
       Version],Reinbek bei Hamburg: Carlsen.

1976   Tom Sawyers Abenteuer. Huckleberry Finns Abenteuer, Munchen:
       Deutscher Taschenbuch.

1976   Tom Sawyer. Huckleberry Finn. [2nd Edition] Freiburg-im-Breisgau:
       Herder.

1976   Same. [2nd Edition] Berlin: Neues Leben.

1976   Tom Sawyer, Heidelberg: Ueberreuter.

                            Tom Sawyer Abroad

1894   Tom Sawyer Abroad. Copyright edition. Collection of British
       Authors, Nr. 2984. Leipsic: Tauchnitz. [English]

1959   Tom Sawyer in Ausland [Tom Sawyer Abroad], Berlin: Holz.

1960   Same. [2nd edition] Berlin: Holz.

1960   Same. Darmstad: Progress.

1965   Same. Berlin: Neues Leben.

1969   Tom Sawyers Neue Abenteuer: Die Reise im Ballon. Tom Sawyer als
       Detektiv [Tom Sawyer's New Adventures: The Journey in Balloon.
       Tom Sawyer as Detective], Reutlingen: Ensslin und Laiblin.

1970   Tom Sawyer auf Weltreise [Tom Sawyer on World Journey], Heidelberg:
       Ueberreuter.

1971   Tom Sawyers Neue Abenteuer: Die Reise im Ballon. Tom Sawyer als
       Detektiv, Reutlingen: Ensslin & Laiblin.

1973   Same. Reutlingen: Ensslin & Laiblin.

Tom Sawyer, Detective

1897   Tom Sawyer, Detective, as Told by Huck Finn, and Other Tales. Copy-
       right edition. Collection of British Authors, Nr. 3184. Leipsic:
       Tauchnitz. [English]

1898   Der Junge Detektiv und Andere Kriminalgeschichten [The Young Detec-
       tive and Other Criminal Stories]. Von Mark Twain und Edgar Allen
       [sic] Poe. Amerikanische Detektivromane, Bd. 6. Berlin: Jacobs-
       thal.

1901   Tom, der Kleine Detektiv. Nebst Zwei Erzahlungen von Bret Harte
       [Tom, the Little Detective. Besides Two Stories of Bret Harte].
       Sammlung Ausgewahlter Kriminal- und Detektiv- Romane, Bd. 25.
       Stuttgart: Lutz.

1903   Same. Stuttgart: Lutz.

1907   Same. Stuttgart: Lutz.

1908   Same. Stuttgart: Lutz.

1911   Tom Sawyer als Detektiv. Wie es Huck Finn Erzahlt [Tom Sawyer As
       Detective. As So Related by Huck Finn]. Saturn. Illustr.
       Universal-Bibliothek, Bd. 6. Stuttgart: Saturn.

1916   Tom Sawyer, Detective, As Told by Huck Finn. Copyright edition.
       Tauchnitz Pocket Library, Nr. 75. Leipsic: Tauchnitz. [English]

1916   Tom, der Kleine Detektiv. Nebst Zwei Erzahlungen von Bret Harte
       [Tom, the Little Detective. Besides Two Stories of Bret Harte].
       Sammlung Ausgewahlter Kriminal- und Detektiv- Romane, Bd. 25.
       Stuttgart: Lutz.

1918   Same. [7th edition] Stuttgart: Lutz.

1958   Tom Sawyer, der Detektiv. Als Ob's Huck Finn Erzahlte [Tom Sawyer,
       the Detective. As Told by Huck Finn], Munchen: Lentz.

1959   Same. [extracts] [5th edition] Berlin: Holz.

1967   Detektiv am Mississippi. Huck Finn Erzahlte. Abenteuer mit Tom
       Sawyer [Detective on the Mississippi. Huck Finn Related. Adventures
       with Tom Sawyer], Wurzburg: Arena.

1969   Detektiv am Mississippi [Detective on the Mississippi]. [2nd
       edition] Wurzburg: Arena.

1969 Tom Sawyers Neue Abenteuer: Die Reise im Ballon. Tom Sawyer als
      Detektiv [Tom Sawyer's New Adventures: The Trip in Balloon. Tom
      Sawyer as Detective], Reutlingen: Ensslin und Laiblin.

1970 Tom Sawyer als Detektiv [Tom Sawyer as Detective], Stuttgart: Boje.

1971 Tom Sawyers Neue Abenteuer: Die Reise im Ballon. Tom Sawyer als
      Detektiv, Reutlingen: Ensslin & Laiblin.

1973 Same. Reutlingen: Ensslin & Laiblin.

1973 Tom Sawyer, Der Detektiv. Als ob's Huck Finn Erzahlte [Tom Sawyer,
      the Detective. As Told by Huck Finn]. [8th Edition] Berlin:
      Holz.

1974 Detektiv am Mississippi: Tom Sawyer und Huckleberry Finn auf
      Verbrecherjagd [Detective on the Mississippi: Tom Sawyer and
      Huckleberry Finn on Criminal Hunt], Wurzburg: Arena.

Tom Sawyer: extracts

1906 Mark Twain: Wie Tom den Zaun Anstrich [Mark Twain: How Tom Painted
      the Fence]. Lutz Kriminal- und Detektiv-Romane, Bd. 47. Stuttgart:
      Lutz.

1907 Same. [2nd edition] Stuttgart: Lutz.

1908 Same. [3rd edition] Stuttgart: Lutz.

1916 Same. [4th edition] Stuttgart: Lutz.

1946 Tom Sawyer, der Seerauber [Tom Sawyer, the Pirate]. Volk und
      Wissen. Berlin, Leipzig: Ilgenfritz.

1947 Tom Sawyer, der Schatzgraber [Tom Sawyer, the Treasure Digger],
      Berlin, Leipzig: Volk und Wissen.

1949 Tom Sawyer, der Seerauber [Tom Sawyer, the Pirate]. Volk und
      Wissen Sammelbucherei. Gruppe 1, Serie H. 5. Berlin, Leipzig:
      Volk und Wissen.

1952 Zeuge Tom [Witness Tom], Kaldenkirchen Rheinland: Steyler.

1974 Tom Sawyer: Seine Abenteuerlichsten Lausbubengeschichten [Tom
      Sawyer: His Adventurous Devilish Boy Stories]. [extracts]
      Munchen: F. Schneider.

1975 Neue Spannende Geschichten mit Tom Sawyer [New Interesting Stories
      with Tom Sawyer], Munchen: F. Schneider.

Tramp Abroad

1880 A Tramp Abroad. Authorized edition. Collection of British Authors,
      Nr. 1899-1900. Leipsic: Tauchnitz. [English]

1901   A Tramp Abroad. [school edition] [excerpts] Leipsic: Freytag.
       Vienna: Tempsky. [English]

1922   Bummel durch Europa [Stroll through Europe], Berlin: Ullstein.

1963   Zu Fuss durch Europa [On Foot through Europe], Gottingen: Vanden-
       hoeck und Ruprecht.

1963   Same. [2nd edition] Gottingen: Vandenhoeck und Ruprecht.

1966   Same. Berlin, Darmstadt: Buchgemeinschaft.

1966   Flosshahrt auf dem Neckar [Rafting on the Neckar]. [extract]
       Heidelberg: Europaishe Kulturstalten.

1966   Rafting down the Neckar - From Heilbronn to Heidelberg [extract]
       Heidelberg: European Places of Culture. [English]

1967   Mark Twain Bummelt durch Europa [Mark Twain Strolls through Europe],
       Munchen: Deutscher Taschenbuch.

1967   Zu Fuss durch Europa. [3rd edition] Gottingen: Vandenhoeck und
       Ruprecht.

1969   Ein Bummel durch Europa [A Stroll through Europe], Frankfurt:
       Ullstein.

1969   Mark Twain Bummelt durch Europa. [3rd edition] Munchen: Deutscher
       Taschenbuch.

1971   Mark Twain Bummelt durch Europa: Aus die Reiseberichten [Mark
       Twain Strolls through Europe: from the Travel Accounts]. [4th
       Edition] Munchen: Deutscher Taschenbuch.

1973   Same. [5th Edition] Munchen: Deutscher Taschenbuch.

1975   Same. [6th Edition] Munchen: Deutscher Taschenbuch.

Travel Sketches

1886   Unterwegs und Daheim [On the Way and at Home], Stuttgart: Lutz.

Miscellaneous Writings

1924   Kriegsgebet [War Prayer]. Die Weltbuhne [World Scene], Jg. 20,
       Nr. 47, November 1924, S. 758.

1927   Cecil Rhodes. [school edition] Aschendorffs Moderne Auslands-
       bucherei, nr. 5. Munster: Aschendorffsche Verlaghandlung.
       [English]

Selections

1960 Your Personal Twain... Seven Seas Books, 7. Berlin: Seven Seas,
      [English]

1967 Das Schonste von Mark Twain [The Finest of Mark Twain], Hannover:
      Fackeltrager.

1970 Das Mark-Twain-Buch [The Mark Twain Book], Gutersloh, Bertelsmann,
      Stuttgart: Europaisch Buch-und Phonoklub.

Collected Works*

   Mark Twain's exposure to German readers would be found to be
   appreciably greater than that reflected by the preceding record of
   his single editions if the numerous German publications of his
   collected works could be taken into account. Almost all of these
   collected editions were reissued at later dates. The Lutz editions
   in particular appeared so frequently in revised editions and reprints that many cannot be identified accurately by dates. Twain's
   major writings, in most instances, were included in the following
   editions of his selected and collected works:

1892 Mark Twains Ausgewahlte Humoristische Schriften [Mark Twain's
      Selected Humorous Writings]. 6 Bande [6 volumes]. Stuttgart:
      Lutz.

1898 Same. Illustrierte Ausgabe [Illustrated Edition]. 6 Bande [6
      volumes]. Stuttgart: Lutz.

1899-1900 Same. Eisenbahn Ausgabe [Railway Edition]. 6 Bande [6
      volumes]. Stuttgart: Lutz.

1903 Mark Twains Humoristische Schriften [Mark Twain's Humorous Writings].
      Neue Folge [New Series]. 6 Bande [6 volumes]. Stuttgart: Lutz.

1910 Mark Twains Ausgewahlte Werke [Mark Twain's Selected Works].
      Auswahl in Drei Banden [Selection in Three Volumes]. Romane der
      Weltliteratur [Novels of World Literature]. Leipzig: Hesse &
      Becker.

1911 Same. 6 Bande [6 volumes]. [also issued in Hesses Volksbucherei,
      nr. 649-660]. Leipzig: Hesse & Becker.

1925 Mark Twains Werke [Mark Twain's Works]. [3 volumes] Leipzig:
      Hesse & Becker.

   *Sources of information for the collected editions are found princi-
   pally in Edgar Hemminghaus' Mark Twain in Germany, in Jahresverzeichnis des Deutschen Schrifttums, and in the Index Translationum,
   supplemented by Heinsius' Algemeines Bucher-Lexikon, Kanser's
   Bucher-Lexikon, and Deutsche Bibliographie. Halbjahres-Verzeichnis
   (see "Bibliographical Sources").

1940-1949 Same. [Mark Twain's Works]. [5 volumes] Stuttgart: Lutz.

1949 Same. Reutlingen: Ensslin und Laiblin.

1960-1965 Mark Twains Ausgewahlte Werke in Zwolf Banden [Mark Twain's Selected Works in Twelve Volumes], Berlin, Weimar: Aufbau.

1965 Mark Twains Gesammelte Werke in Funf Banden [Mark Twain's Collected Works in Five Volumes], Munchen, Darmstadt: Hanser.

1971-1972 Mark Twains Werke in Zwei Banden [Mark Twain's Works in Two Volumes], Darmstadt: Deutsche Buch-Gemeinschaft. Gutersloh: Bertelsman. Stuttgart: Europa Bildungsgemeinschaft. Munchen: Hanser.

1972-1973 Mark Twains Ausgewahlte Werke. [4? volumes] Berlin: Aufbau.

1974 Mark Twains Ausgewahlte Werke: in 12 Banden, Berlin, Weimar: Aufbau.

1975 Same. [2nd Edition] Berlin, Weimar: Aufbau.

The Tauchnitz Editions

The Leipsic publisher Bernhard Tauchnitz included in his extensive "Collection of British Authors" English-language editions of all of Mark Twain's major works except The Gilded Age. Since they were not published as a collected edition, they are entered as single works in the preceding bibliography. Appearing in most instances shortly after their first American publication, the Tauchnitz editions gave many European readers early access to Mark Twain before the later foreign language translations of his writings. This formidable collection, issued in twenty-seven titles over a forty-three-year-period, gave an added dimension to Mark Twain's international popularity.

1876 The Adventures of Tom Sawyer. CBA Nr. 1622.

1879 The Innocents Abroad or The New Pilgrim's Progress. 2 vols. CBA Nr. 1812-1813.

1880 A Tramp Abroad. 2 vols. CBA Nr. 1899-1900.

1880 Roughing It. CBA Nr. 1929.

1881 Innocents at Home. CBA Nr. 1948.

1881 The Prince and the Pauper. A Tale for Young People of All Ages. 2 vols. CBA Nr. 2027-2028.

1882 The Stolen White Elephant and Other Stories. CBA Nr. 2077.

1883 Life on the Mississippi. 2 vols. CBA Nr. 2143-2144.

1883 Sketches. CBA Nr. 2162.

1885 The Adventures of Huckleberry Finn (Tom Sawyer's Comrade). 2 vols.
      CBA Nr. 2307-2308.

1886 Selections from American Humour. CBA Nr. 2529.

1890 A Yankee at the Court of King Arthur. 2 vols. CBA Nr. 2638-2639.

1892 The American Claimant. CBA Nr. 2863.

1893 The Million-Pound Bank-Note, and Other New Stories. CBA Nr. 2907.

1894 Tom Sawyer Abroad. CBA Nr. 2984.

1895 Pudd'nhead Wilson. CBA Nr. 3039.

1896 Personal Recollections of Joan of Arc.... 2 vols. CBA Nr. 3138-
      3139.

1897 Tom Sawyer, Detective, As Told by Huck Finn, and Other Tales.
      CBA Nr. 3184.

1897 More Tramps Abroad [Following the Equator]. 2 vols. CBA Nr. 3252-
      3253.

1900 The Man That Corrupted Hadleyburg, and Other Stories and Sketches.
      2 vols. CBA Nr. 3453-3454.

1902 A Double-Barrelled Detective Story. Two Little Tales. The Death
      Disk. A Defense of General Funston. CBA Nr. 3591.

1907 The $30,000 Bequest and other Stories. CBA Nr. 3959.

1907 Christian Science. With Notes Containing Corrections to Date.
      CBA Nr. 3979.

1910 Extract from Captain Stormfield's Visit to Heaven, and Is Shakespeare
      Dead? CBA Nr. 4209.

1916 Sketches. Series 1. English Textbooks, Nr. 32.

1916 Tom Sawyer, Detective, As Told by Huck Finn, and Other Tales.
      Pocket Library Nr. 75.

1918 Sketches. Series 2. Pocket Library Nr. 88.

Iceland

Sources: IT/NUC

1930 Milljon-arsedillinn [Million-Banknote], Reykjavik: Prentamidjan a
      Bergstadastreti 19.

1931 Sjo Skopsogur [Seven Stories], Reykjavik: Erlingsson.

1957 <u>Tumi A Fer og Flugi</u> [Tom Sawyer Abroad], Reykjavik: Leiftur.

1965 <u>Sagan af Tuma Litla</u> [Tale of Little Tom], Reykjavik: Leiftur.

1967 <u>Milljonarsedillinn og Fleiri Sogur</u> [Million Banknote and More
      Stories], Reykjavik: Leiftur.

1971 <u>Bref fra Jordu</u> [Letters from the Earth], Reykjavik: Prentrim.

Italy

Sources: BNF/BNI/BNR/CC/IT/NUC/UnP

Autobiography

1963 <u>Autobiografia</u>. Tradizione Americana. 3. Venezia: Pozza.

Captain Stormfield's Visit to Heaven

1926 <u>Rapporto della Visita di Capitan Tempesta in Paradiso</u> [Report of
      the Visit of Captain Tempest to Heaven]. Collezione de Scrittori
      Italiani e Stranieri, n. 4. Aquila: Vecchioni.

1945 <u>Relazione del Viaggio di Capitan Tempesta in Paradiso</u> [Report of
      the Voyage of Captain Tempest in Heaven], Milano: Denti.

Connecticut Yankee

1952 <u>Un Americano alla Corte di Re Artu</u> [An American at the Court of
      King Arthur], Milano: Vallardi.

1955 Same. Biblioteca Universale Rizzoli, 944-947. Milano: Rizzoli.

1957 Same. Milano: Fabbri.

1958 <u>Un Yankee del Connecticut alla Corte del Re Artu</u> [A Yankee from
      Connecticut at the Court of King Arthur]. <u>La Banconota da
      1.000.000 di Sterline</u> [The Bank-note of 1,000,000 of Pounds Ster-
      ling]. Collana dei Grandi Narratori. 6. Milano: Club del Libro.

1961 <u>Un Americano alla Corte di Re Artu</u>. Superverdi S.A.I.E. 50.
      Torino: S.A.I.E.

1962 <u>Un Yankee del Connecticut alla Corte del Re Artu</u>. <u>La Banconota
      da 1.000.000 di Sterline</u>. I Classici di Tutti i Tempi. 5. Serie
      Grandi. Narratori 2. Novara: I.G.D.A.

1966 <u>Un Americano alla Corte di Re Artu</u>, Roma: Paoline.

1970 Same. Milano: Fabbri.

1972 Same. Milano: Club degli Editori.

1972 Same. Firenze: Vallecchi.

Gilded Age

1954 L'Eta dell'Oro e Altri Racconti [The Golden Age and Other Stories].
      I Grandi Maestri, 18. Roma: Casini.

1960 L'Eta dell'Oro e Racconti [The Golden Age and Stories]. I Grandi
      Maestri, 18. Roma, Firenze: Casini.

Huckleberry Finn

1915 Le Avventure di Huckleberry Finn [The Adventures of Huckleberry
      Finn]. [2 vols.] Firenze: Bemporad e Figlio.

1930 Same. [2 vols.] Collezione di Capolavori Straniere Tradotti per la
      Gioventu' Italiana, n. 30. Firenze: Bemporad e Figlio.

1934 Le Avventure di Huck Finn [The Adventures of Huck Finn], Torino:
      Frassinelli.

1935 Le Avventure di Huck Finn: Romanzo [The Adventures of Huck Finn:
      Novel]. Collana Selene, n. 46. Milano: Minerva.

1935 Le Avventure di Huckleberry Finn. [2nd edition]. Firenze:
      Bemporad e Figlio.

1939 Le Avventure di Huck Finn, Torino: Frassinelli.

1943 Same. Torino: n. pub.

1949 Le Avventure di Tom Sawyer e di Huckleberry Finn, Torino: Einaudi.

1952 Le Avventure di Huck Finn, Milano: A.P.E.

1953 Same. Milano: Fabbri.

1953 Same. Torino: Frassinelli.

1953 Le Avventure di Huckleberry. Nettuno Omnia. Bologna: A.E.G.M.

1953 Le Avventure di Huccle [sic] Finn, Milano: La Sorgente.

1955 Le Avventure di Huck Finn, Milano: Fabbri.

1955 Same. Milano: Piccoli.

1963 Tom Sawyer, Huckleberry Finn. I Millenni. Torino: Einaudi.

1964 Le Avventure di Huckleberry Finn. Biblioteca Universale Rizzoli.
      2101/2104. Milano: Rizzoli.

1965 Same. I Grandi Libri: 34. Firenze: Salani. Vicenza: Stoccherio.

MARK TWAIN

UN AMERICANO
ALLA CORTE DI
RE ARTÙ

Biblioteca Universale
Rizzoli

Fig. 29. *Un Americano all Corte di Re Artù,* cover of 1955 Italian edition published by Rizzoli (Courtesy of Rizzoli Editore [Milan])

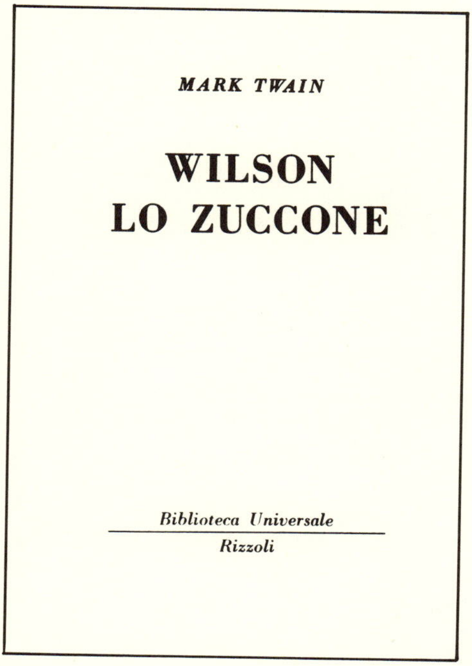

MARK TWAIN

WILSON
LO ZUCCONE

Biblioteca Universale
Rizzoli

Fig. 30. *Wilson Lo Zuccone,* cover of 1949 Italian edition published by Rizzoli (Courtesy Rizzoli Editore [Milan])

MARK TWAIN

IL RANOCCHIO SALTATORE

E ALTRI RACCONTI

Biblioteca Universale
Rizzoli

Fig. 31. *Il Ranocchio Saltatore e Altri Racconti,* cover of 1950 Italian edition published by Rizzoli (Courtesy Rizzoli Editore [Milan])

1966   Same. Scuola del Leggere 4. Palermo: Palumbo (Telestar).

1966   Same. Il Picchio. 44. Milano: Bietti.

1966   La Saga di Tom Sawyer [including Tom Sawyer, Huckleberry Finn, and Tom Sawyer, Detective]. La Biblioteca. 11. Milano: Mursia.

1967   Le Avventure di Huckleberry Finn. Scuala del Leggere. 4. Palermo: Palumbo (Telestar).

1969   Same. Brescia: La Scuola.

1969   Same. Firenze: Salani.

1969   Le Avventure di Huck Finn, Bologna: Capitol.

1971   Le Avventure di Huckleberry Finn, Milano: Bietti.

Innocents Abroad

1959   The Innocents Abroad, or the New Pilgrims' Progress (A Selection). Scrittori Inglesi. Roma: Signorelli. [English]

1960   Gli Innocenti all'Estero Ovvero. Il Viaggio dei Novelli Pellegrini [The Innocents Abroad or The Voyage of the New Pilgrims]. Collana Narrativa. 10. Milano: Lerici.

King Leopold's Soliloquy

1960   Il Soliluquio di Re Leopoldo... [The Soliloquy of King Leopold]. Nostro Tempo. Roma: Riuniti.

Letters from the Earth

1964   Lettre dalla Terra [Letters from the Earth]. A Cura di [Edited by] Bernard DeVoto. I Classici della Letteratura. 1. Roma: Riuniti. Novara: Stella Alpina.

Life on the Mississippi

1962   Vita sul Mississippi [Life on the Mississippi]. La Caravelle. 1. Roma: Opere Nuove.

1967   Same. L'oblo. Messina-Firenze: G. D'Anna.

Man That Corrupted Hadleyburg

1972   L'Uomo Che Corruppe Hadleyburg [The Man That Corrupted Hadleyburg], Torino: Einaudi.

Mysterious Stranger

1954 Il Forestiero [The Stranger]. Edizioni Librarie Italiane. Milano: Eli.

Prince and the Pauper

1891 Masino e Il Suo Re: Amena Lettura pei Fanciulli [Pauper and His King: Pleasant Reading for the Boys], Milano: Rechiedei.

1893 Re e Mendico, Novella per Grandi e Piccini [King and Pauper, Short Story for Adults and Children], Roma: Brielli.

1907 Masino e Il Suo Re: Amena Lettura pei Fanciulli, Milano: Carrara.

1914 Principe e Mendico. Romanzo [Prince and Pauper. Novel]. Biblioteca dei Ragazzi, n. 20. Milano: Instituto Editoriale Italiano.

1927 Masino e Il Suo Re: Amena Lettura pei Fanciulli, Milano: Giovanni.

1931 The Prince and the Pauper. Scrittori Inglesi e Americani Commentati per le Scuole, n. 3. Torino: Societa Editrice Internazionale. [English]

1933 Masino e Il Principe: Racconto per i Ragazzi di Tutti i Tempi [Pauper and the Prince: Tale for the Boys of Every Time], Torino/Milano/Firenze: Paravia.

1936 Principe e Mendico. Romanzo, Torino: Unione Tipografico - Editrice Torinese.

1939 The Prince and the Pauper. Scrittori Inglesi e Americani Commentati per le Scuoli. Torino: Societa Editrice Internazionale. [English]

1939 Masin e Il Principe. Racconto per i Ragazzi di Tutti i Tempi, Torino/Milano/Padova: Paravia.

1941 Same. Torino/Milano/Padova: Paravia.

1945 Il Principe ed Il Mendico [The Prince and the Pauper], Milano: Corticelli.

1946 Same. Milano: Corticelli.

1948 Il Principe e Il Mendico [The Prince and the Pauper], Firenze: Marzocco.

1949 Il Principe e Il Povero [The Prince and the Pauper], Milano: Carroccio.

1949 Same. Roma: Societa Apostolato Stampa.

1950   Il Principe e Il Povero. Romanzo. [The Prince and the Pauper.
       Novel], Milano: La Sorgente.

1952   Same. Firenze: Franceschini.

1952   Same. Torino: Societa Apostolato Stampa.

1953   Same. Romanzo per Ragazzi [Novel for Boys]. Milano: Carroccio.

1953   Il Principe e Il Povero, Milano: Carroccio.

1953   Same. Milano: Fabbri.

1954   I Due Re [The Two Kings], Bergamo, Milano: Minerva Italica.

1954   Il Principe e Il Povero, Torino: S.A.I.E.

1954   Il Principe e Il Povero. Romanzo per Ragazzi, Milano: Boschi.

1954   Il Principe e Il Mendicante [The Prince and the Beggar]. Torino:
       Societa Editrice Internazionale.

1955   Il Principe e Il Povero, Milano: Fabbri.

1955   Same. Torino: S.A.I.E.

1958   Principe e Mendico. Romanzo. La Scala d'Oro, Biblioteca Graduata
       per Ragazzi, Ser. 5, n. 5. Torino: Unione Tipografico-Editrice
       Torinese.

1959   Il Principe e Il Mendico. Storia per i Giovani di Tutti le Eta
       [The Prince and the Pauper. Tale for the Youth of All Ages].
       Capolavori Stranieri per la Gioventu. [6th edition]. Firenze:
       Bemporad-Marzocco.

1959   Masino e Il Principe. Le Gemme d'Oro. Torino/Milano/Padova:
       Paravia.

1959   Il Principe e Il Povero, Milano: Lucchi.

1960   Le Prince et le Pauvre [The Prince and the Pauper]. Editions de
       l'Iris. Rosa d'Oro. 350, 4. Montreal, Milano: A.L.T. [French]

1963   Il Principe e Il Povero. I Birilli. S.III: per i Ragazzi dai 10
       ai 13 Anni. 52 [Ninepins. Series III: for the Boys from 10 to
       13 Years. 52]. Milano: AMZ.

1963   Same. Milano: AMZ.

1964   Same. [In a collection of stories by Mark Twain, Rudyard Kipling,
       John Ruskin, and Herman Melville]. I Capolavori. Milano:
       Mondadori.

1964   Le Prince et le Pauvre. Les Grands Classiques Illustres. 3. Paris:
       Del Duca. Bologne: Steb. [French]

1965 Il Principe e Il Povero. Colana Salaria, 5. Bologna: Capitol.

1965 Same. Classica Mondiale. 7. Milano: Europea Editrice.

1965 Il Principe e Il Mendicante. Narratori Moderni per la Scula
Media. 23. Torino: Societa Editrice Internazionale.

1966 Il Principe e Il Povero. Margherita. Milano: Aristea.

1966 Same. Classici Malipiero. 11. Bologna: Malipiero.

1966 Same. Racconti e Avventiere. 11. Bologna: Malipiero.

1966 Same. I Grandi Capolavori. 11. Bolgna: Malipiero.

1966 Same. La 500 Ep. 31. Roma: Paoline.

1966 Same. Strenne Corticelli. 8. Milano: Mursia.

1967 Same. Tiberina. 20. Bologna: Capitol. Firenze: B.B.D.M.

1967 Same. I Birilli. S. III. Per i Ragazzi dai 10 ai 14 Anni. 52
[Nine Pins. Series III. For the Boys from 10 to 14 Years. 52].
Milano: AMZ. Torino. Marietti.

1967 Same. Classici per Ragazzi. 13. Milano: Fabbri.

1968 The Prince and the Pauper. After the Story by Mark Twain. A Ward
Lock Classic in Color. London: Ward Lock. Bologna: STEB.
[English]

1968 Il Principe e Il Povero. Classici per Ragazzi. Firenze: Vallecchi.

1969 Same. Milano: Fabbri.

1973 Masino e il Principe, Napoli: Il Tripode.

Pudd'nhead Wilson

1949 Wilson Lo Zuccone [Wilson the Dunce]. Biblioteca Universale
Rizzoli, 28-29. [14th edition] Milano: Rizzoli.

1965 Same. Primavera. 13. Padova: R.A.D.A.R.

Report from Paradise

1953 Viaggio in Paradiso; L'Angelo del Protocollo [Voyage to Heaven;
The Angel of Protocol], Milano: Longanesi.

1956 Viaggio in Paradiso di Mark Twain [Voyage to Heaven by Mark Twain],
Milano: [Longanesi?]

1965 Viaggio in Paradiso. Nuova ed. [New edition], Milano: Longanesi.

Roughing It

1959 Vita Dura [Hard Life]. I Narratori del Realismo. 9. Roma: Riuniti.

Stories and Sketches

1900 Racconti Americani [American Stories], Milano: Corriere della Sera.

1910 Il Biglietto di L.25 Milioni ed Altri Racconti Umoristici [The Note of 25 Million Lira and Other Humorous Stories], Firenze: Bemporad e Figlio.

1919 Same. Firenze: Bemporad e Figlio.

1920 Il Romanzo di la Giovane Esquimese [The Romance of the Esquimo Girl], Milano: n. pub.

1922 Il Romanzo d'Una Giovane Esquimese [The Romance of An Esquimo Girl], Milano: Corticelli.

1927 Un Biglietto di Banca da Venticinque Milioni: Romanzo [A Bank Note for Twenty-five Million: Novel], Firenze: n. pub.

1930 The Million Pound Bank-Note. English and American Literary Works, n. 2. Firenze: Riggio. [English]

1931 Tom Sawyer. The L.1.000.000 Bank-note [an abridgement]. Collezione di Classici Inglesi. Palermo: Gino. [English]

1934 Racconti Umoristici [Humorous Stories]. I Capolavori dell' Umorismo. Milano: Sonzogno.

1934 The 1.000.000 Bank-note. Tom Sawyer, Palermo: Gino. [English]

1934 Il Biglietto di 25.000.000. Novelle [The Note for 25,000,000. Short Stories]. Collana Letteraria Minerva, 32. Milano: Minerva.

1935 Il Biglietto da Venticinque Milioni di Lire ed Altri Umoristici [The Note for Twenty-five Million Lira and Other Humorous Stories]. Collezione di Capolavori, n. 39. Firenze: Bemporad.

1936 Same. Firenze: Bemporad e Figlio.

1939 Sherlock Holmes Battuto [Sherlock Holmes Defeated]. In Ultragiallo delle Rivelazioni. Cinque Capolavori Gialli [Ultra Thriller of Detections. Five Thriller Masterpieces]. Milano: Attualita.

1945 Il Biglietto da Un Milione di Sterline [The Note for A Million Sterling], Milano: n. pub.

1949 La Rivincita dell'Asino [The Revenge of the Donkey]. In Jack London: Un Naso per Il Re [A Nose for the King]. Lanciano: Carabba.

1950   Il Ranocchio Saltatore e Altri Racconti [The Jumping Frog and
       Other Stories]. Biblioteca Universale Rizzoli. [8th edition]
       Milano: Rizzoli.

1951   Tom Sawyer Poliziotto, e Il Biglietto da Venticinque Milioni di
       Lire [Tom Sawyer Detective, and The Bank-note for Twenty-five
       Million Lira], Firenze: Marzocco.

1952   Il Furto dell'Elefante Bianco, e Altri Racconti [The Theft of the
       White Elephant, and Other Stories]. Biblioteca Universale Rizzoli,
       n. 399-400. Milano: Rizzoli.

1954   L'Eta dell'Oro e Racconti [The Gilded Age and Stories], Roma:
       Casini.

1958   Un Yankee del Connecticut alla Corte del Re Artu, La Banconota
       de 1,000,000 di Sterline [A Yankee from Connecticut at the Court
       of King Arthur, The Bank-note for 1,000,000 Sterling], Milano:
       Il Club del Libro.

1960   L'Eta dell'Oro e Racconti [The Gilded Age and Stories]. I Grandi
       Maestri. 18. Roma: Casini.

1961   Eva Cosi Scriveva [Eve As Writer (Eve's Diary)], Milano: Elmo.

1961   I Racconti sul Fiume [Stories concerning the River]. I Grandi
       Libri delle Fiave. Bologna: A.M.Z.

1962   Same. Collana Azzurra. Milano: A.M.Z.

1962   Un Yankee del Connecticut alla Corte del Re Artu, La Banconota da
       1.000.000 di Sterline. I Classici di Tutti i Tempi. 5. Serie
       Grandi Narratori. 2. Novara: I.G.D.A.

1963   Racconti sul Fiume. Penne d'Oro. Milano: A.M.Z.

1965   Short Stories, A Selection. Biblioteca di Classici Stranieri.
       Sezione Inglese e Americana. 21. Milano: Mursia (Ferrari).
       [English]

1966   Il Biglietto da un Milione di Sterline e Altre Novelle [The Note
       for A Million Sterling and Other Short Stories]. I Libri del
       Sabato. Grandi Romanzi. 49. Roma: Casini. Bologna: Steb.

1967   Racconti [Stories]. I Grandi Scrittori Stranieri. 278. Torino:
       Unione Tipografico-editrice Torinese.

1972   23 [Venitre] Racconti [23 Stories], Milano: Club degli Editori.

1972   L'Uomo Che Corruppe Hadleyburg, Torino: Einaudi [volume includ-
       ing three stories]

1973   Il Frontiere dell'Allegria: Tutte le Novelle e i Racconti
       Umoristici [The Frontier of Mirth: All the Short Stories and
       the Humorous Tales], Milano: Mursia.

Tom Sawyer

1909 <u>Le Avventure di Tom Sawyer</u> [The Adventures of Tom Sawyer], Firenze: Bemporad.

1918 Same. Firenze: Bemporad e Figlio.

1930 Same. Collezione di Capolavori Stranieri Tradotti per la Gioventu Italiana, n. 26. [2nd edition]. Firenze: Bemporad e Figlio.

1931 <u>Tom Sawyer. The L.1.000.000 Bank-Note.</u> [abridgement] Collezione di Classici Inglesi. Palermo: Gino. [English]

1934 <u>Le Avventure di Tom Sawyer. Romanzo</u> [The Adventures of Tom Sawyer. Novel]. Collana Letteraria Minerva, 17. Milano: Minerva.

1934 <u>The 1.000.000 Bank-Note. Tom Sawyer</u>, Palermo: Gino. [English]

1937 <u>Le Avventure di Tom Sawyer.</u> [3rd edition] Firenze: Bemporad e Figlio.

1938 <u>Le Avventure di Tom Sawyer. Romanzo.</u> I Corvi Collana Universale Moderna, n. 91. della Serie Viola. Milano: Corbaccio.

1939 <u>Le Avventure di Tom Sawyer: Romanzo per Ragazzi</u> [The Adventures of Tom Sawyer: Novel for Boys]. Libri Belli. Collezione per Ragazzi, 3. Milano: Lucchi.

1939 <u>Le Avventure di Tom Sawyer.</u> Collezione di Capolavori Stranieri Tradotti per la Gioventu Italiana, n. 26. [4th edition] Firenze: Marzocco.

1947 <u>The Adventures of Tom Sawyer.</u> The Albatross Modern Continental Library, Vol. 1622. Verona, Milano: London, Paris: Mondadori. [English]

1947 Same. Milano: Signorelli. [English]

1948 <u>Le Avventure di Tom Sawyer</u>, Milano: Lucchi.

1948 Same. Milano: Baldini e Castoldi.

1949 <u>Le Avventure di Tom Sawyer e di Huckleberry Finn</u> [The Adventures of Tom Sawyer and of Huckleberry Finn], Torino: Einaudi.

1950 <u>Le Avventure di Tom Sawyer.</u> I Libri della Gioventu, 5. Firenze: Salani.

1951 Same. Firenze: Franceschini.

1952 <u>Tom Sawyer. Romanzo</u>, Milano: La Sorgente.

1953 <u>Le Avventure di Tom Sawyer</u>, Milano: Carroccio.

1953 Same. Milano: Fabbri.

1953 Same. Nettuno Omnia. Bologna: A.E.G.M.

1953 Same. Torino: Societa Apostolato Stampa.

1953 Same. Torino: Societa Apostolato Stampa.

1953 Same. Milano: A.P.E.

1954 Le Avventure di Tom Sawyer. Romanzo per Ragazzi. Milano: Boschi.

1954 Le Avventure di Tom Sawyer, Torino: S.A.I.E.

1955 Same. Milano: Lucchi.

1955 Same. Milano: Fabbri.

1955 Same. Roma: Curcio.

1956 Same. Firenze: Curcio.

1956 Same. [18th edition] Firenze: Marzocco.

1958 Same. Il Bosco. 36. Milano, Verona: Mondadori.

1960 Same. Superverdi. 22. Torino: S.A.I.E.

1962 Same. Torino, Genova, Milano: S.E.I.

1962 Same. Libri Belli. Collezione per Ragazzi. 3. Milano: Fabbri.

1963 Tom Sawyer, Huckleberry Finn. I Millenni. Torino: Einaudi.

1963 Le Avventure di Tom Sawyer. I Birilli. S. III: per i Ragazzi
      dai 10 ai 13 anni. [for Boys from 10 to 13 years] 46. Milano:
      AMZ.

1964 Same. I Grandi Libri. 30. Firenze: Salani. Vicenza: A.G.V.

1964 Same. Torino, Roma, Napoli: Mezzogiorno.

1964 Tom Sawyer. Caleidoscopio. 28. Verona: Mondadori.

1964 Tom Sawyer. Romanzo, Milano: La Sorgente.

1965 Le Avventure di Tom Sawyer. Miniclassici per la Gioventu Malipiero.
      8. Bologna: Malipiero.

1965 Same. Collana Salaria, 11. Bologna: Capitol.

1965 Same. I Classici per la Gioventu. Milano: AMZ.

1965 Same. Classici per Ragazzi. 5. Milano: Fabbri.

1966 La Saga di Tom Sawyer [The Saga of Tom Sawyer (Adventures of Tom
      Sawyer, Adventures of Huckleberry Finn, Tom Sawyer Detective)].
      La Biblioteca. 11. Milano: Mursia.

1966   Tom Sawyer. Bestsellers per i Giovani. 4. Torino: Albero.

1966   Le Avventure di Tom Sawyer, Milano: Europea.

1966   Same. Napoli, Casoria: Istituto Editoriale del Mezzogiorno.

1966   Same. La 500 ep. 22. Roma: Paoline.

1966   Same. I Grandi Classici Illustrati. 17. Bologna: Steb.

1966   Same. Tiberina 8. Bologna: Capitol. Firenze: BBDM.

1966   Les Adventures de Tom Sawyer [The Adventures of Tom Sawyer]. Les
       Grands Classiques Illustres. Paris: Mondiales. Bologne: Steb.
       [French]

1967   Le Avventure di Tom Sawyer. I Birilli. S. III. Per i Ragazzi
       dai 10 ai 14 anni [For Boys from 10 to 14 years]. 46. Milano:
       AMZ. Torino: Marietti.

1967   Same. [new edition] Milano: AMZ.

1967   Same. Classica Mondiale. 39. Milano: Europea. Bologna: Steb.

1967   Same. L'Oblo. Messina-Firenze: D'Anna.

1967   Same. Narrativa Moderna. 15. Padova: R.A.D.A.R. Vicenza:
       Stocchiero.

1968   Same. Italenti 6. Bologna: Malipiero.

1968   Same. Classici Italiani e Stranieri per la Scuola Media. Brescia:
       La Scuola.

1968   Same. Firenze: Salani.

1968   Tom Sawyer. Milano: Fabbri.

1970   Le Avventure di Tom Sawyer. Bologna: Capitol.

1971   Same. Torino: SEI.

1973   Same. Milano: Bietti.

1974   Same. Padova: EMP.

Tom Sawyer Abroad

1911   Tom Sawyer L'Aeronauta [Tom Sawyer the Aeronaut], Firenze: Bemporad
       e Figlio.

1918   Same. Firenze: Bemporad e Figlio.

1935   Same. Collezione di Capolavori, n. 28. Firenze: Bemporad e
       Figlio.

1953   Le Nuove Avventure di Tom Sawyer, Milano: [Mursia?]

1957   Tom Sawyer a Volo per il Mondo [Tom Sawyer in Flight over the World],
        Milano: Lucchi.

1965   Le Nuove Avventure di Tom Sawyer. Tom Sawyer all'esterno, Tom
        Sawyer Detective [The New Adventures of Tom Sawyer. Tom Sawyer
        Abroad, Tom Sawyer Detective]. Strenne Corticelli. Milano:
        Mursia.

                        Tom Sawyer, Detective

1920   Tom Sawyer, Poliziotto [Tom Sawyer, Detective], Firenze: Bemporad.

1921   Same. Firenze: Bemporad.

1936   Tom Sawyer Poliziotto e Altri Novelle [Tom Sawyer Detective and
        Other Short Stories]. Collezione di Capolavori, n. 27. Firenze:
        Bemporad e Figlio.

1951   Tom Sawyer Poliziotto, e Il Biglietto da Venticinque Milioni di
        Lire [Tom Sawyer Detective, and the Note for Twenty-five Million
        Lire]. [2nd edition] Firenze: Marzocco.

1953   Le Nuove Avventure di Tom Sawyer [The New Adventures of Tom Sawyer],
        Milano: [Mursia?]

1954   Tom Sawyer Poliziotto. (Romanzo per Ragazzi) [Tom Sawyer Detective.
        (Novel for Boys)], Milano: La Sorgente.

1956   Altre Avventure di Tom Sawyer [Other Adventures of Tom Sawyer],
        Milano: Fabbri.

1965   Le Nuove Avventure di Tom Sawyer: Tom Sawyer all'estero, Tom
        Sawyer Detective [The New Adventures of Tom Sawyer: Tom Sawyer
        Abroad, Tom Sawyer Detective], Milano: Mursia.

1966   La Saga di Tom Sawyer [The Saga of Tom Sawyer (Adventures of Tom
        Sawyer, Adventures of Huckleberry Finn, Tom Sawyer Detective)].
        La Biblioteca. 11. Milano: Mursia.

                        Travel Sketches

1959   Naples Revisited. Portrait of A City As Seen by American Novelists
        of the XIX Century [Cooper, Melville, Twain (extract from The
        Innocents Abroad), H. James, Botta, Guido], Roma: Fischer.
        [English]

1961   La Citta Sepolta di Pompei [The Buried City of Pompey]. Sta in:
        Testimonianze Americane sull'Italia del Risorgimento [Published
        in: American Testimony about the Italy of the Movement for Poli-
        tical Unity (an extract from The Innocents Abroad)], Milano:
        Edizioni di Comunita.

Selections

1928 Selections. Collezione di Classici Inglesi. Palermo: Gino.
[English]

Netherlands

Sources: BCB/BCCB/IT/NUC

American Claimant

1893 De Amerikaansche Pretendent [The American Claimant], Leiden:
Blankenberg.

1908 De Erfgenaam in Amerika [The Heir in America]. Zie Bibliotheek,
No. 3/4. n.p.: Blauwe.

1951 De Erfgenaam uit Amerika [The Heir from America]. [2nd edition]
Amsterdam, Antwerp: Wereldbibliotheek.

1955 Same. Amsterdam: Wereldbibliotheek.

1968 De Amerikaansche Pretendent, Amsterdam: Wereldbibliotheek.

Autobiography

1907 Uit het Leven van Mark Twain. Autobiographie [From the Life of
Mark Twain. Autobiography], Haarlem: Loosjes. Amsterdam: Zonen.

Huckleberry Finn

1885 De Lotgevallen van Huckleberry Finn (Tom Sawyer's Makker) [The
Adventures of Huckleberry Finn (Tom Sawyer's Comrade)], Arnheim:
Rinkes. Amsterdam: Van Holkema & Warendorf.

1894 Same. [2nd edition] Amsterdam: Van Holkema & Warendorf.

1908 De Lotgevallen van Huckleberry Finn. Zie Kameraad, Deel X
[Volume X]. n.p.: De Golde.

1919 De Lotgevallen van Huckleberry Finn (Tom Sawyer's Makker).
[6th edition] Amsterdam: Van Holkema & Warendorf.

1927 Same. Amsterdam: Van Holkema & Warendorf.

1950 De Lotgevallen van Huckleberry Finn. [2nd edition] Haarlem: De
Sleutel.

1954 Huckleberry Finn; de Vriend van Tom Sawyer [Huckleberry Finn; the
Friend of Tom Sawyer], 'S-Gravenhage: Van Goor Zonen.

1958 Same. [2nd edition] 'S-Gravenhage: Van Goor Zonen.

1961 De Avonturen van Huckleberry Finn [The Adventures of Huckleberry Finn], 'S-gravenhage: Zuid-Holland. U.M.

1965 De Lotgevallen van Huckleberry Finn, Amsterdam: Veen.

1968 Huckleberry Finn; de Vriend van Tom Sawyer. [3rd edition] 'S-Gravenhage: Van Goor Zonen.

1973 Omnibus: Tom Sawyer. Huckleberry Finn, 'S-Gravenhage: Van Goor.

Innocents Abroad

1879 Reizigers van over See [Travellers beyond the Seas]. 2 deelen [2 volumes]. Arnheim: Rinkes.

1880 Een Moderne Pelgrimstocht [A Modern Pilgrimage]. 2 deelen. Arnheim: Rinkes.

Joan of Arc

1897 Persoonlijke Herinneringen van Jeanne d'Arc [Personal Recollections of Joan of Arc]. 2 deelen. Amsterdam: Van Dantzig.

King Leopold's Soliloquy

1961 Koning Leopold's Alleenspraak [door] Mark Twain. Belgie's Kolonialisme in de Congo [King Leopold's Soliloquy. Belgium's Colonialism in the Congo], Amsterdam: Pegasus.

Prince and the Pauper

1882 Prins en Bedelknaap. Een Verhaal voor Jongelieden [Prince and Beggar Boy. A Tale for Young People], Arnheim: Rinkes.

1896 Same. [2nd edition] Amsterdam: Van Holkema & Warendorf.

1911 Prins en Bedelknaap. Zie Kameraad. Deel XII. [Vol. XII]. [3rd edition] n.p.: De golde.

1918 The Prince and the Pauper. Zie Library (Meulenhoff's English), No. 2. 'S-Gravenhage. [English]

1925 Prins en Bedelknaap, Amsterdam: Van Holkema & Warendorf.

1934 Same. Amsterdam: Van Holkema & Warendorf.

1952 De Prins en de Straatjongen [The Prince and the Streetboy], Utrecht: Cantecleer.

1954 Same. [2nd edition] Utrecht: Cantecleer.

1961 Prins en Bedelknaap, 'S-Gravenhage: Van Goor Zonen.

1969 Same. 'S-Gravenhage: Muelenhoff.

1975 Same. Rotterdam: Lekturama.

Roughing It

1878 Door Dik en Dun. Een Amerikaansch Reisverhaal [Through Thick and
      Thin. An American Travel Account], Arnheim: Rinkes.

Stories and Sketches

1892 Spoorweg-kannibolen [Railway-cannibals]. Zie Warendorf's Novellen-
      bibliotheek. No. 31. Amsterdam: Warendorf.

1898 Een Merkwaardig Voorval [A Remarkable Incident]. Zie Warendorf's
      Novellen-bibliotheek. No. 103. Amsterdam: Warendorf.

1900 Het Bankbiljet van een Mil'joen Pond en Andere Verhalen [The Bank-
      note for A Million Pounds and Other Tales]. Zie Universum
      (Literair). No. 16. n.p.

1902 Archy Stillman, de Detective, Hilversum: Vleming. Rotterdam:
      Bolle.

1907 Grappen en Grillen [Drolleries and Whims]. Zie Kunst. Deel V
      [Vol. V]. n.p.: Blijde.

1907 Het Bankbiljet van Tien Mil'joen [The Bank-note for Ten Million].
      Zie Voor Decoupe, No. 162. n.p.: n.pub.

1908 De Geschiedenis van een Paard, gevolgd door De Geschiedenis van
      een Hond [The Story of A Horse, followed by The Story of A Dog],
      'S-Gravenhage: Hols.

1908 "De Landbouw," Weekblad voor Chicago. Farce in 2 Tafereelen
      ["The Agriculture," Weekly Paper for Chicago. Farce in 2 Scenes].
      Zie Tooneel-bibliotheek. No. 17. n.p.: Mosman's.

1922 Same. [2nd edition] Zie Tooneel-bibliotheek. No. 17. n.p.:
      Mosman's.

1971 Een Praatje Bij Het Vuur in Het Jaar 1601 [A Chat by the Fire in
      the Year 1601], Amsterdam: Arbeiderspers.

Tom Sawyer

1877 De Lotgevallen van Tom Sawyer [The Adventures of Tom Sawyer],
      Arnheim: Rinkes.

1879 Same. [2nd edition] Arnheim: Rinkes.

1883 Same. [3rd edition] Arnheim: Rinkes.

1890 Same. [5th edition] Amsterdam: Van Holkema & Warendorf.

1896 Same. [6th edition] Amsterdam: Van Holkema & Warendorf.

1903 Same. Zie Kameraad. [6th edition] n.p.: De Golde.

1908 Streeken en Avonturen van Tom Sawyer [Pranks and Adventures of Tom Sawyer], Amsterdam: Bekker.

1909 De Lotgevallen van Tom Sawyer. Zie Kameraad. Deel II [Vol. II]. [7th edition] n.p.: De Golde.

1930 Same. Amsterdam: Van Holkema & Warendorf.

1950 The Adventures of Tom Sawyer. [abridged] Amsterdam: Muelenhoff. [English]

1953 De Avonturen van Tom Sawyer, 'S-Gravenhage: Van Goor Zonen.

1955 Same. [2nd edition] 'S-Gravenhage: Van Goor Zonen.

1955 The Adventures of Tom Sawyer. [abridged] Amsterdam: Muelenhoff. [English]

1957 De Avonturen van Tom Sawyer, Haarlem: De Sleutel.

1958 Same. Haarlem: Gottmer.

1958 The Adventures of Tom Sawyer. [abridged] Amsterdam: Meulenhoff. [English]

1960 De Avonturen van Tom Sawyer. [12th edition] 'S-Gravenhage: Kramers.

1961 Tom Sawyer, Amsterdam: Van Holkema & Warendorf.

1961 De Avonturen van Tom Sawyer. [3rd edition] 'S-Gravenhage: Van Goor Zonen.

1962 Same. 'S-Gravenhage: Van Goor.

1962 The Adventures of Tom Sawyer. [abridged] Amsterdam: Meulenhoff. [English]

1963 De Avonturen van Tom Sawyer, 'S-Gravenhage: Kramers.

1965 Same. Amsterdam: Veen.

1967 Same. 'S-Gravenhage: Van Goor.

1968 Same. [abridged] 'S-Gravenhage: Meulenhoff.

1968 Same. Nederlandse Boekclub (Prinsevin-kempark 2). 'S-Gravenhage: Succes.

1968   Omnibus. Tom Sawyer als Kwajongen. Tom Sawyer als Zeerover. Tom
        Sawyer als Speurder [Omnibus. Tom Sawyer as Mischievous Boy. Tom
        Sawyer as Pirate. Tom Sawyer as Tracker]. [abridged edition]
        'S-Gravenhage: Meulenhoff.

1968   Tom Sawyer. Easy Readers. Serie B [simplified for use in schools].
        Groningen: Wolters-Noordhoff. [English]

1973   Omnibus: Tom Sawyer. Huckleberry Finn, 'S-Gravenhage: Van Goor.

1974   Avonturen van Tom Sawyer. [4th edition] 'S-Gravenhage: Van Goor.

1976   Tom Sawyer, Amsterdam: Lanoo.

Tom Sawyer Abroad

1894   Tom Sawyer's Reisavonturen [Tom Sawyer's Travel Adventures],
        Amsterdam: Van Holkema & Warendorf.

1905   Same. Zie Kameraad. VI. n.p.: De Golde.

1925   Same. Amsterdam: Van Holkema & Warendorf.

Tom Sawyer, Detective

1899   De Jonge Detective [The Young Detective]. Zie Detective-romans,
        No. 3. n.p.: Amerikaansche.

Tramp Abroad

1881   Door Stad en Land [Through Town and Country]. 2 deelen. Sneek:
        Van Druten.

1884   Ontmoetingen op een Voltreis [Encounters upon A Hike]. 2 deelen.
        [2nd edition of Door Stadt en Land]. Sneek: Van Druten.

Travel Sketches

1938   Letters from the Sandwich Islands; Written for the Sacramento
        Union, by Mark Twain, The Hague: Nijhoff. [English]

Miscellaneous Writings

1899   Eenden-John [John of the Ducks]. Naar't Engels [After the English].
        Zie Reisbibliotheek, 2e serie, No. 1. n.p.: Slothouwer.

1965   Epigrammen [Epigrams], 'S-Gravenhage: Boucher.

Selections

1912 Selections. Zie Up-to-date-series, Vol. 4. n.p.: n.pub.[English]

Norway

Sources: IT/NB

Huckleberry Finn

1889 Huck Finns Eventyr [Huck Finn's Adventures], Oslo: Omtvedt.

1930 Huck Finns Opplevelser [Huck Finn's Adventures]. Verdens Beste
       Romaner. Oslo: Gyldendal.

1939 Huck Finns Bedrifter [Huck Finn's Exploits], Oslo: Ascheboug.

1949 Huck Finn, Bergen: Eides.

1959 Huck Finns Opplevelser. Hjemmenes Boksamling. Oslo: Reistad &
       Sonn.

1959 Same. Gyldendals Familiebibliotek. Verdensromaner. Oslo:
       Gyldendal.

1963 Same. Oslo: Gyldendal.

1969 Huckleberry Finns Eventyr, Oslo: De Unge.

1969 Huckleberry Finn, Oslo: Tveitan.

1974 Huck Finn og Eventyra Hans [Huck Finn and His Adventures], Oslo:
       Norsk Barneblad.

Innocents Abroad

1940 Troskyldige Globetrottere (Inocense [sic] Abroad) [Simple Globe-
       trotters (Innocents Abroad)], Oslo: Petlitz.

Joan of Arc

1913 Jeanne d'Arc. Orleans-moyi [Joan of Arc. Orleans Maid], Oslo:
       Samlaget.

Man That Corrupted Hadleyburg

1947 Skandalen i Hadleyburg og Andere Historier [Scandals in Hadleyburg
       and Other Stories], Oslo: Dybwad.

Prince and the Pauper

1917 Tiggerprinsen. En Fortaelling for Ungdom i Alle Lande [Beggar Prince. A Tale for Young People in All Lands], Oslo: Ascheboug.

1928 Prinsen og Fattigguten [Prince and Pauper Boy], Oslo: Jorgensen.

1937 Tiggerprinsen, Oslo: Gyldendal.

1945 Prinsen og Fattigguten, Oslo: Jorgensen.

1951 Same. Oslo: Tiden.

1956 Tiggerprinsen, Oslo: Gyldendal.

1972 Prinsen og Fattiggutten, Oslo: Tiden.

Pudd'nhead Wilson

1971 Den Tvilsomme Tvilling [The Doubtful Twin], Oslo: Den Norske Bokklubben.

Stories and Sketches

1947 Skandalen i Hadleyburg og Andere Historier, Oslo: Dybwad.

1962 Fransk Duell [French Duel], Oslo: Fredhoi.

Tom Sawyer

1922 Tom Sawyer og Eventyri Haus [Tom Sawyer and His Adventures], Oslo: Jorgensen.

1929 Tom Sawyer, Oslo: Damm.

1929 Tom Sawyers Bedrifter [Tom Sawyer's Exploits], Oslo: Ascheboug.

1945 Tom Sawyer og Eventyri Haus, Oslo: Jorgensen.

1949 Tom Sawyer, Bergen: Eides.

1961 Same. Udodelige Ungdomsboker. Oslo: Damm.

1961 Tom Sawyers Bedrifter. Verdens Beste Ungdomsboker. 15. Stavanger: Stabenfeldt.

1966 Tom Sawyer, Oslo: De Unge.

1968 Same. Oslo: Tveitan.

1969 Same. [2nd edition] Oslo: Tveitan.

1975 Tom Sawyer og Eventyra Hans [Tom Sawyer and His Adventures], Larvik:
Norsk Barneblad.

Selections

1963 Mark Twains Beste [Mark Twain's Best]. Omnibus-bokene. 7. Oslo:
Erichsen.

Portugal

Sources: IT/NUC/PBP/SPT

American Claimant

1946 O Conde Americano [The American Count], Lisboa: Inquerito.

1963 O Pretendente Americano [The American Claimant], Porto: Civilizacao.

Connecticut Yankee

1962 Um Americano na Corte do Rei Artur [An American at the Court of
King Arthur]. Coleccao Juvenil. Lisboa: Portugalia.

Huckleberry Finn

1944 As Aventuras de Huckleberry Finn [The Adventures of Huckleberry
Finn], Lisboa: Inquerito.

1952 Aventuras de Huckleberry Finn. Biblioteca dos Rapazes. Lisboa:
Portugalia.

1956 Same. [2nd edition] Lisboa: Portugalia.

Prince and the Pauper

1945 O Principe e O Pobre [The Prince and the Pauper], Lisboa: Inquerito.

1963 Same. Porto: Civilizacao.

1965 Same. Porto: Civilizacao.

1967 Same. [3rd edition] Porto: Civilizacao.

1967 Same. Lisboa: Inquerito.

1976 Same. [6th edition] Porto: Civilizacao.

Roughing It

1949   Uma Viagem em Mala-posta [A Journey in A Mail-coach], Lisboa: Severo, Freitas, Mega.

Stories and Sketches

191-?   Contos [Stories]. Coleccao Lilas, 4. Porto: Da Silva.

1946   O Roubo de Elefante Branco [The Theft of White Elephant]. Coleccao Romances e Contos, 5. Lisboa: Inquerito.

1947   A Heranca do Tio [The Legacy of the Uncle]. [The $30,000 Bequest] Coleccao Claridade. Lisboa: Lisboneuse.

Tom Sawyer

1952   As Aventuras de Tom Sawyer [The Adventures of Tom Sawyer], Lisboa: Portugalia.

1961   Same. [5th edition] Coleccao Biblioteca dos Rapazes. Lisboa: Portugalia.

1962   Aventuras de Tom Sawyer. [4th edition] Lisboa: Portugalia.

1968   Same. [6th edition] Lisboa: Portugalia.

Tom Sawyer Abroad

1953   Viagems de Tom Sawyer [Journeys of Tom Sawyer]. Biblioteca dos Rapazes. Lisboa: Portugalia.

1958   Viagems de Tom Sawyer. Tom Sawyer, Detective. [2nd edition] Lisboa: Portugalia.

Tom Sawyer, Detective

1958   Viagems de Tom Sawyer. Tom Sawyer, Detective. [2nd edition] Lisboa: Portugalia.

1962   Tom Sawyer, Detective. [2nd edition] Lisboa: Portugalia.

Collected Works

1944   Obras Completas de Mark Twain [Complete Works of Mark Twain], Lisboa: Inquerito.

Spain

Sources: AEHA/BE/BON/CGLE/CGLEH/IT/LE/LEV/MLH/NUC/PBS/SPT

American Claimant

1925 El Pretendiente Americano [The American Pretender], Madrid:
Biblioteca Nueva.

1944 El Conde Americano [The American Count] y Otros Cuentes [and
Other Stories]. Coleccion Humor y Aventura, 1. Barcelona: Del
Junco.

Captain Stormfield's Visit to Heaven

1951 Una Visita al Cielo y Otras Narraciones [A Visit to Heaven and
Other Stories]. El Trebol de Cuatro Hojas. Barcelona: Arimany.

Connecticut Yankee

1943 Un Yanqui en la Corte del Rey Artus [A Yankee in the Court of the
King Arthur]. [2nd edition] Barcelona: La Academica.

1944 Same. Madrid: Diana.

1950 Un Yanqui en el Corte del Rey Arturo. Juvenil Cadete. Barcelona:
Mateu.

1951 Same. Coleccion Juvenil Cadete, 10. Barcelona: Mateu.

1957 Same. [adaptation] Barcelona: Bruguera.

1958 Un Yanqui en la Corte del Rey Artur, Barcelona: Mateu.

1959 Un Yanqui en la Corte del Rey Arturo, Barcelona: Bruguera.

1963 Un Yanqui en la Corte del Rey Artur. Coleccion Para tu Hijo.
Barcelona: Mateu.

1965 Un Ianqui a la Corte del Rei Artur, Barcelona: Bruguera.

1967 Un Yanqui en la Corte del Rey Artus, Barcelona: Circulo de
Lectores.

1970 Un Yanqui en la Corte del Rey Arturo, Barcelona: Bruguera.

1971 Same. [4th edition] Barcelona: Bruguera.

1971 Same. Barcelona: Mateu.

1973 Same. [5th edition] Barcelona: Bruguera.

1974 Same. Barcelona: AFHA International.

1974 Same. Barcelona: Bruguera.

1975 Same. Barcelona: Bruguera.

Fig. 32. *Tom Sawyer*, cover of 1964 Spanish edition published by Plaza & Janes (Courtesy Plaza & Janes, S. A. [Barcelona])

1975 Same. Barcelona: Bruguera.

1975 Same. Barcelona: Sopena.

1976 Same. [2nd edition] Barcelona: AFHA International.

1976 Same. [6th edition] Barcelona: Bruguera.

Huckleberry Finn

1923 Las Aventuras de Huck [The Adventures of Huck]. [2 vols.] Libreria Rivadeneyra. Madrid: Raggio.

1940 Aventuras de Huck, Madrid: Diana.

1942 Huck Finn. Continuacion de las Aventuras de Tom Sawyer [Huck Finn. Continuation of the Adventures of Tom Sawyer]. Ediciones Nausica. Barcelona: La Poligrafa.

1943 Same. [2nd edition] Barcelona: La Poligrafa.

1944 Las Aventuras de Huckleberry Finn. Famosas Novelas. Barcelona: Molino.

1949 Same. Coleccion Crisol. Madrid. Aguilar.

1953 Huck Finn, el Negro y Tom Sawyer [Huck Finn, the Negro and Tom Sawyer]. Coleccion Juvenil Cadete, 42. Barcelona: Mateu.

1957 Las Aventuras de Huckleberry Finn. Coleccion Historias, 94. Barcelona: Bruguera.

1957 Same. Barcelona: Juventud.

1957 Tom Sawyer y Huck Finn [Tom Sawyer and Huck Finn], Barcelona: Arimany.

1959 Aventuras de Huck Finn, Barcelona: Bruguera.

1960 Huck Finn, el Negro y Tom Sawyer, Barcelona: Mateu.

1961 Aventuras de Tom Sawyer. Aventuras de Huckleberry Finn. Grandes Novelas de la Literatura Universal, 19. Barcelona: Exito.

1962 Las Aventuras de Huckleberry Finn (El Camarada de Tom Sawyer) [The Adventures of Huckleberry Finn (The Comrade of Tom Sawyer)]. Coleccion Crisol, 264. [3rd edition] Madrid: Aguilar.

1962 Tom Sawyer y Huckleberry Finn, Barcelona: Zeus.

1963 Las Aventuras de Huckleberry Finn (El Camarada de Tom Sawyer), Barcelona: Sopena.

1963 Huckleberry Finn, Barcelona: Arimany.

1963 Las Aventuras de Tom Sawyer, Huckleberry Finn, Tom Sawyer Detective, y Tom Sawyer de Viaje, Barcelona: Arimany.

1967 Aventuras de Huck Finn, Barcelona: Bruguera.

1970 Same. [2nd edition] Barcelona: Bruguera.

1970 Huckleberry Finn, Barcelona: Circulo de Lectores.

1972 Same. Barcelona: Salvat. Madrid: Alianza.

1972 Aventuras de Huck Finn, Barcelona: Bruguera.

1972 Same. Barcelona: Bruguera.

1973 Same. [4th edition] Barcelona: Bruguera.

1974 Same. [5th edition] Historias Seleccion. Barcelona: Bruguera.

1974 Las Aventuras de Huckleberry Finn, Barcelona: Planeta.

1975 Las Aventuras de Huck Finn, Valladolid: Ediva.

1975 Aventuras de Huck Finn, Barcelona: Bruguera.

1975 Same. [3rd edition] Barcelona: Bruguera.

1976 Same. [6th edition] Barcelona: Bruguera.

1976 Aventuras de Huckleberry Finn, Madrid: Magisterio Espanol.

Innocents Abroad

1923 Viajes Humoristicos [Humorous Voyages], Madrid: Calleja.

1925 Same. [2nd edition] Madrid: Calleja.

1925 Viajes Absurdos y Aventuras Inverosimiles [Absurd Voyages and Improbable Adventures]. [2 vols.] Madrid: Castilla.

1943 Viajes Humoristicos, n.p.: Anaconda.

1945 Los Inocentes en el Extranjero [The Innocents Abroad]. Ediciones Nausica, 16. Barcelona: La Poligrafa.

Joan of Arc

1910 Juana de Arco (Novela Historica) [Joan of Arc (Historical Novel)], Madrid: Tesoro.

1949 Same. Coleccion la Jirafa, E.2. Madrid: Tesoro.

1950 Same. Barcelona: Alas.

1952 Same. Madrid: Tesoro.

1955 Juana de Arco, Barcelona: Molino.

1956 Same. Popular Literaria. Barcelona: Tesoro.

1956 Juana de Arco (Novela Historica), Madrid: C.P.L.

Life on the Mississippi

1974 Viejos Tiempos en el Mississippi [Old Times on the Mississippi],
      La Coruna: Adara.

Man That Corrupted Hadleyburg

1953 El Hombre que Corrompio a una Ciudad [The Man Who Corrupted A
      City], Madrid: Diana.

1953 Same. Madrid: Dolar.

1961? Same. Coleccion Austral, 649. Madrid: Espasa-Calpe. Austral.

1972 El Corruptor de Hadleyburg. Cuento Political de Doble Fondo
      [The Corrupter of Hadleyburg. Political Story of Double Nature],
      Madrid: Mauricio D'ors.

Mysterious Stranger

1936 El Forastero Misterioso [The Mysterious Stranger], n.p.: Letras.

Prince and the Pauper

1909 Same. Coleccion Selecta Internacional. Barcelona: Domenech
      (Maucci).

1925 Same. Barcelona: Domenech (Maucci).

1925 Same. Barcelona: Gili.

1943? Principe y Mendigo [Prince and Beggar]. Ediciones La Nave. Madrid:
      Lopez.

1943 Same. Famosas Novelas. Barcelona: Molino.

1944 Same. Novela Complete, 23. Barcelona: Ameller.

1945 El Principe y el Mendigo [The Prince and the Beggar]. Coleccion
      Oasis, 34. Barcelona: Reguera.

1946 Principe y Mendigo, Madrid: Diana.

1952 Same. Coleccion Juvenil Cadete, 24. Barcelona: Mateu.

1958 El Principe y el Mendigo. Juvenil Cadete. Barcelona: Mateu.

1958 Same. Madrid: Pia Sociedad de San Pablo.

1958 Same. Madrid: Paulinas.

1958 Principe y Mendigo, Barcelona: Bruguera.

1959 Same. Barcelona: Bruguera.

1960 Same. Coleccion Iris, 34. Barcelona: Bruguera.

1961 Same. [2nd edition] Barcelona: Bruguera.

1963 Same. Barcelona: Bruguera.

1963 El Principe y el Mendigo, Barcelona: Mateu.

1966 Principe y Mendigo, Barcelona: Bruguera.

1969 Same. Barcelona: Bruguera.

1970 Same. [5th edition] Barcelona: Bruguera.

1970 El Principe y el Mendigo, Barcelona: Rodegar.

1971 Principe y Mendigo, Barcelona: Bruguera.

1971 Same. Madrid: Libra.

1972 Same. Barcelona: Molino.

1973 Same. Barcelona: Bruguera.

1974 Same. Barcelona: Bruguera.

1975 Same. [2nd edition] Barcelona: Bruguera.

1975 Same. [7th edition] Barcelona: Bruguera.

1976 Same. Barcelona: Bruguera.

1976 Same. [8th edition] Barcelona: Bruguera.

Pudd'nhead Wilson

1944 Cabezahueca Wilson [Empty Head Wilson], Barcelona: Nausica.

1959 Wilson, el Simple [Wilson, the Simple], Barcelona: Bruguera.

Roughing It

1944 Los Inocentes en sus Pais [The Innocents in their Country],
      Barcelona: Nausica.

1944 La Vida Dura [The Hard Life], Barcelona: Lauro.

1944 Same. Barcelona: Janes.

1945 En el Pais del Oro y de la Plata [In the Country of the Gold and
      of the Silver]. Coleccion Retablo. Barcelona: Nausica.

1948 Pasada Fatigas [Past Hardships], Barcelona: Reguera.

1960 Aventuras en el Far-West [Adventures in the Far West], Barcelona:
      Bruguera.

1965 Los Inocentes en el Pais del Oro [The Innocents in the Country of
      Gold], Madrid: Dedalo.

1970 Aventuras en el Far-West. [2nd edition] Barcelona: Bruguera.

1972 Aventura en el Oeste [Adventure in the West], Barcelona: Bruguera.

1972 Adventuras en el Far West. [3rd edition] Barcelona: Bruguera.

1973 Same. [4th edition] Barcelona: Bruguera.

1976 Same. [6th edition] Barcelona: Bruguera.

1976 Aventura en el Oeste, Barcelona: Bruguera.

Stories and Sketches

1895 Bosquejos Humoristicos [Humorous Sketches], Barcelona: Castillo.

1901 Cuentos Humoristicos [Humorous Stories], Madrid, Barcelona:
      Lezcano y Cia.

1903 Cuentos Escogidos [Selected Stories]. Primera Serie [First Series].
      Madrid: Libreria Moderna.

1903? Same. [2nd edition] Madrid: Helencia.

1904 El Prometido de Aurelia. Narraciones Humoristicas [The Betrothed
      of Aurelia. Humorous Narrations]. Coleccion Alegria. Vol. VII.
      Madrid: Palacios.

1907? El Prometido de Aurelia. [2nd edition] Madrid: Palacios?

1910 Cuentos Humoristicos. Biblioteca de los Cuentos. Madrid: Admini-
      stracion del Noticiero-Guia de Madrid.

1912 Cuentos Escogidos. Coleccion Alegria, Vol. XVIII. [2nd edition]
      Madrid: Noticiero-guia de Madrid.

1918 L'elefante Blanc Robat [The Stolen White Elephant]. Biblioteca
      Literaria. Barcelona: Catalana.

1920 El Diario de Eva [The Diary of Eve], Madrid: Pueyo.

1920 L'elefante Blanc Robat y La Burra en las Coles [The Stolen White
      Elephant and the Donkey in the Cabbages], Madrid: Pueyo.

1920? Same. Madrid: Mundo Latino.

1920 Narraciones Humoristicas, Madrid: Rivadeneyra.

1922? Rayos, Truenos y Centellas; y Otros Cuentos Humoristicos [Thunder-
      bolts, Explosions and Flashes; and Other Humorous Stories],
      Barcelona: Guerrero.

1923? Bosquejo Humoristico [Humorous Sketches]. Biblioteca Ilustrada
      Economica. Barcelona: Bauza.

1923 ¿Ha Muerto Shakespeare? (Satiras) [Is Shakespeare Dead? (Satires)].
      Biblioteca Nueva. Madrid: Rivadeneyra.

1923 Mas Sagaz que Sherlock Holmes [More Shrewd than Sherlock Holmes],
      Barcelona: Maucci.

1924 El Diario de Eva, Madrid: Rivadeneyra.

1925? Narraciones Humoristicas. Biblioteca Nueva. Madrid: Rivadeneyra.

1929 El Disco de la Muerte [The Death Disk]. Revista Literaria Semanal,
      49. Madrid.

1929 La Herencia del Tio [The Inheritance of the Uncle]. Revista
      Literaria Semanal, 211. Madrid.

1929 Sherlock Holmes, Derrotado [Sherlock Holmes Defeated]. Revista
      Literaria Semanal, 176. Madrid.

1931 Narraciones Humoristicas. Coleccion Mundial de Obras Selectas.
      [3rd edition] Biblioteca Nueva. Madrid: Rivadeneyra.

1933 La Herencia del Tio, Madrid: Diana.

1934 La Ranota Saltadera del Comtat de Calaveras. El Desortat Promes
      d'Aurelia [The Jumping Frog of the Contest of Calaveras. The
      Disordered Fiance of Aurelia], Barcelona: Portada de Junceda.

1934 Tom Sawyer, Detective. El Romance de l'Esquimaleta. Un Reportage
      Sobre la Mort de Juli Cesar. La Ranota Saltadera del Comtat de
      Calaveras. El Desortat Promes d'Aurelia [Tom Sawyer, Detective.
      The Romance of the Esquimo Maiden. A Report about the Death of
      Julius Cesar. The Jumping Frog of the Contest of Calaveras. The
      Disordered Fiance of Aurelia], Barcelona: Portada de Junceda.

1934   El Disco de la Muerte, y Otros Cuentos [The Death Disk and Other Stories], Barcelona: Catalana.

1941? Diario de Adan [Diary of Adam], Madrid: Dedalo.

1941   Diario Adan, Barcelona: Grano de Arena.

1941   Diario de Eva [Diary of Eve], Barcelona: Grano de Arena.

1941   Un Deulo Historico [An Historical Duel], Barcelona: Agencia Distribuidora de Obras Selectas.

1942   Dos Detectives ante un Barril [Two Detectives before A Barrel], Barcelona: Alba.

1942   El Periodismo en Tennessee [Journalism in Tennessee].   Ediciones de la Gacela.   Barcelona: Atlantida.

1943   Cuentos Humoristicos, n.p.:   Anaconda.

1943   El Robo del Elefante Blanco y Otras Narraciones [The Theft of the White Elephant and Other Narrations].   Coleccion Anfora.   Madrid: Anfora.

1943   El Nino Malo y el Nino Bueno [The Bad Boy and the Good Boy (Sketches New and Old)], Barcelona: Janes.

1943   Las Mas Divertidas Aventuras [The Most Amusing Aventures], n.p.:   Anaconda.

1944   El Conde Americano y Otros Cuentos [The American Earl and Other Stories].   Coleccion Humor y Aventura, 1.   Barcelona: El Junco.

1944   Narraciones Humoristicas.   Coleccion Mundial de Obras Selectas.   Madrid: Biblioteca Nueva.

1945   El Disco de la Muerte, y Otros Cuentos, Barcelona: Albon.

1947   Aventuras de un Illuso [Adventures of a Visionary].   Novelas y Cuentos, Madrid: Diana.

1948   Cabeza de Chorlito [Hairbrained Person].   Novelas y Cuentos, Madrid: Diana.

1948? El Diario de Eva, Segovia: Biblioteca Nueva.

1950   El Robo del Elefante Blanco y Otras Narraciones.   La Novela Selecta, 4.   Madrid: Union Distribuidora de Ediciones.

1951   Una Visita al Cielo y Otras Narraciones [A Visit to Heaven and Other Stories], Barcelona: Arimany.

1953   El Robo del Elefante Blanco.   Excritores Celebres, 60.   Madrid: Dolar.

1954   Una Extrana Aventura [A Strange Adventure], Barcelona: G.P.
       [Guada].

1955   La Revolucion de Pitcairn [The Revolution of Pitcairn], Barcelona:
       G.P. [Guada].

1955   El Robo del Elefante Blanco, Barcelona: G.P. [Guada].

1955   L'Elefant Blanc, Robot [The White Elephant, Theft], Barcelona:
       Selecta. [Catalan]

1955   Una Apuesta de Millonario [A Bet of A Millionaire], Barcelona:
       G.P. [Guada].

1958   El Diario de Eva, Barcelona: Guada.

1958   Los Amores de Alonso Fitz Clarence [The Loves of Alonso Fitz
       Clarence], Barcelona: G.P. [Guada].

1961   Cabeza de Chorlito [Hairbrained Person]. Juvenil Cadete.
       Barcelona: Mateu.

1961   Fragmentos del Diario de Adan y Diario de Eva [Fragments of the
       Diary of Adam and Diary of Eve]. [3rd edition] Coleccion Austral
       679. Madrid: Espasa-Calpe.

1963? Nuevos Cuentos [New Stories]. Coleccion Austral 713. Madrid:
       Espasa-Calpe.

1963? Fragmentos de Diario de Adan, Madrid: Espasa-Calpe.

1966? Un Reportaje Sensacional y Otros Cuentos [Sensational Reporting
       and Other Stories]. Coleccion Austral 698. [4th edition]
       Madrid: Espasa-Calpe.

1968   El Robo del Elefante Blanco, Barcelona: Dima.

1970   Cabeza de Chorlito, Madrid: Del Hoyo.

1972   Nuevos Cuentos. [3rd edition] Madrid: Espasa-Calpe.

1973   El Elefante Blanco Robado [The Stolen White Elephant], Barcelona:
       La Gaya Ciencia.

Tom Sawyer

1903   Aventuras de Masin Sawyer. Novela de un Nino [Adventures of Master
       Sawyer. Novel of a Boy]. Biblioteca Humoristica. Vol. 1. Madrid:
       Serra.

1918   Les Aventures de Tom Sawyer [The Adventures of Tom Sawyer],
       Barcelona: Catalana. [French]

1923 Las Aventuras de Tom Sawyer [The Adventures of Tom Sawyer], Madrid: Espasa-Calpe.

1929 Same. Madrid: Revista Literaria Semanal: 123.

1933? Same. Barcelona: Catalana.

1943 Same. Barcelona: Molino.

1943 Same. Barcelona: Nausica.

1945 Same. Coleccion Retablo. [2nd edition] Barcelona: Nausica.

1946 Las Aventuras de Tom Sawyer. Coleccion Oases, 49. Barcelona: Reguera.

1948 Aventuras de Tom Sawyer. Tom Sawyer Detective. Tom Sawyer en el Extranjero [Adventures of Tom Sawyer. Tom Sawyer Detective. Tom Sawyer Abroad], Madrid: Aguilar.

1948 Aventuras de Tom Sawyer. Coleccion Tesoro Viejo, 14. Barcelona: Baguna.

1949 Las Aventuras de Tom Sawyer, Barcelona: Baguna.

1950? Same. Barcelona: Ameller.

1952 Same. Juvenil Cadete, 30. Barcelona: Mateu.

1953 Same. [2nd edition] Biblioteca Selecta Universal, 10. Barcelona: Selecta.

1953 Aventuras de Tom Sawyer. Escritores Celebres, 42. Madrid: Dolar.

1956 Same. [adaptation] Barcelona: Bruguera.

1957 Las Aventuras de Tom Sawyer. Biblioteca Infantil Juventud. Barcelona: Juventud.

1957 Las Aventuras de Tom Sawyer. Tom Sawyer, Detective. Tom Sawyer en el Extranjero, Barcelona: Juventud.

1957 Same. Coleccion Crisol, 242. [3rd edition] Madrid. Aguilar.

1957 Tom Sawyer y Huck Finn [Tom Sawyer and Huck Finn], Barcelona: Arimany.

1957 Aventuras de Tom Sawyer, Barcelona: Arimany.

1957 Same. Barcelona: G.P.

1958 Same. [2nd edition] Barcelona: Bruguera.

1959 Same. Coleccion Historias, 26. [3rd edition] Barcelona: Bruguera.

1960   Same. Coleccion Iris, 32. Barcelona: Bruguera.

1960   Same. [4th edition] Madrid: Aguilar.

1960   Same. Bilbao: Felicidad.

1960   Las Aventuras de Tom Sawyer, Barcelona: Mateu.

1960   Aventuras de Tom Sawyer, Tom Sawyer Detective, Tom Sawyer en el
       Extranjero. Coleccion Crisol. [4th edition] Madrid: Aguilar.

1961   Aventuras de Tom Sawyer. Aventuras de Huckleberry Finn. Grandes
       Novelas de la Literatura Universal, 19. Barcelona: Exito.

1961   Aventuras de Tom Sawyer, Bilbao: Felicidad.

1962   Same. Bilbao: Felicidad.

1962   Same. Coleccion Corinto. [3rd edition] Barcelona: Bruguera.

1962   Las Aventuras de Tom Sawyer. Coleccion Franja Escarlata, Vol. 6.
       Bilbao: Felicidad.

1962   Tom Sawyer y Huckleberry Finn, Barcelona: Zeus.

1963   Aventuras de Tom Sawyer, n.p.: Ferma.

1963   Same. Barcelona: Mateu.

1963   Las Aventuras de Tom Sawyer, Barcelona: Libros Bolivar.

1963   Las Aventuras de Tom Sawyer, Huckleberry Finn, Tom Sawyer Detective,
       y Tom Sawyer de Viaje, Barcelona: Arimany.

1965   Aventuras de Tom Sawyer, Barcelona: Bruguera.

1965   Same. [6th edition] Madrid: Espasa-Calpe.

1968   Aventuras de Tom Sawyer. Tom Sawyer Detective. Tom Sawyer en el
       Extranjero. [6th edition] Madrid: Aguilar.

1969   Aventuras de Tom Sawyer, Barcelona: Bruguera.

1969   Las Aventuras de Tom Sawyer. [7th edition] Madrid: Espasa-Calpe.

1969   Same. [2nd edition] Barcelona: Juventud.

1969   Same. Clasicos Juveniles, 4. Barcelona: Molino.

1970   Same. Barcelona: Salvat.

1971   Aventuras de Tom Sawyer. [4th edition] Barcelona: Bruguera.

1971   Same. Madrid: Escuelas Profesionales Sagrado Corazon.

1972   Same. [5th edition] Barcelona: Bruguera.

1972 Same. Barcelona: Sopena.

1973 Same. [6th edition] Barcelona: Bruguera.

1973 Same. Madrid: Edaf.

1973 Same. Leon: Everest.

1974 Same. [2nd edition] Barcelona: Bruguera.

1974 Same. [7th edition] Barcelona: Bruguera.

1974 Same. Barcelona: Sopena.

1974 Las Aventuras de Tom Sawyer. [8th edition] Madrid: Espasa-Calpe.

1974 Same. [3rd edition] Barcelona: Juventud.

1974 Same. 2 vols. Barcelona: La Gaya Ciencia.

1974 Same. Madrid: Paulinas.

1974 Same. Madrid: Rodas.

1974 Same. Barcelona: Toray.

1975 Same. [8th edition] Barcelona: AFHA.

1975 Same. Madrid: Alonso.

1975 Same. Valladolid: Edival.

1975 Aventuras de Tom Sawyer. [8th edition] Barcelona: Bruguera.

1975 Same. [2nd edition] Madrid: Everest.

1975 Same. Bilbao: Vasco Americano.

1975 Tom Sawyer, Bilbao: Laida.

1975 Same. Barcelona: Noguer.

1976 Same. Bilbao: Fher.

1976 Aventuras de Tom Sawyer. [9th edition] Barcelona: Bruguera.

1976 Same. Madrid: Maves.

1976 Same. Bilbao: Sima.

1976 Las Aventuras de Tom Sawyer. [9th edition] Barcelona: Afha Internacional.

1976 Same. Bilbao: Maves.

Tom Sawyer Abroad

1943   Tom Sawyer a traves del Mundo [Tom Sawyer across the World].
        Coleccion Retablo. Barcelona: Nausica.

1948   Aventuras de Tom Sawyer. Tom Sawyer Detective. Tom Sawyer en el
        Extranjero [Adventures of Tom Sawyer. Tom Sawyer Detective. Tom
        Sawyer Abroad], Madrid: Aguilar.

1951   Tom Sawyer a traves del Mundo, Madrid: Diana.

1957   Las Aventuras de Tom Sawyer. Tom Sawyer, Detective. Tom Sawyer
        en el Extranjero, Barcelona: Juventud.

1957   Aventuras de Tom Sawyer, Tom Sawyer Detective, Tom Sawyer en el
        Extranjero. Coleccion Crisol, 242. [3rd edition] Madrid: Aguilar.

1960   Same. Coleccion Crisol. [4th edition] Madrid: Aguilar.

1961   Tom Sawyer, Detective. Tom Sawyer, en el Extranjero. Coleccion
        Austral, 1049. [3rd edition] Madrid: Espasa-Calpe.

1961   Tom Sawyer a traves del Mundo, Barcelona: Bruguera.

1963   Las Aventuras de Tom Sawyer, Huckleberry Finn, Tom Sawyer Detective,
        y Tom Sawyer de Viaje, Barcelona: Arimany.

1967   Tom Sawyer a traves del Mundo, Barcelona: Bruguera.

1968   Aventuras de Tom Sawyer. Tom Sawyer Detective. Tom Sawyer en el
        Extranjero. [6th edition] Madrid: Aguilar.

1970   Tom Sawyer a traves del Mundo. [3rd edition] Madrid: Bruguera.

1970   Tom Sawyer Detective. Tom Sawyer en el Extranjero. [4th edition]
        Madrid: Espasa-Calpe.

1971   Tom Sawyer a Traves del Mundo, Barcelona: Bruguera.

1971   Same. [4th edition] Barcelona: Bruguera.

1972   Same. [5th edition] Barcelona: Bruguera.

1972   Tom Sawyer Detective. Tom Sawyer en el Extranjero, Barcelona:
        Sopena.

1973   Tom Sawyer a Traves del Mundo. [6th edition] Barcelona: Bruguera.

1974   Same. [3rd edition] Barcelona: Bruguera.

1974   Same. Historias Seleccion. [7th edition] Barcelona: Bruguera.

1976   Same. [8th edition] Barcelona: Bruguera.

Tom Sawyer Detective

1904   Una Pesquisa Policial de Masin Sawyer, contada por Huck Jiun [sic]
[A Police Investigation by Master Sawyer, told by Huck Finn].
Segunda parte de las Aventuras de Masin Sawyer. Biblioteca
Humoristica, Vol. III. Madrid: Serra.

1909   Tom Sawyer, Detective, Barcelona: Domenech (Maucci).

1909   Hazanas de Tom Sawyer (Detective), contadas por Su Amigo Huck
Jiun [sic] [Exploits of Tom Sawyer (Detective), told by His
Friend Huck Finn], Barcelona: Orbi.

1934   Tom Sawyer, Detective, Barcelona: Portada de Junceda.

1943   Same. Barcelona: Nausica.

1948   Aventuras de Tom Sawyer. Tom Sawyer Detective. Tom Sawyer en el
Extranjero. Coleccion Crisol, 242. Madrid: Aguilar.

1950   Tom Sawyer, Detective, Madrid: Diana.

1951   Same. Coleccion Juvenil Cadete, 21. Barcelona: Mateu.

1952   Same. Escritores Celebres, 34. Madrid: Dolar.

1957   Las Aventuras de Tom Sawyer. Tom Sawyer, Detective. Tom Sawyer
en el Extranjero, Barcelona: Juventud.

1957   Aventuras de Tom Sawyer, Tom Sawyer Detective, Tom Sawyer en el
Extranjero. [3rd edition] Madrid: Aguilar.

1958   Tom Sawyer Detective. Coleccion Juvenil Cadete. Barcelona: Mateu.

1959   Same. Barcelona: Bruguera.

1960   Aventures de Tom Sawyer, Tom Sawyer Detective, Tom Sawyer en el
Extranjero. Coleccion Crisol. [4th edition] Madrid: Aguilar.

1961   Tom Sawyer, Detective, y Tom Sawyer, en el Extranjero. Coleccion
Austral, 1049. [3rd edition] Madrid: Espasa-Calpe.

1962   Tom Sawyer Detective. Coleccion Historias, vol. 81. [2nd edition]
Barcelona: Bruguera.

1963?   Same. Barcelona: Arimany.

1963?   Las Aventuras de Tom Sawyer, Huckleberry Finn, Tom Sawyer, Detective,
y Tom Sawyer de Viaje, Barcelona: Arimany.

1967   Tom Sawyer Detective, Barcelona: Bruguera.

1968   Aventuras de Tom Sawyer. Tom Sawyer Detective. Tom Sawyer en el
Extranjero. [6th edition] Madrid: Aguilar.

1969 Tom Sawyer, Detective, Barcelona: Bruguera.

1970 Tom Sawyer, Detective. [2nd edition] Barcelona: Bruguera.

1970 Tom Sawyer Detective. Tom Sawyer, en el Extranjero. [4th edition]
      Madrid: Espasa-Calpe.

1972 Same. Barcelona: Sopena.

1972 Tom Sawyer Detective, Barcelona: Bruguera.

1972 Same. [3rd edition] Barcelona: Bruguera.

1973 Same. Barcelona: Bruguera.

1973 Same. [4th edition] Barcelona: Bruguera.

1973 Same. Barcelona: La Gaya Ciencia.

1973 Same. Barcelona: Mateu.

1974 Same. Barcelona: Bruguera.

1974 Same. Historias Seleccion. [5th edition] Barcelona: Bruguera.

1975 Same. Bilbao: Fher.

1976 Same. Barcelona: Bruguera.

1976 Same. [2nd edition] Barcelona: Bruguera.

1976 Same. [6th edition] Barcelona: Bruguera.

What Is Man?

1946 ¿Que es el Hombre? Oraclum, 1. Barcelona: Delfos.

Selections

1975 Las Tres Erres: Raza, Religion y Revolucion [Mark Twain and the
      Three R's: Race, Religion and Revolution]. [Ed. Maxwell D.
      Geismar] Madrid: Guadarrama.

Collected Works

1945 La Obra Perdurable. Todas Las Novelas de Mark Twain [The Ever-
      lasting Work. Entire Novels of Mark Twain]. 1 vol. Ediciones
      Lauro. Barcelona: Janes. Subsequent edition (Plaza & Janes):
      1964.

1953 Novelas Completas y Ensayos [Complete Novels and Essays]. Obras
      Eternas. 2 vols. Madrid: Aguilar. Subsequent editions: 1957,
      1962, 1967, 1972, 1973.

1957 Las Cinco Mejores Obras de Mark Twain [The Five Best Works of Mark
      Twain]. Coleccion Las Cinco Mejores Obras. 1 vol. [2nd edition]
      Barcelona: Mateu. Subsequent edition: 1959.

Sweden

Sources: ASB/IT/NL/NUC/SBF/SBK/SF

American Claimant

1892 Arfvingen fran Amerika [Heir from America]. Humoristisk Bibliotek
      10. Stockholm: Seligmann.

1909 Amerika-Grefen [Duke from America]. Froleens Bokskatt. Vol. 33.
      Stockholm: Froleen.

Connecticut Yankee

1890 En Yankee [A Yankee]. Humoristisk Bibliotek No. 7. Stockholm:
      Seligmann.

1916 En Yankee vid Kung Arturs Hov [A Yankee at King Arthur's Court].
      Beromda Bocker 60-61. Stockholm: Bjorck & Borjesson.

1954 Same. [2nd edition] Stockholm: Lindqvist.

1962 Same. Sohlmans Klassikerbibliotek. [3rd edition] Stockholm:
      Lindqvist.

Following the Equator

1898 En Landstrykares Anteckningar [A Tramp's Notes]. [New Series]
      Stockholm: Geber.

1946 Same. Stockholm: Natur och Kultur.

Gilded Age

1877 Kattguld. Humorist Roman [Gold-glimmer. Humorous Novel], Karls-
      krona: Bjurman.

1877 Kattguld. Humoristisk Roman, Norrkoping: Randel.

Huckleberry Finn

1885 Huckleberry Finns Afventyr [Huckleberry Finn's Adventures], Stock-
      holm: Seligmann.

1885 Same. Stockholm: Geber

1893 Same. [2nd edition] Stockholm: Geber.

1897 Tom Sawyers och Huckleberry Finns Afventyr [Tom Sawyer's and
      Huckleberry Finn's Adventures], Stockholm: Silen.

1906 Huckleberry Finns Afventyr. Beromdu Bocker. 9. Stockholm:
      Bjorck & Borjesson.

1907 Same. [2nd edition] Stockholm: Bjorck & Borjesson.

1913 Same. Stockholm: Nord.

1915 Same. Beromda Bocker. 9. Stockholm: Bjorck & Borjesson.

1919 Same. Beromda Bocker. 9. Stockholm: Bjorck & Borjesson.

1928 Same. Stockholm: Wohlstrom.

1936 Same. Barnbiblioteket Saga 166. Stockholm: Hammarlund.

1940 Same. Stockholm: Bjorck & Borjesson.

1943 Same. De Ododliga Ungdomsbockerna 29. Stockholm: Bonnier.

1943 Same. Barnbiblioteket Saga 166. Stockholm: Hammarlund.

1945 The Adventures of Huckleberry Finn. Zephyr Books. A Library of
      British and American Authors. No. 35. Stockholm: Continental
      Book Co. [English]

1946 Huckleberry Finns Aventyr, Stockholm: Lindqvist.

1948 Same. Stockholm: Ardor.

1950 Huckleberry Finns Aventyr. Berattad for Saga [Huckleberry Finn's
      Adventures. Related As A Saga]. [3rd edition] Stockholm: Svensk
      Lararetidning.

1952 Huckleberry Finns Aventyr. De Ododliga Ungdomsbockerna 29.
      Stockholm: Bonnier.

1955 Same. Stockholm: Lindqvist.

1957 Same. Saga 166. [4th edition] Stockholm: Svensk Lararetidning.

1957 Huckleberry Finn. Tidens Bokklubb. Stockholm: Tiden.

1960 Huckleberry Finns Aventyr. De Ododliga Ungdomsbockerna 29. Stock-
      holm: Bonnier.

1960 Same. Sohlmans Klassikerbibliotek. Stockholm: Sohlman.

1964 Huckleberry Finn, Stockholm: Tiden.

1964 Huckleberry Finns Aventyr. Sagas Beromda Bocker. Saga 166.
      Stockholm: Svensk Lararetidning.

1965 Same. De Ododliga Ungdomsbockerna 29. Stockholm: Bonnier.

1965 Same. Stjarnbockerna. Stockholm: Lindqvist.

1965 Same. Stockholm: Raben & Sjogren.

1967 Huckleberry Finn. Litteraturserien. 14. Stockholm: Liber,
      Seelig.

1968 Same. Stockholm: Tiden.

1968 Huckleberry Finns Aventyr, Malmo: Norden.

1969 Same. Stockholm: Lindqvist.

1971 Huckleberry Finn, Stockholm: Lindblad.

1971 Huckleberry Finns Aventyr, Goteborg: Data-reprografi.

1973 Same. Stockholm: Lindblad.

Innocents Abroad

1876 En Tripp kring Gamla Verlden [A Trip around the Old World], Stock-
      holm: Flodin.

Joan of Arc

1945 Jeanne d'Arc [Joan of Arc], Stockholm: Lindfors.

1945 Same. n.p.: Rossel.

1957 Jeanne d'Arc. Roman [Joan of Arc. Novel]. Wohlstroms Romanbiblio-
      tek. Bla Elitserien [3]. Stockholm: Wohlstrom.

Letters from the Earth

1966 Brev fran Jorden [Letters from the Earth], Stockholm: Raben &
      Sjogren.

Life on the Mississippi

1883 Fran Mississippifloden [From the Mississippi River], Stockholm:
      Seligmann.

1910 Fran Mississippifloden och Andra Berattelser [From the Mississippi
      River and Other Tales], Stockholm: Geber.

1919 Pa Mississippifloden. Minnen, Handelser och Aventyr [On the
      Mississippi River. Memories, Occurrences and Adventures]. Beromda
      Bocker 87. Stockholm: Bjorck & Borjesson.

1959 Mississippi, Stockholm: Christofers Bokforlag [Seelig].

1970 Livet pa Mississippi [Life on the Mississippi], Stockholm: Prisma.

                    Prince and the Pauper

1885 Prinsen och Tiggargossen [Prince and the Beggar Boy]. En
      Berattalse for Unga Personer af Alla Aldrar [A Tale for Young
      People of All Ages]. Stockholm: Askerberg.

1912 Same. Stockholm: Askerberg.

1912 Prinsen och Tiggargossen. Efter Mark Twain [Prince and the Beggar
      Boy. After Mark Twain]. Barnbiblioteket Saga. Stockholm: Svensk
      Larraretidning.

1918 Same. Barnbiblioteket Saga. 41. Stockholm: Svensk Larraretidning.

1919 Prinsen och Tiggargossen. En Berattelse for Unga Personer af Alla
      Aldrar. Beromda Bocker. 84. Stockholm: Bjorck & Borjesson.

1926 Prinsen och Tiggargossen. Efter Mark Twain Fritt Berattad [Prince
      and the Beggar Boy. After Mark Twain Freely Told]. Barnbiblio-
      teket Saga. 41. Lasebok i Hem och Skola [Reading Book at Home
      and School]. Stockholm: Svensk Larraretidning.

1928 Prinsen och Tiggaren. En Berattelse for Unga Personer av Alla
      Aldrar, Stockholm: Wohlstrom.

1943 Prinsen och Tiggargossen. Barnbiblioteket Saga 41. Stockholm:
      Hammarlund.

1947 Prinsen och Tiggargossen. Efter Mark Twains Berattelse [Prince
      and the Beggar Boy. After Mark Twain's Tale], Stockholm: Ahlen
      & Akerlund (Bonnier).

1952 Prinsen och Tiggargossen. Barnbibliotek Saga 41. Stockholm:
      Hammarlund.

1952 Same. [5th edition] Stockholm: Svensk Larraretidning.

1957 Prinsen och Tiggargossen. En Barattelse for Ungdom i Alla Aldrar
      [Prince and the Beggar Boy. A Tale for Young People of All Ages].
      Aladdinbockerna. 3. Stockholm: Aladdinklubben/Folket i Bild
      [Seelig].

                    Pudd'nhead Wilson

1918 En Droppe Negerblod [One Drop Negro Blood]. Kriminalhistoria
      [Criminal Stories]. Stockholm: Bjorck & Borjesson.

1919 Same. Kriminalhistoria. Beromda Bocker. 78. Stockholm: Bjorck
      & Borjesson.

1929 Same. Stockholm: Wohlstrom.

1959 Same. Stockholm: Ruhnforlag [Seelig].

1961 Same. Sagas Beromda Bocker. Saga 408. Stockholm: Svensk
      Larraretidning.

1961 Daniel M. McKeithan. The Morgan Manuscript of Mark Twain's
      Pudd'nhead Wilson [facsimile]. Essays and Studies on American
      Language and Literature, Uppsala: Lundequist. [English]

Roughing It

1874 Pa Mafa eller Huru Ledes en Tre Manaders Lusttripp [Haphazard or
      How To Be Bored in Three Months Pleasure Trip], Norrkoping:
      Randel.

1948 Slita Hund [Worn and Torn Dog (Have To Rough It)], Stockholm:
      Fahlcrantz & Gumaelius.

Stories and Sketches

1874 Valda Skizzer [Choice Sketches], af Mark Twain, Upsala: Schultz.

1874 Bilder och Dikter af Mark Twain [Pictures and Poems by Mark Twain].
      In Amerikanska Humorister. Stockholm: n. pub.

1877 Valda Skizzer [2nd edition] Upsala: Schultz.

1878 Bilder och Skizzer av Artemus Ward, Charles D. Warner, Mark Twain,
      Bret Harte, The Danbury Newsman, Thomas Bailey Aldrich [Pictures
      and Sketches by...]. Humorister, Amerikanska II. Ny Foljd
      [New Series]. Stockholm: Seligmann.

1882 [The Stolen White Elephant] in Valda Stycken ur Amerikanska
      Humorister, V. [Choice Pieces from American Humorists, V.].
      Stockholm: Seligmann.

1883 Valda Skizzer, Upsala: Schultz.

1883 Bilder och Dikter [Pictures and Poems] af Artemus Ward, Bret Harte,
      Mark Twain, Sam Slick. Humorister, Amerikanska I. Stockholm:
      Seligmann.

1884 Den Stora Revolutionen pa Pitcairn och Andra Skizzer [The Great
      Revolution on Pitcairn and Other Sketches], Stockholm: Askerberg.

1889 Nya Humoresker [New Humorous Pieces], Stockholm: Johnson.

1893 Nya Reseskisser. Om Allehanda Slags Fartyg. Sedeln pa en Million
      Pund [New Travel Sketches. About All Sorts and Conditions of
      Ships. Bank-note for A Million Pounds], Stockholm: Seligmann.

1900 Frestaren och Andra Nya Skisser och Berattelser [The Tempter and
      Other New Sketches and Stories], Stockholm: Seligmann.

1902 Ocksa en Detektivhistoria [Also A Detective Story], Stockholm:
      Geber.

1903 Dodssigillet jamte Flera Berattelser och Skizzer [Death's Little
      Seal and Several More Stories and Sketches], Stockholm: Geber.

1907 Den Hoppande Grodan och Andra Humoresker [The Jumping Frog and
      Other Humorous Pieces]. Urval ur Varldslitteraturen [Selected
      from World Literature], Stockholm: Svithiod.

1909 Same. Stockholm: Svithiod.

1910 Den Stora Revolutionen pa Pitcairn och Andra Nya Skisser, Stockholm:
      Askerberg.

1910 Den Stulna Elefanten och Andra Skisser [The Stolen Elephant and
      Other Sketches]. Illustreradt Bibliotek. Vol. 18. Stockholm:
      Holmquists Boktryckeri.

1910 Frestaren, och Andra Nya Skisser och Berattelser, af Mark Twain
      [Tempter and Other New Sketches and Stories, by Mark Twain],
      Stockholm: Wahlstrom & Widstrand.

1912 Lustiga Historier [Funny Stories]. Beromda Bocker 37. Stockholm:
      Bjorck & Borjesson.

1918 "Jag ar Vid Kriget" jamte Andra Berattelser av Alfred de Vigny,
      Alphonse Daudet, Mark Twain, Ruskin, Wilde och Wells ["I Am
      Tired of War" together with Other Stories by...], Stockholm:
      Norstedt.

1918 Spionen fran Louisiana och Andra Humoresker [Spies from Louisiana
      and Other Humorous Pieces]. Overs. Kronebibliotek 17. Stockholm:
      Nutiden.

1919 Guldgravarkatten [Gold-digger Cat], Stockholm: Dahlberg.

1922 Lustige Historier [Funny Stories]. Beromda Bocker 37. Stockholm:
      Bjorck & Borjesson.

1944 En Amerikansk Valkampanj och Andra Humoresker [An American Election
      Campaign and Other Humorous Pieces], Stockholm: Raben & Sjogren.

1949 Snalla Gossar och Stygga [Stingy and Bad Boy]. Forumbiblioteket.
      36. Stockholm: Forum.

1949? Tvenne Jarnvagsverteraners Lavnadsoden [Wasted Lives of Two
      Railway Veterans], n.p.: F.B. Grondahl.

1949   The Jumping Frog, Stockholm: The Polyglot Club [Seelig].   [English]

1950   Spoket pa Canterville Saut Andra Noveller av Oscar Wilde, Theodor
Storm, R.L. Stevenson & Mark Twain [The Ghost at Canterville and
Other Short Stories by ...], Stockholm: Lindquist.

1958   En Amerikansk Valkampanj, Stockholm: Raben & Sjogren.

1961   Mark Twain Beratter [Mark Twain Story-Teller].   Omnibusbockerna.
Stockholm: Folket i Bild [Seelig].

1961   Snalla Gossar och Stygga.   Forumbiblioteket.   36.   Stockholm:
Forum.

1965   Den Stora Franska Duellen och Andra Historier [The Great French
Duel and Other Stories], Stockholm: Prisma.   Seelig.

1966   Miljonpundsedeln [Million Pound Bank-note], Goteborg: Bergendahls
Boktryckeri.

1969   Miljonpundsedeln och Andra Historier, Stockholm: Prisma, Solna,
Seelig.

1971   Snalla Gossar och Stygga [Stingy and Bad Boy], Stockholm: Forum.

Tom Sawyer

1877   Tom Sawyer.   En Skolpojkhistoria [Tom Sawyer.   A Schoolboy's Story],
Stockholm: Seligmanns.

1882   Tom Sawyer, Stockholm: Geber.

1895   Tom Sawyer.   En Skolpojkhistoria, Stockholm: Geber.

1897   Tom Sawyers och Huckleberry Finns Afventyr [Tom Sawyer's and
Huckleberry Finn's Adventures], Stockholm: Silen.

1906   Tom Sawyer; en Skolpojkhistoria.   [5th edition] Stockholm: Geber.

1906   Tom Sawyers Afventyr Inom och Utom Skolam [Tom Sawyer's Adventures
within and outside School].   Ungdomens Bibliotek.   Vol. 97.
Stockholm: Johnson.

1907   Tom Sawyers Afventyr [Tom Sawyer's Adventures].   Beromda Bocker.
19.   Stockholm: Bjorck & Borjesson.

1913   Same.   2 vols.   Stockholm: Nord.

1915   Same.   Beromda Bocker.   19.   Stockholm: Bjorck & Borjesson.

1919   Same.   Beromda Bocker.   19.   Stockholm: Bjorck & Borjesson.

1920   Same.   Stockholm: Ahlen & Askerlund.

1928   Same.   Stockholm: Wohlstrom.

1937   Same. De Ododliga Ungdomsbockerna. Vol. 2. Stockholm: Bonnier.

1938   Tom Sawyer. Berattelsen om en Skolpojke [Tom Sawyer. Stories about A Schoolboy]. Barnbiblioteket Saga 146. Stockholm: Hammarlund.

1939   Tom Sawyers Aventyr, Stockholm: Lindquist.

1940   Same. Stockholm: Bjorck & Borjesson.

1947   Same. De Ododliga Ungdomsbockerna. 2. Stockholm: Bonnier.

1948   The Adventures of Tom Sawyer. Zephyr Books. A Library of British and American Authors. 106. Stockholm: The Continental Book Co. [English]

1948   Tom Sawyer. Barnbiblioteket Saga 146. Stockholm: Hammarlund. Svensk Larraretidning.

1948   Tom Sawyers Aventyr, Stockholm: Ardor.

1949   Same. Lindqvists Ungdomsbibliotek. 391. Stockholm: Lindqvist.

1949   Same. Schildts Ungdomsbocker, 101. Harnosand: Schildt.

1950   Tom Saweri Imelikud Juhtumused [Tom Sawyer's Strange Adventures], Goteborg: Orto. [Estonian]

1951   Tom Sawyers Aventyr. De Ododliga Ungdomsbockerna. 2. Stockholm: Bonnier.

1953   Tom Sawyer. Barnbiblioteket Saga 146. Stockholm: Hammarlund.

1953   Tom Sawyers Aventyr, Stockholm: Lindqvist.

1955   Same. De Ododliga Umdomsbockerna. 2. Stockholm: Bonnier.

1956   Same. De Klassika Ungdomsbockerna. Uppsala: Lindblad.

1956   Tom Sawyer. Tidens Bokklubb. Stockholm: Tiden.

1961   Same. Sagas Beromda Bocker. Stockholm: Svensk Lararetidning.

1962   Tom Sawyers Aventyr. De Ododliga Ungdomsbockerna. 2. Stockholm: Bonnier.

1963   Same. Stjarnbockerna. Stockholm: Lindqvist.

1964   Tom Sawyer. Sagas Beromda Bocker. Saga 146. [6th edition] Stockholm: Svensk Lararetidning.

1965   Same. Litteraturserien. 3. Stockholm: Liber.

1965   Same. Tidens Bokklubb. Stockholm: Tiden.

1965   Tom Sawyers Aventyr. De Ododliga Ungdomsbockerna. 2. Stockholm: Bonnier.

1966   Tom Sawyer. Sagas Beromda Bocker. Saga 146. [7th edition]
       Stockholm: Svensk Lararetidning.

1967   Same. Litteraturserien. 3. Stockholm: Libera, Seelig.

1968   Tom Sawyer. Simplified for Use in Schools and for Private Study.
       Easy Readers. B. Stockholm: Svensk Bokforlag (Bonnier). [English]

1969   Tom Sawyer. Litteraturserien. 3. Stockholm: Liber, Solna,
       Seelig.

1969   Same. Stockholm: Tiden.

1971   Tom Sawyers Aventyr, Stockholm: Lindblad.

1973   Same. Goteborg: Data-reprografi.

1974   Same. Stockholm: Bonnier.

1976   Tom Sawyer, Hoganas: Bra Bocker.

1976   Same. Gambleby: Forlagstjanst.

1976   Same. Gambleby: Forlagstjanst.

Tom Sawyer Abroad

1894   Tom Sawyer pa Resa [Tom Sawyer upon A Journey], Stockholm: Geber.

1894   Tom Sawyer pa Stroftag [Tom Sawyer on Excursion], Stockholm:
       Seligmann.

1906   Tom Sawyer pa Resa, Stockholm: Geber.

1911   Tom Sawyer som Detektiv och Tom Sawyer pa Resa [Tom Sawyer As
       Detective and Tom Sawyer upon A Journey]. Beromda Bocker. 36.
       Stockholm: Bjorck & Borjesson.

1919   Tom Sawyer som Detektiv och Tom Sawyer pa Resa. Fortsattning pa
       Tom Sawyer och Huckleberry Finn [Tom Sawyer As Detective and Tom
       Sawyer upon A Journey. Continuation upon Tom Sawyer and Huckle-
       berry Finn]. Beromda Bocker. 36. Stockholm: Bjorck & Borjesson.

1940   Same. Stockholm: Bjorck & Borjesson.

1940   Tom Sawyer pa Resa. Barnbiblioteket Saga 194. Stockholm: Hammar-
       lund.

1946   Same. Stockholm: Lindqvist.

1948   Same. Barnbiblioteket Saga 194. Stockholm: Hammarlund.

1962   Tom Sawyer pa Flygfard [Tom Sawyer on A Flying Journey]. Wohl-
       stroms Ungdomsbocker. Jurybockerna. 9. Stockholm: Wohlstrom.

1971 Tom Sawyer pa Resa, Stockholm: Lindqvist.

1975 Tom Sawyer pa Flygfard, Stockholm: Lindblad.

Tom Sawyer, Detective

1896 Tom Sawyer som Detektiv [Tom Sawyer as Detective], Stockholm:
      Geber.

1911 Tom Sawyer som Detektiv och Tom Sawyer pa Resa [Tom Sawyer as
      Detective and Tom Sawyer upon A Journey]. Beromda Bocker. 36.
      Stockholm: Bjorck & Borjesson.

1919 Tom Sawyer som Detektiv och Tom Sawyer pa Resa. Fortsattning pa
      Tom Sawyer och Huckleberry Finn [Tom Sawyer as Detective and Tom
      Sawyer upon A Journey. Continuation upon Tom Sawyer and Huckle-
      berry Finn]. Beromda Bocker. 36. Stockholm: Bjorck & Borjesson.

1929 Tom Sawyer som Detektiv, Stockholm: Wohlstrom.

1939 Same. Barnbiblioteket Saga 190. Stockholm: Hammarlund.

1940 Tom Sawyer som Detektiv och Tom Sawyer pa Resa. Fortsattning pa
      Tom Sawyer och Huckleberry Finn, Stockholm: Bjorck & Borjesson.

1945 Tom Sawyer som Detektiv, Stockholm: Lindqvist.

1950 Same. Barnbiblioteket Saga 190. Stockholm: Hammarlund.

1950 Same. [2nd edition] Stockholm: Svensk Lararetidning.

1961 Same. Wohlstroms Ungdomsbocker. Jury-bockerna. 5. Stockholm:
      Wohlstrom.

1974 Same. Stockholm: Lindblad.

Tramp Abroad

1882 Ur En Landstrykares Anteckningar [Out of A Tramp's Notes]. Valda
      Stycken ur Amerikanska Humorister, V [Choice Pieces from American
      Humorists, V], Stockholm: Seligmann.

Miscellaneous Writings

1948 Min Van Rogers [My Friend Rogers], Stockholm: Forum.

Selections

1925 Selections from Mark Twain, Stockholm: Bergvoll. [English]

1960 Mark Twains Basta [Mark Twain's Best]. Omnibusbockerna. 1. Stock-
      holm: Folket i Bild. [Seelig].

Switzerland

Sources: ABL/Bib/CGLF/DB/ECB/HV/IT/JDS/LC/LF/MTG/NUC/SB/SLVS/ZBZ

American Claimant

1955 Noblesse Oblige. (Roman) [Nobility Obligates. (Novel)].
Collection Connaitre. Geneve: Connaitre.

Autobiography

1962 Selbstbiographie [Self Biography], Zurich: n. pub.

Captain Stormfield's Visit to Heaven

1954 Vom Umgang mit Engeln. Kapitan Stromfield's [sic] Himmelische
Erfahrungen [Of Going around with Angels. Captain Stormfield's
Heavenly Experience], Zurich: Sanssoucci: Barmerlea. [German
Spoerli]

Huckleberry Finn

1943 Huckleberry Finn, Zurich: Tena.

1944 Huckleberry Finns Fahrten und Abenteuer [Huckleberry Finn's Travels
and Adventures], Zurich: Schweizer Druck-und-Verlagshaus.

1950 Die Abenteuer des Tom Sawyer und Huckleberry Finn [The Adventures
of Tom Sawyer and Huckleberry Finn], Zurich: Atrium.

1953 Huckleberry Finns Abenteuer [Huckleberry Finn's Adventures], Zurich:
Buchergilde Gutenberg.

1962 Les Aventures d'Huckleberry Finn [The Adventures of Huckleberry
Finn]. Collection La Guilde des Jeunes. Serie Romans, 15.
Lausanne: La Guilde des Jeunes.

1965 Same. Collection Sommets de Roman Americain. Lausanne: Rencontres.

1966 Tom Sawyer und Huckleberry Finn, Zurich: Buchergilde Gutenberg.

1970 Les Aventures de Hucklberry Finn, Geneve: Edito Service.

1971 Die Abenteuer des Huckleberry Finn, Basel: Herder.

c1973 Tom Sawyers Abenteuer; Huckleberry Finns Fahrten und Abenteuer,
Zurich: Schweizer Verlagshaus.

1975 Tom Sawyer, Huckleberry Finn, Basel: Herder.

Prince and the Pauper

1946 Le Prince et le Pauvre [The Prince and the Pauper]. Collection
      Pour la Jeunesse. Lausanne: Payot.

1948 Prinz und Bettelknabe [Prince and Beggar Boy], Zurich: Artemis.

1966 Same. Neue Schweizer Bibliothek. Zurich: Schweizer Verlagshaus.

1970 Same. Zurich, Stocker-Schmid.

Pudd'nhead Wilson

1969 Querkopf Wilson [Crank Wilson]. Roman Dietikon. Zurich: Stocker-
      Schmid.

Stories and Sketches

1881 Sketches. English Library, Nr. I. Zurich: Rudolphi & Klemm.
      [English]

1914 Die Verschworung von Fort Trumbull. Das Todeslos [The Conspiracy
      of Fort Trumbull. The Death Ticket]. Verein fur Verbreitung
      guter Schriften, Nr. 95 [Union for the Spread of Good Writing,
      No. 95]. Zurich.

1940 Locht, Bruder, Locht! Humoresken und Satirein [Punch, Brothers
      Punch! Humorous and Satirical Pieces], Wadenswil/Zurich: Villiger.

1946 Journal d'Eve et d'Adam [Diary of Eve and Adam], Lausanne: La
      Tramontane.

1953 Tagebuch von Adam und Eva [Diary of Adam and Eve], Zurich:
      Sanssouci.

1960 Schone Geschichten. 28 Ausgewahlte Humoristische. Skizzen und
      Erzahlungen [Fine Stories. 28 Selected Humorous Pieces. Sketches
      and Stories], Zurich: Diogenes.

1961 Journal d'Eve et d'Adam. Collection L'Eventail, 21. Lausanne:
      Marguerat.

1962 Der Gefoppte Eichelhaher [The Hoaxed Jay], Zurich: n.pub.

1962 Le Journal d'Eve et le Journal d'Adam, suivis d'Autres Contes
      [The Diary of Eve and the Diary of Adam, followed by Other Stories].
      Collection Plaisir de Lire, 114. Lausanne: Plaisir de Lire.

1964 Tagebuch von Adam und Eva, Zurich: Sanssouci.

1966 Adams Tagebuch. 28 Ausgewahlte Skizzen und Erzahlungen [Adam's
      Diary. 28 Selected Sketches and Stories], Zurich: Diogenes.

1966 The £1,000,000 Bank Note. After A Story by Mark Twain. En-
      glischszenen fur die Schule. Bern: Staatliche Lehrmittelverlag.
      [English]

1967 Wilde, O.; Poe, E.A.; Twain, Mark. The Happy Prince und Andere
      Kurzgeschichten [Ocar Wilde, Edgar Allan Poe, Mark Twain. The
      Happy Prince and Other Short Stories], Stuttgart, Berlin, Zurich:
      Junker.

1969 Adams Tagebuch und Andere Heitere Geschichten [Adam's Diary and
      Other Cheerful Stories], Freiburg im Breisgau, Basel, Wien: Herder.

1973 Das Tagebuch von Adam & Eva, Zurich-Hottingen: Cesar Keiser.

1975 Schone Geschichten: Skizzen und Erzahlungen. Neuauflage [New
      Edition], Zurich: Diogenes.

1976 Tagebuch von Adam und Eva. [extracts] Zurich: Sanssouci.

Tom Sawyer

1926 Les Aventures de Tom Sawyer [The Adventures of Tom Sawyer],
      Lausanne: Spes.

1943 Tom Sawyers Abenteuer: Frei Nacherzahlt [Tom Sawyer's Adventures:
      Freely Told], Zurich: n.pub.

1944 Les Aventures de Tom Sawyer, Geneve: Meyer.

1950 Die Abenteuer des Tom Sawyer und Hucklberry Finn [The Adventures
      of Tom Sawyer and Huckleberry Finn], Zurich: Atrium.

1951 Tom Sawyers Abenteuer. Frei Nacherzahlt, Zurich: Buchergilde
      Gutenberg.

1958 Die Abenteuer des Tom Sawyer, Munchen, Zurich: Droemer/Knaur.

1959 Same. [8th edition] Munchen, Zurich: Droemer/Knaur.

1959 Same. [9th edition] Munchen, Zurich: Droemer/Knaur.

1959 Les Aventures de Tom Sawyer. La Guilde du Livre. Lausanne: La
      Guilde des Jeunes.

1966 Tom Sawyer und Huckleberry Finn, Zurich: Buchergilde Gutenberg.

1970 Tom Sawyers Abenteuer, Basel: Herder.

1973 Tom Sawyers Abenteuer; Huckleberry Finns Fahrten und Abenteuer
      [Tom Sawyer's Adventures; Huckleberry Finn's Travels and Adventures].
      [adapted] Zurich: Schweizer Verlagshaus.

1975 Tom Sawyer. Huckleberry Finn, Basel: Herder.

Travel Sketches

1946 Rigireise [Rigi Trip] [extracted from A Tramp Abroad, Vol.1, Chaps. 25-29]. Schweizerische Bibliothek. 38. Zurich: Rascher.

1948 Same. Zurich: Rascher.

1954 Same. Zurich: Rascher.

1960 Same. Zurich, Stuttgart: Rascher.

1961 Same. Das Schweizer Buch, 76. Zurich.

1971 Eine Rigibesteigung [An Ascent of the Rigi], Zurich: Diogenes.

Collected Works

1971 Werke in Zwei Banden [Works in Two Volumes], Olten: Schweitzer Buchzentrum.

EASTERN EUROPE

Albania

Sources: IT/NUC

1957 Aventurat e Hekelber Finit [Adventures of Huckleberry Finn], Tirane: Ndermarrja Shteterore e Botimeve.

1962 Vjedhja e Elefantit Te Bardhe [Theft of the White Elephant]. Naim Frasheri. Tirane: Ndermarrja Shteterore e Botimeve.

1964 Princi dhe i Varfiri [Prince and the Pauper], Tirane: Drejtoris e Botimene Shkollore.

1967 Aventurat e Hekelber Finit, Tirane: Ndermarrja Shteterore e Botimeve.

1972 Nje Amerikan Ne Oborrin e Mbretit Artur [An American at the Court of King Arthur], Tirane: Naim Frasheri.

Bulgaria

Sources: IT/LC/NUC

Autobiography

1969 Autobiografija [Autobiography], Sofija: Mladez.

Connecticut Yankee

1947   Edin Ianki pri Dvora na Kral Artur [A Yankee at the Court of King
       Arthur], Sofija: Orps.

1963   Edin Janki v Dvora na Kral Artur [A Yankee at the Court of King
       Arthur]. [2nd edition] Sofija: Kultura.

Huckleberry Finn

1951   Prikliucheniiata na Khububeri Fin [Adventures of Huckleberry Finn],
       Sofija: Mladez.

1960   Hik Fin'in Basindan Gelenler [The Things That Happened to Huck
       Finn]. [extract] Sofya: Prosveta. [Turkish]

1965   Haklberi Fin [Huckleberry Finn], Sofija: Mladez.

1974   Tom Sojer. Hakalberi Fin. [4th edition] Sofija: Mladez.

King Leopold's Soliloquy

1963   Monologat na Kral Leopold [Monologue of King Leopold], Sofija:
       NSOF.

Letters from the Earth

1966   Pisma ot Zemjata [Letters from the Earth], Plovdiv: Danov.

1969   Same. [2nd edition] Plovdiv: Danov.

Life on the Mississippi

1960   Zhivotut po Misisipi [Life on the Mississippi], Sofija: Kultura.

Prince and the Pauper

1947   Printsut i Prostiakut [Prince and Pauper], Sofiy: Chipyv.

1963   Princat i Prisekat [Prince and Pauper], Sofija: Mladez.

1963   Prinsut i Prosekut [Prince and Pauper], Sofia: Mladez.

1969   Princat i Prosekat [Prince and Pauper]. [2nd edition] Sofija:
       Mladez.

Stories and Sketches

1950   Chovekut, Koito Zhivei v Tuminan [The Man Who Lived in the Darkness],
       Sofija: Mladez.

1955 Kandidat za Gubernator [Candidate for Governor]. (Isbrani Razkazi)
      [(Selected Stories)], Sofija: Kultura.

Tom Sawyer

1954 Prikljucenijata na Tom Sojer [Adventures of Tom Sawyer], Sofija:
      Mladez.

1962 Same. [2nd edition] Sofija: Mladez.

1965 Tom Sojer [3rd edition] Sofija: Mladez.

1974 Tom Sojer. Hakalberi Fin. [4th edition] Sofija: Mladez.

Miscellaneous

1966 Da ne se Otvarja do 2406 Godina [Do Not Open until the Year 2406],
      Sofija: NSOF.

Selections

1975 Izbrano [Selections], Sofija: Kultura.

Czechoslovakia

Sources: CPL/IT/NUC

American Claimant

1951 Americky Nopadnik [American Claimant], Praha: Prace.

1962 Same. Praha: Dilia.

Connecticut Yankee

1947 Yankee na Dvore Krale Artuse [Yankee at the Court of King Arthur],
      n.p. n.pub. [Bohemian]

1954 Same. Praha, Nase Vojsko. [Bohemian]

1955 Yankee z Connecticutu na Dvore Krale Artusa. [Yankee from
      Connecticut at the Court of King Arthur], Bratislava: SVKL.
      [Bohemian]

1957 Princ a Chudas [Prince and Pauper, including the Connecticut
      Yankee], Praha: SNKLHU.

1961 Yankee z Connecticutu na Dvore Krale Artuse. Praha. Kapka
      Knihovna Pro Kazdelo: [Bohemian]

1970   Same. [5th edition] Praha: Prace. [Bohemian]

1972   Same. Bratislava: Tatran.

1976   Princ a Chudas. Yankee z Connecticutu na Dvore Krole Artuse
       [Prince and Pauper. Yankee from Connecticut at the Court of
       King Arthur], Praha: Odeon.

Gilded Age

1962   Pozlaceny Vek; Pribeh Nasich Dnu [The Gilded Age; A Tale of Today].
       Knihovna Klasiku. Praha: SNKLU. [Bohemian]

Huckleberry Finn

1901? Dobrodruzstvi Frantika Finna (Kamarada Toma Sawyera) [Adventures
       of Huckleberry Finn (Comrade of Tom Sawyer)], Praha: Otto.

1935   Dobrodruzstvi Hucka Finna [Adventures of Huck Finn]. Knihovna
       Vesele Mladi Sv. 2. Praha: Janu. [Bohemian]

1953   Same. Praha: Prace. [Bohemian]

1954   Tom Sawyer; Huckleberry Finn, Praha: SNKLHU.

1955   Dobrodruzstvi Huckleberryho Finna [Adventures of Huckleberry Finn],
       Praha: SNDK.

1955   Same. Bratislava: SNDK.

1956   Same. Praha: SNDK.

1956   Same. [2nd edition] Praha: SNKLHU

1957   Same. [2nd edition] Bratislava: Mlade Leta.

1961   Same. Praha: SNDK.

1963   Same. [4th edition] Praha: SNDK.

1964   Huckleberry Finn, Bratislava: SVKL.

1965   Dobrodruzstvi Huckleberryho Finna. [5th edition] Praha: Mlada
       Fronta.

1965   Same. [5th edition] Praha: SNDK.

1966   Huckleberry Finn Kalandjai [Huckleberry Finn Adventures], Bratislava:
       Mlade Leta. [Magyar]

1966   Dobrodruzstva Huckleberryho Finna, Bratislava: Mlade Leta.

1970   Dobrodruzstvi Toma Sawyera. Dobrodruzstvi Huckleberryho Finna
       [Adventures of Tom Sawyer. Adventures of Huckleberry Finn].
       [4th edition]   Praha: Odeon.

1971   Dobrodruzstva Huckleberryho Finna. [4th edition] Bratislava:
       Mlade Leta.

1972   Huckleberry Finn Kalandjai. [6th edition] Bratislava: Madach.
       [Magyar]

1973   Dobrodruzstvi Huckleberryho Fina. [6th edition] Praha: Albatros.

Innocents Abroad

1953   Nasinci na Castach [Innocents Abroad], Praha: Melantrich.

1971   Same. [2nd edition] Praha: Melantrich.

Joan of Arc

1951   Panna vr Zbroji [Joan of Arc], Praha: Vysehrad.

1957   Same. [2nd edition] Praha: Lidova Demokracie.

1972   Same. Praha: Svoboda.

Letters from the Earth

1968   Listy zo Zeme [Letters from the Earth], Bratislava: VPL.

Life on the Mississippi

1912   Zivot na Mississippi [Life on the Mississippi], Praha: Tille.

1952   Same. Martin: Matica Slovenska. [Slovenian]

1955   Zivot na Mississippi; Jak Jsem Se Protloukol[Life on the
       Mississippi; Roughing It], Praha: SNKLHU.

1963   Zivot na Mississippi. [2nd edition] Praha: SNDK.

1971   Elet a Mississipin [Life on the Mississippi], Bratislava: Madach.
       [Magyar]

Mysterious Stranger

1961   Tajomny Cizinec; Vybor z Providek [Mysterious Stranger; Selected
       Stories], n.p. n.pub. [Bohemian]

1968 Tajomny Cudzinec [Mysterious Stranger], Bratislava: Tatram. [Bohemian]

Prince and the Pauper

1947 Princ a Zobrak, Povest [Prince and Pauper, Tale], n.p.: Transoscius.

1957 Princ a Chudas [Prince and Pauper], Praha: SNKLHU.

1958 Same. Praha: SNDK.

1962 Princ a Bedar [Prince and Beggar], Bratislava: Mlade Leta.

1968 Princ a Chudas. [2nd edition] Praha: SNDK. New York and London: Harper & Brothers.

1976 Princ a Chudas. Yankee z Connecticutu na Dvore Krole Artuse [Prince and Pauper. Yankee from Connecticut at the Court of King Arthur], Praha: Odeon.

Roughing It

1955 Zivot na Mississippi; Jak Jsem Se Protloukol [Life on the Mississippi; Roughing It], Praha: SNKLHU.

Stories and Sketches

n.d. Prvni Milion; Kniha Humoru z Americkeho Prostredi [The First Million; Humorous Book out of the American Setting], Praha: Vilimek. [Slovnik]

1891 Vybrane Humoresky [Selected Humor], Praha: Otty.

1922 Humoresky a Orty [Humorous Stories], Tatran, Martin: Turciansky. [Slovenian]

1952 Ze Zeme Dolaru [From the Land of Dollars], Praha: Prace.

1953 Humoresky a Satiry [Humor and Satire]. Kniznica Rohaca, Sv. 8. Bratislava, Praca: Vydavotel'stvo ROH. [Slovak]

1961 Tajomny Cizinec; Vybor z Providek [The Mysterious Stranger; Selected Stories], n.p. n.pub.

1966 Tom Sawyer na Cestach a Jene Prozy [Tom Sawyer Abroad and Other Stories], Praha: Odeon. [Bohemian]

1975 Tom Sawyer Detektivem a Jine Povidky [Tom Sawyer Detective and Other Stories], Praha: Albatros.

Tom Sawyer

19--? Cesty Toma Sawyer, Praha: J. Otto.

1921 Mali Klatez Tom Sawyer [Little Vagabond Tom Sawyer], n.p. n.pub.
      [Slovak]

1927 Dobrodruzstvi Toma Sawyera [Adventures of Tom Sawyer], n.p. n.pub.
      [Bohemian]

1937 Cesty Tom Sawyera [Reputation of Tom Sawyer]. Knihovna Vesele
      Mladi Sv. 5. Praha: Janu.

1937 Dobrodruzstvi Toma Sawyera. Universalni Knihovna Sv. 1. Mistek na
      Morave. Bilek. [Bohemian]

1949 Same. Praha: Vysehrad. [Bohemian]

1953 Tom Sawyer a Jeho Dobrodruzstva [Tom Sawyer and His Adventures],
      Bratislava: SNDK. [Slovak]

1954 Tom Sawyer; Huckleberry Finn, Praha: SNKLHU.

1955 Dobrodruzstvi Toma Sawyera, Praha: SNDK. [Bohemian]

1956 Same. [2nd edition] Praha: SNDK. [Bohemian]

1956 Same. [2nd edition] Praha: SNKLHU.

1957 Tom Sawyer a Jeho Dobrodruzstva. [2nd edition] Bratislava: Mlade
      Leta. [Slovak]

1960 Dobrodruzstvi Toma Sawyera, Praha: Dilia.

1960 Vel'ke Dobrodruzstvo Toma Sawyera [Grand Adventures of Tom Sawyer],
      Bratislava: Diliza.

1962 Dobrodruzstvi Tom Sawyera, Praha: Orbis.

1963 Same. [4th edition] Praha: SNDK.

1963 Tom Sawyer Kalandjai [Tom Sawyer's Adventures]. [8th edition]
      Bratislava: Konyvkiado. [Magyar]

1964 Dobrodruzstvi Toma Sawyera. [7th edition] Praha: Mlada Fronta.

1965 Tom Sawyer a Jeho Dobrodruzstva. [3rd edition] Bratislava: Mlade
      Leta.

1965 Dobrodruzstvi Toma Sawyera. [5th edition] Praha: SNDK.

1970 Same. [6th edition] Praha: Albatros.

1970 Dobrodruzstvi Toma Sawyera. Dobrudruzstvi Huckleberryho Finna
      [Adventures of Tom Sawyer. Adventures of Huckleberry Finn].
      [4th edition] Praha: Odeon.

1971   Tom Sawyer Kalandjai. [6th edition] Bratislava: Madach. [Magyar]

1971   Tom Sawyer a Jeho Dobrodruzstva [Tom Sawyer and His Adventures].
       [4th edition] Bratislava: Mlade Leta.

Tom Sawyer Abroad

19--? Cesty Toma Sawyera [Reputation of Tom Sawyer], Praha: Otto.

1966   Tom Sawyer na Cestach a Jene Prozy [Tom Sawyer Abroad and Other
       Stories], Praha: Odeon.

Tom Sawyer, Detective

n.d.   Tom Sawyer Detektivem [Tom Sawyer Detective], Praha: Hejda &
       Tucek.

1937   Same. Knihovna Vesele Mladi Sv. 6. Praha: Janu.

1956   Ukradnute Diamanty [Stolen Diamonds], Bratislava: Smena.

1959   Tom Sawyer Detektivem, Praha: SNDK.

1975   Tom Sawyer Detektivem a Jine Povidky [Tom Sawyer Detective and
       Other Stories], Praha: Albatros.

Finland

Sources: IT/KSLF/NUC/SK/SKFL

Connecticut Yankee

1923   En Yankee vid Kung Arturs Hov [A Yankee at King Arthur's Court],
       Helsingfors: Soderstrom. [Swedish title]

1925   Jankki Kunningas Arthurin Hovissa [Yankee at King Arthur's Court],
       Helsinki: Koursanvalta.

1953   En Yankee vid Kung Arthurs Hov. Beromda Romaner, 7. Helsingfors.
       [Swedish title]

1974   Jenkki Kunigas Arthurin Hovissa, Hameenlinna: Karisto.

Huckleberry Finn

1927   Huckleberry Finnin Seikkailut [Huckleberry Finn's Adventures],
       Porvoo: Soderstrom.

1940 Same. Porvoo: Soderstrom.

1943 Same. Helsinki: Soderstrom.

1948 Same. Helsinki: Soderstrom.

1955 Huckleberry Finns Aventyr [Huckleberry Finn's Adventures], Helsing-
      fors: Sid. [Swedish title]

1956 Huckleberry Finnin Seikkailut. [6th edition] Nuorten Toivekkirjasto
      79. Porvoo, Helsinki: Soderstrom.

1965 Same. [8th edition] Porvoo, Helsinki: Soderstrom.

1968 Same. [9th edition] Porvoo, Helsinki: Soderstrom.

1971 Same. [10th edition] Porvoo: Soderstrom.

1972 Same. Helsinki: Ex Libris.

1972 Same. Helsinki: Otava.

1972 Same. [new edition] Helsinki: Suuri Suomalainen Kirjakerho.

1973 Same. [2nd edition] Helsinki: Otava.

1973 Same. [11th edition] Porvoo: Soderstrom.

1973 Same. [2nd-3rd editions] Helsinki: Suuri Suomalainen Kirjakerho.

1976 Same. [12th edition] Porvoo: Soderstrom.

Innocents Abroad

1922 Jenkkeja Maailmalla; Heidan Toivioretkensa Pyhalle Maalle
      [Innocents Abroad; the New Pilgrim's Progress]. 2 vols. Porvoossa:
      Soderstrom.

Joan of Arc

1910 Johanna d'Arc [Joan of Arc], Porvoossa: Soderstrom.

1948 Orleansin Neitsyt [Maid of Orleans], Helsinki: Fennia.

Letters from the Earth

1963 Matkakirjeita Maasta [Letters from the Earth]. [extracts] [2nd-3rd
      editions] Helsinki: Weilin & Goos.

1976 Same. Helsinki: Weilin & Goos.

Life on the Mississippi

1900 Luotsina Mississippi-Joella [Mississippi Pilot], Hameenlinna: Karisto.

1913 Same. Hameenlinna: Karisto

1920 Luotsina Mississippi; Humoristinen Kertomus Kirjottanut Mark Twain [Mississippi Pilot; Humorous Stories Written by Mark Twain], Hameenlinna: Karisto.

1935 Luotsina Mississippi-Joella. Humoristinen Kertomus. Hameenlinna?: Karisto?

1963 Mississippi, Helsinki: Soderstrom.

Prince and the Pauper

1908 Prinssi ja Kerjalaispoika [Prince and the Pauper], Helsingissa: Otava.

1951 Same. Porvoo: Soderstrom.

1951 Same. Nuorten Towekujasto, 7. Porvoo: Varho.

1953 Same. [2nd edition] Nuorten Toivekirjasto, 7. Porvoo, Helsinki: Soderstrom.

1958 Same. [3rd edition] Porvoo, Helsinki: Soderstrom.

1967 Same. [4th edition] Porvoo, Helsinki: Soderstrom.

1975 Same. [5th-6th editions] Porvoo: Soderstrom.

Pudd'nhead Wilson

1932 Veren Perinto [Blood Inheritance], Hameenlinna: Karisto.

1963 Same. [2nd edition] Hameenlinna: Karisto.

Report from Paradise

1958 Kapteeni Taivaassa [Captain Heaven], Hameenlinna: Karisto.

Roughing It

1948 Slita Hund [Worn and Torn Dog (Have To Rough It)], Helsingfors: Soderstrom.

1957 Koiranelamaa. Alkuteoksen Nimi [Roughing It. Original Title]. Olli Nuorto. Porvoo, Helsinki: Soderstrom.

Stories and Sketches

1935 Mark Twain, Humoreskeja. 13 Jutelmaa ja Pakinaa [Mark Twain,
      Humorous Stories. 13 Narrations and Comments], Hameenlinna:
      Karisto.

1963 Mark Twainin Parhaat [Mostly Mark Twain], Helsinki: Tammi.

Tom Sawyer

1909 Tom Sawyerin Seikkailut [Tom Sawyer's Adventures], Helsingissa:
      Kustannus.

1926 Same. Porvoo: Soderstrom.

1933 Same. [2nd edition] Porvoo: Soderstrom.

1943 Tom Sawyers Aventyr [Tom Sawyer's Adventures]. Schildts Ungdoms-
      bocker, 42. Helsingfors: [Swedish title]

1949 Tom Sawyerin Seikkailut. [4th edition] Porvoo: Soderstrom.

1953 Tom Sawyers Aventyr. Soderstroms Favoritbocker. Helsingfors:
      Soderstrom. [Swedish title]

1956 Tom Sawyerin Seikkailut. Alkuteoksen Nimi [Tom Sawyer's Adventures.
      Original Title]. [5th edition] Nuorten Toivekirjasto 78. Porvoo,
      Helsinki: Soderstrom.

1956 Tama Sawyerin Viimeiset Seikkailut; Tom Sawyer, Ilmailija; ja
      Tom Sawyer, Salapoliisi [Tom Sawyer's Adventures; Tom Sawyer
      Abroad; and Tom Sawyer, Detective]. Joka Kodin Tahtikirjasto 39.
      Helsinki: Otava.

1959 Tom Sawyerin Seikkailut, Porvoo, Helsinki: Soderstrom.

1962 Same. [8th edition] Helsinki: Soderstrom.

1965 Same. [9th edition] Porvoo, Helsinki: Soderstrom.

1967 Same. [10th edition] Porvoo, Helsinki: Soderstrom.

1970 Same. [12th edition] Porvoo, Helsinki: Soderstrom.

1972 Same. [13th edition] Porvoo: Soderstrom.

1973 Same. Helsinki: Otava.

1973 Same. [14th edition] Porvoo: Soderstrom.

1973 Same. [15th edition] Porvoo: Soderstrom.

1973 Same. [new edition] Helsinki: Suuri Suomalainen Kirjakerho.

Tom Sawyer Abroad

n.d.   Tom Sawyer Matkalla [Tom Sawyer on the Way], n.p.:   Suomensi
       Aatto S.

1909   Tom Sawyer Ilmailija (Huckleberry Finn'in Jatko) [Tom Sawyer
       Aeronaut (Huckleberry Finn's Continuation)], Helsingissa: Kustannus.

1956   Tom Sawyerin Viimeiset Seikkailut; Tom Sawyer, Ilmailija; ja
       Tom Sawyer, Salapoliisi [Tom Sawyer's Adventures; Tom Sawyer
       Abroad; and Tom Sawyer, Detective].   Joka Kodin Tahtikirjasto 39.
       Helsinki: Otava.

1971   Tom Sawyer Vierailla Mailla [Tom Sawyer Abroad].   [2nd edition]
       Hameenlinna: Karisto.

Tom Sawyer, Detective

1950   Tom Sawyer Solapoliisina.   Huck Finnin Kertomus [Tom Sawyer
       Detective.   Huck Finn's Narration], Hameenlinna: Karisto.

1951   Same.   [2nd edition] Hameenlinna: Valkeila.

1956   Tom Sawyerin Viimeiset Seikkailut; Tom Sawyer, Ilmailija; ja
       Tom Sawyer, Salapoliisi [Tom Sawyer's Adventures; Tom Sawyer
       Abroad; and Tom Sawyer, Detective].   Joka Kodin Tahtikirjasto 39.
       Helsinki: Otava.

1957   Tom Sawyer Salapoliisina.   Huck Finnin Kertomus.   [3rd edition]
       Hameenlinna: Karisto.

1971   Tom Sawyer Salapoliisina [4th edition] Hameenlinna: Karisto.

1971   Same.   [5th edition] Hameenlinna: Karisto.

Miscellaneous

1972   Kaksipippuinen Jutto Ja Merkillisia Tarinoita ⌈Adventures in
       Remote Seas], Helsinki: Weilin & Goos.

Greece

Sources: IT/NUC

Connecticut Yankee

1952   Enas Giankes tou Kounektikat Sten Aule tou Basilea Arthourou [A
       Yankee of Connecticut at the Court of King Arthur], Athenai:
       Pekhlibanides.

Huckleberry Finn

1950 Khok Phinn, O Philos tou Tom Soger [Huck Finn, Comrade of Tom Sawyer], Athenai: Vlessas.

1953 Hock Finn [Huck Finn], Athenai: Pekhlibanidis.

1953 Oi Peripeteies tou Chok Phinn [The Adventures of Huck Finn], Athenai: Alikiotis.

Life on the Mississippi

1964 Zoe Ston Mississipe [Life on the Mississippi], Athenai: Atlantis.

Prince and the Pauper

1950 Basilopoulo Kai Zutianopoulo [Prince and Pauper], Athenai: Alikiotis.

1951 Prigkips Kai Phtokhos [Prince and Pauper], Athenai: Pekhlibanides.

1970 Prinkepas Kai Phtochos [Prince and Pauper], Athenai: Pekhlibanides.

Tom Sawyer

1949 Tom Soger [Tom Sawyer], Athenai: Ulessas.

1952 Oi Peripeteies tou Tom Soger [The Adventures of Tom Sawyer], Athenai: Pekhlibanides.

1953 Same. Athenai: Alikiotis.

1972 Same. Athenai: Papadopoulos.

Tom Sawyer, Detective

1962 O Tom Soyer Astynomikos [Tom Sawyer Detective], Athenai: Vlessas.

Hungary

Sources: CPL/IT/MK/NUC

American Claimant

1893 Az Amerikai Orokos Regeny egy Kotetben [The American Heir. Novel in Two Volumes], Budapest: Legrady.

Autobiography

1968 Oneletrajz [Autobiography], Budapest: Europa.

Captain Stormfield's Visit to Heaven

191-? Stormfield Kapitany Latogatasa a Mennyorszagban [Captain Storm-field's Visit to Heaven]. Ld. Tevan-kvtar, 90-91. n.p. n.pub.

Connecticut Yankee

1956 Egy Jenki Artur Kiraly Udvaraban [A Yankee at the Court of King Arthur], Budapest: Uj Magyar.

1957 Same. 2 vols. Budapest: Szepirodalmi.

Following the Equator

1963 Utazas az Egyenlito Korul [Journey around the Equator]. [3rd edition] Vilagjarok Klasszikus Utleirasok, 4. Budapest: Gondolat.

Gilded Age

1876 Az Aranyozott Kor. Amerikai Regeny [The Gilded Age. American Romance]. 3 vols. Budapest: Athenaeum.

1957 Az Aranykor [The Gilded Age], Budapest: Europa.

Huckleberry Finn

1887 Huckleberry Finn Kalandjai [Huckleberry Finn's Adventures], Buda-pest: Revai.

190-? Huckleberry Finn Vandorlasai es Kalandjai [Huckleberry Finn's Mi-grations and Adventures], Budapest: Athenaeum.

1904 Same. [Bound with volumes entitled Tamas Urfi Isinyei es Kalandjai [Master Tom's Pranks and Adventures]. Budapest: Tarasag Kiadasa.

1905 Same. Budapest: Revai.

1921 Huckleberry Finn Kalandjai, Budapest: Athenaeum.

1935 Same. Budapest: Tolnai.

1936 Huckleberry Finn es Tom Sawyer Kalandjai, Budapest: Revai.

1949 Huckleberry Finn Kalandjai, Budapest: Szikra.

1954   Same. Budapest: Ifjusagi.

1956   Tom Sawyer Kalandjai; Huckleberry Finn, Budapest: Ifjusagi.

1960   Huckleberry Finn, Budapest: Mora.

1964   Huckleberry Finn; Regeny [Huckleberry Finn; Romance], Budapest:
       Mora Ferenc.

1972   Huckleberry Finn Kalandjai. [6th edition] Budapest: Mora.

1975   Same. [7th edition] Budapest: Mora.

Innocents Abroad

1954   Jambor Lelkek Kulfoldon [Innocent Spirits Abroad], Budapest:
       Muveit Nep.

Joan of Arc

1964   Jeanne d'Arc [Joan of Arc], Budapest: Magveto.

Life on the Mississippi

n.d.   Hajoselet a Mississippin [Seafaring Life on the Mississippi],
       Budapest: Revai.

1971   Elet a Mississippin [Life on Mississippi], Budapest: Gondolat.

Man That Corrupted Hadleyburg

1951   A Lovatett Varos; Elbeszelesek [A City Fooled; Stories], Budapest:
       Szepirodalmi.

1955   Same. Budapest: Szepirodalmi.

1973   A Lovatett Varos, Budapest: Magyar Helikon.

Mysterious Stranger

n.d.   A Titokzatos Idegen [The Mysterious Stranger], Budapest: Genius.

Prince and the Pauper

1885   Koldus es Kiralyfi [Beggar and Prince], Budapest: Bela.

1897   Same. [2nd edition] Budapest: Revai.

19--? Same. Budapest: Revai.

1906   Koldus es Kiralyfi. Ifjusagi Elbeszeles [Beggar and Prince.
        Youthful Story], Budapest: Athenaeum.

1920   Koldus es Kiralyfi. Klasszikus Regenytar, uz Sorozat. Budapest:
        Revai.

1930   Same. Budapest: Revai.

1955   Same. Budapest: Ifjusagi.

1962   Same. Budapest: Mora Ferenc.

1970   Same. Budapest: Mora.

1974   Same. [2nd edition] Budapest: Mora.

Pudd'nhead Wilson

n.d.   Az Ostoba Wilson [Stupid Wilson], Budapest: Legrady.

191-?   Same. 4. kiad. [4th edition] Budapest: Legrady.

1920   Same. [4th edition] Budapest: Legrady.

1956   Puddingfeju Wilson [Puddinghead Wilson], Budapest: Szepirodalmi.

Stories and Sketches

n.d.   Az en Oram [My Watch]. Ld: Humoros Zsebkonyvtar I. n.p. n.pub.

n.d.   Hogyan Szerksztettem Egy Gazdasagi Lapot [How I Edited An Agricul-
        tural Newspaper]. Ld: Humoros Zsebkonyvtar II. n.p. n.pub.

n.d.   Tapasztalalok a Difteritisz Korul [Experiences around Diphtheria].
        Ld: Humoros Zsebkonyvtar V. n.p. n.pub.

n.d.   Rajzok [Sketches]. Ld: Utkozben VI. n.p. n.pub.

19--?   Az 1,000,000 Fontos Banko e Mas Novellak [The 1,000,000 Pound
        Bank-note and Other New Stories]. [2nd edition] Budapest:
        Athenaeum.

1905   A Vereb es Egyeb Elbeszelesek [The Sleuth and Other Stories]. [2nd
        edition] Budapest. Baer.

1920   Wicklow, a kem, es mas Tortenetek [Wicklow, the Spy, and Other
        Stories], Budapest: Athenaeum. [Wendish]

1949   Az Ellopott Feher Elefant [The Stolen White Elephant], Budapest:
        Hungaria.

1950   Embertelen Vilag. 14 Amerikai Elbeszeles [Monstrous World. 14
        American Stories (Twain, London, Howard Fast, et al.)]. [2nd edi-
        tion] Budapest: Athenaeum.

1951   A Lovatett Varos; Elbeszelesek [A City Fooled; Stories], Budapest:
       Szepirodalmi.

1955   Same. Budapest: Szepirodalmi.

1957   Adam es Eva Noploja [Adam and Eve's Diary], Budapest: Europa.

1957   Az Egymillio Fontos Bankjegy es Egyeb Frasok [The One Million
       Pounds Bank-note and Other Stories], Budapest: Europa.

1958   Megszeliditem A. Kerekpart [Taming the Bicycle], Budapest: Terra.

1961   Nincs Mindenre Paragrafus. Novelette Kisregeny es Elbeszelesek
       [Not Everything Articles. Short Stories, Romances and Accounts],
       Budapest: Szepirodalmi.

1966   Embereves a Vonaton. Humoreszkek, Elbeszelesek [Cannibalism in the
       Cars. Humorous Sketches, Stories], Budapest: Magveto.

                              Tom Sawyer

1886   Tamas Urfi Kalandjai [Master Tom's Adventures], Budapest: Revai.

1904   Tamas Urfi Csinjei es Kalandjai [Master Tom's Pranks and Adventures],
       Budapest: Magyar.

1912   Same. Regenyes Elbeszeles. Budapest: Athenaeum.

1922   Tamas Urfi Kalandjai, Budapest: Athenaeum.

1933   Same. Budapest: Athenaeum.

1936   Huckleberry Finn es Tom Sawyer Kalandjai, Budapest: Revai.

1954   Tom Sawyer Kalandjai, Budapest: Ifjusagi.

1956   Tom Sawyer Kalandjai; Huckleberry Finn, Budapest: Ifjusagi.

1959   Tom Sawyer Kalandjai. 2 vols. Budapest: Mora.

1962   Same. Budapest: Mora.

1962   Same. [8th edition] Budapest: Europa.

1963   Same. Budapest: Regeny.

1971   Same. [6th edition] Budapest: Mora.

1975   Tom Sawyer Kalandjai: Regeny [Tom Sawyer's Adventures: Romance].
       [7th edition] Budapest: Mora.

Tom Sawyer Abroad

1920 Tamas Urfi Leghajon [Master Tom Aeronaut]. Elbesseli Huck Finn [Related by Huck Finn], Budapest: Athenaeum.

1934 Same. Budapest: Athenaeum.

1956 Tom Sawyer Mint Detektiv; Tom Sawyer Leghajon [Tom Sawyer As Detective; Tom Sawyer Aeronaut], Budapest: Ifjusagi.

Tom Sawyer, Detective

1920 Tamas Urfi Mint Detektiv; Elbeszeli Huck Finn [Master Tom As Detective; Related by Huck Finn], Budapest: Athenaeum.

1922 Same. n.p.: Halasz Gyula.

1934 Tamas Urfi, Mint Detektiv, Budapest: Athenaeum.

1956 Tom Sawyer Mint Detektiv; Tom Sawyer Leghajon [Tom Sawyer As Detective; Tom Sawyer Aeronaut], Budapest: Ifjusagi.

1961 Tom Sawyer Kozbelep [Tom Sawyer Intervenes], Budapest: Nepmuv. Int.

Travel Sketches

1955 Utirajzok [Travel Descriptions], Budapest: Muvelt Nep.

Miscellaneous

1962 Emlekek, Gondolatok [Memories, Reflections], Budapest: Gondolat.

Selections

1885? Amerikai Humoristak [American Humorists], n.p.: Mulatsagos Tortenetek alott is.

Poland

Sources: BBPo/BP/CPL/IT/NUC/PB/SWPP

Captain Stormfield's Visit to Heaven

1949 Podroz Miedzyplanetarna [Interplanetary Journey]. In Humoreski, Vol. I. Warszawa: Panstwowy Instytut Wydawniczy.

1951 Same. In Humoreski, Vol. I. Warszawa: Pantswowy Instytut Wydawniczy.

Connecticut Yankee

1936 Yankes na Dworze Krola Artura [A Yankee at the Court of King
      Arthur], Warszawa: Roj.

1948 Same. Spoldzielnia Wydawnicza Wiedza, Nr. 5. Warszawa: Wiedza.

1949 Same. Warszawa: Ksiazka i Wiedza.

Huckleberry Finn

n.d. Prihodi Juka [Adventures of Huck], n.p.: Derzhiruka.

1898 Przygody Hucka [Adventures of Huck]. Biblioteka dziel Wyborow, Nr.
      56-57. Warszawa: Granowskiego i Sikorskiego.

1912 Same. Warszawa: n.pub.

1933 Same. Warszawa: Przeworski.

1934 Przygody Hucka, Powiesc dla Mlodziezy [Adventures of Huck, Novel
      for Youths], Warszawa: Przeworski.

1936 Przygody Hucka, Warszawa: Przeworski.

1937 Przygody Keklberry Finna [Adventures of Huckleberry Finn], Kijow:
      Ukrderznacmeuwydawniczy.

1938 Przygody Hucka, Warszawa: Przeworski.

1946 Same. Lodz: Lodzski Instytut Wydawniczy.

1955 Same. Warszawa: Iskry.

1956 Same. [2nd edition] Warszawa: Iskry.

1966 Same. [3rd edition] Warszawa: Iskry.

1973 Same. [4th edition] Warszawa: Iskry.

Letters from the Earth

1966 Listy z Ziemi [Letters from the Earth], Warszawa: Ksiazka i
      Wiedza.

Life on the Mississippi

1967 Zycie na Missisipi [Life on the Mississippi], Warszawa: Czytelnik.

Man That Corrupted Hadleyburg

1968   Cztlowiek Ktory Zdemoralizowal Hadleyburg [Man Who Demoralized
       Hadleyburg], Warszawa: Ksiazka i Wiedza.

Prince and the Pauper

1899   Krolewicz-zebrak, Opowiadanie Historyczne [Prince-Pauper, Historical
       Tale], Warszawa: Thiella.

1933   Ksiaze i Zebrak [Prince and Pauper], Warszawa: Przeworski.

1936   Same. Warszawa: Przeworski.

1938   Same. Warszawa: Przeworski.

1939   Same. Warszawa: Przeworski.

1947   Ksiaze i Zebrak; Powiesc dla Mlodziezy [Prince and Pauper; Novel
       for Young People], Lodz: Lodzski Instytut Wydawniczy.

1950   Tom Canty, Poznan: Michaekowa.

1954   The Prince and the Pauper, Warszawa: Panstwowy Zakl. Wydawniczy
       Szkol. [English]

1954   Krolewicz i Zebrak, Warszawa: Iskry.

1955   Same. [2nd edition] Warszawa: Iskry.

1956   Same. [3rd, 4th editions] Warszawa: Iskry.

1958   Same. Warszawa: Iskry.

1960   Same. [6th edition] Warszawa: Iskry.

1962   Same. Warszawa: Iskry.

1964   Same. [8th edition] Warszawa: Iskry.

1966   Same. [9th edition] Warszawa: Iskry.

1967   Same. [9th, 10th editions] Warszawa: Iskry.

1972   Same. [11th edition] Warszawa: Iskry.

1975   Prigkepas Kai Zetianos [Prince and Pauper], Warszawa: Wydawniczy
       Szkol.

Roughing It

1960   Pod Golym Niebem [Under Naked Sky], Warszawa: Iskry.

1965   Same. [2nd edition] Warszawa: Iskry.

Stories and Sketches

1881 Humoreski [Humorous Sketches]. 3 vols. Wydawnictwo A. Wislickiego,
      Nr. 31. Warszawa: Przegladu.

1899 Bajeczski dla Starych Dzieci [Tales for Old Children]. Dod. do
      Graz. Polskiej, Nr. 34. Warszawa: n.pub.

1899 Humoreski i Opowiadania [Humorous Sketches and Stories]. Warszawa:
      Csernoka.

1899? Humoreski. 3 vols. Wydawnictwo A. Wislickiego, Nr. 12, 25, 31.
      Warszawa: Wydawniczy.

19--? Same. I. Biblioteka Powszechna. Lwow: Zukerkandla.

1913 Di Tage Bikhlekh fun Odem un Haveh [Extracts from the Diary of
      Adam and Eve], Bapmaza, Varshava [Warsaw]: n.pub. [Yiddish]

1913 Bialy Slon i Inne Humoreski [White Elephant and Other Humorous
      Sketches], Krakow: Kwasniew-skiego.

1923 Opowiadania [Stories], Warszawa: Slonimski.

1925 Ma'aseh Be-'orekh Shavu'on Hakla'i [How I Edited An Agricultural
      Paper Once]. Warszawa: n.pub. [Yiddish]

1949 Humoreski. 2 vols. I. Podroz Miedzplanetarna [The Interplanetary
      Journey]. II. Bajeczki dla Starych Dzieci [Tales for Old Children],
      Warszawa: Panstwowy Instytut Wydawniczy.

1951 Opowiadania i Humoreski. Biblioteca Zolnierza. Warszawa:
      Wydawniczy.

1951 Selected Stories, Warszawa: n.pub. [English]

1954 Krol i Osiol, oraz Inne Opowiadania [The King and the Donkey, and
      Other Stories]. Spoldzielnia. Warszawa: Czytelnik.

1954 Same. Warszawa: Czytelnik.

1956 Pamflety [Lampoons], Warszawa: Ksiazka i Wiedza.

1660 Nieszczesny Narzeczony Aurelii [The Unhappy Fiance of Aurelia; Short
      Stories]. Biblioteca Powszechna. Warszawa: Panstwowy Instytut
      Wydawniczy.

1962 Same. [2nd edition] Warszawa: Panstwowy Instytut Wydawniczy.

1965 Same. [3rd edition] Warszawa: Instytut Wydawniczy.

1973 Trzydziesci Trzy Opowiesci [Complete Short Stories], Warszawa:
      Czytelnik.

Tom Sawyer

1925 Przygody Tomka Sawyera [Adventures of Tom Sawyer], Lwow-Poznan: Nakladem Wydawnictava Polskiego.

1933 Same. Warszawa: Przeworski.

1936 Przygody Tomka Sojera [Adventures of Tom Sawyer], Kijow: Ukrderznacmeu.

1936 Przygody Tomka Sawyera, Warszawa: Przeworski.

1938 Same. Warszawa: Przeworski.

1939 Same. Warszawa: Przeworski.

1949 Same. Warszawa: Ksiazka i Wiedza.

1951 Same. Warszawa: Ksiazka i Wiedza.

1953 Same. [5th edition] Warszawa: Iskry.

1955 Same. Warszawa: Iskry.

1956 Same. [3rd edition] Warszawa: Iskry.

1963 Same. Warszawa: Iskry.

1965 Same. [6th edition] Warszawa: Iskry.

1968 Same. [7th edition] Warszawa: Iskry.

1971 Same. [8th edition] Warszawa: Iskry.

1972 Same. [9th edition] Warszawa: Iskry.

1973 Same. [10th edition] Warszawa: Iskry.

1975 Same. [11th edition] Warszawa: Iskry.

Romania

Sources: IT/MTR/NUC

American Claimant

1922 Porcul in Trifoi [Pig in the Clover], Bucuresti: Caragiale.

1940 Pretendentul American [American Claimant], Bucuresti: Traducatorului.

1964 Same. Bucuresti: Pentru Literatura Universala.

Connecticut Yankee

1961 Un Yankeu La Curtea Regelui Arthur [A Yankee at the Court of King
      Arthur]. Biblioteca Pentru Toti, no. 55. Buceresti: Editura
      Literatura Universala.

1961 Egy Jenki Artur Kiraly Usvaraban [A Yankee at the Court of King
      Arthur]. 2 vols. Bukarest: Allanie Irodalmi es Muveszeti Kiado.
      [Magyar]

1966 A Connecticut Yankee in King Arthur's Court. [abridged] Bucuresti:
      Editura Didactica si Pedagogica. [English]

1975 Un Iankeu la Curtea Regelui Arthur [A Yankee at the Court of King
      Arthur], Cluj-Napoca: Dacia.

Huckleberry Finn

1942 Aventurile Si Calatoriile Lui Huckleberry Finn [Adventures of
      Huckleberry Finn]. Editura Cugetarea. Bucuresti: Delafras.

1950 Aventurile Lui Huckleberry Finn [Adventures of Huckleberry Finn],
      Bucuresti: Editura Tineretului.

1956 Aventurile Lui Tom Sawyer; Aventurile Lui Huckleberry Finn
      [Adventures of Tom Sawyer; Adventures of Huckleberry Finn]. [2nd
      edition] Bucuresti: Editura de Stat Pentru Literatura si Arta.

1957 Aventurile Lui Huckleberry Finn. Bucuresti: Editura Tineretului.

1959 Same. [2nd edition] Bucuresti: Editura Tineretului.

1964 Same. [3rd edition] Bucuresti: Editura Tineretului.

1969 Same. Bucuresti: Editura Pentru, Literatura Universala.

1975 Same: Bucuresti: Editura Ion Creanga.

King Leopold's Soliloquy

1961 Monologul Regelui Leopold [Monologue of King Leopold], Bucuresti:
      Editura Politica.

Life on the Mississippi

1964 Viata Pe Mississippi [Life on the Mississippi], Bucuresti: Editura
      Tineretului.

Man That Corrupted Hadleyburg

1951 Omul Care A Corupt Hadleyburgul [The Man That Corrupted Hadleyburg].
In Pagini Alese [Choice Pages]. Biblioteca Pentru Toti. Bucuresti:
Editura de Stat Pentru Literatura si Arta.

1964 Same. In Bancnota de un Milion de Lire. Schite. Povestiri.
Nuvele [Bank-note for A Million Lire. Sketches. Short Stories.
Pamphlets]. Biblioteca Pentru Toti, no. 262. Bucuresti: Editura
Pentru. Literatura.

Prince and the Pauper

1937 Print si Cersetor [Prince and Pauper]. Noua Colectie Delafras.
Bucuresti: Delafras.

1937 Same. Noua Colectie Delafras. Bucuresti: Editura Librariei
Principele Mircea.

1943 Same. Biblioteca Bucuria Copiilor, n. 39. [adaptation] Bucuresti:
Editura Bucur Ciobanul.

1955 Same. Bucuresti: Editura Tineretului.

1956 Same. [2nd edition] Bucuresti: Editura Tineretului.

1956 Kroljevic i Prosjak [Prince and Pauper], Bukurest: Omladinsko
Izdavacko Preduzece. [Serbian]

1957 Koldus es Kiralyfi [Beggar and Prince], Bukarest: Ifjusagi.
[Magyar]

1959 Print si Cersetor. [3rd edition] Bucuresti: Editura Tineretului.

1960 Same. [4th edition] Bucuresti: Editura Tineretului.

1967 Same. [5th edition] Bucuresti: Editura Tineretului.

1976 Same. Bucuresti: Editura Ion Creanga.

Stories and Sketches

1895 Novele si Schite de Alarcon, Bret Harte, Mark Twain [Short Stories
and Sketches by Alarcon, Bret Harte, Mark Twain]. Biblioteca
Pentru Toti, no. 10. Bucuresti: Editura Librariei Carol Muller.

1897 Broasca Minunata [Jumping Frog]. Colectia Saraga, no. 64. Jassy:
Editura Librariei Scoalelor, Fratii Saraga.

1902 Novele ai Schite de Alarcon, Bret Harte, Mark Twain. [2nd edition]
Biblioteca Pentru Toti, no. 10. Bucuresti: Editura Librariei
Leon Alcalay.

1904   Istoria Unui Baiat Rau Care [Story of the Bad Little Boy].   In
       Nuvele Umoristice si Satirice din Toate Literaturile [Humorous and
       Satirical Short Stories from World Literature].   Autorii Celebri.
       Piatra-Neamt: n.pub.

1909   Furtul Elefantului Alb [Theft of the White Elephant].   Colectiunea
       Lumen, no. 9.   Bucuresti: n.pub.

1909   Un Ramasag Intre Miliardari si Alte Schite [The £1,000,000 Bank-
       note and Other Sketches].   Biblioteca Pentru Toti, no. 397-398.
       Bucuresti: Editura Librariei Alcalay.

1912   Drepturile Femeei [Women's Rights].   Biblioteca Pentru Toti, no.
       799.   Bucuresti: Editura Librariei Leon Alcalay.

1915   Broasca Minuata [Jumping Frog].   In I.L. Caragiale, Reminiscente
       [Reminiscences], Bucuresti: Institutul de Editura si Arte Grafice
       Facla.

1916   Schite Umoristce [Humorous Sketches].   Biblioteca Literara si
       Stiintifica, no. 6.   Bucuresti: Editura Librariei H. Steinberg.

1922   Same.   [2nd edition] Biblioteca Literara si Stiintifica, no. 6.
       Bucuresti: Editura Librariei H. Steinberg si Fiul.

1925   Bancnota de 1.000.000 Lire Sterline [Bank-note for 1,000,000 Lire
       Sterling].   Floarea Literaturilor Straine, no. 3.   Bucuresti:
       Editura Adeverul.

1931   Broasca Minunata.   In I.L. Caragiale, Opere.   Vol. II.   Nuvele si
       Schite.   Bucuresti: Editura Cultura Nationala.

1932   Despre Barbieri [About Barbers].   Floarea Literaturilor Straine,
       no. 356.   Bucuresti: Editura Adeverul.

1936   Curierul Amator [Playing Courier].   Floarea Literaturilor Straine,
       no. 82.   Bucuresti: Editura Adeverul.

1943   Risul in Ceata [Laughing in Mist].   [Sketches and Tales by Mark
       Twain and Stephen Leacock] Lectura Pentru Toti, no. 17.   Bucuresti:
       Editura Curentul.

1945   Novele si Schite de Alarcon, Bret Harte, Mark Twain.   [3rd edition]
       Biblioteca Pentru Toti, no. 10.   Bucuresti: Editura Biblioteca
       Pentru Toti.

1946   Goana Dupa Elefant [Stolen White Elephant].   [adaptation] Teatru
       Satesc.   Buzau: Editura Librariei Ioan Calinescu.

1951   Pagini Alese [Choice Pages (Sketches and Stories)].   Biblioteca
       Pentru Toti.   Bucuresti: Editura de Stat Pentru Literatura si
       Arta.

1964   Bancnota de un Milion de Lire.   Schite.   Povestiri.   Nuvele [Bank-
       note for a Million Lire.   Sketches.   Short Stories.   Pamphlets].
       Biblioteca Pentru Toti, no. 262.   Bucuresti: Editura Pentru Litera-
       tura.

Tom Sawyer

1940 Aventurile Lui Tom Sawyer [Adventures of Tom Sawyer]. Editura
Cugetarea. Bucuresti: Delafras.

1942 Same. Bucuresti: Editura Ioan Lazareanu.

1949 Same. Bucuresti: Editura de Stat Literatura Pentru Tineret.

1956 Aventurile Lui Tom Sawyer; Aventurile Lui Huckleberry Finn
[Adventures of Tom Sawyer; Adventures of Huckleberry Finn]. [2nd
edition] Bucuresti: Editura de Stat Pentru Literatura si Arta.

1957 Aventurile Lui Tom Sawyer. [2nd edition] Bucuresti: Editura
Tineretului.

1959 Same. [2nd edition] Bucuresti: Editura Tineretului.

1964 Same. [3rd edition] Bucuresti: Editura Tineretului.

1968 Same. Bucuresti: Editura Tineretului.

1972 Tom Sawyer Kalandjai [Tom Sawyer's Adventures], Bukarest: Ion
Creanga. [Magyar]

1973 Aventurile Lui Tom Sawyer, Bucuresti: Ion Creanga.

Tom Sawyer Abroad; Tom Sawyer, Detective

1970 Tom Sawyer Detectiv. Tom Sawyer in Strainatate [Tom Sawyer,
Detective. Tom Sawyer Abroad], Bucuresti: Editura Ion Creanga.

Miscellaneous

1898 Parizianul [Paris Notes], Craiova: Benvenisti.

1911 Furnica [The Ant]. In Literatura Americana. Biblioteca Facla,
No. 9. Bucuresti: Societatea de Editura Facla.

1962 Vorbesc Din Mormint [I Speak from the Grave (extracts from Mark
Twain's Autobiography and Mark Twain in Eruption)]. Bucuresti:
Editura Pentru Literatura Universala.

1968 Dui Copilarie [Sweet Childhood], Bucuresti: Editura Tineretului.

Collected Works

1954-58   Opere Mark Twain [Works of Mark Twain]. 4 vols. Clasicii
Literaturii Universale. Bucuresti: Editura de Stat Pentru
Literatura si Arta.

Yugoslavia

Sources: BJ/IT/NUC

Autobiography

1962 Autobiografija [Autobiography]. [Ed. Charles Neider] Zagreb: Naprijed. [Serbo-Croatian]

Connecticut Yankee

1948 Jenki Na Dvoru Kralja Artura [Yankee at the Court of King Arthur], Beograd: Novinska Izdavacko Preduzece Saveza Novinara FNRJ. [Serbo-Croatian]

1958 Yankee Na Dvoru Kralja Arthura, Zagreb: Mladost. [Serbo-Croatian]

1975 Jenki iz Connecticuta na Dvoru Kralja Arturja [Yankee from Connecticut at the Court of King Arthur], Ljubljana: Mladinska. [Slovene]

Huckleberry Finn

1948 Pustolvoscine Huckleberryja Finna [Adventures of Huckleberry Finn], Ljubljana: Mladinska. [Serbian]

1948 Pustolovine Huckleberrya Finna [Adventures of Huckleberry Finn], Zabreb: Hrvatske. [Serbo-Croatian]

1949 Huckleberry Finn Kalandjai [Huckleberry Finn's Adventures], Subotica: Hid. [Magyar]

1949 Tom Sojer i Fin Haklberi [Tom Sawyer and Huckleberry Finn], Beograd: Novo Pokolenje. [Serbo-Croatian]

1952 Dozivljaji Haklberi Fina (druga Toma Sojera)[Experiences of Huckleberry Finn (comrade of Tom Sawyer)], Beograd: Novo Pokolenje. [Serbo-Croatian]

1956 Huckleberry Finn Kalandjai, Novi Sad: Konyvkiado Vallalat. [Magyar]

1960 Dozivljaji Haklberi Fina, Beograd: Sportska Knjiga. [Serbo-Croatian]

1962 Prigode Huckleberryja Finna [Adventures of Huckleberry Finn]. [2nd edition] Ljubljana: Mladinska Knjiga. [Slovenian]

1962 Same. Ljubljana: Mladinska Knjiga. [Slovenian]

1962 Dozivljaji Huckleberry Finna, Zagreb: Skolska Knjiga. [Serbo-Croatian]

1963 Dozivljaji Haklberi Fina, Beograd: Sportska Knjiga. [Serbo-Croatian]

1964 Dozivljaji Huckleberryja Finna, Zagreb: Skolska Knjiga. [Serbo-Croatian]

1965 Pustolovine Haklberi Fina [Adventures of Huckleberry Finn], Sarajevo: Veselin Maslesa. [Serbo-Croatian]

1965 Same. Sarajevo: Veselin Maslesa. [Serbo-Croatian]

1966 Dozivljaji Huckleberryja Finna, Zagreb: Skolska Knjija. [Serbo-Croatian]

1967 Dozivljaji Haklberi Fina, Sarajevo: Veselin Maslesa. [Serbian]

1968 Dozivljaji Huckleberryja Finna. [4th edition] Zagreb: Skolska Knjiga. [Serbo-Croatian]

1969 Hoklberi Fin [Huckleberry Finn], Skopje: Kultura. [Macedonian]

1970 Dozivljaji Huckleberryja Finna [5th edition] Zagreb: Skolska Knjija. [Serbo-Croatian]

1973 Same. Zagreb: Skolska Knijiga. [Serbo-Croatian]

1974 Prigode Huckleberryja Finna. 2 vols. Ljubljana: Mladinska. [Slovene]

1974 Pustolovine Huckleberryja Finna, Zagreb: Mladost. [Serbo-Croatian]

1975 Dozivljaji Huckleberryja Finna: Izbor [Adventures of Huckleberry Finn: Various Languages], Zagreb: Skolska Knjiga. [Serbo-Croatian]

1976 Same. [8th edition] Zagreb: Skolska Knjiga. [Serbo-Croatian]

1976 Dozivljaji Haklberi Fina. [3rd edition] Sarajevo: Veselin Maslesa. [Serbian]

Innocents Abroad

1964 Naivcine Na Putovanju ili Novo Hodocasce [Innocents on A Voyage or the New Pilgrimage]. [2 vols.] Zagreb: Matica Hrvotska. [Serbo-Croatian]

Life on the Mississippi

1949 Zivot na Misisipiju. Roman [Life on the Mississippi. Novel], Zagreb: Novo Polkojenje. [Serbo-Croatian]

1957 Same. Beograd: Turkisticka Stampa. [Serbo-Croatian]

1961 Zivljenje Na Misisipiju [Life on the Mississippi], Ljubljana:
      Mladinska Knjiga. [Slovenian]

Man That Corrupted Hadleyburg

1957 Covjek Koji Je Pokvario Hadleyburg [Man That Corrupted Hadleyburg],
      Zagreb: Sloga. [Serbo-Croatian]

Mysterious Stranger

1960 Tajanstveni Stranac [Mysterious Stranger], Sarajevo: Svjetlost.
      [Serbo-Croatian]

1961 Same. Beograd: Rad. [Serbo-Croatian]

Prince and the Pauper

n.d. Princ a Nuzak; povidka pro mladez kazdeho stari [Prince and Pauper;
      a tale for youth of all ages], Zagreb?: n.pub. [Croatian]

1951 Kraljevic i Prosjak. Prica za Mlade Ljude Svih Uzrasta [Prince
      and Beggar; Tale for Young People of All Ages], Beograd: n.pub.
      [Serbo-Croatian]

1952 Kraljevic i Prosjak, Sarajevo: Svjetlost. [Serbo-Croatian]

1953 Kraljevic in Berac [Prince and Pauper], Ljubljana: Mladinska
      Knjiga. [Slovene]

1953 Kraljevic i Prosjak, Sarajevo: Svjetlost. [Serbo-Croatian]

1954 Same. Sarajevo: Svjetlost. [Serbo-Croatian]

1954 Koldus es Kiralyfi. (Regeny az Ifjusag Szamara) [Beggar and
      Prince. (Romance for Young Generations)], Novi Sad: Testveriseg-
      Egyseg. [Magyar]

1955 Kraljevic i Prosjak. (Prica za Mlade Ljude Svih Uzrasta), Beograd:
      Sportska Knjiga. [Serbo-Croatian]

1957 Kraljevic i Prosjak, Sarajevo: Svjetlost. [Serbo-Croatian]

1957 Same. Sarajevo: Svjetlost. [Serbo-Croatian]

1958 Same. Beograd: Sportska Knjiga. [Serbo-Croatian]

1958 Koldus es Kiralyfi. Regeny az Ifjusag Szamara, Novi Sad:
      Bratstvo-Jedininstvo. [Magyar]

1958 Princi dhe Lypsi [Prince and Pauper], Prishtine: Rilindja.
      [Albanian]

1959   Koldus es Kiralyfi, Novi Sad: Forum. [Magyar]

1962   Kraljevic i Prosjak, Zagreb: Mladost. [Serbo-Croatian]

1963   Same. Sarajevo: Svjetlost. [Serbo-Croatian]

1964   Kraljevic i Prosjak. Prica za Hiljada Ljudi Svih Uzrasta [Prince
        and Pauper. A Tale for Young People of All Ages], Zagreb: Mladost.
        [Serbo-Croatian]

1965   Kraljevic i Prosjak: Pripovest za Mladey Svoke Dobi [Prince and
        and Beggar: Tale for the Young of All Ages], Zagreb: Matica
        Hrvatska. [Croatian]

1966   Kraljevic i Prosjak, Beograd: Sportska Knjiga. [Serbo-Croatian]

1966   Same. Sarajevo: Svjetlost. [Serbo-Croatian]

1967   Same. [2nd edition] Zagreb: Mladost. [Serbo-Croatian]

1972   Kraljevic i Prosjak. Prica za Hiljade Ljudi Svih Uzrasta.
        [3rd edition] Zagreb: Mladost. [Serbo-Croatian]

1974   Same. Zagreb: Mladost. [Serbo-Croatian]

Pudd'nhead Wilson

1957   Opasna Detektivska Prica. Mamlaz Vilson [A Double-barrelled
        Detective Story. Pudd'nhead Wilson], Sarajevo: Dzepna Knjiga.
        [Croatian]

Roughing It

1962   Kroz Sito i Reseto [Going Through A Lot], Subotica-Beograd:
        Minerva. [Serbo-Croatian]

1964   7 Godina Pustolovina [7 Years of Adventures]. [2 vols.] Zagreb:
        Matica Hrvatska. [Croatian]

Stories and Sketches

n.d.   Saljive Price Marka Twain-a i Drugih Americkih Humorista [Humorous
        Stories of Mark Twain and Other American Humorists]. Klasici
        Humora...Urednik, Joe Matosic, v. 2. Zagreb: Danice. [Croatian]

1948   Na Onome Svetu [In the Other World], Beograd: Prosveta. [Serbo-
        Croatian]

1950   Satiricne Price [Satirical Stories], Beograd: Novo Pokolenje.
        [Croatian]

1952   Bankovecza za Milijon Funtov; Humoreske [Bank-note for a Million
       Pounds; Humorous Pieces]. Mala Knjiznica, 55. Ljubljana:
       Slovenski Knjizni Zavod. [Slovene]

1953   Satiricne i Humoristicne Pripovetke [Satirical and Humorous Stories],
       Beograd: Narodna Knjiga. [Serbo-Croatian]

1954   Novcanica od Milion Funti [Bank-note for a Million Pounds], Beograd:
       Biro za Stamparske. Uslufe. [Serbo-Croatian]

1955   Novcanica od 1.000.000 Funti, Cetinje: Narodna Knjiga. [Serbo-
       Croatian]

1956   Novcanica od Milijun Funti i Druge Pripovijetke [Bank-note for
       a Million Pounds and Other Stories], Zagreb: IBI. [Serbo-
       Croatian]

1957   Dnevnik Adama i Eve [Private Life of Adam and Eve], Beograd:
       Sportska Knjiga. [Serbo-Croatian]

1957   Opasna Detektivska Prica. Mamlaz Vilson [A Double-barreled
       Detective Story. Pudd'nhead Wilson], Sarajevo: Dzepna Knjiga.
       [Croatian]

1959   Cudan Dozivljaj i Druge Price [Strange Encounter and Other Stories],
       Beograd: Mlado Pokolenje. [Serbo-Croatian]

1959   Ljubavni Roman Mlade Eskimke i Druge Pripovetke [The Eskimo Maiden's
       Romance and Other Stories], Beograd: Rad. [Serbo-Croatian]

1959   Zivotinje u Ogledalu [Animals in A Mirror], Zagreb: Mladost.
       [Croatian]

1963   Izabrane Pripovetke [Selected Stories], Beograd: Narodna Knjiga.
       [Serbo-Croatian]

1963   Sistem Protiv Provalnika [System against the Burglars], Zagreb:
       Stvarnost. [Serbo-Croatian]

1964   Lov Na Dvolicnu Puru [Hunting the Deceitful Turkey], Zagreb:
       Naprijed. [Serbo-Croatian]

1964   Novcanica od 1,000,000 Funti i Druge Pripovijetke, Sarajevo:
       Svjetlost. [Serbo-Croatian]

1964   Dnevnik Adama i Eve, Zagreb: Matica Hrvatska. [Serbo-Croatian]

                              Tom Sawyer

1921   Maili Klatez; Tom Sawyer [Little Vagabond; Tom Sawyer], Ljubljana:
       Zalozila in Izdala. Omladina. [Croatian]

1926   Pustolovine Malog Tome. Roman Jednog Nevaljanca sa Slikama
       [Adventures of Tom Sawyer. Novel of A Rascal Boy in Pictures],
       Zagreb: Jeronima. [Serbo-Croatian]

1948   Tom Savijer [Tom Sawyer], Beograd: Novo Pokolenje. [Serbian]

1949   Tom Sojer i Fin Haklberi [Tom Sawyer and Huckleberry Finn], Beograd: Novo Pokolenje. [Serbo-Croatian]

1949   Tom Sojer [Tom Sawyer], Skopje: Novo Pokolenje. [Macedonian]

1952   Dozivljaji Toma Sojera [Adventures of Tom Sawyer], Beograd: Novo Pokolenje. [Serbo-Croatian]

1953   Tom Sawyer Kalandjai [Tom Sawyer's Adventures], Novi Sad: Testveriseg-Egyseg. [Magyar]

1956   Tom Savijer [Tom Sawyer], Novi Sad: Matica Srpska. [Serbian]

1957   Tom Sojer, Beograd: Sportska Knjiga. [Serbo-Croatian]

1960   Prigode Toma Sawyerja [Adventures of Tom Sawyer], Ljubljana: Mladinska Knjiga. [Slovene]

1960   Dozivljaji Toma Sojera, Sarajevo: Svjetlost. [Serbo-Croatian]

1961   Same. Sarajevo: Svjetlost. [Serbo-Croatian]

1962   Pustolovine Toma Sojera [Adventures of Tom Sawyer], Beograd: Branko Djonovic. [Serbo-Croatian]

1963   Same. Beograd: Branko Djonovic. [Serbo-Croatian]

1963   Dozivljaji Toma Sojera, Sarajevo: Svjetlost. [Serbo-Croatian]

1963   Tom Sojer, Beograd: Sportska Knjiga. [Serbo-Croatian]

1963   Pustolovine Toma Sawyera, Zagreb: Mladost. [Serbo-Croatian]

1963   Tom Solr [Tom Sawyer], Skopje: Kultura. [Macedonian]

1963   Dozivljaji Toma Sojera, Beograd: Prosveta. [Serbo-Croatian]

1964   Same. Sarajevo: Svjetlost. [Serbo-Croatian]

1965   Prigode Toma Sawyera, Ljubljana: Mladinska Knjiga. [Slovene]

1965   Aventurat e Tome Sojerit [Adventures of Tom Sawyer], Prishtine: Rilindja. [Albanian]

1965   Pustolovine Toma Sojera, Sarajevo: Veselin Maslesa. [Serbo-Croatian]

1965   Pustolovine Toma Sawyera, Zagreb: Matica-Hrvatska. [Serbo-Croatian]

1966   Pustolovine Toma Sojera, Beograd: Nolit. [Serbo-Croatian]

1966   Same. Sarajevo: Veselin Maslesa. [Serbo-Croatian]

1966   Tom Sojer, Skopje: Kultura. [Macedonian]

1966   Dozivljaji Toma Sojera, Beograd: Mlado Pokolenje. [Serbo-Croatian]

1966   Same. Beograd: Prosveta. [Serbo-Croatian]

1967   Same. Sarajevo: Svjetlost. [Serbo-Croatian]

1967   Pustolovine Toma Sojera, Sarajevo: Veselin Maslesa. [Serbo-Croatian]

1968   Pustolovine Toma Sawyera. [2nd edition] Zagreb: Mladost. [Serbo-Croatian]

1968   Dozivljaji Toma Sojera, Beograd: Mlado Pokolenje. [Serbo-Croatian]

1968   Same. Beograd: Prosveta. [Serbo-Croatian]

1970   Same. Beograd: Mlado Pokolenje. [Serbo-Croatian]

1971   Dozivljaji Toma Sojera, Beograd: Prosveta. [Serbo-Croatian]

1971   Prigode Toma Sawyera, Ljubljana: Jugoreklam, Murska Sobota; Pomurska Zalozba. [Slovene]

1971   Tom Soer. [3rd edition] Skopje: Kultura. [Macedonian]

1971   Tom Sojer, Beograd: Mlado Pokolenje. [Serbo-Croatian]

1971   Pustolovine Toma Sojera, Ljubljana: Jugoreklam. Novi Sad: Forum. [Serbo-Croatian]

1971   Same. Sarajevo: Veselin Maslesa. [Serbo-Croatian]

1972   Prigode Toma Sawyerja, Ljubljana: Mladinska Knjiga. [Slovene]

1973   Pustolovine Toma Sawyera. [4th edition] Zagreb: Mladost. [Serbo-Croatian]

1973   Dozivljaji Toma Sojera, Beograd: Nolit. [Serbo-Croatian]

1973   Tom Soer, Skopje: Kultura. [Macedonian]

1973   Same. Skopje: Nasa Kniga. [Macedonian]

1975   Same. Skopje: Kultura. [Macedonian]

1975   Same. Skopje: Makedouska; Nasa. [Macedonian]

1975   Pustolovine Toma Sawyera. [5th edition] Zagreb: Mladost. [Serbo-Croatian]

1976   Dozivljaji Toma Sojera, Beograd: Nolit. [Serbo-Croatian]

1976 Tom Soer, Skopje: Nova Makedonija; Detska Radost. [Macedonian]

Tom Sawyer Abroad

1952 Mali Toma u Balonu [Little Tom in A Balloon]. Zabavna Biblioteka.
8. Sarajevo: Seljacka Knjiga. [Serbo-Croatian]

Tom Sawyer, Detective

1952 Tom Sojer Detektiv [Tom Sawyer Detective], Novi Sad: Brastvo-
Jedinstvo. [Serbo-Croatian]

1953 Tom Sojer Detektiv: Po Pricanju Huka Fina [Tom Sawyer Detective:
Told by Huck Finn], Subotica: Minerva. [Serbo-Croatian]

1957 Tom Sawyer, Detektiv, Ljubljana: Mladinska Knjija. [Slovene]

Miscellaneous

1962 Izbor [Various Languages]. Mark Twain, Fran Levstik, Nikolaj
Gogol, Victor Hugo, Skopje: Narodna Zadruga. [Macedonian]

1975 Dozivljaji Huckleberryja Finna: Izbor [Adventures of Huckleberry
Finn: Various Languages], Zagreb: Skolska Knjiga. [Serbo-
Croatian]

EUROPEAN AND ASIATIC RUSSIA

Sources: ALRT/BN/CGBN/CGLEs/CPL/GSRT/IT/LC/MTRT/NUC/RSAL/SK/UnC

The following titles of Mark Twain's writings published in European
and Asiatic Russia are transliterations of the original titles in
Russian and other Slavic and Turkic languages. Variants of transliterations among bibliographical sources have been regularized for
the sake of consistency. In a few instances English translations
are approximate rather than literal, in order to identify the
writings with their American titles. Publications in the Baltic
states are included with those of European Russia in order to
indicate the regional rather than national distribution of Mark
Twain editions.

American Claimant

1930 Amerikanskii Pretendent [American Claimant], Moskva: Biblioteka
Zhurnola "Ogonyok."

Autobiography

1935 Avtobiografiya [excerpts]. International Literatoora [Inter-
      national Literature], 1935, No. 11, 85-97; 1936, No. 1, 92-103.
      Moskva.

1961 Iz Avtobiografiya..., Moskva: Goslitizdat Izd-vo Khudozh. Lit-ry.

                         Captain Stormfield

1926 Kapten Stormfilt Taewas [Captain Stormfield's Visit], Tartu
      [Estonian SSR]: Hermann. [Estonian]

1926 Puteshestviye Kapitana Stormfilda na Nebo [Visit of Captain
      Stormfield to Heaven], Leningrad: Seyatel.

1935 Same. Moskva: Goslitizdat.

1938 Vizit Kapitana Stormfilda na Nebesa [Visit of Captain Stormfield
      to Heaven], Moskva: Voyenizdat Molodaja Gvardija.

1940 Same. Moskva: Voyenizdat Molodaja Gvardija.

1944 Same. In Ukroshcheniye Velosipeda [Taming the Bicycle], Moskva:
      Voyenmorizdat.

1955 Kapitana Stormfildo Kelione i Roju [Captain Stormfield's Visit to
      Heaven], Vilnjus [Lithuanian SSR]: Goslitizdat. [Lithuanian]

1963 Puteshestviye Kapitana Stormfilda v Raj [Visit of Captain Storm-
      field to Paradise]. [extract] Moskva: Gospolitizdat.

1964 Keletoriia Kepitomuluj Stormfield yn Raj [Visit of Captain Storm-
      field to Paradise], Kisinev: Voyenmorizdat. [Moldavian]

                        Connecticut Yankee

1926 Ianki pri Dvore Korolia Artura [Yankee in Court of King Arthur],
      Petrograd, Leningrad, Moskva: Kupernik.

1927 Same. Kharkov: n.pub.

1928 Same. Moskva: Zif.

1928 Same. Leningrad: Krasniy Gazyeta.

1945 Same. Moskva, Leningrad: Detizdat.

1950 Same. Riga [Latvian SSR]: Latgosizdat.

1953 Same. Moskva: n.pub.

1955 A Connecticut Yankee in King Arthur's Court, Moscow: Foreign
      Languages Publishing House? [English]

Марк ТВЕН

СОБРАНИЕ СОЧИНЕНИЙ
В **12** ТОМАХ

Под общей редакцией
А. А. ЕЛИСТРАТОВОЙ
М. О. МЕНДЕЛЬСОНА
А. И. СТАРЦЕВА

ГОСУДАРСТВЕННОЕ ИЗДАТЕЛЬСТВО
ХУДОЖЕСТВЕННОЙ ЛИТЕРАТУРЫ
Москва

Fig. 33. *Sobranie Sochinenii,* title page of 1959 Russian edition
published by Goslitizdat

1956 Ianki pri Dvore Korolia Artura, Minsk: Ucpedgiz BSSR.

1959 Janki Kuningas Arthuri Oukonnas [Yankee in Court of King Arthur],
      Tallin [Estonian SSR]: Estgosizdat. [Estonian]

1970 Janki iz Konnektikuta pri Dvore Korolja Artura [Yankee from
      Connecticut in Court of King Arthur], Erevan [Armenian SSR]:
      Ajastan. [Armenian]

1971 Yn Jankeu La Kurtja Rezeluj Artur [A Yankee at the Court of
      King Arthur], Kisinev: Kartja Moldovenjaske. [Moldavian]

1973 Janki iz Konnektikuta pri Dvore Korolja Artura. In Izbrannye
      Romany [Selected Novels], Vol. 2. Moskva: Hudoz Literatura.

1976 Konektikutas Jenkis Karala Artura Galma [Connecticut Yankee
      at the Court of King Arthur], Riga [Latvian USSR]: Liesma.
      [Lettish]

Gilded Age

1874 Mishurnyi Viek [Gilded Age], St. Petersburg: A.A. Krayevskago.

1963 Pozoloceny Vik [Gilded Age], Kiev: Goslitizdat Ukrainy.
      [Ukrainian]

Huckleberry Finn

1888 Prikljucenija Finna [Adventures of Finn], St. Petersburg: Soovina.

1926 Prikljucenija Gekkelberri Finna i Beglovo Negra Dzhima [Adventures
      of Huckleberry Finn and Runaway Negro Jim], Leningrad: Molodaja
      Gvardija.

1927 Prikljucenija Finna, Leningrad: Krasniy Gazyeta.

1928 Prikljucenija Gekkelberri Finna, Moskva, Leningrad: Gosizdat.

1928 Prygody Heka Finna [Adventures of Huck Finn], n.p. n.pub.
      [Ukrainian]

1930 Prikljucenija Gekkelberri Finna, Moskva, Leningrad: Gosizdat.

1933 Same. Moskva: Molodaja Gvardija.

1935 Same. Leningrad: Goslitizdat Izd-vo Detskoilitry.

1936 Same. Moskva, Leningrad: Detizdat.

1936 Huckleberry Finnin Seikkailut [Huckleberry Finn's Adventures],
      Petrozavodsk [Karelo-Finnish SSR]: n.pub. [Finnish]

1937 Prikljucenija Gekkelberri Finna, Moskva, Leningrad: Detizdat.

1937 Same. Oblastnoye Izdatelstvo. Saratov: Izd-vo Oblemestproma.

1942 Same. Moskva, Leningrad: Detizdat.

1948 The Adventures of Tom Sawyer and The Adventures of Huckleberry
      Finn, Moscow: Foreign Languages Publishing House. [English]

1950 Prikljucenija Gekkelberri Finna, Moskva, Leningrad: n.pub.

1952 Heklberija Fina Piedzivojumi [Adventures of Huckleberry Finn],
      Riga [Latvian SSR]: Latvijas Valsts Izdevnieciba. [Lettish]

1954 Prikljucenija Gekkelberri Finna, Moskva: Goslitizdat.

1955 Same. Moskva: Detizdat.

1955 Same. Moskva: Goslitizdat.

1956 Same. Minsk: Gosizdat BSSR.

1956 Tom Sawyeri. Huckleberri Finni Seiklused [Adventures of Tom
      Sawyer and Huckleberry Finn], Tallin [Estonian SSR]: Estgosizdat.
      [Estonian]

1956 Prygody Gekl'berri Finna [Adventures of Huckleberry Finn], Kiev:
      Molod. [Ukrainian]

1956 Gekl'berri Finn Madzaralary [Huckleberry Finn's Adventures], Kazan
      [Tatar SSR]: Tatknigoizdat. [Tatar]

1956 The Adventures of Tom Sawyer. The Adventures of Huckleberry Finn,
      Moscow: Foreign Languages Publishing House? [English]

1957 Prikljucenija Gekkelberri Finna, Tashkent [Uzbek SSR]: Ucpedgiz
      UzSSR.

1958 Prikljucenija Toma Soiyera. Prikljucenija Gekkelberri Finna
      [Adventures of Tom Sawyer. Adventures of Huckleberry Finn],
      Moskva: Detizdat.

1959 Aventurile lui Heklberi Fin [Adventures of Huckleberry Finn],
      Kisinev: Skoala Sovetike. [Moldavian]

1959 Prikljucenija Toma Soiyera. Prikljucenija Gekkelberri Finna.
      Biblioteka Prikljuchenii, 2. Tbilisi [Georgian SSR]: Detjunizdat
      GSSR. [Georgian]

1959 Heklberri Finnin Ma'Arolary [Adventures of Huckleberry Finn], Baku
      [Azerbaidzhan SSR]: Detjunizdat. [Azerbaidjan]

1960 Heklberio Fino Nuotykiai [Huckleberry Finn's Adventures], Vilnjus
      [Lithuanian SSR]: Goslitizdat. [Lithuanian]

1960 Gekl'berri Finnin' Basyndam Gecirenleri [Huckleberry Finn's
Adventures], Ashabad [Turkmen SSR]: Turkmengosizdat. [Turkmen]

1960 Gekl'berri Finning Bosidan Kecirganlari [Huckleberry Finn's Adven-
tures], Tashkent [Uzbek SSR]: Es Gvardija. [Uzbek]

1961 Prikljucenija Toma Soiyera; Prikljucenija Gekkelberri Finna; Toma
Soiyerza Granitsei; Tom Soiyer-Syshshik [Adventures of Tom
Sawyer; Adventures of Huckleberry Finn; Tom Sawyer Abroad; Tom
Sawyer, Detective], Moskva: Moskovskii Rabochii.

1962 Prikljucenija Gekkelberri Finna, Moskva: Detizdat.

1966 Same. Erevan [Armenian SSR]: Ajastan. [Armenian]

1966 Prygody Geklberri Finna, Kiev: Veselka. [Ukrainian]

1966 Prikljucenija Gekkelberri Finna [included in Prikljucenija Toma
Sojera], Tbilisi [Georgian SSR]: Nakaduli. [Georgian]

1967 Prikljucenija Toma Soiyera. Prikljucenija Gekkelberri Finna,
Moskva: Detskaia Lit-ra.

1967 Gekl'berri Finnin Basyman Kesenderf [Huckleberry Finn's Adven-
tures]. [2nd edition] Alma-Ata [Kazakh SSR]: Zazusy. [Kazakh]

1969 Gekl'berri Findin Zoruktary [Huckleberry Finn's Adventures], Frunze
[Kirgiz SSR]: Mektep. [Kirgiz]

1970 Huckleberry Finni Seiklused [Hucklberry Finn's Adventures], Tallin
[Estonian SSR]: Eesti Raamat. [Estonian]

1970 Haklberija Fina Piedzivojumi [Huckleberry Finn's Adventures], Riga
[Latvian SSR]: Liesma. [Lettish]

1971 Prikljucenija Toma Sojera. Prikljucenija Gekl'berri Finna, Moskva:
Detskaia Lit-ra.

1971 Same. Petrozavodsk [Karelo-Finnish SSR]: Karelija.

1971 Prikljucenija Toma Sojera. Prikljucenija Gekl'berri Finn.
Rasskazy [Adventures of Tom Sawyer. Adventures of Huckleberry
Finn. Stories], Moskva: Hudoz Literatura.

1972 Prikljucenija Gekl'berri Finna. Tom Sojerza Granicej [Adven-
tures of Huckleberry Finn. Tom Sawyer Abroad], Orzonikidze: Ir.

1972 Prikljucenija Toma Sojera. Prikljucenija Gekl'berri Finna.
Jumoristiceskie Rasskazy i Pamflety [Adventures of Tom Sawyer.
Adventures of Huckleberry Finn. Humorous Stories and Pamphlets],
Tbilisi [Georgian SSR]: Subcota Sakartvelo. [Georgian]

1973 Prikljucenija Toma Sojera. Prikljucenija Gekl'berri Finna.
Princ i Nishchi [Adventures of Tom Sawyer. Adventures of Huckleberry Finn. Prince and Pauper], Kisinev: Lumina.

1974 Prikljucenija Toma Sojera. Prikljucenija Gekl'berri Finna, Moskva: Detskaia Lit-ra.

1974 Prikljucenija Gekl'berri Finna, Leningrad: Lenizdat.

1974 Same. In Izbrannye Romany [Selected Novels, Vol.1], Moskva: Hudoz Literatura.

1975 Same. Moskva: Detskaia Lit-ra.

1976 Heklberri Finnin Madcaralary [Adventures of Huckleberry Finn], Baku [Azerbaidzhan SSR]: Gjandzlik. [Azerbaidzhan]

Innocents Abroad

1928 Prostaki za Granitsei ili Novoye Stranstviye Pilgrima [Simpletons Abroad or New Pilgrim's Progress], Moskva, Leningrad: Gosizdat.

1936 Same. [excerpts] Moskva: Goslitizdat.

1963 Vohikud Voorsil, Ehk Unt Palverandurite Teekond [Innocents Abroad, the New Pilgrim's Progress], Tallin [Estonian SSR]: Estgosizdat. [Estonian]

Joan of Arc

1897 Vospominaniia o Ioannie d'Ark [Recollections of Joan of Arc], St. Petersburg: A.S. Soovorina.

1902 Lichnye Vospominaniia o Zhanne d'Ark [Personal Recollections of Joan of Arc], St. Petersburg: Izd-va Idbiia.

1902 Zhanna d'Ark [Joan of Arc], St. Petersburg: A. Iavina.

1961 Zhanna d'Ark. Roman [Joan of Arc. Novel], Minsk: Goslitizdat izd-vo BSSR.

1965 Zanna d'Ark [Joan of Arc], Tashkent [Uzbek SSR]: Es Gvardija. [Uzbek]

Letters from the Earth

1963 Pis'ma s Zemli [Letters from Earth], Moskva: Gospolitizdat izd-vo Polit Lit-ry.

1964 Vestules no Zemes [Letters from Earth], Riga [Latvian SSR]: Latgosizdat. [Lettish]

1964 Laiskai is Zemes [Letters from Earth], Vilnjus [Lithuanian SSR]: Vaga. [Lithuanian]

1966   Kirjad maa Pealt [Letters from Earth], Tallin [Estonian SSR]:
       Eesti Raamat. [Estonian]

Life on the Mississippi

1910   Zhizn'na Missisipi [Life on Mississippi], Moskva: n.pub.

1935   Luotsina Missippi-joella. Humoristinen Kertomus [Mississippi Pilot.
       Humorous Stories], Petrozavodsk [Karelo-Finnish SSR]: n.pub.
       [Finnish]

1960   Zhizn'na Missisipi, Petrozavodsk [Karelo-Finnish SSR]: Gosisdot
       izd-vo Karel-skoi. ASSR. [Finnish]

Man That Corrupted Hadleyburg

1925   Doloy Chestnost! Chelovek, Kotoryi Razoblachil Gedliburg [Hollow
       Honesty! Man Who Exposed Hadleyburg], n.p.: n.pub.

1925   Chelovek Podkupivshi Gedliburg [Man Who Bribed Hadleyburg],
       Leningrad: Seyatel.

1966   Celovek, Kotoryj Sovratil Gedliberg [Man Who Corrupted Hadleyburg],
       Tbilisi [Georgian SSR]: Izd-vo CKKP Gruzii. [Georgian]

Prince and the Pauper

1884   Prints i Nishchi [Prince and Pauper], St. Petersburg: A.S.
       Soovorina.

1897   Same. Moskva: I.D. Sntina.

1901   Same. [3rd edition] St. Petersburg, Moskva: n.pub.

1918   Same. Petrograd: Priroda i Lyudi.

1918   Same. Moskva: I.D. Sytin.

1918   Same. [new edition] Moskva: I.D. Sytin.

1922   Same. Petrograd: Gosizdat.

1922   Same. Petrograd: Editions d'Etat de Litterature Universelle.

1922   Princas ir Elgeta, Laisvai [Prince and Pauper, Novel]. Kulturos
       Bendroves Isleistosios, 33. Siauliai [Lithuania]: Kulturos
       b-'es Leidings. [Lithuanian]

1930   Ishkana yev Mouratzge [Prince and Pauper], Erevan [Armenian SSR]:
       n.pub. [Armenian]

1936   Prints i Nishchi, Moskva, Leningrad: Detizdat.

1937 Same. Moskva, Leningrad: Detizdat.

1938 Same. Oblastnoye Izdatelstvo (Kuybyshev). Kuybyshev: Ablgizdat.

1941 Same. Moskva, Leningrad: Detizdat.

1946 Same. Moskva, Leningrad: Detizdat.

1951 Kraljevic i Prosjak [Prince and Pauper], Belgorod: n.pub.
      [Slovak-Croatian]

1954 Prints i Nishchi, Moskva: Goslitizdat izd-vo Khudozh. Lit-ry.

1955 Same. Kazan [Tatar SSR]: Tatknigoizdat.

1956 Same. Moskva: Detizdat.

1956 Same. Rostov-on-Don: Knigoizdat.

1956 Prints ja Kerjus [Prince and Pauper], Tallin [Estonian SSR]:
      Estgosizdat. [Estonian]

1956 Princis un Ubaga Zeus [Prince and Pauper], Riga [Latvian SSR]:
      Latgosizdat. [Lettish]

1956 Princ i Nishchi [Prince and Pauper], Tashkent [Uzbek SSR]:
      Ucpedgiz Uz SSR.

1957 Prync i Zlydar [Prince and Pauper], Kiev: Detizdat. [Ukrainian]

1957 Princ i Niscij, Tbilisi [Georgian SSR]: Detjunizdat. [Georgian]

1957 Princ si Cersetor [Prince and Pauper], Kisinev: Skoala Sovetike.
      [Moldavian]

1959 Prints i Nishchi. [3rd edition] Moskva: Goslitizdat Ucheb.-
      pedagog. izd-vo.

1959 Princas ir Elgeta, Vilnjus [Lithuanian SSR]: Goslitizdat.
      [Lithuanian]

1961 Prints i Nishchi, Moskva: Detizdat.

1962 Saghzoda na Gado [Prince and Pauper], Tashkent [Uzbek SSR]:
      Es Gvardija. [Uzbek]

1963 Pasctyh'yk Uembra Fak Yremre [Prince and Pauper], Nalcik
      [Kabardino-Balkarian SSR]: Kobard-Bolkar. [Kabardin]

1965 Prints i Nishchi, Moskva: Detskaia Lit-ra.

1966 Same. Moskva: Detskaia Lit-ra.

1966 Princ i Niscij, Tbilisi [Georgian SSR]: Nakaduli. [Georgian]

1968   Prints i Nishchi. Shkol'naia Biblioteca. Moskva: Detskaia
Lit-ra.

1969   Prync i Zlydar, Kiev: Veselka. [Ukrainian]

1969   Sahzada va Dilanci [Prince and Pauper], Baku [Azerbaidzhan SSR]:
Gjandzlik. [Azerbaidzhan]

1970   Princ ham Telance [Prince and Pauper]. [2nd edition] Kazan
[Tatar SSR]: Tatknigoizdat. [Tatar]

1970   Princis un Ubaga Zeus, Riga [Latvian SSR]: Liesma. [Lettish]

1970   Prints i Nishchi, Moskva: Detskaia Lit-ra.

1973   Princ i Niscij, Moskva: Detskaia Literatura.

1973   Same. In Izbrannye Romany [Selected Novels, Vol. 2], Moskva:
Hudoz Lit-ra.

1973   Prikljucenija Toma Sojera. Prikljucenija Gekl'berri Finna. Princ
i Niscij [Adventures of Tom Sawyer. Adventures of Huckleberry
Finn. Prince and Pauper], Kisinev: Lumina.

1974   Princ si Cersetor [Prince and Pauper], Kisinev: Lumina.[Moldavian]

1975   Princ i Niscij, Moskva: Detskaia Literatura.

1975   Soqhzoda va Gado [Prince and Pauper], Dushanbe [Tadzhik SSR]:
Irfon.[Tadzhik]

1975   Prinz i Niscij, Petrozavodsk [Karelo-Finnish SSR]: Karelija.

Pudd'nhead Wilson

1929   Pustogolovyi Uil'son [Empty-headed Wilson], Leningrad: n.pub.

Report from Paradise

1955   Engela Vestule un Citi Stasti [Angel Letter and Other Stories],
Riga [Latvian SSR]: Latgosizdat. [Lettish]

1957   Lyst Angela-Hranytelja [Leaves of the Guardian Angel], Kiev:
Goslitizdat Ukrainy. [Ukrainian]

1958   Same. Kiev: Molod. [Ukrainian]

Stories and Sketches

1888   Ocherki i Rasskazy [Essays and Stories], Moskva: n.pub.

1896 Yumoristicheskye Rasskazy [Humorous Stories], St. Petersburg: Panteleevech.

1908 Dnevnik Adama [Adam's Diary], St. Petersburg: n.pub.

1918 Razgovor s Intervyurom i Drugiye Yumoristicheskiye Rasskazy [Encounter with Interviewer and Other Humorous Stories], Moskva: Universelle Biblioteka.

1925 Strashnoye Proisshestviye [A Frightful Incident], Leningrad: Seyatel.

1926 Lyudoyedstvo v Poyezde [Cannibalism in the Cars], Moskva, Leningrad: Zif.

1926 Neizdannyie Rasskazy [Unpublished Stories], Leningrad: Smekhach.

1926 Rasskazy [Stories], Moskva: Biblioteka Zhurnala "Ogonyok."

1926 Roman Eskimoski [Eskimo Maiden's Romance], Leningrad: Seyatel.

1928 Rasskazy, Leningrad: Krasniy Gazyeta.

1929 Moi Chasy [My Watch], Moskva: Biblioteka Zhurnola "Ogonyok."

1930 Pokhishcheniye Belova Slona [Stolen White Elephant], Moskva, Leningrad: Gosizdat.

1934 Bankovy Bilet Million Funtov Sterlingov [Bank-note of Million Pounds Sterling], Moskva: Zhurnal-gazeta Obyedinenija.

1935 Pokhishcheniye Belova Slona, Moskva: Zhurnal-gazeta Obyedinenija.

1936 Dzhim Vulf i Koty [Jim Wolf and the Cats]. In 30 Dbei, 1936. No. 5, 58-60. Leningrad.

1936 Izbrannye Rasskazy [Selected Stories], Moskva: Goslitizdat.

1937 Prygayushchaya Lyagushka [Jumping Frogs], Moskva, Leningrad: Detizdat.

1937 Rasskazy, Moskva: Goslitizdat.

1938 Amerikanskiye Rasskazy [American Stories], Leningrad: Goslitizdat.

1939 Izbrannye Rasskazy, Moskva, Leningrad: Detizdat.

1939 Prygayushchaya Lysgushka, Syktyvkar: Komigizdat.

1940 Rasskazy, Moskva: Pravda.

1943 Znamenitaya Skachushchaya Lyagushka i Drugiye Rasskazy [Famous Leaping Frog and Other Stories], Moskva: Goslitizdat izd-vo Khudozh. Lit-ry.

1944   Ukroshcheniye Velosipeda [Taming the Bicycle], Moskva: Voyen-morizdat. [six stories and sketches, including "Captain Storm-field's Visit to Heaven."]

1947   Rasskazy. Biblioteka Sholnika. Moskva, Leningrad: Goslitizdat-vo Detskoi Lit-ry.

1949   Rasskazy i Pamfleti [Stories and Pamphlets], Moskva: Goslitizdat.

1950   Rasskazy, Riga [Latvian SSR]: Latgosizdat.

1951   Izbrannye Rasskazy i Pamfleti, Moskva: Goslitizdat izd-vo Khudozh. Lit-ry.

1951   Rasskazy i Pamfleti, Leningrad: n.pub.

1951   Same. Moskva: Goslitizdat.

1952   Same. Moskva, Leningrad: Gazetno-Zhurnal'noe Knizoe izd-vo.

1952   Same. Leningrad: English and American Authors. [English]

1955   Opovidannja [Stories], Kiev: Goslitizdat Ukrainy. [Ukrainian]

1955   Engela Vestule un Citi Stasti [Angel Letter and Other Stories], Riga [Latvian SSR]: Latgosizdat. [Lettish]

1955   Yumoristicheskye Rasskazy [Humorous Stories], Kiev: Goslitizdat USSR.

1956   Same. Kiev: Goslitizdat Ukrainy.

1957   Rasskazy, Moskva: Volnizdat.

1959   Qhikoja va Pamfletaer [Stories and Pamphlets], Tashkent [Uzbek SSR]: Goslitizdat UzSSR. [Uzbek]

1959   Rasskazy i Pamfleti, Tashkent [Uzbek SSR]: Goslitizdat UzSSR.

1960   Aadama ja Eeva Palvikud, ja Mind Jutte [Journal of Adam and Eve, and Other Stories], Tallin [Estonian SSR]: Gazetno-zhurnal'noe izd-vo. [Estonian]

1960   Yumoristicheskye Rasskazy, Tbilisi [Georgian SSR]: Izd-vo CKKP Gruzii. [Georgian]

1961   Miljon Funt Sterlinglik Bank Bileti [Million Pound Sterling Bank-note], Baku [Azerbaidzhan SSR]: Detjunizdat. [Azerbaidzhan]

1962   Moi Chasy [My Watch], Erevan [Armenian SSR]: Ajpetrat. [Armenian]

1965   Yumoristicheskye Rasskazy i Pamfleti, Tbilisi [Georgian SSR]: Literatura de Helovneba. [Georgian]

1968   Krasnyj Kruzok [Bright Tankard], Tbilisi [Georgian SSR]: Nakaduli. [Georgian]

1968 An'Gimeler [Stories], Alma-Ata [Kazakh SSR]: Zazusy. [Kazakh]

1969 Gurrin'ler [Stories], Nukus [Uzbek SSR]: Karakalpakija.
[Karakalpak]

1969 Bankovyj Bilet v 1000000 Funtov Sterlingov [Bank-note for 1,000,000
Pound Sterling], Tbilisi [Georgian SSR]: Nakaduli. [Georgian]

1971 Prikljucenija Toma Sojera. Prikljucenija Gekl'berri Finna.
Rasskazy [Adventures of Tom Sawyer. Adventures of Huckleberry
Finn. Stories], Moskva: Hudoz Literatura.

1971 Utajmavanne Velosipeda; Apaviadanni [Taming the Bicycle; Stories],
Minsk: Vyd-va Belarus'. [Belorussian]

1972 Opovidannja Ta Pamflety [Stories and Pamphlets], Kiev:
Dnipro.

1972 Prikljucenija Toma Sojera. Prikljucenija Gekl'berri Finna.
Jumoristiceskie Rasskazy i Pamflety [Adventures of Tom Sawyer.
Adventures of Huckleberry Finn. Humorous Stories and Pam-
phlets], Tbilisi [Georgian SSR]: Subcota Sakartvelo. [Georgian]

1973 Opovidannja [Stories], Kiev: Molod'. [Ukrainian]

1975 Rasskazy [Stories], Moskva: Hudoz Literatura.

Tom Sawyer

1886 Prikljucenija Thoma [Adventures of Tom], St. Petersburg: Soovorina.

1918 Same. n.p.: n.pub.

1919 Same. St. Petersburg: Vsemir. Lit.

1923 Same. Petrograd, Moskva: Vsemir. Lit.

1924 Tom Sawyeri Imelikud Juhtumised [Tom Sawyer's Strange Adventures],
Tallin [Estonia]: Rahvaulikool. [Estonian]

1927 Tom Soiyer [Tom Sawyer], Kiev: n.pub. [Yiddish]

1927 Prikljucenija Toma Soiyera [Adventures of Tom Sawyer], Moskva,
Leningrad: Gosizdat.

1927 Prikljucenija Toma [Adventures of Tom], Leningrad: Vokrug Sveta.

1928 Same. Moskva, Leningrad: Gosizdat.

1928 Prikljucenija Toma Soiyera, Moskva: Biblioteka Zhurnala "Ogonyok."

1929 Same. Moskva, Leningrad: Gosizdat.

1930 Same. Moskva, Leningrad: Gosizdat.

1931   Same. Moskva, Leningrad: Gosizdat.

1933   Same. Leningrad, Moskva: Molodaja Gvardija.

1934   Same. Goslitizdat Detskaia Lit-ra. Leningrad: Detizdat.

1934   Tom Soiers [Tom Sawyer], Valmera [Latvia]: Dumis. [Lettish]

1935   Prikljucenija Toma Soiyera, Leningrad: Lendetizdat.

1936   Same. Moskva, Leningrad: Detizdat.

1936   Same. [excerpts] Moskva, Leningrad: Uchpedgiz.

1937   Same. Kirov: Oblastnoye Izdatelstvo.

1937   Same. Saratov: Sarablgizdat. Oblastnoye Izdatelstvo.

1938   Same. 4 vols. Moskva: Uchpedgiz.

1938   Same. Moskva, Leningrad: Detizdat.

1939   Same. Khabarovsk: Dalgiz.

1940   Same. Moskva, Leningrad: Detizdat.

1946   Same. Leningrad: Lenizdat.

1948   The Adventures of Tom Sawyer and The Adventures of Huckleberry
       Finn, Moscow: Foreign Languages Publishing House. [English]

1948   Prikljucenija Toma Soiyera, Moskva, Leningrad: n.pub.

1950   Same. Stalingrad: Oblastnoe Izdatel'stva.

1953   Same. Moskva, Leningrad: n.pub.

1953   Aventures de Tom Sawyer [Adventures of Tom Sawyer], Moscou, Lenin-
       grad: Editions d'Etat de Litterature Enfantine. [French]

1954   Prikljucenija Toma Soiyera, Moskva: Detizdat.

1954   Same. Minsk: n.pub.

1954   Same. Tallin [Estonian SSR]: Gosizdat EsSSR.

1955   Same. Moskva: Goslitizdat.

1955   Same. Petrozavodsk [Karelo-Finnish SSR]: Gosizdat KFSSR.

1955   Prigodi Toma Sojera [Adventures of Tom Sawyer], Kiev: Molod.
       [Ukrainian]

1956   The Adventures of Tom Sawyer. The Adventures of Huckleberry Finn,
       Moscow: n.pub. [English]

1956 Tom Sawyeri Seiklused. Huckleberri Finni Seiklused [Tom Sawyer's
      Adventures. Huckleberry Finn's Adventures], Tallin [Estonian SSR]:
      Estgosizdat. [Estonian]

1957 Prikljucenija Toma Soiyera, Krasnodar: Knigoizdat.

1957 Tom Sojir Madzaralary [Tom Sawyer's Adventures], Kazan [Tatar SSR]:
      Tatknigoizdat. [Tatar]

1957 Aventurile lui Tom Sojir [Adventures of Tom Sawyer], Kisinev:
      Skoala Sovetike. [Moldavian]

1957 Tom Sojerdin Zoruktary [Tom Sawyer's Adventures], Frunze [Kirgiz
      SSR]: Kirgizucpediz. [Kirgiz]

1957 Prikljucenija Toma Soiyera, Tashkent [Uzbek SSR]: Ucpedgiz
      Uz SSR.

1958 Prikljucenija Toma Soiyera. Prikljucenija Gekkelberri Finna.
      Biblioteka Prikliuchenii, 12. Moskva: Detizdat.

1959 Same. Biblioteka Prikliuchenii, 2.   Tbilisi [Georgian SSR]:
      Detjunizdat GSSR. [Georgian]

1959 Tom Sojjerin Madzaralary [Tom Sawyer's Adventures], Baku [Azer-
      baidzhan SSR]: Detjunizdat. [Azerbaidzhan]

1959 Tom Sojerin' Basyndan Gecirenleri [Tom Sawyer's Adventures],
      Ashabad [Turkmen SSR]: Turkmengosizdat. [Turkmen]

1960 Tomo Sojerio Nuotykiai [Tom Sawyer's Adventures], Vilnjus
      [Lithuanian SSR]: Goslitizdat. [Lithuanian]

1960 Tom Sojerding Basynan Kesirgenberi [Tom Sawyer's Adventures],
      Nukus [Uzbek SSR]: Karakalpakgiz. [Karakalpak]

1961 Prikljucenija Toma Soiyera; Prikljucenija Gekkelberri Finna; Tom
      Soiyer za Granitsei; Tom Soiyer-Syshchik [Adventures of Tom
      Sawyer; Adventures of Huckleberry Finn; Tom Sawyer Abroad; Tom
      Sawyer Detective], Moskva: Moskovskii Rabochii.

1962 Prigodi Toma Sojera [Adventures of Tom Sawyer], Kiev: Detizdat.
      [Ukrainian]

1964 Prikljucenija Toma Soiyera [Adventures of Tom Sawyer], Erevan
      [Armenian SSR]: Ajepetrat. [Armenian]

1965 Same. Moskva: Detskaia Lit-ra.

1965 Tom Sojerdin' Tan'gazajyp Isteri [Tom Sawyer's Adventures], Alma-Ata
      [Kazakh SSR]: Zazusy. [Kazakh]

1966 Prikljucenija Toma Soiyera, Tbilisi [Georgian SSR]: Nakaduli.
      [Georgian]

1967 Prikljucenija Toma Soiyera. Prikljucenija Gekkelberri Finna,
      Moskva: Detskaia Lit-ra.

1967 Tom Soiyer, Kiev: n.pub. [Yiddish]

1968 Toma Sojera Piedzivojumi [Tom Sawyer's Adventures], Riga [Latvian
      SSR]: Liesma. [Lettish]

1970 Tom Sawyeri Seiklused [Tom Sawyer's Adventures], Tallin [Estonian
      SSR]: Eesti Raamat. [Estonian]

1970 Prikljucenija Toma Soiyera, Groznyy: Ceceno-Ingus.

1970 Same. Ordzhonikidze: Ir.

1971 Prikljucenija Tom Soiyera. Prikljucenija Gekl'berri Finna, Moskva:
      Detskaia Lit-ry.

1971 Same. Petrozavodsk [Karelo-Finnish SSR]: Karelija.

1971 Prikljucenija Toma Soiyera. Prikljucenija Gekl'berri Finna.
      Rasskazy [Adventures of Tom Sawyer. Adventures of Huckleberry
      Finn. Stories], Moskva: Hudoz Literatura.

1971 Prikljucenija Toma Soiyera, Ordzonikidze: Ir.

1971 Same. Saratov: Privolz.

1972 Same. Kaliningrad: Knigoizdat.

1972 Prikljucenija Toma Soiyera. Prikljucenija Gekl'berri Finna.
      Jumoristiceskie Rasskazy i Pamflety [Adventures of Tom Sawyer.
      Adventures of Huckleberry Finn. Humorous Stories and Pam-
      phlets], Tbilisi [Georgian SSR]: Subcota Sakartvelo. [Georgian]

1973 Prikljucenija Toma Soiyera, Moskva: Detskaia Literatura.

1973 Same. Leningrad: Lenizdat.

1973 Same. Minsk: Nar. Asveta.

1973 Same. Sverdlovsk: Sred.-Ural'sk. Knigoizdat.

1973 Prikljucenija Toma Soiyera. Prikljucenija Gekl'berri Finna.
      Princ i Niscij [Adventures of Tom Sawyer. Adventures of Huckle-
      berry Finn. Prince and Pauper], Kisinev: Lumina.

1974 Prikljucenija Toma Soiyera. Prikljucenija Gekl'berri Finna,
      Moskva: Detskaia Literatura.

1974 Prikljucenija Toma Soiyera, Tbilisi [Georgian SSR]: Nakaduli.
      [Georgian]

1974 Same. In Izbrannye Romany [Selected Novels, Vol. 1]: Moskva:
      Hudoz Literatura.

1975 Same. Novosibirsk: Zap.-Sib. Knigoizdat.

1976 Same. Mahackala: Dagucpedgiz.

1976 Same. Vladivostok: Dal'nevost.

1976 Same. Perm': Knigoizdat.

1976 Same. Stavropol: Stavrop Knigoizdat.

1976 Same. Novosibirsk: Zap.-Sib. Knigoizdat.

Tom Sawyer Abroad

1934 Tom Soiers, A. Melnalkana Tulkojuma [Tom Sawyer Abroad], Valmera
     [Latvia]: Dumis. [Lettish]

1961 Tom Soyer za Granitsei [Tom Sawyer Abroad]. In Prikljucenija
     Toma Soyera; Prikljucenija Geklberri Finna..., Moskva: Moskovskii
     Rabochii.

1972 Prikljucenija Gekl'berri Finna. Tom Sojerza Granicej [Adventures
     of Huckleberry Finn. Tom Sawyer Abroad], Ordzonikidze: Ir.

Tom Sawyer, Detective

1923 Tom Sawyer Salauurijana. Huck Finni Jutustused [Tom Sawyer's
     Secret. Told by Huck Finn], Tallinna [Estonia]: Rahvaulikool.
     [Estonian]

1928 Tom Soiyer-Syshchik [Tom Sawyer-Detective], Moskva, Leningrad:
     Gosizdat.

1961 Same. In Prikljucenija Toma Soyera; Prikljucenija Geklberri
     Finna..., Moskva: Moskovskii Rabochii.

Miscellaneous

1899 Mark Tven o Vseobshchem Mire [Mark Twain about Universal Peace].
     In Novoe Vremia, January 23/February 4, 1899 [Illustrated
     supplement].

1961 Iz Avtobiografiya [Autobiography]; Iz Zapianykh Knizhek [Note Book];
     Izbrannye Pis'ma [Selected Letters], Moskva: Goslitizdat Izd-vo
     Khudozh. Lity-ry.

1964 Razmyshleniia o Religii [Reflections on Religion], Moskva:
     Politizdat.

1969   Na Prieme u Prezidanta; Fel'etony i Rechi [At the Reception of the
       President; Satires and Speeches], Moskva: Pravda.

1969   Soyedinennye Linchuiushchie Shtaty [United States of Lynchdom].
       Narodnata Biblioteka. Moskva: Khudozh Lit-ra.

Selections

1898   Izbrannye Sochinenii. Eskizy [Selected Works. Sketches], St.
       Petersburg: n.pub.

1924   Naljaleht Linnukasvatusest [Droll Leaves], Tartu [Estonia]:
       Esto-Reklaam. [Estonian]

1935   Dva Mapka Tvena [Two of Mark Twain]. In International Litratoorny,
       1935, No. 11, 3-10.

1937   Izbrannye Proizvedenya [Selected Works], Moskva: Goslitizdat.

1938   Odnotomnik Marka Tvena [One-volume Edition of Mark Twain], n.p.:
       n.pub.

1939   Izbrannye Proizvedenya, Moskva: Goslitizdat.

1949-50   Izbrannoe [Selections]. 2 vols. Moskva: Goslitizdat.

1950   Same. Rostov: Rostizdat.

1953   Izbrannye Proizvedenya. 2 vols. Moskva: Goslitizdat izd-vo
       Khudozh. Lit-ry.

1954   Izbrannoe, Moskva: Goslitizdat?

1958   Same. Moskva: Moskovskii Rabochii.

1961   Same. Moskva: Moskovskii Rabochii.

1962   Ocherki. Tvorchystvo [Essays. Creative Works], Moskva: Goslitiz-
       dat.

1973   Izbrannye Romany v Dvukh Tomakh [Selected Novels in Two Volumes],
       Moskva: Khudozhestvennaia Literatura.

Collected Works

1898-99   Sobranie Sochinenii [Collected Works]. 5 vols. St.
           Petersburg: Panteleevech. Subsequent editions: 1906, 1910.

1911-18   Palnoe Sobranie Sochinenii [Complete Collected Works], St.
           Petersburg: Soikin.

1927-29   _Sobranie Sochinenii_. 6 Vols. Moskva, Leningrad: Gosizdat.

1954   _Sobranie Sochinenii_. 12 vols. Moskva: n.pub.

1957   _Tvorchystvo Marka Tvena_ [Creative Works of Mark Twain], Saratov: n. pub.

1959-61   _Sobranie Sochinenii_. 12 vols. Moskva: Goslitizdat izd-vo Khudozh. Lit-ry.

LATIN AMERICA

Argentina

Sources: AEHA/BBA/BE/BON/CGLEH/CPL/IT/LEV/NUC/PBS/SPT

Connecticut Yankee

1945   _Un Yanqui en la Corte del Rey Arturo_ [A Yankee in the Court of King Arthur]. Coleccion La Rosa de los Vientos. Buenos Aires: Veinte.

1947   Same. Colleccion Robin Hood. Buenos Aires: Poseidon.

1947   Same. Coleccion Robin Hood. Buenos Aires: Acme.

1947   Same. Buenos Aires: Acme.

1949   Same. Buenos Aires: Acme.

1951   Same. [3rd edition] Buenos Aires: Acme.

1963   Same. Buenos Aires: Acme.

1963   Same. Buenos Aires: Plaza & Janes.

Huckleberry Finn

1939   _Las Aventuras de Huck_ [The Adventures of Huck], Buenos Aires: Losada.

1940   _Aventuras de Huck Finn, Novela_ [Adventures of Huck Finn, Novel]. Biblioteca Mundial Sopena. Buenos Aires: Sopena.

1941   _Aventuras de Huck Finn_, Buenos Aires: Sopena.

1941   Same. Biblioteca Belliken. Buenos Aires: Atlantida.

1943   _Las Aventuras de Huck_. [2nd edition] Buenos Aires: Losada.

1943 Aventuras de Huck Finn. Novela. Biblioteca Mundial Sopena: Buenos Aires. Sopena.

1944 Aventuras de Huck. Coleccion Robin Hood. Buenos Aires: Acme.

1945 Las Aventuras de Huck. Biblioteca Contemporanea, No. 51. Buenos Aires: Losada.

1945 Aventuras de Huck Finn. Novela. Biblioteca Mundial Sopena. Buenos Aires: Sopena.

1946 Aventuras de Huck. Coleccion Robin Hood. Buenos Aires: Poseidon.

1948 Same. [3rd edition] Buenos Aires: Acme.

1949 Aventuras de Huck Finn. Novela. Biblioteca Mundial Sopena. Buenos Aires: Sopena.

1950 Aventuras de Huck Finn. Biblioteca Bellekin. [3rd edition] Buenos Aires: Atlantida.

1950 Aventuras de Huck. [4th edition] Buenos Aires: Acme.

1951 Same. [5th edition] Buenos Aires: Acme.

1953 Las Aventuras de Huckleberry Finn, Buenos Aires: Peuser.

1958 Same. Buenos Aires: Peuser.

1958 Las Aventuras de Huck. [4th edition] Buenos Aires: Losada.

1960 Aventuras de Huck. [8th edition] Buenos Aires: Acme.

1963 Las Aventuras de Huck Finn. Buenos Aires: Atlantida.

1964 Aventuras de Huck. [9th edition] Buenos Aires: Acme.

Innocents Abroad

1943 Viajes y Cuentos Humoristicos [Travels and Humorous Stories], Buenos Aires: Colomino.

Life on the Mississippi

1947 La Vida en el Misisipi [Life on the Mississippi]. Coleccion El Navio. Buenos Aires: Emece.

1963 Same. Buenos Aires: Emece.

Man That Corrupted Hadleyburg

1947 El Hombre que Corrompio a Una Ciudad [The Man Who Corrupted A City]. [2nd edition] Coleccion Austral. Buenos Aires: Espasa-Calpe.

Mysterious Stranger

1950   El Forastero Misterioso [The Mysterious Stranger].   Grandes
       Novelistas Contemporaneos.   Buenos Aires: Veinte.

Prince and the Pauper

1942   El Principe y el Mendigo [The Prince and the Beggar].   Famosas
       Novelas.   Buenos Aires: Molino.

1947   Principe y Mendigo.   Coleccion Robin Hood.   Buenos Aires: Acme.

1948   Same.   Buenos Aires: Sopena.

1950   Same.   Coleccion Robin Hood.   [4th edition] Buenos Aires: Acme.

1951   El Principe y el Mendigo, Buenos Aires: Codex.

1952   Principe y Mendigo.   Coleccion Robin Hood.   [5th edition] Buenos
       Aires: Acme.

1957   El Principe y el Mendigo.   Buenos Aires.   Acme.

1963   Same.   Buenos Aires: Atlantida.

1963   Principe y Mendigo: Buenos Aires.   Acme.

1963   Same.   Buenos Aires: Peuser.

1963   Same.   Buenos Aires: Tor.

1969   El Principe y el Mendigo.   Coleccion Platero.   Buenos Aires:
       Almendros.

Pudd'nhead Wilson

1957   Wilson el Simpla [Wilson the Simpleton], Buenos Aires: Acme.

Stories and Sketches

1939   Las Mas Divertidas Historias [The Most Amusing Stories].   Biblio-
       teca Pluma de Oro.   Coleccion de Grandes Obras Universales.   Buenos
       Aires: Porter.

1939   Cuentos Humoristicos [Humorous Stories], Buenos Aires: Tor.

1942   Same.   Buenos Aires: Tor.

1942   ¿Ha Muerte Shakespeare? [Is Shakespeare Dead?] Buenos Aires: Tor.

1943   Viajes y Cuentos Humoristicos [Travels and Humorous Stories],
       Buenos Aires: Colomino.

1943   El Robo del Elefante Blanco [The Theft of the White Elephant].
Ediciones de Grandes Autores. Buenos Aires: Tor.

1945   Cuentos Humoristicos. Ediciones de Grandes Autores. Buenos Aires:
Tor.

1945   Novelas Cortas, Cuentos y Relatos [Abridged Novels, Stories, and
Narratives]. Biblioteca Cuspide. Buenos Aires: Gil.

1947   Same. Biblioteca Cuspide. [2nd edition] Buenos Aires: Gil.

1947   Un Reportaje Sensacional y Otros Cuentos [Sensational Reporting
and Other Stories]. Coleccion Austral, 698. Buenos Aires: Espasa-
Calpe.

1947   Same. Coleccion Austral, 698. [2nd edition] Buenos Aires: Espasa-
Calpe.

1947   Fragmentos del Diario de Adan y Diario de Eva [Fragments of the
Diary of Adam and Diary of Eve]. Coleccion Austral. Buenos Aires:
Espasa-Calpe.

1947   Nuevos Cuentos [New Stories]. Coleccion Austral. Buenos Aires:
Espasa-Calpe.

1947   Same. Coleccion Austral. [2nd edition] Buenos Aires: Espasa-Calpe.

1954   Un Reporatje Sensacional y Otros Cuentos. Coleccion Austral, 698.
[3rd edition] Buenos Aires: Espasa-Calpe.

1963   El Billete de un Millon de Libras [The Banknote for A Million
Pounds], Buenos Aires: Plaza & Janes.

Tom Sawyer

1938   Las Aventuras de Tom Sawyer [The Adventures of Tom Sawyer], Buenos
Aires: Losada.

1940   Same. Buenos Aires: Losada.

1941   Same. Buenos Aires: Espasa-Calpe.

1941   Same. Buenos Aires: Espasa-Calpe.

1941   Aventuras de Tom Sawyer, Buenos Aires: Sopena.

1943   Las Aventuras de Tom Sawyer. Coleccion Austral, 212. [2nd edition]
Buenos Aires: Espasa-Calpe.

1943   Aventuras de Tom Sawyer, Buenos Aires: Atlantida.

1944   Same. Buenos Aires: Acme.

1945   Las Aventuras de Tom Sawyer, Buenos Aires: Atlantida.

1948   Same. Buenos Aires: Losada.

1948   Same. Buenos Aires: Mundo Moderno.

1948   Aventuras de Tom Sawyer; Novela [Adventures of Tom Sawyer; Novel].
       Coleccion Topacio. Buenos Aires: Sopena.

1949   Aventuras de Tom Sawyer. [3rd edition] Buenos Aires: Acme.

1949   Same. [4th edition] Buenos Aires: Acme.

1949   Same. Biblioteca Billeken. [3rd edition] Buenos Aires: Atlantida.

1950   Tom Sawyer, Buenos Aires: Mundo Moderno.

1950   Aventuras de Tom Sawyer [5th edition] Buenos Aires: Acme.

1951   Las Aventuras de Tom Sawyer. Coleccion Lecturas Juveniles. Buenos
       Aires: Peuser.

1953   Aventuras de Tom Sawyer, Buenos Aires: Acme.

1956   Same. [5th edition] Buenos Aires: Atlantida.

1957   Same. Buenos Aires: Acme.

1957   Las Aventuras de Tom Sawyer, Buenos Aires: Peuser.

1958   Same. [5th edition] Buenos Aires: Losada.

1963   Same. Buenos Aires: Atlantida.

1963   Same. [5th edition] Buenos Aires: Peuser.

1963   Aventuras de Tom Sawyer, Buenos Aires: Acme.

1963   Same. Buenos Aires: Difusion.

1963   Same. Buenos Aires: Sopena.

1963   Same. Buenos Aires: Tor.

1967   Las Aventuras de Tom Sawyer. [6th edition] Buenos Aires: Losada.

1976   Aventuras de Tom Sawyer. [11th edition] Buenos Aires: Atlantida.

Tom Sawyer Abroad

1943   Tom Sawyer en el Extranjero [Tom Sawyer Abroad], Buenos Aires:
       Acme.

1943   Same. Buenos Aires: Acme.

1946   Same. Coleccion Robin Hood. Buenos Aires: Poseidon.

1947 Same. Coleccion Robin Hood [2nd edition] Buenos Aires: Acme.

1949 Same. [3rd edition] Buenos Aires: Acme.

1950 Same. [4th edition] Buenos Aires: Acme.

1951 Tom Sawyer, Detective; Tom Sawyer en el Extranjero. Coleccion
      Austral. Buenos Aires: Espasa-Calpe.

1953 Tom Sawyer en el Extranjero, Buenos Aires: Acme.

1953 Tom Sawyer, Detective y Argonauta [Tom Sawyer, Detective and
      Adventurer], Buenos Aires: Poseidon.

1964 Tom Sawyer en el Extranjero. [8th edition] Buenos Aires: Acme.

Tom Sawyer, Detective

1943 Tom Sawyer Detective, Buenos Aires: Acme.

1951 Tom Sawyer, Detective; Tom Sawyer en el Extranjero [Tom Sawyer,
      Detective; Tom Sawyer Abroad], Buenos Aires: Espasa-Calpe.

1953 Tom Sawyer, Detective y Argonauta [Tom Sawyer, Detective and Adven-
      turer], Buenos Aires: Poseidon.

Collected Works

1946 Novelas y Cuentos [Novels and Stories]. [1 vol.] Buenos Aires: Gil.

1962 Obras de Mark Twain [Works of Mark Twain]. [1 vol.] Coleccion
      Maestros del Humors. Buenos Aires: Plaza & Janes.

Brazil

Sources: BB/BBA/IT/PBP/SPT

American Claimant

1961 O Pretendente Norte-americano. Romance [The North American
      Claimant. Novel]. Coleccao as Obras Eternas. Rio de Janeiro:
      Vecchi.

Autobiography

1946 Aventuras de Mark Twain [Adventures of Mark Twain]. Introducio de
      Albert Bigelow Paine [Introduction by Albert Bigelow Paine].
      Coleccao Memorias, Diarios e Confissaos, V. 21. Rio de Janeiro:
      Olympio.

Connecticut Yankee

1945 Um Ianque na Corte do Rei Artur [A Yankee at Court of King Arthur].
      Coleccao A Marcha do Tempo, 5. Sao Paulo: Brasiliense.

1949 Same. Coleccao Os Maiores Exitos de Tela. Rio de Janeiro: Vecchi.

1951 Same. Coleccao A Marcha do Tempo, 5. [2nd edition] Sao Paulo:
      Brasiliense.

1957 Same. [3rd edition] Sao Paulo: Brasiliense.

1959 Same. [4th edition] Biblioteca Literatura Moderna, 6. Sao Paulo:
      Brasiliense.

1960 Same. Coleccao Madrigal. Rio de Janeiro: Scala.

1973 Same. Rio de Janeiro: Tecnoprint.

Huckleberry Finn

1934 Aventuras de Huck [Adventures of Huck]. Coleccao Terra Ma Rear,
      19. Sao Paulo: Nacional.

1945 As Aventuras de Huck. Coleccao Os Audazes. Rio de Janeiro: Vecchi.

1949 Same. [2nd edition] Rio de Janeiro: Vecchi.

1949 Aventuras de Huck, Sao Paulo: Brasiliense.

1954 As Aventuras de Huck. (Companheiro de Tom Sawyer). Romance [The
      Adventures of Huck. (Companion of Tom Sawyer). Novel]. [3rd
      edition] Rio de Janeiro: Vecchi.

1954 Aventuras de Huck, Sao Paulo: Brasiliense.

1958 Same. [4th edition] Sao Paulo: Brasiliense.

1958 As Aventuras de Huck (Companheiro de Tom Sawyer) (Romance). [4th
      edition] Rio de Janeiro: Vecchi.

1959 As Aventuras de Huck. Coleccao A Marcha do Tempo. [5th edition]
      Sao Paulo: Brasiliense.

1962 As Aventuras de Huck - Companheiro de Tom Sawyer. Coleccao es
      Audazes, 12. [5th edition] Rio de Janeiro: Vecchi.

1969 Aventuras de Huck, Rio de Janeiro: Ouro.

1970 Same. Rio de Janeiro: Ouro.

1973 Same. [7th edition] Sao Paulo: Brasiliense.

1975 Aventuras de Huck, Huckleberry Finn, Rio de Janeiro: Tecnoprint.

Prince and the Pauper

1933 O Principe e O Pobre [The Prince and the Pauper]. Coleccao Terra
Marear. Sao Paulo: Nacional.

1945 O Principe e O Pobre. Historia para Criancas de Todas as Idades
[The Prince and the Pauper. Story for Children of All Ages].
Coleccao A Marcha do Tempo, 6. Sao Paulo: Brasiliense.

1946 O Principe e O Pobre. Coleccao Os Audazes. Rio de Janeiro:
Vecchi.

1948 O Principe e O Mendigo (Um Romance para Jovens de Todas as Idades)
[The Prince and the Beggar (A Novel for Youths of All Ages)].
Coleccao Os Audazes, n. 13. [2nd edition] Rio de Janeiro: Vecchi.

1953 Same. Coleccao Os Audazes, n. 13. [3rd edition] Rio de Janiero:
Vecchi.

1954 O Principe e O Pobre. Historia para Criancas de Todas as Idades.
Coleccao A Marcha do Tempo, 7. [3rd edition] Sao Paulo:
Brasiliense.

1955 O Principe e O Mendigo (Um Romance para Jovens de Todas as Idades).
Coleccao Os Audazes, n. 13. [4th edition] Rio de Janeiro: Vecchi.

1957 O Principe e o Pobre, Sao Paulo: Brasiliense.

1958 O Principe e O Mendigo. Coleccao os Audazes, 13. Rio de Janeiro:
Vecchi.

1959 O Principe e O Pobre. Coleccao A Marcha do Tempo. [5th edition]
Sao Paulo: Brasiliense.

1960 O Principe e O Mendigo. Coleccao Primavera, 4. Sao Paulo:
Paulinas.

1962 Same. Rio de Janeiro: Lux.

1963 Principe e Mendigo, Rio de Janeiro: Bruguera.

1970 O Principe e O Pobre, Rio de Janeiro: Ouro.

Pudd'nhead Wilson

1961 O Pateta Wilson [Simpleton Wilson]. Coleccao as Obras Eternas.
Rio de Janeiro: Vecchi.

Stories and Sketches

1956 Locuras de Milionario [Madness of A Millionaire]. Coleccao
Maiores Exitos da Tela. Rio de Janeiro: Vecchi.

1958 Alegres Historias [Merry Tales], Sao Paulo: Cultrix.

1974   O Diario de Adao e Eva [The Diary of Adam and Eve], Rio de
       Janeiro: Tecnoprint.

1974   O Roubo de Elefante Branco [The Theft of White Elephant], Rio de
       Janeiro: Tecnoprint.

Tom Sawyer

1933   As Aventuras de Tom Sawyer [The Adventures of Tom Sawyer].
       Coleccao de Livre-film, 2. Rio de Janeiro: Civilizacao
       Brasileira.

1942   Same. Coleccao Os Audazes. Rio de Janeiro: Vecchi.

1945   Same. [2nd edition] Coleccao Os Audazes. Rio de Janeiro: Vecchi.

1948   Same.   Coleccao O Marcha do Tempo, 17. Sao Paulo: Brasiliense.

1949   Same. [3rd edition] Coleccao Os Audazes. Rio de Janeiro: Vecchi.

1951   Same. [2nd edition] Coleccao O Marcha de Tempo, 17. Sao Paulo:
       Brasiliense.

1953   Same. [4th edition] Coleccao Os Audazes. Rio de Janeiro: Vecchi.

1954   Same. Sao Paulo: Clube Livro.

1956   Same. [5th edition] Coleccao Os Audazes. Rio de Janeiro: Vecchi.

1957   Same. Coleccao a Marcha do Tempo. [3rd edition] Sao Paulo:
       Brasiliense.

1959   Same. Coleccao a Marcha do Tempo. [4th edition] Sao Paulo:
       Brasiliense.

1960   Same. Coleccao Os Audazes, 11. [6th edition] Rio de Janeiro:
       Vecchi.

1970   Aventuras de Tom Sawyer, Rio de Janeiro: Ouro.

1971   Same. Rio de Janeiro: Ouro.

1973   Same. [7th edition] Sao Paulo: Brasiliense.

1974   Same. [8th edition] Sao Paulo: Brasiliense.

Tom Sawyer Abroad

1933   Autras Aventuras de Tom Sawyer [Other Adventures of Tom Sawyer],
       Rio de Janeiro: Civilizacao.

1934   As Viagens de Tom Sawyer Narradas por Huck Finn [The Travels of Tom
       Sawyer Told by Huck Finn]. Coleccao Terra Morear, 28. Sao Paulo:
       Nacional.

1955 Aventuras de Tom Sawyer no Estrangeiro, Romance [Adventures of Tom Sawyer Abroad, Novel]. Coleccao Os Audazes, 28. Rio de Janeiro: Vecchi.

1960 Same. [3rd edition] Coleccao Os Audazes, 28. Rio de Janeiro: Vecchi.

1974 As Viagens de Tom Sawyer, Rio de Janiero: Tecnoprint.

Tom Sawyer, Detective

1933 Autras Aventuras de Tom Sawyer [Other Adventures of Tom Sawyer], Rio de Janeiro: Civilizacao.

1955 Tom Sawyer, Detective; Romance [Tom Sawyer, Detective; Novel]. Coleccao Os Audazes, 27. Rio de Janeiro: Vecchi.

1960 Same. Coleccao Os Audazes, 27. [3rd edition] Rio de Janeiro: Vecchi.

1973 Tom Sawyer Detective, Rio de Janeiro: Tecnoprint.

Chile

Sources: BON/LEV/NUC/PBS

Huckleberry Finn

1940 Las Aventuras de Huck [The Adventures of Huck], Santiago: Zig-Zag.

Mysterious Stranger

1936 El Forastero Misterioso [The Mysterious Stranger]. Los Grandes Escritores. Santiago: Zig-Zag.

1942 Same. Santiago: Zig-Zag.

Prince and the Pauper

1927 Principe y Mendigo [Prince and Beggar]. Los Grandes Escritores. Santiago de Chile: Letras.

1937 Same. Santiago: Zig-Zag.

Stories and Sketches

1934 La Herencia del Tio [The Inheritance of the Uncle], Santiago de Chile: Letras.

1936   Las Mas Divertidas Historias [The Most Amusing Stories]. Biblio-
       teca Amanta, v. 2. Santiago: Ercilla.

1945   El Diario de Eva [The Diary of Eve]. Los Grandes Escritores.
       Santiago: Zig-Zag.

1972   El Robo de Elefante Blanco [The Theft of the White Elephant],
       Santiago: Quimantu.

                            Tom Sawyer

1940   Las Aventuras de Tom Sawyer [The Adventures of Tom Sawyer].
       Coleccion Aventura. Santiago: Zig-Zag.

                            Colombia

Sources: BON/LEV

                         Huckleberry Finn

1963   Huckleberry Finn [English language edition], Bogota?: Albon.
       [English]

                       Stories and Sketches

1895? La Novela de Una Virgen Esquimal y La Celebre Rana Saltadora
       [The Story of An Eskimo Maiden and The Celebrated Jumping Frog].
       Biblioteca Popular, 6. Bogota: Libreria Nueva.

1896? Bocetos Humoristicos [Humorous Sketches]. Biblioteca Popular, 58.
       Bogota: Libreria Nueva.

                          Miscellaneous

1907? Humoradas [Humorous Sayings], Bogota: La Luz.

                              Cuba

Sources: ABC/BC

1944   Principe y Mendigo [Prince and Beggar]. Supplemento de Guerra y
       Literario a Informacion, No. 59. Habana: Cooperativa de
       Suscriptores de Informacion.

1962   Huckleberry Finn. Ediciones Juveniles. Biblioteca del Pueblo.
       Habana: Nacional de Cuba.

1962 Aventuras de Tom Sawyer [Adventures of Tom Sawyer]. Seccion de
      Bibliotecas Escolares. Ministerio de Educacion. Habana: Nacional
      de Cuba.

Mexico

Sources: ABM/BON/CLIM/IT/LEV/MB/NUC/PBS/SPT

Connecticut Yankee

1952 Un Yanqui en la Corte del Rey Artus [A Yankee in the Court of
      King Arthur]. Coleccion Juventud. Mexico: Latino Americana.

Gilded Age

1952 La Edad Dorada [The Gilded Age], Mexico: Latino Americana.

Huckleberry Finn

1952 Huck Finn; Continuacion de las Aventuras de Tom Sawyer [Huck Finn;
      Continuation of the Adventures of Tom Sawyer]. Coleccion Juventud.
      Mexico: Latino Americana.

1953 Huck Finn, el Negro y Tom Sawyer [Huck Finn, the Negro and Tom
      Sawyer], Mexico: Latino Americana.

1953 Aventuras de Huck por Mark Twain [Adventures of Huck by Mark Twain],
      Mexico: Diana.

1963 Aventuras de Huck, Mexico: Diana.

Prince and the Pauper

1952 Principe y Mendigo [Prince and Beggar]. Coleccion Gigantes en
      Miniatura 11. Mexico: Compania General de Ediciones.

1956 Same. Mexico: Novara-Mexico.

1962 Same. [5th edition] Mexico: Diana.

1963 Same. Mexico: Diana.

Pudd'nhead Wilson

1953 Cabezahueca Wilson [Empty-head Wilson]. Coleccion Juventud.
      Mexico: Latino Americana.

Stories and Sketches

1940 La Celebrada Rana Saltarina [The Celebrated Jumping Frog]. Pequena
      Coleccion Mirasol, 2. Mexico: Talleres Tipograficos Modelo.

1940 La Celebrada Rana Cantarina y Otros Cuentos [The Celebrated
      Jumping Frog and Other Stories], Mexico: Campania General Editora.

1943 Mark Twain's "1601." Conversation As It Was...by the Social Fire-
      side in the Time of the Tudors, Mexico City: Privately printed.
      [English]

1952 El Robo del Elefante Blanco y Otras Narraciones [The Theft of the
      White Elephant and Other Narrations], Mexico: Diana.

1953 Narraciones Humoristicos [Humorous Narrations], Mexico: Diana.

1963 ¿Ha Muerto Shakespeare? [Is Shakespeare Dead?], Mexico: Nacional.

Tom Sawyer

1953 Las Aventuras de Tom Sawyer [The Adventures of Tom Sawyer].
      Coleccion Juventud. Mexico: Latino Americana.

1953 Aventuras de Tom Sawyer, Mexico: Diana.

1956 Same. Ilustrada de Obras Immortales. Mexico: Cumbre.

1956 Las Aventuras de Tom Sawyer. [3rd edition] Mexico: Novaro-
      Mexico.

1959 Aventuras de Tom Sawyer. [2nd edition] Coleccion Ilustrada de
      Obras Immortales. Mexico: Cumbre.

1960 Tom Sawyer. Clasicos de Oro Ilustrados, 4. Mexico: Novaro-
      Mexico.

1962 Aventuras de Tom Sawyer [5th edition] Mexico: Diana.

1967 Same. Mexico: Cumbre.

1972 Las Aventuras de Tom Sawyer, Mexico: Porrua.

1973 Same. Naucalpan: Organizacion Editorial Novaro.

Tom Sawyer Abroad

1953 Tom Sawyer a Traves del Mundo [Tom Sawyer across the World].
      Coleccion Juventud. Mexico: Latino Americana.

1954 Tom Sawyer en el Extranjero [Tom Sawyer Abroad], Mexico: Diana.

1963 Same. Mexico: Diana.

Tom Sawyer, Detective

1952   Tom Sawyer Detectivo, Mexico: Latino Americana.

Tramp Abroad

1953   Aventuras de un Vagabundo [Adventures of A Vagabond], Mexico:
       Latino Americana.

Selections

1919   Mark Twain Seleccion [Mark Twain Selections]. Cultura, tomo 10,
       no. 3. Mexico: Cultura.

1967   Seleccion de Obras de Mark Twain [Selection of Works by Mark Twain].
       Ed. Bernard De Voto. [Spanish translation of The Portable Mark
       Twain] Mexico: Wiley.

Peru

Sources: NUC

1964   El Hombre que Corrompio a Hadleyburg [The Man Who Corrupted
       Hadleyburg]. Populibros Peruanos, 6 ser., 29. Lima: Populibros
       Peruanos.

Uruguay

Sources: BON

1921   Cuentos Escogidos [Selected Fables], Motevideo: Garcia.

1943   Same. [2nd edition] Montevideo: Garcia.

NEAR EAST

Iran

Sources: IT

Huckleberry Finn

1960   Madjerahaye Huckleberry Finn [Adventures of Huckleberry Finn],
       Tehran: n.pub.

1970   Hakelberifin [Huckleberry Finn], Tehran: Rowzan.

Prince and the Pauper

1958   Shahzadeh Va Geda [Prince and Pauper], Tehran: Amir Kabir.

1962   Shazade O Geda [Prince and Pauper]. [3rd edition] Tehran: Pocket
Books.

1973   Shahzade Va Geda, Tehran: Mehregan.

Tom Sawyer

1958   Tam-Sayer [Tom Sawyer], Tehran: n.pub.

1962   Tom Sayer [Tom Sawyer], Tehran: Pocket Books.

1970   Tam Sayer, Tehran: Ketabha-ge Jibi.

Israel

Sources: IT/LC/NUC

Connecticut Yankee

1952   Yaki be-hatsar ha-melekh Artur [A Yankee in the Court of King
Arthur], Tel-Aviv: n.pub.

1953   Yanky Be-hazar Ha-Melekh Arthur, Tel-Aviv: Tevel.

Huckleberry Finn

1954   Meoraot Huckleberry Finn [Adventures of Huckleberry Finn], Tel-
Aviv: Omanut.

1954   Hakelberi Fin [Huckleberry Finn], Tel-Aviv: Cecik.

1969   Alilot Huckleberry Finn [Adventures of Huckleberry Finn], Tel-Aviv:
Mizrahi.

Innocents Abroad

1975   Massa Taanugot Le'erez ha-qodesh [Innocents Abroad], Tel-Aviv:
Levinson.

Prince and the Pauper

1941   Ben Hamelekh wehe-'ani [Prince and the Pauper]. [abridged] Tel-
Aviv: n.pub.

1952   Ben Ha-melekh Wehe-'ani, Tel-Aviv: Yizr'el.

1953 Same. Tel-Aviv: Cecik.

1954 Same. Tel-Aviv: Massada.

1959 Same. Tel-Aviv: Cecik.

1967 Same. Tel-Aviv: Mizrahi.

Pudd'nhead Wilson

1954 Wilson Ha-tembl [Simpleton Wilson], Tel-Aviv: Cecik.

Stories and Sketches

1954 Ketavim (I) [Stories (I)], Tel-Aviv: Karmi & Naor.

1964 Ma'ase Be-orek Sel Itton Haklai [How I Edited An Agricultural
Paper], Tel-Aviv: Cherikowĕr.

Tom Sawyer

1940 Tom Sawyer. [2 vols.] Tel-Aviv: n. pub.

1952 Same. Tel-Aviv: Yizr'el.

1954 Same. Tel-Aviv: Cecik.

1960 Harpatkaotaw Shel Tom Sawyer [Adventures of Tom Sawyer]. [abridged]
Tel-Aviv: Fridman.

1962 Me'ora' ot Tom Sawyer [Adventures of Tom Sawyer], Tel-Aviv: Niv.

1968 Harpatqeot Tom Sawyer [Adventures of Tom Sawyer]. [abridged] Tel-
Aviv: Mizrahi.

Tom Sawyer Abroad

1955 Tom Soyer Ba-Derakhim [Tom Sawyer Abroad], Tel-Aviv: Yavneh.

1974 Tom Sawyer Ballash. Tom Sawyer Bashehaqim [Tom Sawyer Detective.
Tom Sawyer Abroad], Jerusalem: Keter.

Tom Sawyer, Detective

1974 Tom Sawyer Ballash. Tom Sawyer Bashehaqim [Tom Sawyer Detective.
Tom Sawyer Abroad], Jerusalem: Keter.

Turkey

Sources: IT/NUC/TB

Huckleberry Finn

1957 Huck Finn'in Basindan Gelenler [The Things That Happened to Huck
Finn], Istanbul: Varlik.

1970 Same. [2nd edition] Istanbul: Varlik.

1973 Kahraman Finn [Huckleberry Finn], Istanbul: Dogan Kardes
Matbaacilik Sanayi.

Life on the Mississippi

1965 Misisipi'de Hayat [Life on the Mississippi], Istanbul: Varlik.

Mysterious Stranger

1963 Esrarengiz Yabanci [Mysterious Stranger], Istanbul: Iyigiin.

Prince and the Pauper

1953 Calinan Tac. (Roman) [False Crown. (Novel)], Istanbul: Dogan
Kardes.

1955 Same. [2nd edition] Istanbul: Dogan Kardes.

1962 Same. Istanbul: Gur.

1962 Kucek Prenshe Fakir Cocuk [Plucky Prince Pauper Boy], Istanbul:
Isil Kitabevi.

1966 Calinan Tac. [2nd edition] Istanbul: Duran Ofset.

1966 Same. Istanbul: Iyigiin.

1972 Same. Istanbul: Itimat Kitabevi.

1974 Sehzade ile Dilenci [Prince and Pauper], Istanbul: Yaylacik
Matbassi.

Stories and Sketches

1941 Uykusuz Gece, Amerikali Mark Twain 'den Secme Hikayeler [Sleepless
Night, Selected Stories of the American Mark Twain]. Hilminin
Kolekalyonu, No. 69. Istanbul: Hilmi Kitabevi.

1948 Ademin Hatira Defteri [Extracts from Adam's Memoirs], Istanbul:
Yenicag.

1959 Sigir Sozlesmesi [Beef Contract], n.p.: Yeni Matbaa.

1960 Karnaval [Carnival], Istanbul: Ar-El Matbaasi.

1963 Beyaz Fil [White Elephant], Istanbul: Iyigiin.

1972 Adem ile Havva'nin Cennet Gunlugu [Adam and Eve's Paradise
      Day-words], Istanbul: Milliyet Yayin.

Tom Sawyer

19--? Tom Sawyer'in Maceralari [Tom Sawyer's Adventures], Istanbul:
       Nebioglu.

1949 Tom Soyer'in Basindan Gelenler [The Things That Happened to Tom
      Sawyer], Istanbul: Turkiye Yayinevi.

1950 Tom Sawyer'in Maceralari, Istanbul: Nebioglu.

1954 Same. Istanbul: Varlik.

1957 Same. [2nd edition] Istanbul: Varlik.

1960 Same. Istanbul: Iyigun.

1960 Same. Istanbul: Ceylan.

1962 Tom Sawyer, Istanbul: Gur.

1963 Tom Sawyer'in Maceralari, Istanbul: Nebioglu.

1963 Same. [3rd edition] Istanbul: Varlik.

1965 Same. Istanbul: Iyigun.

1967 Same. Istanbul: Kutulmus Matbaasi.

1968 Same. [4th edition] Istanbul: Varlik.

1970 Tom Sawyer, Istanbul: Nes Riyat Anonim Sirketi.

1971 Tom Sawyer'in Maceralari, Istanbul: Itimat Kitabevi.

1974 Tom Sawyer, Istanbul: Altin Kitaplar Basimevi.

1975 Same. Istanbul: Halk El Sanatlar.

Miscellaneous

1963 Kirk yil Sonra [Forty Years Afterwards], Istanbul: Iyigiin.

AFRICA

Egypt

Sources: BN/CGBN/IT/NUC

1948 Al-Amir wa l-faqir [The Prince and the Pauper]. Awladona. Nos Enfants, 5. Le Caire [Cairo]: Dar al-Ma'arif.

1960 10 Qisas Amrikiyyah [10 American Stories], -al-Qahirah [Cairo]: Maktabit-al-Nahdah al Misriyyah.

1961 'Ashr Qisas li Mark Twin [Selected Stories of Mark Twain], -al-Qahirah: n.pub.

1963 Tum Suyir; Qissat Bayat Tin [Tom Sawyer], n.p.: n.pub.

1968 Mughamarat Hakilbry Fin [Adventures of Huckleberry Finn], -al-Qahirah: Maktabat Misriyyah.

1972 Al-'Amir Wal-Faqir [The Prince and the Pauper], al-Qahirah: Dar Al-Ma'auf.

1974 Tum Suwir [Tom Sawyer], al-Qahirah: Dar al-Ma'arif.

Morocco

Sources: BE/SPT

1959 Aventuras de Tom Sawyer [Adventures of Tom Sawyer]. Biblioteca Adan y Eva. Tetuan, Ceuta: Cremades. [Spanish]

South Africa

Sources: IT

1953 Die Avonture van Tom Sawyer [The Adventures of Tom Sawyer], Pretoria: Van Schaik. [Afrikaans]

1963 Die Avonture van Huckleberry Finn [The Adventures of Huckleberry Finn], Kaapstad: Malherbe. [Afrikaans]

1968? Die Verhaal van Tom Sawyer [The Story of Tom Sawyer], Roodepoort: Baanbrekeruitgewers. [Afrikaans]

1970 Tom Sawyer word Speurder [Tom Sawyer Becomes Detective], Pretoria: Van Schaik. [Afrikaans]

INDIAN SUBCONTINENT

Ceylon (Sri Lanka)

(Sources: IT)

1962 <u>Dangakaraya</u> [Tom Sawyer], Colombo: Wijesena & Bros. [Singhalese]

India

Sources: INB/IRC/IT/MTI/NBIL/NUC

Following the Equator

n.d. <u>More Tramps Abroad: India</u>, Bombay: Modern Publishing Co. [English]

1970 <u>Ayamang di Indiyans</u> [Among the Indians]. [extracts from <u>Following</u>
      <u>the Equator</u>] Calcutta: Mandal Book House. [Bengali]

Huckleberry Finn

n.d. <u>Huckleberry Finn</u>, Bombay: Tripathi. [Gujarati]

1952 Same. Madras: Granthamala. [Telugu]

1964 <u>The Adventures of Hucklberry Finn. Adapted and Retold</u>, New Delhi:
      Eurasia. [English]

1966 <u>Bhatak Bahaddar</u> [Floating Earth?], Bombay: Majestic Book Stall.
      [Marathi]

1966 <u>Haklberi Finera Duhsahasika Abhiyana</u> [Adventures of Huckleberry
      Finn], n.p.: n.pub. [Bengali]

1966 <u>Hakkilperifin Viracceyalkal</u> [Adventures of Huckleberry Finn], Madras:
      Sarvasiddhanta. [Tamil]

1967 <u>Huckleberry Finnam Parakramo</u> [Adventures of Huckleberry Finn],
      Bombay: Vora. [Gujarati]

1967 <u>Huckleberry Finintal Albutha Vikramangal</u> [Adventures of Huckleberry
      Finn], Kottayam: Sahitya Pravarthak C.S. [Malayalam]

1968 <u>Bahati Dhara</u> [Floating Earth], Delhi: Rajpal. [Hindi]

1971 <u>[The Adventures of Huckleberry Finn]</u>, Gauhati: Ranjit Kakati.
      [Assamese]

1975 <u>Huckleberry Finn</u>, Delhi: Radhakrishna Prakashan [Hindi]

Life on the Mississippi

n.d. Mississippi no Jeewano [Life on the Mississippi], Bombay: Tripathi.
      [Gujarati]

1966 Ei Nadi Micicipi [Life on the Mississippi], Calcutta: Shri Bhumi.
      [Assamese]

1966 Mohander Panchali [Life on the Mississippi], Calcutta: Mitralaya.
      [Bengali]

1967 Mississippivaril Mushaphari [Life on the Mississippi], Bombay:
      Majestic. [Marathi]

Prince and the Pauper

1908 Rank Ani Rao [Prince and Pauper], Wai: Damodar Modavritta.
      [Marathi]

1950 Raju-Peda [Prince and Pauper], Madras: Granthamala. [Telugu]

1952 Same. Madras: Granthamala. [Telugu]

1956 Same. Madras: Granthamala. [Telugu]

1961 The Prince and the Pauper. Retold, Madras: Orient Longmans.
      [English]

1969 Rajaputra o Bhikari [Prince and Pauper], Cuttack: Grantha Mandir.
      [Oriya]

1973 Bhikhari Aur Rajakumar [Pauper and Prince], Delhi: Paramount.
      [Hindi]

Roughing It

1970 Yadom ki Ghatiyam [Recollection of Mountains], Delhi: Rajpal.
      [Hindi]

1971 Same. Delhi: Rajpal. [Hindi]

Tom Sawyer

1951 Dhadasi Chandu [Adventures of Tom]. [abridged adaptation] Bombay:
      Majestic Book Stall. [Marathi]

1952 Tom Sawyer, Madras: Granthamala. [Telugu]

1955 Tomsayer [Tom Sawyer], n.p.: n.pub. [Malayalam]

1955 Tam Cayar [Tom Sawyer], Madras: Aruna Books (India). [Tamil]

Fig. 34. *Bahati Dhara,* jacket of 1968 Indian edition published by Rajpal & Sons (Courtesy Rajpal & Sons [Delhi])

बहती धारा

अध्याय—१

'टाम सायर के कारनामे' किताब को पढ़े बिना आपको मेरे बारे में कुछ मालूम नहीं हो सकता, लेकिन कोई बात नहीं। उस किताब को मिस्टर मार्क ट्वेन ने लिखा और आम तौर पर सच्ची घटनाओं का ही वर्णन किया है। वैसे कुछ बातों को बढ़ा-चढ़ाकर भी लिख दिया है, लेकिन उन्होंने अधिकतर सचाई से काम लिया है। थोड़े-से भूठ या बात को जरा-सा बढ़ाकर लिखने में कोई बुराई नहीं; क्योंकि मुझे तो आज तक एक भी ऐसा आदमी नहीं मिला जो कभी भूठ न बोला हो। हां, एक पौली मौसी जरूर थीं, या वह विधवा और शायद मेरी भी, जो भूठ से हमेशा दूर रहीं। पौली मौसी से मतलब है टाम की मौसी पौली और मेरी और विधवा डगलस—इन सबके बारे में उस किताब में लिखा है; वह 'टाम सायर के कारनामे' नाम की किताब जिसके बारे में ऊपर बता आया हूं कि थोड़े-से बात-बढ़ाव के सिवा उसमें आम तौर पर सचाई से काम लिया गया है।

वह किताब इस तरह खत्म होती है: डाकुओं ने जो रुपया गुफा में छिपाया था वह मुझे और टाम को मिल गया। हरएक के हिस्से छह-छह हजार डालर आये और सबके सब सोने के—इस तरह हम दोनों खासे अमीर हो गए। उन रुपयों को अब समेटकर रखा तो डालरों का बहुत बड़ा ढेर लग गया था। तब न्यायाधीश थेचर साहब ने उस रकम को ब्याज पर उठा दिया और हमें सालोंसाल एक डालर रोज के हिसाब से आमदनी होने लगी। इतना पैसा आने लगा कि समझ में नहीं आता था, उसका क्या करें! विधवा डगलस ने मुझे गोद ले लिया और कहा कि वह मुझे सिखाए-पढ़ाएगी। लेकिन उसके साथ रहना मेरे लिए अच्छी-खासी मुसीबत हो गई—हर घड़ी का जंजाल! वह विधवा अपने हर काम में इतनी चौकस और कानन-कायदे की इतनी पाबन्द थी कि उसकी कट्टरता के मारे मेरा दम

Fig. 35. *Bahati Dhara,* first page of text of Hindi translation of Huckleberry Finn, 1968 edition published by Rajpal & Sons (Courtesy Rajpal & Sons [Delhi])

1955 Tom Sawyer, Madras: Granthamala. [Telugu]

1957 Dhadshi Chandu [Adventures of Tom]. [2nd abridged edition] Bombay: Siddharth Sahitya. [Marathi]

1957 Tom Sawyerchi Dhadase [Adventures of Tom Sawyer], Bombay: Samstha. [Marathi]

1958 Tam Saiyara [Tom Sawyer], Calcutta: Grantham. [Bengali]

1958 Tam Sayyara [Tom Sawyer], Calcutta: Ravindranath Dutta Grantham. [Bengali]

1960 Tom Soyar na Parakramo [The Adventures of Tom Sawyer], Bombay: Anaud. [Gujarati]

1960 The Adventures of Tom Sawyer. Adapted and Simplified, Madras: Umadevan. [English]

1960 Same. [abridged] Madras: Raja Ramchander. [English]

1961 The Adventures of Tom Sawyer, Retold, Bombay: Blackie. [English]

1962 Tam Chayarar Kanda [Tom Sawyer Story], Gauhati: New Book Stall. [Assamese]

1964 Tam Cayar [Tom Sawyer]. [Abridged] Madras: Saivasiddhanta. [Tamil]

1971 Tom Sawyer, Cuttack: Granthamandir. [Oriya]

1972 Natakhat Nandu, Delhi: National Publishing House. [Hindi]

1973 Tom Enna Kutti, Kozhikode: Poorna. [Malayalam]

Tom Sawyer, Detective

1972 Detective Tom Sawyer, Calcutta: Abhyerday Prakas Mandir. [Bengali]

Pakistan

Sources: IT

n.d. Mark Twain in India. [pamphlet] Indisier, Series V, No. 1. [2nd edition] Ed. B.J. Vaswani. Karachi. [excerpts from Following the Equator] [English]

194-? Same. [3rd edition] [English]

1964 The Prince and the Pauper. [2nd edition] Dacca: Book Promotion. [English]

SOUTHEAST ASIA

Burma

Sources: IT

Prince and the Pauper

1969 Bayiut Thar Tau Hnint Thitsar Shi Sin Ye Thar Lay, Rangoon:
Varsity Sarpag. [Burmese]

Indonesia

Sources: IT/NUC

Huckleberry Finn

1950 Pengalaman Huckleberry Finn [Adventures of Huckleberry Finn],
Djakarta: Noordhoff-Kolff. [Indonesian]

1976 Petualangan Huck Finn [Adventures of Huck Finn], Jakarta:
Gramedia [Indonesian]

Stories and Sketches

1963 Uaug Kertas Djutaan [Money Paper Million (Million Pound Bank-
note)], Djakarta: Jajasan Kebudajaan Sadar. [Indonesian]

Tom Sawyer

1948 Tom Sawyer, Anak Amerika, oleh Mark Twain [Tom Sawyer, American
Child, by Mark Twain], Djakarta: Balai Pustaka. [Indonesian]

1957 Same. [3rd edition] Djakarta: Balai Pustaka. [Indonesian]

Malaysia

Sources: IT/NUC

Huckleberry Finn

1964 Huckleberry Finn, Kuala Lumpur: Malaysia Publications.

Prince and the Pauper

1965   Cherita Anak Raja Dengan Anak Papa [Story of the Child Prince and
        Child Pauper]. Di-Melayukan Oleh Z'aba. Chet. 4. Kuala Lumpur:
        Dewan Behasa dan Pustaka, Kementerian Pelajaran. [Malay]

Philippines

Sources: IT

1974   Tom Sawyer, Quezon City: Alewar-Phoenix. [Filipino]

Thailand

Sources: NUC

1963   Chaochay Kap Yachok [Prince and Pauper], Bangkok: Ongkankha
        Khurusapha.   [Thai]

1975   Huck Pachon Pai [Adventures of Huckleberry Finn], Bangkok: Graffic
        Art.   [Thai]

FAR EAST

China

Sources: HKL

Gilded Age

1957   The Gilded Age [translated Chinese Title], Peking: Jen Min Wen
        Hsueh Press.

Huckleberry Finn

1956   The Adventures of Huckleberry Finn [translated title], Peking:
        China Youth Press.

1956   Same.   Shanghai: Hsin Wen-I Press.

Joan of Arc

1958   Personal Recollections of Joan of Arc [translated title], Shanghai:
        Hsin Wen-I Press.

Life on the Mississippi

1958 Life on the Mississippi [translated title], Peking: Jen Min Wen
      Hsueh Press.

Prince and the Pauper

1937 The Prince and the Pauper [translated title], Shanghai: Shang Wu
      Press.

Stories and Sketches

1937 Selections of the American Short Story [translated title]. [In-
      cludes The Celebrated Jumping Frog by Mark Twain along with stories
      by eleven other American writers: Irving, Hawthorne, Emerson, Poe,
      Harte, Bierce, H. James, O. Henry, Dreiser, Cather, Lewis] Shanghai:
      Shang Wu Press.

1955 Eve's Diary (Private Life of Adam and Eve; Being Extracts from
      Their Diaries) [translated title], Shanghai: Hsin Wen-I Press.

1955 The Story of A Salesman [translated title]. [A collection of
      Mark Twain's short stories] Shanghai: P'ing Mong Press.

Tom Sawyer

1936 The Adventures of Tom Sawyer [translated title], Shanghai: Shang
      Wu Press.

Hong Kong

Sources: HKL

Huckleberry Finn

1958 The Adventures of Huckleberry Finn [translated title], Hong Kong:
      Chung Liu Press.

1961 Same. Hong Kong: Wen T'ung Book Co.

1963 Same. Hong Kong: World To-day Press.

1964 Same. Hong Kong: Hai Yen Press.

1965 Same. [2nd edition] Hong Kong: World To-day Press.

Life on the Mississippi

1961   Life on the Mississippi [translated title], Hong Kong: Chien Wen
       Book Co.

Prince and the Pauper

1959   The Prince and the Pauper [translated title], Hong Kong: Chin Tai
       Book Co.

Stories and Sketches

1957   Selections of American Writers' Works [translated title]. [The
       Celebrated Jumping Frog and The Story of the McWilliams Couple
       together with selections from O. Henry, Saroyan, Dreiser, Poe,
       Hawthorne, Whitman] Hong Kong: Hong Kong Literary Press.

1960   A Treasury of World Short Stories [translated title]. [2 vols.]
       [Mark Twain's The Death of A Painter together with stories by
       Steinbeck, Hemingway, O. Henry, Hawthorne, and various Russian,
       German, Italian, Spanish, and British writers] Hong Kong: Rh Sin
       Book Co.

Tom Sawyer

n.d.   The Adventures of Tom Sawyer [translated title]. [2 vols.]
       Hong Kong: The Shanghai Book Co.

1957   The Adventures of Tom Sawyer [translated title], Hong Kong: The
       Shanghai Book Co.

1960   Same. [2nd edition] Hong Kong: The Shanghai Book Co.

1960   Same. Hong Kong: Rh Sin Book Co.

1961   Same. Hong Kong: Wen T'ung Book Co.

1964   Same. Hong Kong: World To-day Press.

1964   Same. [2nd edition] Hong Kong: World To-day Press.

1966   Same. [2nd edition] Hong Kong: Wen T'ung Book Co.

Selections

1958   Selections of Mark Twain's Works [translated title], Hong Kong:
       Hong Kong Literary Press.

1961   Mark Twain [translated title], Hong Kong: Shanghai Book Co.

Japan

Sources: IT MTJ NUC

Autobiography

1975 Jiden [Autobiography]. Amerika Koten Bunko, 6. Tokyo: Kenkyu-sha.

Connecticut Yankee

1951 Yume No Kyutei, Tokyo: Okakura.

1962 Arthur-o Kyutei No Yankee, Tokyo: Hayakawa.

1962 Kuso Kishi No Boken, Tokyo: Iwasaki.

1971 Asa o Atta Otoko, Tokyo: Iwasaki.

1976 Arthur-o Kyutei no Yanki, Tokyo: Hayakawa.

1976 Same. Tokyo: Tokyo Sogensha.

Huckleberry Finn

1923 The Adventures of Huckleberry Finn. Kenkyusha English Classics.
      Tokyo: Kenkyusha. [English]

1941 [The Adventures of Huckleberry Finn], n.p.: n.pub.

1950 Huckleberry Finn No Boken. [2 vols.] Tokyo: Iwanami.

1958 Same. Tokyo: Kenkyusha Shuppan.

1959 Same. Tokyo: Shincho-sha.

1962 Same. [2 vols.] Tokyo: Kadokawa.

1966 Tom Sawyer No Boken. Huckleberry Finn No Boken, Tokyo: Kawade.

1968 Huckleberry Finn No Boken, Tokyo: Poplar-sha.

1970 Same. Tokyo: Kodausha.

1971 Hakkuru Beri Fin No Boken, Tokyo: Kodausha.

1976 Huckleberry Finn No Boken, Tokyo: Gakushukenkyusha.

1976 Same. Tokyo: Iwasaki.

1976 Same. 2 vols. Tokyo: Kaiseisha.

1976 Same. Tokyo: Kodausha.

Fig. 36. *Tom Sawyer No Boken*, title page of 1953 Japanese edition published by Shinchosha (Courtesy Shinchosha Company [Tokyo])

Fig. 37. *Tom Sawyer No Boken*, cover of revised 1953 Japanese edition published by Shinchosha (Courtesy Shinchosha Company [Tokyo])

Innocents Abroad

1951 Aka Getto Gaiyu-ki. [2 vols.] Tokyo: Iwanami.

1962 Oshu Yumoa Ryoko, Tokyo: Iwasaki.

King Leopold's Soliloquy

1968 Leopold O No Dokuhaku, Tokyo: Rironsha.

Life on the Mississippi

1960 Mississippi No Hitobito, Tokyo: Kagaminra.

1962 Mississippi No Boken, Tokyo: Iwasaki.

Man That Corrupted Hadleyburg

1959 [Man That Corrupted Hadleyburg]. In Mark Twain Tanpen Zenshu [The Complete Short Stories of Mark Twain, ed. Charles Neider]. Tokyo: Kyoho.

Mysterious Stranger

1969 Fushigina Shonen, Tokyo: Iwanami.

Prince and the Pauper

1899 [The Prince and the Pauper], n.d.: n.pub.

1950 Oji To Kojiki, Tokyo: Iwanami.

1952 Same. Tokyo: Kadokawa.

1954 Same. Tokyo: Shincho-sha.

1958 Same. Tokyo: Iwanami.

1965 Same. Tokyo: Kodausha.

1965 Same. Tokyo: Shogakukan.

1966 Same. Tokyo: Kodausha.

1967 Tom Sawyer No Boken. Oji To Kojiki, Tokyo: Kodausha.

1970 Oji To Kojiki, Tokyo: Kadokawa.

1975 Same. Tokyo: Gakushu Kenkyu.

1976 Same. Tokyo: Tamagawadaigaku.

Roughing It

1969 Seibu Ryoko Kidan, Tokyo: Chikuma.

Stories and Sketches

1877? 1601. [privately printed]

1903 [Three Mark Twain stories in Western Strange Stories], n.p.:
      Hoichian Hara.

1907 [Adam's Diary], n.p.: Kyushiro Honma.

1912? [The £1,000,000 Bank Note in Humorous Stories in Various Countries],
       n.p.: n.pub.

1916 [Stories and anecdotes in Ten Humorous Stories], n.p.: Kuni
      Sasaki.

1926 [Stories, tales, anecdotes, and humorous lectures, in Witty Stories
      That Let the World Laugh], n.p.: Rinnosuke Kagaya.

1952 Eve No Nikki [Eve's Diary, etc.], Tokyo: Iwanami.

1955 Kimyona Keiken [A Curious Experience]. Sekai Taishu Shosetsu
      Zenshu, 3. Tokyo: Oyama.

1959 Mark Twain Tanpen Zenshu [The Complete Short Stories of Mark Twain,
      ed. Charles Neider]. [5 vols.] Tokyo: Kyoho.

1960 Calaveras Gun No Nadakaki Tobi-Gaeru [Celebrated Jumping Frog of
      Calaveras County, etc.], Tokyo: Nan'un-do.

1965 ...Hanegaeru [Celebrated Jumping Frog of Calaveras County, etc.].
      Shonen Shojo Sekai No Meisaku Bungaku, 12. Tokyo: Shogakukan.

1976 Adamu to Ibu No Nikki [Adam and Eve's Diary], Tokyo: Obunsha.

Tom Sawyer

1950 Tom Sawyer No Boken [Adventures of Tom Sawyer], Tokyo: Iwanami.

1951 Same. Tokyo: Mikasa.

1952 Same. Tokyo: Iwanami.

1952 Same. Tokyo: Mikasa.

1953 Same. Tokyo: Shincho-sha.

1964 Same. Tokyo: Kadokawa.

1965 Same. Tokyo: Shogakukan.

1966 Tom Sawyer No Boken. Huckleberry Finn No Boken, Tokyo: Kawade.

1967 Tom Sawyer No Boken, Tokyo: Kaiseisha.

1967 Tom Sawyer No Boken. Oji To Kojiki, Tokyo: Kodausha.

1968 Tom Sawyer No Boken, Tokyo: Shogakukan.

1971 Tomu-Soya No Boken, Tokyo: Bunken Shuppan.

1974 Tom Sawyer No Boken. Junia-ban Sekai no Bungaku, 6. Tokyo:
Shueisha.

1975 Same. Tokyo: Fukuin-kan.

1975 Same. Tokyo: Gakushu Kenkyu.

1976 Same. Tokyo: Jitsugyo no Nihonsha.

1976 Same. Tokyo: Kaiseisha.

Tom Sawyer Abroad

1955 Tom Sawyer No Tantei, Tanken [Tom Sawyer, Detective. Tom Sawyer
Abroad], Tokyo: Shincho-sha.

1962 Tom Sawyer No Kuchu Ryoko [Tom Sawyer Abroad], Tokyo: Iwasaki.

Tom Sawyer, Detective

1955 Tom Sawyer No Tantei, Tanken [Tom Sawyer, Detective. Tom Sawyer
Abroad], Tokyo: Shincho-sha.

1962 Tom Sawyer No Meitautei [Tom Sawyer Detective], Tokyo: Iwasaki.

1976 Meitantei Tom Sawyer [Detective Tom Sawyer], Tokyo: Jitsugyo
no Nihonsha.

What Is Man?

1973 Ningen Towa Nanika [What Is Man], Tokyo: Iwanami.

Selections

1975 Jigoku no Pen [A Pen Warmed-up in Hell]. [Ed. Frederick Anderson]
Tokyo: Heibou.

Korea

Sources: IT

1960   Tomsoya Eui Moheom [Adventures of Tom Sawyer], Seoul: Gyemongsa.

1962   Wangjawa Geogi [The Prince and the Pauper], Seoul: Jeongilchulpansa.

1967   Huckle Berry-eui Moheom [Adventures of Huckleberry Finn], Seoul:
       Seongmunsa.

1967   Tom Sawyer-eui Gongjung Yeohyaeng [Adventures of Tom Sawyer],
       Seoul: Seongmunsa.

1972   Tomsoyeolui Moheom [Adventures of Tom Sawyer], Seoul: Beourhan.

What Is Man?

1974   In-ganiran Mu-conya [What Is Man], Seoul: Yugmunsa.

Taiwan

Sources: HKL/IT

Huckleberry Finn

1957   The Adventures of Huckleberry Finn [translated title], Taipei:
       The Great China Book Co.

Innocents Abroad

1959   Sha Tzu Lu Hsing Chi [The Innocents Abroad], Taipei: Wen Hua Book
       Co.

Prince and the Pauper

1963   Ch'i Kai Wang Tzu [Prince and the Pauper], Taipei: Kuo Yii Book
       Co.

1974   Ch'i Kai Yu Wang Tsu [Prince and the Pauper], Taipei: Ch'iao Lien
       Tung Fang Book Co.

Stories and Sketches

1959   Selections of the American Short Story [translated title]. [2 vols.]
       Taipei: Shang Wu Press.

Tom Sawyer

1953   T'ang Mu Li Hsien Chi [The Adventures of Tom Sawyer], Taipei: Cheng
       Chung Book Co.

1957   T'ang Mu Sha Ya [The Adventures of Tom Sawyer], Taipei: The Ch'i
       Ming Book Co.

1957 T'ang Mu Li Hsien Chi, Taipei: The Great China Book Co.

1957 Same. Taipei: Hsin Lu Book Co.

1964 Same. Taipei: Wu Chou Public Service.

1964 Same. Taipei: Wen Yuan Book Co.

1965 Same. Taipei: Hsin Ya Public Service.

1967 Same. [2nd edition] Taipei: Wen Yuan Book Co.

1967 Same. Taipei: Fu Han Press.

Selections

1965 Tang Tai Wen Hseuh Ming Chu, Taipei: Hsin Lu Book Co.

Addendum

UNIDENTIFIED SUBSEQUENT EDITIONS

Many foreign publications of Mark Twain's writings reappeared
as new editions or reprints following their original publication.
Many of these subsequent issues have been omitted from the preceding Provisional Bibliography for lack of identifying dates in
the bibliographical sources. However, at least 488 such issues
can be extrapolated from information available in the Bibliography.
These undated subsequent editions, running as high as 141 in Germany alone, if added to those already fully identified, bring Mark
Twain's international editions to a total of over 5,600 published
during the 110 years following Twain's literary emergence in 1867.
Any attempt to make a "final" estimate of his proliferation during
those decades would be conjectural, but the publishing record
speaks for itself. The following addendum indicates the undated
subsequent issues of various editions listed in the Bibliography.

Great Britain

English As She Is Spoke; or, A Jest in Sober Earnest. The Vellum-
    parchment Shilling Series of Miscellaneous Literature no. 1. London:
    Field & Tuer. 1st-3rd eds.

Denmark

Huck Finn, Kobenhavn: Ungdommens. 2nd-5th eds.

Nye Skitser, Kjobenhavn: Nyt Dansk Forlagskonsortium. 1st ed.

France

Le Pretendant Americain, Roman, Paris: Mercure de France. 1st, 2nd
    eds.

Le Prince et le Pauvre, Paris: Gedalge. 2nd, 3rd eds.

Un Pari de Milliardaires et Autres Nouvelles, Paris: Mercure de France.
    1st-3rd eds.

Le Legs de 30.000 Dollars, et Autres Contes, Paris: Mercure de France.
    2nd-4th,6th, 7th eds.

Les Peterkins, et Autres Contes, Paris: Mercure de France. 1st-12th eds.

Plus Fort que Sherlock Holmes, Paris: Mercure de France. 3rd-13th eds.

Exploits de Tom Sawyer, Detective, et Autres Nouvelles, Paris: Mercure
    de France. 2nd-10th eds.

Germany

Huck Finns Fahrten und Abenteuer, Stuttgart: Lutz. 2nd-5th eds.

Die Abenteuer des Huckleberry Finn, Munchen: Droemer/Knaur. 2nd-6th eds.

Die Abenteuer des Huckleberry Finn, Ravensburg: Maier. 1st, 3rd eds.

Huckleberry Finn, Reutlingen: Ensslin & Laiblin. 1st-12th, 14th-19th
    eds.

Prince und Bettelknabe, Stuttgart: Loewes. 2nd, 5th, 7th-11th eds.

Der Prinz und der Bettlerknabe, Berlin: Kinderbuchverlegen. 1st, 3rd-
    5th eds.

Prinz und Betteljunge, Ravensburg: Maier. 2nd, 4th eds.

The Death-Disk, Frankfurt: Diesterweg. 2nd-4th eds.

Die Besten Geschichten, Bremen: Schunemann. 2nd ed.

Ein Geheimnisvoller Besuch: Skizzen, Leipzig: Reclam. 1st-4th eds.

Heitere Geschichten, Herrenalb/Schwarzwald: 1st ed.

Sechs Erstaunliche Kurzgeschichten, Munchen: Langewiesche-Brandt. 2nd-
    3rd eds.

Das Tagebuch von Adam und Eva und Andere Geschichten, Weimar: Kiepenheuer.
    1st ed.

Tom Sawyer und Huckleberry Finn: Abenteuer am Mississippi, Reutlingen: Ensslin & Laiblin. 2nd-13th eds.

Tom Sawyers Abenteuer und Streiche, Stuttgart: Lutz. 2nd, 3rd, 6th eds.

Tom Sawyers Abenteuer und Streiche, Berlin: Aufbau. 5th, 6th, 8th eds.

The Adventures of Tom Sawyer Simplified, Hamburg: Westermann. 2nd ed.

Die Abenteuer des Tom Sawyer, Munchen, Zurich: Droemer/Knaur. 3rd-7th eds.

Tom Sawyers Abenteuer, Berlin und Weimar: Aufbau. 1st ed.

Tom Sawyers Abenteuer, Ravensburg: Maier. 1st-2nd eds.

Tom Sawyers Abenteuer, Berlin: Neues Leben. 3rd-8th eds.

Tom Sawyers Abenteuer, Leipzig: Reclam. 1st-2nd eds.

Tom Sawyer, Reutlingen: Ensslin & Laiblin. 1st-11th eds.

Tom Sawyers Abenteuer: Eine Mississipi-Erzahlung, Reutlingen: Ensslin & Laiblin. 2nd-21st eds.

Tom, der Kleine Detektiv. Nebst Zwei Erzahlungen von Bret Harte, Stutgart: Lutz. 6th ed.

Tom Sawyer, der Detektiv. [extracts] Berlin: Holz. 1st-4th, 6th-7th eds.

Mark Twain Bummelt durch Europa, Munchen: Deutscher Taschenbuch. 2nd ed.

Italy

Un Americano alla Corte di Re Artu, Milano: Rizzoli. 1st-5th eds.

Il Principe e Il Mendico, Firenze: Bemporad-Marzocco. 2nd-5th eds.

Wilson Lo Zuccone, Milano: Rizzoli. 1st-13th eds.

Le Avventure di Tom Sawyer, Firenze: Marzocco. 1st-3rd, 5th-17th eds.

Il Ranocchio Saltatore, Milano: Rizzoli. 1st-7th eds.

Tom Sawyer Poliziotto, e Il Biglietto da Venticinque Milioni di Lire, Firenze: Marzocco. 1st ed.

Netherlands

De Lotgevallen van Huckleberry Finn, Amsterdam: Van Holkema & Warendorf. 3rd-5th eds.

De Lotgevallen van Huckleberry Finn, Haarlem: De Sleutel. 1st ed.

Prins en Bedelknaap, Amsterdam: Van Holkema & Warendorf. 1st ed.

Prins en Bedelknaap, n.p.: Zie Kameraad (De Golde). 1st, 2nd eds.

De Lotgevallen van Tom Sawyer, Amsterdam: Van Holkema & Warendorf.
    1st-4th eds.

De Lotgevallen van Tom Sawyer, n.p.: Zie Kameraad (De Golde). 1st-5th
    eds.

De Avonturen van Tom Sawyer, 'S-Gravenhage: Kramers. 1st-11th eds.

Portugal

O Principe e O Pobre, Porto: Civilizacao. 4th-5th eds.

As Aventuras de Tom Sawyer, Lisboa: Portugalia. 2nd-4th eds.

Viagems de Tom Sawyer. Tom Sawyer, Detective, Lisboa: Portugalia.
    1st ed.

Tom Sawyer, Detective, Lisboa: Portugalia. 1st ed.

Spain

Un Yanqui en la Corte del Rey Artus, Barcelona: La Academica. 1st ed.

Aventuras de Huck Finn, Barcelona: Bruguera. 4th-5th eds.

Cuentos Escogidos, Madrid: Helencia. 1st ed.

Cuentos Escogidos, Madrid: Noticiero-Gui de Madrid. 1st ed.

Fragmentos del Diario de Adan y Diario de Eva, Madrid: Espasa-Calpe.
    1st, 2nd eds.

Nuevos Cuentos, Madrid: Espasa-Calpe. 2nd ed.

Un Reportaje Sensacional y Otros Cuentos, Madrid: Espasa-Calpe.
    1st-3rd eds.

Aventuras en el Far West, Barcelona: Bruguera. 5th ed.

Las Aventuras de Tom Sawyer, Barcelona: Selecta. 1st ed.

Las Aventuras de Tom Sawyer, Barcelona: AFHA. 1st-7th eds.

Aventuras de Tom Sawyer. Tom Sawyer, Detective. Tom Sawyer en el
    Extranjero, Madrid: Aguilar. 2nd, 5th eds.

Aventuras de Tom Sawyer, Barcelona: Bruguera. 1st ed.

Aventuras de Tom Sawyer, Madrid: Everest. 1st ed.

Aventuras de Tom Sawyer, Madrid: Aguilar. 1st-3rd eds.

Aventuras de Tom Sawyer. Coleccion Corinto. Barcelona: Bruguera.
    1st, 2nd eds.

Aventuras de Tom Sawyer, Madrid: Espasa-Calpe. 1st-5th eds.

Tom Sawyer, Detective, Tom Sawyer, en el Extranjero, Madrid: Espasa-Calpe.
    1st, 2nd eds.

Tom Sawyer Detective, Barcelona: Bruguera. 1st ed.

Sweden

En Yankee vid Kung Arturs Hov, Stockholm: Lindqvist. 1st ed.

Huckleberry Finns Aventyr, Stockholm: Lararetidning. 1st, 2nd eds.

Prisen och Tiggargossen, Stockholm: Svensk Lararetidning.   4th ed.

Tom Sawyer; en Skolpojhistoria, Stockholm: Geber. 3rd, 4th eds.

Tom Sawyer, Stockholm: Svensk Lararetidning. 3rd-5th eds.

Tom Sawyer som Detektiv, Stockholm: Svensk Lararetidning. 1st ed.

Switzerland

Die Abenteuer des Tom Sawyer, Munchen, Zurich: Droemer/Knaur. 1st-6th
    eds.

Bulgaria

Edin Janki v Dvora na Kral Artur, Sofija: Kultura. 1st ed.

Tom Sojer. Hakalberi Fin, Sofija: Mladez. 1st-3rd eds.

Czechoslovakia

Yankee z Connecticutu na Dvore Krale Artuse, Praha: Prace. 1st-4th
    eds. [Bohemian]

Dobrodruzstvi Huckleberryho Fina. Praha: Albatros. 1st-5th eds.

Dobrodruzstvi Huckleberryho Finna, Praha: SNKLHU. 1st ed.

Dobrodruzstvi Huckleberryho Finna, Bratislava: Mlade Leta. 1st ed.

Dobrodruzstvi Huckleberryho Finna, Praha: Mlada Fronta. 1st-4th eds.

Huckleberry Finn Kalandjai, Bratislava: Madach. [Magyar.] 1st-5th eds.

Dobrodruzstvi Toma Sawyera. Dobrodruzstvi Huckleberryho Finna, Praha:
    Odeon. 1st-3rd eds.

Zivot na Mississippi, Praha: SNDK. 1st ed.

Panna ve Zbroji, Praha: Lidova Demokracie. 1st ed.

Tom Sawyer a Jeho Dobrodruzstva, Bratislava: Mlade Leta. [Slovak]
    4th-5th eds.

Dobrodruzstvi Tom Sawyera, Praha: SNDK. 3rd ed.

Tom Sawyer Kalandjai, Bratislava: Konyvkiado. [Magyar] 1st-7th eds.

Tom Sawyer Kalandjai, Bratislava: Madach. [Magyar] 1st-5th eds.

Dobrodruzstvi Toma Sawyera, Praha: Mlade Fronta. 1st-6th eds.

Dobrodruzstvi Toma Sawyera, Praha: Albatros. 1st-5th eds.

Finland

Huckleberry Finnin Seikkailut, Porvoo, Helsinki: Soderstrom. 5th,
    7th eds.

Tom Sawyerin Seikkailut, Porvoo: Soderstrom. 3rd, 7th, 11th eds.

Tom Sawyer Solapoliisina, Hameenlinna: Valkeila. 1st ed.

Tom Sawyer Solapoliisina, Hameenlinna: Karisto, 2nd ed.

Tom Sawyer Vierailla Mailla, Hameenlinna: Karisto. 1st ed.

Hungary

Huckleberry Finn Kalandjai, Budapest: Mora. 1st-5th eds.

Koldus es Kiralyfi, Budapest: Revai. 1st ed.

Az Ostoba Wilson, Budapest: Legrady. 2nd, 3rd eds.

Az 1,000,000 Fontos Banko e Mas Novellak, Budapest: Athenaeum. 1st ed.

Embertelen Vilag. 14 Amerikai Elbeszeles, Budapest: Athenaeum. 1st ed.

Tom Sawyer Kalandjai, Budapest: Mora. 3rd-5th eds.

Tom Sawyer Kalandjai, Budapest: Europa. 1st-7th eds.

Poland

Przygody Tomka Sawyera, Warszawa: Iskry. 1st-4th eds.

Romania

Aventurile lui Tom Sawyer; Aventurile lui Huckleberry Finn, Bucuresti:
   Editura de Stat Pentru Literatura si Arta. 1st ed.

Aventurile lui Tom Sawyer, Bucuresti: Editura Tineretului. 1st ed.

Yugoslavia

Dozivljaji Haklberi Fina, Sarajevo: Veselin Maslesa. [Serbian] 2nd ed.

Pustolovine Toma Sawyera, Zagreb: Mladost. [Serbo-Croatian] 3rd ed.

Russia

Prints i Nishchi, St. Petersburg, Moskva: n.pub. 1st, 2nd eds.

Prints i Nishchi, Moskva: Goslitizdat Ucheb.-pedagog. izd-vo. 1st,
   2nd eds.

Princ ham Telance, Kazan [Tatar SSR]: Tatknigoizdat. [Tatar] 1st ed.

Argentina

Aventuras de Huck, Buenos Aires: Acme. 2nd, 6th, 7th eds.

Aventuras de Huck Finn, Buenos Aires: Atlantida. 2nd ed.

Principe y Mendigo, Buenos Aires: Acme. 2nd, 3rd eds.

El Hombre que Corrompio a Una Ciudad, Buenos Aires: Espasa-Calpe. 1st
   ed.

Un Reportaje Sensacional y Otros Cuentos, Buenos Aires: Espasa-Calpe.
   1st-2nd eds.

Aventuras de Tom Sawyer, Buenos Aires: Acme. 2nd ed.

Aventuras de Tom Sawyer, Buenos Aires: Atlantida. 4th, 7th-10th eds.

Las Aventuras de Tom Sawyer, Buenos Aires: Losada. 4th ed.

Las Aventuras de Tom Sawyer, Buenos Aires: Peuser. 3rd, 4th eds.

Tom Sawyer en el Extranjero, Buenos Aires: Acme. 6th, 7th eds.

Brazil

Aventuras de Huck, Sao Paulo: Brasiliense. 3rd, 6th eds.

O Principe e O Pobre, Sao Paulo: Brasiliense. 2nd ed.

Aventuras de Tom Sawyer, Sao Paulo: Brasiliense. 4th-6th eds.

Aventuras de Tom Sawyer no Estranjeiro, Romance, Rio de Janeiro: Vecchi.
    2nd ed.

Tom Sawyer, Detective; Romance, Rio de Janeiro: Vecchi. 2nd ed.

Mexico

Principe y Mendigo, Mexico: Diana. 1st-4th eds.

Las Aventuras de Tom Sawyer, Mexico: Novaro-Mexico. 1st, 2nd eds.

Aventuras de Tom Sawyer, Mexico: Diana. 2nd-4th eds.

Iran

Sahzada O Geda, Tehran: Pocket Books. 1st, 2nd eds.

Turkey

Calinan Tac, Istanbul: Duran Ofset. 1st ed.

Pakistan

Mark Twain in India, Karachi: Indisier. 1st ed.

The Prince and the Pauper, Dacca: Book Promotion. 1st ed.

Indonesia

Tom Sawyer, Anak Amerika, oleh Mark Twain, Djakarta: Balai Pustaka.
      2nd ed.

ADDITIONAL CHINESE
TRANSLATIONS

Sources: CABCT, NUC

In the search for Far Eastern publications of Mark Twain, Chinese-
language editions have been elusive due to the lack of bibliographical sources covering such editions and lack of reporting to the
Index Translationum from Hong Kong and Mainland China. In 1972
the first inclusive, although not exhaustive, source became available through the efforts of Donald Murray, Chan Wai-Hueng, and
Samuel Huang in "A Checklist of American Books in Chinese Translation," American Book Collector (Chicago), XXII (March-April 1972).
The following items, when combined with those in the preceding
Provisional Bibliography, provide a more comprehensive coverage of
Chinese translations of various Mark Twain works.

Singapore

1952 [A Record of the Adventures of A Mischievous Youth (The Adventures
      of Tom Sawyer)], Singapore: Nan-Yang.

China

1956 [The Gilded Age], Shanghai: Wen-I Lien-Ho.

1947 [A Playful Boy's Adventures (The Adventures of Huckleberry Finn)],
      Shanghai: Kuang-Ming.

1954 [The Adventures of Huckleberry Finn], Shanghai: Wen-I Lien-Ho.

1955 [On the Mississippi River (Life on the Mississippi)], Shanghai:
      Hsin-Wen-I.

1953 [The Man Who Ruined Hadleyburg (The Man That Corrupted Hadleyburg)],
      Shanghai: Hsin-Wen-I.

1957 [Stupid Wilson (Pudd'nhead Wilson)], Shanghai: Hsin-Wen-I.

n.d. Yu-Mo Hsiao-Shuo-Chi [Collected Humorous Stories], Shanghai:
      Chung-Hua Bookstore.

1960 Chung-Tuan-Pien Hsiao-Shuo Hsuan [Selected Medium-Short Stories],
      Peking: Jen-Min Wen-Hsuch.

n.d. [The Adventures of Tom Sawyer], Shanghai: Shih-Chieh.

1955 [The Adventures of Tom Sawyer], Peking: Jen-Min Wen-Hsueh.

1955   [The Record of Tom Sawyer Abroad (Tom Sawyer Abroad)], Shanghai:
       Shanghai Bookstore.

1955   [The Cases of the Detective Tom Sawyer (Tom Sawyer, Detective)],
       Shanghai: Shanghai Bookstore.

1961   Ma-K'e-T'u-Wen [Mark Twain]. [Selections] Shanghai: Shanghai
       Bookstore.

Hong Kong

1968   [A Record of the Wanderings of Huckleberry Finn (The Adventures of
       Huckleberry Finn)], Hong Kong: Hui-T'ung Bookstore.

1956   Ma-k'e-T'u-Wen Tuan-P'ien Hsiao-Shuo-Chi [Collected Short Stories
       of Mark Twain], Hong Kong: Sheng-Huo Bookstore.

1960   [The Cases of the Detective Tom Sawyer (Tom Sawyer, Detective)],
       Hong Kong: Jih Hsin.

1958   Ma-k'e-T'u-Wen Hsilan Chi [Collected Selections from Mark Twain],
       Hong Kong: Wen-Hsueh.

Taiwan

1969   [The Autobiography of Mark Twain], Taipei: Sh-i-Niu.

1969   Ma-k'e-T'u-Wen Min Tso-'in-Hsuan [Selections from the Famous Works
       of Mark Twain], Taipei: Cheng-Wen.

Unidentified

1950   [On the Mississippi River (Life on the Mississippi)], n.p.:   Ch'en-
       Kuang.

1950   [The Beggar and Emperor (The Prince and the Pauper)], n.p.:   Shen-
       Chou Kuo-kuang.

1956   Wang tzu yu p'in erh [The Prince and the Pauper], n.p.: n.pub.

1975   Sha kua Wei-erh-hsun [Pudd'nhead Wilson], n.p.: n.pub.

n.d.   [The Private Life of Adam and Eve; Being Extracts from Their
       Diaries], n.p.: Hu-Feng.

1950   [The Adventures of Tom Sawyer], n.p.: Kuang-Ming.

Tables

Any comprehensive estimate of a writer's international success would need to take into account at least the following factors: the writer's literary merits and defects; appraisals and reappraisals of his works by critics both at home and abroad; shifts in readers' interests over a considerable period of time; mass consumption of the writer's work by an international audience; and the writer's worldwide popularity relative to that of other writers. Literary merits and defects can be readily identified by discriminating readers; professional criticism, however variable, can be resolved into something of a consensus; and readers' interests can be explained by the popular tastes of a particular era. Reading interests and even literary criticism, however, are highly subjective factors and for that reason are difficult to measure. The few dimensions of literary success that can be objectified are the scope of a writer's audience, the frequency of his publication, and his comparative popularity. Publication output and popularity do not, by themselves, produce a total - and certainly not a "final" - estimate of the writer's literary success, but these objective factors can give added dimensions and meaningful perspective to the estimate.

The following tables offer publishing data from which the reader can draw his own conclusions regarding Mark Twain's stature and the degree of his impact on world-wide audiences. Table 1 provides summary information about the total output of Twain's major works in the United States and abroad from 1867 through 1976. Table 2 indicates the proliferation of his international editions during the eleven decades following his first American appearance. Table 3 details the comparative numbers of editions of his various works among fifty-five countries during the same period. Tables 4 and 5 offer a comparison of his international popularity with that of other leading American writers during the middle decades of the 20th Century. All data in Tables 1-3 are extracted from the preceding Provisional Bibliography. Data in Tables 4-5 are derived from two comprehensive sources: the Cumulative Book Index and the international Index Translationum. The Provisional Bibliography extends the American record to 1980, but the tables terminate with 1976 because of the lack of comprehensive source information about foreign translations beyond the latter date.

TABLE 1

Mark Twain's International Editions, 1867-1976

Summary Data

Short Title	Total International Editions	Domestic Editions	Foreign Editions	First Domestic Edition	First Foreign Language Edition	First Foreign Language Translation(s)	Total Countries	Total Languages
American Claimant	43	15	28	1892	1892	German, Swedish	15	12
Autobiography	18	6	12	1924	1907	Dutch	12	9
Captain Stormfield	27	6	21	1907	1909	French	10	12
Christian Science	7	6	1	1907	—	None	2	1
Connecticut Yankee	200	45	155	1889	1890	Danish, Swedish	27	22
Essays	18	18	0	1897	—	None	1	1
Following Equator	26	9	17	1897	1898	Swedish	7	5
Gilded Age	61	37	24	1873	1874	Russian	12	11
Huckleberry Finn	841	145	696	1884	1885	Danish, Dutch, Swedish	47	53
Innocents Abroad	144	51	93	1869	1875	German	21	16
Joan of Arc	52	18	34	1896	1897	Dutch, Russian	13	13
King Leopold	11	3	8	1905	1960	Italian	8	7
Letters	31	26	5	1917-	—	None	3	1
Letters from Earth	18	3	15	1962	1963	Finnish, Russian	11	13
Life on Mississippi	139	54	85	1883	1883	Danish, Swedish	27	24
Man That Corrupted	44	19	25	1900	1900	German	14	11
Mysterious Stranger	28	14	14	1916	1921	German	11	9

Short Title	Total International Editions	Domestic Editions	Foreign Editions	First Domestic Edition	First Foreign Language Edition	First Foreign Language Translation(s)	Total Countries	Total Languages
Notebook	6	6	0	1935	—	None	1	1
Prince and Pauper	551	70	481	1881	1882	Danish, Dutch	44	49
Pudd'nhead Wilson	94	33	61	1894	1898	German	19	13
Report from Paradise	10	1	9	1952	1953	Italian	5	6
Roughing It	102	43	59	1872	1874	German, Swedish	17	14
Speeches	3	3	0	1910	—	None	1	1
Stories and Sketches	921	177	744	1866	1874	Danish, German, Swedish	40	43
Tom Sawyer	1291	155	1136	1876	1876	French, German	46	57
Tom Sawyer Abroad	130	26	104	1894	1894	Dutch, Swedish	23	19
Tom Sawyer, Detective	188	19	169	1896	1896	Swedish	25	20
Tom Sawyer extracts	10	0	10	—	1906	German	1	1
Tramp Abroad	66	13	53	1879	1880	Danish	10	6
Travel sketches	34	16	18	1910	1900	German	9	4
What Is Man?	9	3	6	1917	1946	Spanish	5	2
Miscellaneous	116	80	36	1870	1898	Romanian	15	12
Selections	105	49	56	1873	1875	Danish	16	10
Total single eds.	5344	1169	4175	1866	1874		55	73
Total collected eds.	64	32	32	1891	1892	German	9	6

TABLE 2

Mark Twain's International Editions, 1867-1976 by Titles and Decades

Short Title	Year First Publication	Total International Editions	1867-1869	1870	1880	1890	1900	1910	1920	1930	1940	1950	1960	1970-1976	Un-dated	Unidentified
Stories and Sketches	1866-	921	6	48	52	59	85	61	79	61	89	101	127	68	9	76
Innocents Abroad	1869	144	3	39	20	14	11	8	15	5	5	7	14	3	0	0
Selections	1869-	105	1	14	4	5	3	4	4	10	6	9	27	18	0	0
Miscellaneous	1870-	116	-	2	8	7	15	8	9	6	13	3	21	24	0	0
Roughing It	1872	102	-	15	12	10	12	4	4	1	8	10	12	12	1	1
Gilded Age	1873	61	-	19	7	6	5	3	5	1	1	4	9	1	0	0
Life on Mississippi	1876,1883	139	-	9	12	8	11	14	5	9	11	12	37	8	2	1
Tom Sawyer	1876	1291	-	16	11	14	22	23	56	99	126	231	289	190	6	208
Travel sketches	1878-	34	-	3	2	0	0	1	1	5	4	7	7	4	0	0
Tramp Abroad	1879	66	-	2	28	7	7	3	2	0	0	1	11	3	1	1
Prince and Pauper	1881	551	-	-	26	21	30	20	23	32	43	122	133	57	2	42
Huckleberry Finn	1884	841	-	-	17	14	17	19	31	50	89	171	215	126	2	90
Connecticut Yankee	1889	200	-	-	4	11	7	8	9	4	25	46	33	41	0	12
American Claimant	1892	43	-	-	-	13	6	4	4	1	3	4	5	1	0	2
Pudd'nhead Wilson	1894	94	-	-	-	10	11	7	8	4	3	12	20	3	1	15
Tom Sawyer Abroad	1894	130	-	-	-	9	9	8	7	9	11	22	23	21	2	9
Tom Sawyer, Detective	1896	188	-	-	-	8	15	9	13	8	6	37	32	31	1	28
Joan of Arc	1896	52	-	-	-	10	8	9	4	0	4	9	5	2	0	1

266

Short Title	Year First Publication	Total International Editions	1867-1869	1870	1880	1890	1900	1910	1920	1930	1940	1950	1960	1970-1976	Un-dated	Unidentified
Essays	1897	18	-	-	-	3	6	5	1	1	0	0	1	1	0	0
Following Equator	1897	26	-	-	-	7	3	2	3	1	2	0	2	3	2	1
Man That Corrupted	1900	44	-	-	-	-	9	4	4	4	2	8	8	4	0	1
King Leopold	1905	11	-	-	-	-	3	0	0	0	0	0	7	1	0	0
What Is Man?	1906	9	-	-	-	-	1	3	0	0	1	0	0	3	0	0
Tom Sawyer extracts	1906-	10	-	-	-	-	3	1	0	1	3	1	0	2	0	0
Autobiography	1907	18	-	-	-	-	1	0	2	0	1	1	11	1	0	0
Captain Stormfield	1907	27	-	-	-	-	3	2	3	1	5	6	3	1	0	0
Christian Science	1907	7	-	-	-	-	4	3	0	4	0	0	0	0	0	0
Speeches	1910	3	-	-	-	-	-	1	1	0	0	0	0	1	0	0
Mysterious Stranger	1916	28	-	-	-	-	-	1	2	4	3	5	10	2	1	0
Letters	1917-	31	-	-	-	-	-	1	2	2	4	2	14	6	0	0
Notebook	1935	6	-	-	-	-	-	-	-	2	0	0	1	3	0	0
Report from Paradise	1952	10	-	-	-	-	-	-	-	-	-	8	1	1	0	0
Letters from Earth	1962	18	-	-	-	-	-	-	-	-	-	-	15	3	0	0
Total single eds.	1866-	5344	10	167	203	236	307	236	297	325	468	839	1093	645	30	488
Total collected eds.	1891	64	-	-	15	6	6	8	8	1	5	6	8	7	0	0

TABLE 3

Mark Twain's International Editions, 1867-1976, by Title and Countries

Short Title	Total	USA	Aus	Can	G.B.	N.Z.	Aust	Belg	Den
American Claimant	43	15			1				1
Autobiography	18	6			1				
Captain Stormfield	27	6						1	
Christian Science	7	6							
Connecticut Yankee	200	45		2	11		3	1	2
Essays	18	18							
Following the Equator	26	9			7				
Gilded Age	61	37	1		10				1
Huckleberry Finn	841	145	3	5	63	1	14	5	16
Innocents Abroad	144	51	3	7	46		2		3
Joan of Arc	52	18		1	6				
King Leopold	11	3			1				
Letters	31	26	1		4				
Letters from Earth	18	3							
Life on Mississippi	139	54	1	5	18		2	1	2
Man That Corrupted	44	19			3				
Mysterious Stranger	28	14							
Notebook	6	6							
Prince and Pauper	551	70		7	19		4	2	2
Pudd'nhead Wilson	94	33		1	7				2
Report from Paradise	10	1							2
Roughing It	102	43	2	5	11				
Speeches	3	3							
Stories and Sketches	921	177	1	12	87		3	4	41
Tom Sawyer	1291	155		12	69	1	14	15	21
Tom Sawyer Abroad	130	26			3		1		1
Tom Sawyer, Detective	188	19			6			5	3
Tom Sawyer extracts	10								
Tramp Abroad	66	13	1	8	18		1		5
Travel sketches	34	16	1	3	3				
What Is Man?	9	3			3				
Miscellaneous	116	80		4	10		1		
Selections	105	49			21				4
Unidentified eds.	(488)				3				5
Total single eds.	5344	1169	14	72	431	2	45	34	111
Total collected eds.	64	32			3				

268

TABLE 3 CONTINUED

Short Title	Fr	Ger	Icel	Ital	Neth	Norw	Port	Sp	Swed	Swtz
American Claimant	2	2			5		2	2	2	1
Autobiography		1		1	1					1
Captain Stormfield	1	3		2				1		1
Christian Science		1								
Connecticut Yankee	2	20		10			1	21	4	
Essays										
Following the Equator		2							2	
Gilded Age		1		2					2	
Huckleberry Finn	25	96		26	12	10	3	32	36	11
Innocents Abroad		8		2	2	1		5	1	
Joan of Arc		2			1	1		7	3	
King Leopold		2		1	1					
Letters										
Letters from Earth	1	1	1	1					1	
Life on Mississippi	2	12		2				1	5	
Man That Corrupted		2		1		1		4		
Mysterious Stranger		2		1				1		
Notebook										
Prince and Pauper	29	41		53	11	7	6	31	12	4
Pudd'nhead Wilson	1	11		2		1		2	6	1
Report from Paradise				3						
Roughing It	3	9		1	1		1	13	2	
Speeches										
Stories and Sketches	49	104	3	33	10	2	3	62	35	17
Tom Sawyer	45	124	1	66	31	11	4	78	47	13
Tom Sawyer Abroad	1	9	1	6	3		2	21	12	
Tom Sawyer, Detective	9	20		9	1		2	36	11	
Tom Sawyer extracts		10								
Tramp Abroad		15			2				1	
Travel sketches		1		2	1					6
What Is Man?								1		
Miscellaneous		2			2				1	
Selections		3		1	1	1		1	2	
Unidentified eds.	53	140		47	27		8	43	10	6
Total single eds.	223	644	6	272	112	35	32	362	195	61
Total collected eds.		15					1	3		1

TABLE 3 CONTINUED

Short Title	Alb	Bulg	Czch	Fin	Grc	Hung	Pol	Rom	Yugo	Russ
American Claimant			2			1		3		1
Autobiography		1				1			1	2
Captain Stormfield						1	2			9
Christian Science										
Connecticut Yankee	1	2	8	4	1	2	3	4	3	14
Essays										
Following the Equator						1				
Gilded Age			1			2				2
Huckleberry Finn	2	4	20	16	3	14	13	8	25	53
Innocents Abroad			2	1		1			1	3
Joan of Arc			3	2		1				5
King Leopold		1						1		
Letters										
Letters from Earth		2	1	2			1			4
Life on Mississippi		1	5	5	1	2	1	1	3	3
Man That Corrupted						3	1	2	1	3
Mysterious Stranger			2			1			2	
Notebook										
Prince and Pauper	1	4	6	7	3	10	19	11	23	47
Pudd'nhead Wilson				2		4			1	1
Report from Paradise				1						3
Roughing It			1	2			2		2	
Speeches										
Stories and Sketches	1	2	8	2		16	19	19	18	54
Tom Sawyer		4	24	18	4	14	18	10	51	83
Tom Sawyer Abroad			2	4		3		1	1	3
Tom Sawyer, Detective			5	7	1	5		1	3	3
Tom Sawyer extracts										
Tramp Abroad										
Travel Sketches						1				
What Is Man?										
Miscellaneous		1		1		1		4	2	5
Selections		1				1				14
Unidentified eds.		7	54	8		20	4	3	2	5
Total single eds.	5	30	144	82	13	105	83	68	139	317
Total collected eds.								1		6

TABLE 3 CONTINUED

Short Title	Arg	Braz	Chil	Col	Cuba	Mex	Peru	Uru	Egy	Mor
American Claimant		1								
Autobiography		1								
Captain Stormfield										
Christian Science										
Connecticut Yankee	8	7				1				
Essays										
Following the Equator										
Gilded Age						1				
Huckleberry Finn	21	14	1	1	1	4			1	
Innocents Abroad	1									
Joan of Arc										
King Leopold										
Letters										
Letters from Earth										
Life on Mississippi	2									
Man That Corrupted	1						1			
Mysterious Stranger	1		2							
Notebook										
Prince and Pauper	12	14	2		1	4			2	
Pudd'nhead Wilson	1	1				1				
Report from Paradise										
Roughing It										
Speeches										
Stories and Sketches	16	4	4	2		6		2	2	
Tom Sawyer	31	16	1		1	10			2	1
Tom Sawyer Abroad	10	5				3				
Tom Sawyer, Detective	3	4				1				
Tom Sawyer extracts										
Tramp Abroad						1				
Travel sketches										
What Is Man?										
Miscellaneous				1						
Selections						2				
Unidentified eds.	20	8				9				
Total single eds.	127	75	10	4	3	43	1	2	7	1
Total collected eds.	2									

TABLE 3 CONTINUED

Short Title	SAfr	Iran	Isr	Turk	Cey	Ind	Pak	Bur	Indo	Mal
American Claimant										
Autobiography										
Captain Stormfield										
Christian Science										
Connecticut Yankee			2							
Essays										
Following Equator						2	2			
Gilded Age										
Huckleberry Finn	1	2	3	3		11			2	1
Innocents Abroad			1							
Joan of Arc										
King Leopold										
Letters										
Letters from Earth										
Life on Mississippi				1		4				
Man That Corrupted										
Mysterious Stranger				1						
Notebook										
Prince and Pauper		3	6	8		7	1	1		1
Pudd'nhead Wilson			1							
Report from Paradise										
Roughing It						2				
Speeches										
Stories and sketches			2	6					1	
Tom Sawyer	2	3	6	17	1	18			2	
Tom Sawyer Abroad			1							
Tom Sawyer, Detective	1		1			1				
Tom Sawyer extracts										
Tramp Abroad										
Travel Sketches										
What Is Man?										
Miscellaneous				1						
Selections										
Unidentified eds.		2		1			2		1	
Total single eds.	4	10	23	38	1	45	5	1	6	2
Total collected eds.										

TABLE 3 CONTINUED

Short Title	Phil	Thai	Chin	H.K.	Jap	Kor	Taiw	Unidentified
American Claimant								2
Autobiography					1			
Captain Stormfield								
Christian Science								
Connecticut Yankee					6			12
Essays								
Following Equator								1
Gilded Age			1					
Huckleberry Finn		1	2	5	14	1	1	90
Innocents Abroad					2		1	
Joan of Arc			1					1
King Leopold					1			
Letters								
Letters from Earth								
Life on Mississippi			1	1	2			1
Man That Corrupted					1			1
Mysterious Stranger					1			
Notebook								
Prince and Pauper		1	1	1	12	1	2	42
Pudd'nhead Wilson								15
Report from Paradise								
Roughing It					1			1
Speeches								
Stories and Sketches			3	2	12		1	76
Tom Sawyer	1		1	8	17	3	9	208
Tom Sawyer Abroad					2			9
Tom Sawyer, Detective					3			28
Tom Sawyer extracts								
Tramp Abroad								1
Travel sketches								
What Is Man?					1	1		
Miscellaneous								
Selections				2	1		1	
Unidentified eds.								
Total single eds.	1	2	10	19	77	6	15	
Total collected eds.								

TABLE 4

Comparative International Popularity of Mark Twain
and Other Leading American Writers
during the Mid-20th Century

Sources: CBI/IT

The following American writers, extracted from Table 5, were the
leading contenders for international favor during the middle decades
of the 20th Century, as indicated by editions of their writings published at home and abroad between 1931 and 1976. The war decade of
the 1940's is largely omitted from the tabulation owing to lack of
reporting by the Index Translationum during the period 1940-1947.

	Total Editions	Average per Year	Most Widely Published Work
Jack London	1978	52	The Call of the Wild
Mark Twain	1918	50	The Adventures of Tom Sawyer
Pearl Buck	1874	49	The Good Earth
Erle Stanley Gardner	1489	39	Detective novels
Ernest Hemingway	1417	37	A Farewell to Arms
John Steinbeck	1245	33	The Grapes of Wrath
Ellery Queen	1039	27	Detective novels
Zane Grey	954	25	Western novels
James Fenimore Cooper	931	24	The Last of the Mohicans
Edgar Allan Poe	807	21	Tales
Louisa May Alcott	763	20	Little Women
William Faulkner	725	19	Sanctuary
Edgar Rice Burroughs	691	18	Tarzan series
Herman Melville	574	15	Moby Dick
Vicki Baum	566	15	Novels
Erskine Caldwell	564	15	Tobacco Road
Rex Stout	536	14	Mystery Novels
Louis Bromfield	517	13	Novels
Harriet Beecher Stowe	492	13	Uncle Tom's Cabin
James Oliver Curwood	432	11	Novels
Theodore Dreiser	430	11	An American Tragedy
Sinclair Lewis	426	11	Babbitt

Note: Sixteen other internationally popular writers whose editions fell
below 400 were, in descending order, Hawthorne, Sinclair, Lew Wallace,
Henry James, T.S. Eliot, Stone, Saroyan, Wilder, Fitzgerald, Cather,
Irving, Ferber, Kyne, Harte, Franklin, Thoreau. Slaughter, Spillane, and
Henry Miller eventually became best-sellers in the post-war years.

274

TABLE 5

Comparative International Popularity
of Leading American Writers, 1931-1976

Sources: CBI/IT

The following American writers, based on a survey of forty-two best-
selling authors from the 19th and 20th Centuries, are listed in descending order of international popularity according to their total
international editions published during comparable periods of time.
Country coverage as reported by the sources was limited to the United
States, Great Britain, and thirteen European countries during the
1931-39 period, but expanded world-wide during the post-war periods.

	1931-39 15 countries	1948-54 40 countries	1955-62 63 countries	1963-70 68 countries	1971-76 59 countries
1	Twain	London	Gardner	Buck	London
2	London	Buck	Twain	Twain	Buck
3	Grey	Twain	Buck	Hemingway	Twain
4	Buck	Gardner	London	Steinbeck	Hemingway
5	Burroughs	Cooper	Hemingway	London	Gardner
6	Baum	Grey	Steinbeck	Gardner	Slaughter
7	Lewis	Queen	Queen	Queen	Queen
8	Sinclair	Alcott	Spillane	Faulkner	Steinbeck
9	Alcott	Burroughs	Grey	Slaughter	Burroughs
10	Gardner	Steinbeck	Cooper	Grey	Poe
11	Cooper	Bromfield	Caldwell, E.	Cooper	Cooper
12	Queen	Baum	Poe	Spillane	Miller, H.
13	Curwood	Poe	Faulkner	Poe	Alcott
14	Poe	Hemingway	Bromfield	Alcott	Melville
15	Dreiser	Caldwell, E.	Slaughter	Stout	Grey
16	Kyne	Melville	Alcott	Miller, H.	Stout
17	Cather	Sinclair	Melville	Melville	Faulkner
18	Bromfield	Stowe	Baum	Caldwell, E.	Stowe
19	Faulkner	Slaughter	Dreiser	Burroughs	Fitzgerald
20	Hawthorne	Lewis	Stowe	Stowe	Spillane
21	Caldwell, E.	Curwood	Wallace	James, H.	Curwood
22	Stout	Faulkner	Lewis	Baum	Bromfield
23	Steinbeck	Dreiser	Curwood	Miller, A.	Baum
24	Eliot	Wallace	Saroyan	Dreiser	Stone
25	Ferber	Stout	Hawthorne	Fitzgerald	Caldwell, E.
26	Hemingway	Eliot	Stout	Saroyan	James, H.
27	Melville	Hawthorne	Miller, H.	Hawthorne	Wilder
28	Franklin	Spillane	Wilder	Stone	Dreiser
29	Irving	Saroyan	Miller, A.	Lewis	Eliot
30	Wilder	Stone	James, H.	Wilder	Wallace
31	Stowe	Wilder	Eliot	Bromfield	Hawthorne
32	Harte	Cather	Burroughs	Curwood	Lewis
33	Saroyan	Miller, H.	Stone	Eliot	Irving
34	Thoreau	Kyne	Sinclair	Wallace	Miller, A.
35	Stone	Ferber	Ferber	Irving	Sinclair
36	Wallace	James, H.	Fitzgerald	Harte	Saroyan
37	James, H.	Irving	Irving	Sinclair	Thoreau
38	Fitzgerald	Miller, A.	Harte	Thoreau	Cather

ABOUT THE EDITOR-COMPILER

ROBERT M. RODNEY is a former Dean of Liberal Arts and Emeritus Professor at Eastern Montana College, having taken his Ph.D. at the University of Wisconsin, where he taught English as well as at Pennsylvania State College, Indiana University, and Northern Illinois University. He is co-editor of two other books on the works of Mark Twain, and has published articles in the *Kansas Historical Quarterly* and the *Journal of the Illinois State Historical Society*.

✓